Advance Praise for *Fatal Embrace*

"Mark Braverman has written a courageous, evocative book that merits close attention and continued pondering. It is a book with a critical edge and an urgent summons that calls for fresh decision making. This book is an invitation that must be heeded."
—Walter Brueggemann, Columbia Theological Seminary, and author of *The Prophetic Imagination*

"*Fatal Embrace* sounds the ancient themes of justice, first voiced by Israel's prophets, at a moment when our need to hear them has rarely been more urgent. The terrible paradox of our age is that those religious communities who ordinarily lay compelling claim to the prophetic tradition, progressive Jews and Christians, fall strangely silent in the face of a moral catastrophe—the increasingly brutal occupation of Palestine—against which Isaiah or Jeremiah would have railed in unrelenting protest. No one has drawn up a more damning indictment of that silence than Mark Braverman; few have cried out with as much clarity or passion for Israel's future. Unless we all hear such prophetic voices and respond, now, with real political resolve, it may be too late for Palestinians and Israelis alike."
—Neil Elliott, Acquiring Editor of Fortress Press, and author of *Liberating Paul* and *The Arrogance of Nations*

"A powerful and poetic call for examination and reflection. Courageous, provocative, and greatly deserving of our attention."
—Sara Roy, Senior Research Scholar, Center for Middle Eastern Studies, Harvard University

"Mark Braverman offers us a profound, courageous, and illuminating encounter, from a deeply felt Jewish perspective, with the tragic and intractable conflict in Palestine. It is unsparing in its rejection of Jewish exceptionalism and the practices of the Israeli state, as well as of Euro-American and Christian complicity in the dispossession and violation of the rights of Palestinians. This book is essential reading for all who genuinely care about the future of Israel and the suffering of the Palestinian people."

—Richard Falk, Professor Emeritus of International Law, Princeton University, and UN Special Rapporteur for Human Rights in Occupied Palestinian Territories

"A prophetic voice—clearly pronounced, humanly expressed, courageously raised. Braverman envisions a new shared and universal covenant for all humankind wherein Israelis and Palestinians—Jews, Christians, and Muslims—unite in the pursuit of justice, peace, and reconciliation."

—Naim Ateek, Director, Sabeel Liberation Theology Center, and author of *A Palestinian Christian Cry for Reconciliation*

"In *Fatal Embrace*, Mark Braverman explores the complex and often conflictive relationship between Jewish tradition, Christian theology, and Zionist practice. Drawing on his own experiences and a detailed study of prominent Jewish and Christian writers, Braverman points the way to a future that respects past tragedies but is not imprisoned by them. Both Jews and Christians have much to learn from this thoughtful, courageous, and deeply personal book."

—Stephen Walt, Professor of International Affairs, John F. Kennedy School of Government, Harvard University, and coauthor of *The Israel Lobby and U.S. Foreign Policy*

"Mark Braverman has written a clarion call to action on the future of Israel and Palestine. Calling upon Jews and Christians of Conscience to analyze the past so as to create a future worth bequeathing to our children, Braverman traces his own journey as a Jew into the increasingly difficult terrain of the Middle East."

—Marc Ellis, Director of the Center for Jewish Studies at Baylor University

"Is Zionism entitled to special treatment, given the tragic legacy of anti-Semitism and the Holocaust? Does the Bible trump international law? Mark Braverman insists no exception can be made for Israel. In this courageous book he exposes the dubious roots, erroneous logic, and devastating consequences of Zionist exceptionalism for Middle East peace. Braverman shows that support for Israel is just as strong among well meaning mainstream Christians as it is among fundamentalists and evangelical Christian Zionists who believe the Bible mandates the ethnic cleansing and colonization of Palestine. He shows how the failure of progressive Christians to challenge the inherent racism of Zionism (Jewish and Christian) continues to neutralize and undermine the peace process. Braverman demonstrates convincingly that it is the failure to confront Zionism that perpetuates anti-Semitism not the reverse. Zionism cannot hold interfaith dialogue hostage for ever. Friends must speak plainly if they really care for each other. This courageous book is a wake-up call for Jews and Christians, especially, but for all who yearn for peace and reconciliation in the Middle East."

—Stephen Sizer, author of *Christian Zionism: Road-map to Armageddon?*, *Zion's Christian Soldiers*, and *In the Footsteps of Jesus and the Apostles*

"This is an important book. It needs to be read by both Jews and Christians to help overcome that 'fatal embrace' that has caused so much harm to Jews and now to Palestinians."

—Rosemary Radford Ruether, author of *The Wrath of Jonah*

FATAL EMBRACE

CHRISTIANS, JEWS, AND THE SEARCH FOR
PEACE IN THE HOLY LAND

MARK BRAVERMAN

Synergy Books

To Jan & Glenn
From Love Eve

Fatal Embrace: Christians, Jews, and the Search for Peace in the Holy Land
Published by Synergy Books
P.O. Box 80107
Austin, Texas 78758

For more information about our books, please write us, e-mail us at info@ synergybooks.net, or visit our web site at www.synergybooks.net.

Publisher's Cataloging-in-Publication available upon request.

Library of Congress Control Number: 2009935040

ISBN-13: 978-0-9840760-7-9
ISBN-10: 0-9840760-7-7

Cover photo: Holy Cross Orthodox Benevolent Institution and Israeli separation wall, Bethlehem. Courtesy of Open Bethlehem (www. OpenBethlehem.org).

Please visit www.MarkBraverman.org for more information and a study guide.

10 9 8 7 6 5 4 3 2 1

For Susie

Table of Contents

List of Maps

Foreword

Mark Braverman has written a courageous, evocative book that merits close attention and continued pondering. It is a book with a critical edge and an urgent summons that calls for fresh decision making. I have learned from it and am glad to commend it.

As a passionate Jew with a long and deep love for Israel, Braverman wades into the vexatious enigma of the interface between the state of Israel and the Palestinian people. He recognizes that none of the past or present solutions to the conflict hold any promise for the achievement of a lasting peace unless based on redress of injustices and that fresh thinking presses clear to the theological-ideological foundations of the dispute. Braverman brings to the table his critical thinking as a Jew, his rootage in the lore of Israel, his devotion to Jerusalem, but also his first-hand experience of the antihuman brutality daily enacted on that holy ground that is devastating the future for both parties—consigning Jews to a fortress existence, denying dignity and human rights to Palestinians.

At the bottom of his argument is the thesis, so well considered here, that it is Israel's elemental conviction about being God's one chosen people—and the ensuing social-political exceptionalism—that is the root cause of the conflict. It is that most elemental conviction on the part of Jews that he holds up to scrutiny and about which he insists upon a radical revision. The claim for exceptionalism—held commonly by Israel's most one-dimensional advocates and by Israel's most urbane Jewish critics—makes serious, realistic political thinking impossible and gives warrant for brutalizing policies carried out by the Israeli government that are destructive, self-destructive, and finally irresponsible.

Braverman's primary criticism concerns the defenders of Israel's exceptionalism through which the faith claims of Judaism have been wedded to unbridled military policy. He chooses not to focus on the radical and violent spokespersons for Zionism whom he regards as "straw men," but on more careful serious thinkers who are also trapped in the same self-justifying ideology. Two points are to be noticed in the argument by Braverman. First, he does not discount the impact of the Holocaust upon Israeli thought and policy, and knows about its durable traumatic implications. But he insists that the fault line of exceptionalism is much older and much deeper than the Holocaust. Second, he knows about and cares about the importance of the State of Israel and its security, but insists that current policy rooted in exceptionalism leads not toward but away from achieving security for the State of Israel. And that is because this grounding for self-understanding precludes the kind of political realism that is essential to the survival and well-being of the state, indeed of any state.

This critical conviction about Israel's status as God's chosen people has implications beyond the Jewish devotion to the State of Israel. Braverman also has a chastening word to speak to Christians who want to be friends of and advocates for Israel. I was surprised that Braverman gives very little attention to the Christian Right and its passion for the State of Israel, though he does mention Pastor Hagee. Rather his focus is upon more progressive Christians who bend over backward not to be guilty of "anti-Semitism" and, as a result, give the State of Israel "a pass." Braverman wants such well-meaning Christians to understand that reflective criticism of Zionist policies is not to be confused with anti-Semitism, but is a legitimate critique to be made by responsible Christians who care about Israel's well-being. It is, he proposes, neither legitimate for Christians nor helpful to the State of Israel to refrain from such criticism, or to be mute in the face of its destructive and self-destructive policies. To be sure, the strong advocates of Israeli militarism and territorial entitlement are quick to label any critique of Israel as anti-Semitism, but Braverman makes a clear distinction between anti-Semitism and opposition to the actions of Israel, and urges Christians to be serious and critically reflective. Israeli exceptionalism should provide no exemption from serious critical thought about state policy.

But Braverman goes further in his instruction to well-intentioned Christians. He observes that in an eagerness to find common ground with Judaism, progressive Christians have too easily recast Jewish faith in the categories of Christian faith, most especially concerning "grace," and have thereby "Christianized" Judaism to make it into something other than it is:

> Torah is not Gospel. Election is not grace. The Old Testament covenant is not the New Testament gifting of salvation. *Promise* in Judaism is not about forgiveness from sin. Rather, it is about *blessing*, in the way the ancient world understood that term: peoplehood, progeny, prosperity—and, in the case of the Jewish people—land.

Thus Braverman notices an odd tendency among progressive Christians to be *mute* concerning political extremism that fades into violence while at the same time to be *imperialistic* in theological matters. On both counts, Jews are made to pay a price, respectively, for Christian timidity and for Christian preemption. The great merit of Braverman on this score is to clarify the categories in which the discussion takes place, recognizing that when the categories are clarified, a very different conversation becomes possible.

The central aim of this important book is a critique of exceptionalism, and the insistence that a Jewish sense of being God's one chosen people is rooted in an old tribalism that is no longer viable in a pluralistic world. While this critique of exceptionalism is per force focused on Jewish claims, in fact Braverman's bold words have implication beyond that. On the one hand, his argument invites Christian rethinking about Christian exceptionalism as well, about being the new chosen people of God and followers of the one chosen messiah.

This is not a new thought among some progressive Christians, but Braverman's contextualization of the claim is important and illuminating. Thus by implication, this book is also a summons to Christians to rethink their monopolistic Christological claims that are, in some sense, derivative from Jewish claims.

On the other hand and beyond Braverman's own comment, the critique of exceptionalism may be extended toward U.S. exceptionalism that has eventuated in religious-ideological support for American expansionist imperialism. In an odd sort of way, that nationalist ideology is also rooted in a kind of tribalism, though a very different kind of tribe. I am reminded of the thesis of Regina Schwartz (1997) that monotheism is intrinsically violent, and surely the idea of a chosen people, whether Israel or the church or the United States, evokes the right to absolutism that carries within it the seeds of violence.

Because Braverman has appealed to my own work, I may take the liberty here of thinking again about my own journey around this vexed question. When I published my book, *The Land: Place as Gift, Promise, and Challenge in Biblical Faith* (1977), I was, as were many Christian scholars of the Bible, rather innocent about the extrapolation of the land promises into Israeli ideology. I simply allowed that contemporary Judaism could appeal to the old land promises; and of course much of contemporary Judaism does just that. While I have been criticized for that innocence, it is at least to be noted that I concluded:

> Thus there is a community of concern between Jews and Christians about grasping and waiting, about keeping and losing. Because both Christians and Jews are on both sides of the grasping and waiting, this may be an issue about which there can be new dialogue between them. Neither Jews nor Christians have a monopoly on either side of the issue. For both the question is a difficult and urgent one. For both Christians and Jews it is always a question of self-securing and trust. Self-securing seems to work and yet lead to death. Trust seems unlikely and yet holds promise. This question can never be avoided by either Jews or Christians. For both it is surely the key question of faith. (169)

I had seen then, from the text, that grasping and self-securing lead to death. I did not, however, directly link that grasping certitude to Israeli practice, but the implication is clear.

After that publication, I was duly and rightly chastised in the important work of Michael Prior. As a result, in the newer edition of my book (2002), I made an important revision, concluding, "It is clear on any reading that the modern state of Israel has effectively merged old traditions of land entitlement and the most vigorous military capacity thinkable for a modern state. The outcome of that merger of old traditional claim and contemporary military capacity becomes an intolerable commitment to violence that is justified by reason of state" (xv).

More recently, in a *Christian Century* piece (2009) in response to an assertion that Israel has a "supernatural" entitlement to the land, I wrote, "It strikes me as enormously hazardous to cite a supernatural right in the midst of realpolitik, especially when the right is entwined with military ferociousness and political exclusivism. While such a right may serve self-identity, it makes sense only inside the narrative. Outside the narrative it is no more than ideology, and so offers no basis for the hard work of peace and justice. The capacity to hold together a theological claim (that I as a child of that narrative take not to be in doubt) and the summons of political realism is tricky indeed" (26).

When one considers Jewish exceptionalism in the presence of Palestinians, the claim is not more than a self-serving ideology that will not buy a cup of coffee in a pluralistic world where other ideologies function with equally fervent loyalty. The most such a conviction can do is to "mobilize the base," in this case most especially the "settlers."

Thus while my awareness of the transformation of ancient promises into toxic ideology has been slow in coming, my own sense of matters is fully congruent with that of Braverman. I trace out my learning curve on the subject for two reasons. On the one hand, I want to indicate the way in which I have come to agreement with Braverman's urging. On the other hand, I believe that my own growing awareness of the issue of promise-become-ideology is not atypical, but is reflective of the same learning curve of very many interpreters of the Bible. I am grateful to Braverman for his bold articulation of the demanding work now to be faced in our several interpretive traditions.

In the final chapter of his book, Braverman traces out in concrete, strategic steps what can and must be done. His courage and his wisdom on this matter are urgent, and dare not be dismissed by ideologues, either Jewish or Christian, who are sure to cry out in indignation at his summons. In his own idiom, Braverman echoes the familiar sayings, "When you are in a hole, stop digging" and "Continuing the same actions will produce the same results." Braverman sees that the crisis in the Holy Land is a deep hole, and more digging by the ideologues will not escape that hole. And more occupation violence will only feed the spiral and will never break the nerve of the other party. That is, neither a "two-state solution" nor "one-state solution" will be viable, until Jewish exceptionalism yields to the legitimacy of "the other" on the ground, the Palestinian who is not Jewish but who nonetheless has claims that stand alongside those of Jews, in equal passion and legitimacy. The wish world of ideology will not change that reality on the ground.

It is time, very late, but time for new initiatives. While there may be some glimmer of hope from the new U.S. administration under President Obama, Braverman knows that the new initiative will have to come from a movement of generous, caring, insistent people, and not top-down from policy. The critique of the ideology of exceptionalism is urgent. If and when there are steps taken outside that ideology, then the human questions, the human hurts, and the human hopes may take on fresh, effective power. But as long as the ideology of exceptionalism prevails and remains beyond critique, there is no chance for the transformative power of either human hurt or human hope.

It occurs to me that Braverman's articulation is not unlike that of Job. Job runs up against closed ideology that knows all of the answers ahead of time, that assumes high moral ground, and that permits ideology to screen out human data. The intent of the book of Job is to break open such fixed ideology and to create a possibility for new engagement. No doubt breaking the closed pattern of "chosenness" would be like an opening of the world to the voice from the whirlwind who makes all things new.

This book is an invitation that must be heeded. When heeded, there might be peace in Jerusalem soon, if not next year. If not heeded, holy ground will increasingly be reduced to a killing field. There is a time to grasp and a time to relinquish. It is time now, says Braverman, to relinquish an ideology that has been treasured too long. The beginning begins in relinquishment; it always does. Several times Braverman retells the tale of a monkey who could not reach the new limb of the tree alongside his companions because he could not let go of the limb in his hand. And he was left out of the future of his family.

In Christian tradition, the defining word of "relinquishment" is the Greek *kenosis*. It is written in lyrical fashion of Jesus that, "He emptied himself and became obedient unto death…Therefore God has highly exalted him…" (Philippians 2:8). It is at the center of Christian tradition that new life comes in only from losing what is old. That sense of the gift of newness so important to Christians is derived, of course, from Judaism. At the break point of exile, after the destruction of Jerusalem, the poet claims the attention of the Jewish people:

Do not remember the former things,
Nor consider the things of old.
I am about to do a new thing,
Now it springs forth. (Isaiah 43:19)

There is a temptation, in adjudicating the Holy Land, to remember old things too long. As Miroslav Volf judges, there is a time for forgetting and noticing what is newly given (2006). Braverman summons all parties to the dispute to watch for newness that is about to "spring forth." One does not want to miss the newness because one lingers too long in old ideological perception.

Walter Brueggemann
Columbia Theological Seminary
June 2, 2009

Walter Brueggemann is McPheeters Professor of Old Testament Emeritus at Columbia Theological Seminary, Decatur, Georgia, and the author of Theology of the Old Testatment *(1997),* The Prophetic Imagination, *2nd ed. (2001),* The Book That Breathes New Life *(2005), and* Mandate to Difference: An Invitation to the Contemporary Church *(2007), among numerous other books and articles.*

ISRAEL / PALESTINE 2009

LEBANON
Damascus
Tyre
SYRIA
GOLAN HEIGHTS
Israeli occupied
Acre
Haifa
SEA OF GALILEE
Nazareth
Jenin
Nablus
WEST BANK
Israeli occupied
JORDAN RIVER
Tel Aviv
Yaffa
Ramallah
Amman
Jerusalem
Bethlehem
JORDAN
Hebron
DEAD SEA
GAZA
Israeli blockaded
Beersheba
ISRAEL
MEDITERRANEAN SEA
EGYPT

N
W   E
S

1949-1967 border
Line of Israeli control
in Golan Heights

0   10   20   30   miles
0 10 20 30 40   kilometers

Aqaba
GULF OF AQABA
SAUDI ARABIA

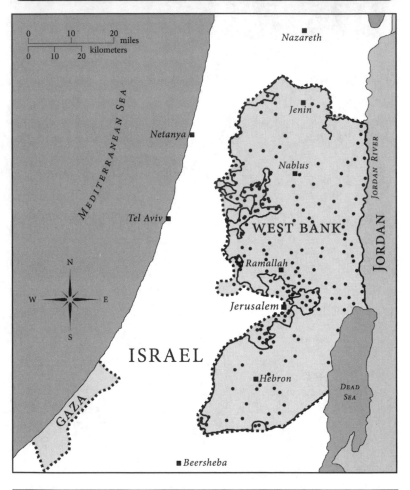

WEST BANK BARRIER WALL AND JEWISH-ONLY SETTLEMENTS

0   10   20 miles
0   10   20 kilometers

MEDITERRANEAN SEA

Nazareth

Jenin

Netanya

Nablus

JORDAN RIVER

Tel Aviv

WEST BANK

JORDAN

Ramallah

Jerusalem

ISRAEL

Hebron

DEAD SEA

GAZA

Beersheba

········ 1949-1967 border   ■ Major cities

——— Israeli separation wall   • Jewish-only settlements

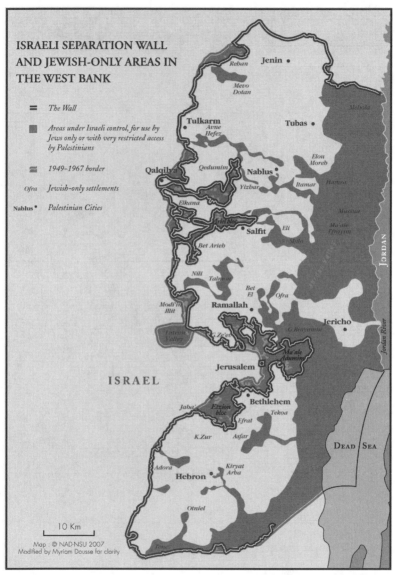

ISRAELI SEPARATION WALL
AND JEWISH-ONLY AREAS IN
THE WEST BANK

= The Wall

■ Areas under Israeli control, for use by
Jews only or with very restricted access
by Palestinians

= 1949–1967 border

Ofra   Jewish-only settlements

Nablus •   Palestinian Cities

Reban

Jenin •

Mevo
Dotan

Meḥola

Tulkarm •
Avne
Hefez

Tubas •

Elon
Moreh

Qalqilya •   Qedumim   Nablus •

Itamar   Ḥamra

Yizhar

Elkana

Massua

Ariel bloc   Ma'ale
Efrayim

Salfit •   Eli
Shilo

Bet Arieh

Nili   Talmon

Bet
El   Ofra

Modi'in
Illit   Ramallah •

Jericho •

Latrun   G.Ze'ev   G.Binyamin

Valley

Ma'ale
Adumim

Jerusalem •

ISRAEL

Jaba'   Etzion   Bethlehem •
bloc   Efrat   Tekoa

K.Zur   Asfar

Adora   Kiryat
Arba

Hebron •

Otniel

JORDAN

Jordan River

DEAD SEA

10 Km

Map : © NAD-NSU 2007
Modified by Myriam Dousse for clarity

ISRAELI-BUILT ROADS IN THE OCCUPIED WEST BANK
Connecting Jewish-only West Bank settlements to one another and to Israel

——— 1949-1967 border ——— Israeli bypass roads (Palestinian use forbidden or restricted)

Prologue

Jesus was preaching and ministering in Galilee, casting out demons and healing the sick. Before long he was surrounded by a crowd of followers. Word of his fame reached his family, and, fearing he would bring trouble on himself from the authorities, they went in search of him:

> Then his mother and his brothers came: and standing outside, they sent to him and called him. A crowd was sitting around him; and they said to him, "Your mother and your brothers and sisters are outside, asking for you." And he replied, "Who are my mother and my brothers?" And looking at those who sat around him, he said, "Here are my mother and my brothers! Whoever does the will of God is my brother and sister and mother." (Mark 3:31–34 [New Revised Standard Version])

Tel Aviv, Israel, 2001. Nurit Peled-Elhanan is the mother of Smadar Elhanan, who was thirteen years old when she was killed by a Palestinian suicide bomber in September 1997. After Smadar's death, Nurit and her husband, Rami, Jewish Israelis, opened their house of mourning to Palestinian supporters and to other bereaved parents. Years later, Nurit said this in a speech in Tel Aviv:

> When my little girl was killed, a reporter asked me how I was willing to accept condolences from the other side. I replied without hesitation that I *had* refused to meet with the other side:

when Ehud Olmert, then the mayor of Jerusalem, came to offer his condolences I took my leave and would not sit with him. For me, the other side, the enemy, is not the Palestinian people. For me the struggle is not between Palestinians and Israelis, nor between Jews and Arabs. The fight is between those who seek peace and those who seek war. My people are those who seek peace. My sisters are the bereaved mothers, Israeli and Palestinian, who live in Israel and in Gaza and in the refugee camps. My brothers are the fathers who try to defend their children from the cruel occupation, and are, as I was, unsuccessful in doing so. Although we were born into a different history and speak different tongues, there is more that unites us than that which divides us.

Introduction

In the early spring of 1916, Daher Nassar stood on a hilltop in central Palestine. To his west he could see the coastal plain stretching to the Mediterranean, to his north the spires and minarets of Jerusalem, and to the east the mountains of Moab. Daher liked this piece of land, the highest point in the fertile hill country south of Bethlehem. For Daher, a Christian, it felt good to be close to the birthplace of Jesus and the ancient "Patriarch's Road" to Hebron. A lover of the land and its bounty, Daher could see in his mind's eye the terraces that would follow the contours of the hill. There he would plant the grapes that would glisten in the summer heat. He could imagine the orchards he would set out in the valley to the south, and the olive and almond trees that would soon range in rows along the crest and on the eastern slope. He thought of the shelter for his family he would find in the caves that dotted the hillside, caves used by Palestinian shepherds and farmers for millennia. Four hundred dunam—a hundred acres. Daher paid the price, signed the papers, and silently mouthed a prayer as he carefully placed the deed to the property for safekeeping: this is for my children and my grandchildren.

Daher Nassar, like his fellow Palestinians, paid taxes to the Ottoman sultan. And, like those other farmers and villagers, he saw the governance of the land pass over to the British Crown at the close of the World War. His sons, Bishara and Naif, who took over stewardship of the farm, saw British troops replaced by

Jordanian regulars in 1948. And, in 1967, Bishara's son Daoud witnessed the blue Star of David hoisted over the territory at the conclusion of the war in which Israel took control of the West Bank. The Nassars have lived and farmed under four occupiers: three kings and now Israel. Only this last ruler has tried to take their land from them.

It was early spring in 2009. I was sitting in a recording studio at the offices of National Public Radio in Chicago. To my right was Daoud Nassar, to my left my friend and colleague Bill Plitt. Bill and I had met Daoud while on an American interfaith delegation to Israel and the Palestinian territories in the summer of 2006. Along with several others, Bill and I founded a nonprofit to support Daoud's continued presence on his ancestral land and his work as director of Tent of Nations, an international peace center he had established on the grounds of the farm. We were on a speaking tour to educate Americans about Daoud's work and to raise funds to help him dig cisterns, install solar power, and buy a backhoe before the Israeli government, frustrated by Daoud's stubborn unwillingness to move off his farm, sealed off the last road providing access to his property. After some introductory questions, the host of the show asked me how it was that I had become involved in this project. "You mean," I responded, "what's a Jewish guy from Philadelphia doing defending the land rights of a Christian Palestinian farmer?" He smiled—of course that is precisely what he meant. I told him I had been horrified by what I saw happening to Daoud and his fellow Palestinians at the hands of the Israeli government. I told him that I had deep family ties in Israel, and that I felt strongly that the future of Israel's citizens depended on safeguarding the human rights of Palestinians in Israel and the occupied territories. Working for justice and coexistence in the Holy Land, I had realized, was the only thing I could see myself doing as a Jew and as an American. The host, apparently no stranger to the heated controversy taking place within the American Jewish community over Israel's policies, followed up with the right question: "What's that been like for you? You must be getting some interesting reactions from your fellow Jews."

I had answered this question countless times since my return from the West Bank, sometimes without being asked. My answer had never been encouraging. The reception that I received from the established Jewish community whenever I talked about my experiences in occupied Palestine had been like a door slamming in my face. When I talked about my horror and deep concern over the injustice I had seen and the catastrophic impact that the conflict was having on both occupier and occupied, I was told by many Jews that I was disloyal to my people, that I had "gone over to the Palestinian side." I was informed that criticizing Israel made me an enemy of the Jewish people and that I was opening the door for the next Holocaust.

Some of the reactions bordered on the bizarre, going back to fears one would have thought we had put behind us: A rabbinical student informed his colleagues that I was obviously a convert to Christianity "masquerading" as a Jew in order to promote the destruction of the Jewish people. A reading of Israeli protest poetry that I had organized to be held at the local Jewish Community Center in Washington, DC, was cancelled when it was discovered that I served on the board of directors of Partners for Peace, an organization that was on the anti-Semitic blacklist of the local Federation of Jewish Agencies. A family friend, a young rabbi who said that he agreed with my assessment of the illegality and immorality of Israeli policy, declined my request to speak at his synagogue. His frank explanation was that if he were to allow me to speak there, he would lose his job. That's why, during the years since returning from my trip, I didn't have good things to say about the position of the American Jewish establishment on the question of Israel. I was hurt and I was angry, and I was aware that this was a problem. How effective could I be as an activist or writer if my anger at my own community leaked out, regardless of how justified that anger was?

But this morning I had a different answer. The previous day we had met in a Chicago suburb with a rabbi who told us that he could not celebrate Israel's Independence Day, the holiday commemorating the founding of the State of Israel, which was observed on the very day we were meeting. Because of Israel's assault on Gaza, its human rights record in the West Bank, and its failure to take responsibility for the expulsion of three-quarters of a million Palestinians to make way for the state in 1948, this was not a day for celebration, he told us. Rather, it was a day for Jewish soul-searching. The story we needed to tell ourselves, he said, was not the story of our victory over our enemies, but the story of what the Palestinian people had lost as a result of our success in founding the Jewish state. The conversation had given me hope—hope that, although this was just a beginning, even the organized Jewish community in the United States might someday come to see that the very future of the Jewish people depended on our achievement of this level of honest self-scrutiny. It gave me some hope that maybe it was not too late to change course. So I had a different answer than my usual one that morning, and I was glad to tell that story to my radio host. Things are starting to shift, I told him.

I had let myself sound more optimistic than I felt. I had been doing a lot of thinking about my people and our national homeland project, and I had not been feeling good about the prospects for peace.

A Fatal Embrace

The Jewish people have always struggled with the tension between the universalism inherent in our ethical code and the particularism so deeply embedded in the cultural and historical narrative that begins with the Old Testament. Global politics is very much at play at this juncture in Jewish history. Since the founding of the State of Israel in 1948, most Jews in the West have believed that their survival depends on establishing and maintaining hegemony in historic Palestine. For that reason, American Jews have erected a powerful apparatus of philanthropic, educational, and lobbying organizations devoted to maintaining the stream of financial and political support for Israel from the U.S. government and from private sources. We Jews want to have our cake and eat it too; we want to see ourselves as universalist and humanitarian, in possession of a religious faith that is based on deep respect for human rights and a fundamental, defining commitment to universal justice. We also, however, persist in supporting the policies of the Israeli government, policies that violate the human rights of Palestinians, support the continuing colonization of occupied territory in violation of international law, and represent the most significant impediment to a peaceful resolution of the half-century-old conflict.

American Jews have not created this situation by ourselves. We have been enabled by our Christian compatriots, who, because of their sense of responsibility for historical anti-Semitism, feel that they have no right to criticize any actions that Israel may take, even when these actions violate principles of human rights and justice cherished by Jews and Christians alike. Buttressed by the vigorous support of the non-Jewish community in America for anything that Israel wants or does, United States government policy over the decades has remained firm in its unqualified support of Israel's policies of de facto colonization of Palestinian lands. These policies remain the main obstacle to a peaceful resolution of the conflict. It's a fatal embrace: these two powerful, deeply-seated forces—Christian atonement and the Jewish search for safety and empowerment—unite to help keep us stuck in Israel/Palestine. The persistence and power of these beliefs—the more powerful because they are unrecognized, unexamined, and even denied—have played a major role in thwarting progress toward a peaceful settlement of the conflict.

Voices of questioning and protest have begun to emerge, however. To an increasing number of Jews, here as well as in Israel, it has become clear that Israel's present course is tragically self-destructive, and must change if Israeli society is to continue and prosper. In addition, Christians on congregational and denominational levels have become concerned about Palestinian human rights based on what they have observed on their pilgrimages to the Holy Land and, increasingly, what they are reading about in the media and seeing on the Internet.

In politics, beliefs and perceptions are just as important as facts. In the case of the conflict in Israel/Palestine, issues of cultural and national identity and of religious faith play a central role. It is therefore crucial that in addition to knowing the facts, we examine the power of those influences that lie at the root of our Western culture and that play a direct role in the continuation of this conflict. The thesis of this book is that these beliefs play a major role in stifling productive dialogue and forward movement in the search for a peaceful resolution to the conflict. We will not have peace in the Holy Land unless we understand the power of these beliefs.

Contrary to the claims of some of my coreligionists, I do not "seek the destruction of the State of Israel." On the contrary, I am in great fear for its peril and seek to preserve Israel's accomplishments, culture, security, and, most of all, its people. I feel like two other Jews must have felt: the prophet Jeremiah and, eight centuries later, Jesus of Nazareth, standing before Jerusalem, weeping over the self-inflicted destruction they saw and the catastrophe to come. As I will discuss in the pages to follow, acknowledging the darkness and weeping over the brokenness is the key to finding a solution. Old Testament scholar Walter Brueggemann writes in *The Land* that "'exile,' as either history or an ideology, has become definitional for Israel's self-discernment" (2002, xvii). Jewish liberation theologian Marc Ellis has written that "we must be willing to embrace Jews of conscience who are willing to…go into exile in order to combat the abusive practices of the Jewish state" (2001). I believe, along with Brueggemann, Ellis, and others who have thought deeply about issues of faith, peoplehood, and history, and who will be our companions on this exploration, that exile can lead to restoration and even renewal. What might be the nature of that renewal, and what it means not only to the Jewish people but to people of all faiths, is the question this book seeks to address.

As Jim Wallis of the Sojourners movement reminds us, when politics fail, great social movements emerge. This book is a call to action. It is my belief that if there is any hope for a lasting peace based on justice in the Holy Land, it will come about as a result of a broad social movement, originating at the grassroots level of faith communities and activist organizations working for peace here and in Israel/Palestine. My hope is that, by calling on Jews to examine our own shadow and by helping Christians overcome their reluctance to question the actions of some Jews, this book will advance the emerging social movement needed to change Israeli and U.S. policy in the region.

A Note on "Balance"

One of the most striking features of this discourse in the United States is the preoccupation with the need for a "balanced" perspective. Here is how this typically plays out: you may not give out information about the abridgement of human rights in occupied Palestine, or talk about targeted assassinations, house demolitions, humiliating and life-threatening restrictions on movement, or any other examples of Palestinian suffering, without presenting what is usually termed the "other side." The "other side" is the recognition of the suffering of the Israelis, who are faced with terrorist attacks and the threat of annihilation. What is important here is not the apparent reasonableness of this argument. Of course, here in America, we are committed to fair play and the airing of all viewpoints. Rather, what is significant is the political context. In my experience, the demand for "balance" is almost always made as a way to invalidate and neutralize scrutiny of those actions of Israel that are, in my view, the root cause of the threat to its own well-being and survival.

The discourse, therefore, is handicapped by the seemingly unassailable position that there are "two sides:" the Israeli (or Jewish) and the Palestinian (or Arab). The world is thus divided into two camps, the "pro-Israel" and the "pro-Palestine." One must belong to one or the other. I am frequently assigned to the "pro-Palestinian" camp because I criticize Israel and talk about the abridgement of Palestinian rights. I reject this designation. This is not a struggle between good guys and bad guys, with the Jews as villains and the Palestinians as blameless victims, any more than it is the opposite. The issue is justice. The issue is the fact that there will never be an end to the conflict until there is a full recognition and redress of the massive abrogation of human rights that accompanied the birth of the State of Israel and that continues to the present day. To tell the story correctly, you have to include the story that until recently has not been reported in our media, or from the pulpits of our churches (for the most part) or our synagogues. It is a story in which the power difference between the two parties to the conflict is painfully apparent, and the evidence of Israel's systematic project to accomplish the goal of ethnic cleansing and political and economic control over the non-Jewish inhabitants of historic Palestine is horrifyingly clear.

I am not alone in this; anyone who goes to see for him or herself—from former U.S. presidents, to South African human rights workers, to Israeli journalists, to American Christian tourists—arrives at the same conclusion. Christiane Amanpour, the award-winning CNN international correspondent, recently talked about the question of "objectivity" in reporting: "Objectivity means reporting the truth. It doesn't mean creating a false equivalent. It doesn't mean saying 'on the one hand this and on the other hand that.' It doesn't mean equating victim with aggressor. If we do that, then we are accomplices" (NPR "Fresh Air" interview, December 3, 2008). Amanpour here is describing the sleight of hand commonly employed to deflect and derail the discussion: presenting a situation in which the rights of one group are being denied by another as a "conflict between two rights."

Events and experiences drive our intellectual endeavors, our research, and our search for answers. This book arises from what I have seen with my eyes and felt in my heart. It is a response to horror and deep sadness. It comes from a Jew who is overwhelmed by the reality of Israel's ethnic cleansing of Palestine, a project begun in the period 1947–1949, in the lead-up to and aftermath of the establishment of the State of Israel. The project to rid the land of its indigenous people continued with the opportunity afforded by Israel's victory in the Six-Day War of 1967, and was further advanced through the blueprint for annexation and control served up by the Oslo Accords of 1993.[1] It continues to the present day in what can only be described as an orgy of settlement activity and rush to establish the necessary facts on the ground to precede the inevitable political settlement to come. This is the reality that drives and informs the writing in the chapters to follow. It is the reality that has set me on this journey.

About This Book

This book is organized in three parts. Part 1 sets out the basics of what I believe to be the barriers to achieving peace in the Holy Land. Chapter 1 provides an overview of the discourse in the U.S. over how to resolve the half-century-long conflict, and the issues it raises for the Christian and Jewish communities. In chapter 2, I tell the story of growing up Jewish in postwar America, and the crisis of identity and spirit that resulted from my encounter with Israel's occupation of Palestine. Chapter 3 focuses on the impact of anti-Semitism on Jewish history and Jewish experience today, while chapter 4 is a discussion of Zionism—its origins, consequences, critics, and defenders. This last chapter covers the efforts of several Jewish writers to understand the historical, psychological, and spiritual forces driving the actions of the State of Israel and world Jewry's support of those policies that many regard as barriers to peace.

---

1. The 1993 Oslo Accords, or "Declaration of Principles," was the first agreement between Israel and political representatives of the Palestinians. It was meant to be the first step leading to an autonomous Palestinian state in the West Bank and Gaza and to normal relations with Israel. The Accords created the Palestinian Authority (PA), which would exercise various degrees of control over some of the area occupied by Israel. The Accords also established three zones: Area A, under complete control of the PA; Area B, under Palestinian civil control and Israeli military control; and Area C, completely controlled by Israel. Area C consists of Jewish-only settlements and "security zones" off limits to Palestinians. The Accords set a transitional period of five years leading to the resolution of the "permanent issues" of Jewish settlements, Jerusalem, and the return of refugees, which were excluded from the 1993 agreement. The outbreak of the *Al Aqsa Intifada* (or "Second Intifada") is generally understood as the result of the Palestinians' frustration at the failure of the Accords to achieve its promised goals and a reaction to the enormous growth of Jewish-only settlements throughout the West Bank and Gaza.

In part 2, we undertake a consideration of Christianity's post-WWII project to atone for anti-Semitism. Chapters 5 and 6 are a review of the effort by Christians to reverse the theology complicit in two millennia of Western anti-Semitism. We'll pay particular attention to the implications of this project for Christian attitudes toward modern political Zionism. In chapters 7 and 8, we explore the thinking of a number of contemporary progressive Christian theologians regarding the Holy Land and the Jewish people. We'll see that even in those thinkers who have been passionately devoted to universalism, equality, and social justice, we can detect a reluctance to deny the Jewish people a superior right to the land.

In part 3, I propose that a return to the model of community that characterized early Christianity can provide the key to achieving peace in the Holy Land today. Chapter 9 opens with a consideration of several Jewish progressive writers. We'll see that even as they struggle with the ethical and theological issues raised by political Zionism, their thinking reveals a persistent sense of entitlement with respect to the Jewish claim to the land. Chapter 10 considers the voices of social critics within Israel and frames this discussion through a consideration of contemporary work on nonviolence. Chapters 11 and 12 continue the discussion of alternatives to violence as a solution to the conflict in the Holy Land. We will explore the work of contemporary scholars who see the Gospels as the record of a movement of social transformation.

Finally, in chapter 13, we consider the key role of the faith communities, in particular the American church, in the mounting of a broad, grassroots movement to guide the political change needed to bring peace. This chapter includes a prescription for action and a vision for a new interfaith agenda based on a commitment to universal justice.

PART 1

Breaking the Spell

Hillel says, "If I am not for myself, who will be for me? But if I am only for myself, who am I?"
—*Ethics of the Fathers* 1:14

Two terrible things happened to the Jewish people this century: the Holocaust and the lessons learned from it.
—Israeli writer Boaz Evron, 1981

I'm afraid of what the past
Will do to my future.
—Yehuda Amichai, *From Man You Came and to Man You Shall Return*

Chapter 1

The Moment of Truth

Suddenly I knew that the first step toward reconciling Jew and Palestinian was the restoration of human dignity. Justice and righteousness were what I had been hungering and thirsting for: If I were really committing my life to carry God's message to my people, I would have to lift up, as Jesus had, the men and women who had been degraded and beaten down.

—Father Elias Chacour, *Blood Brothers*

When I was a boy in the 1950s attending Hebrew school in Philadelphia, once a year we received cardboard folders equipped with slots for dimes. The folders were distributed by the Jewish National Fund, a nonprofit corporation founded in 1901 by the World Zionist Organization to buy and develop land in Palestine for Jewish settlement. On the cover was a picture of a tree being planted by handsome, tanned people wearing shorts. When the card was full, you sent it in and in return received a certificate with your name on it and a bigger picture of a tree—the tree you had planted in Israel. It was fun and it was a thrill; I was reclaiming the homeland. I saw pictures of kibbutzim and orange groves filling the valleys. I dreamed of going there someday.

Four decades later, now a middle-aged man, I saw pictures of Israeli bulldozers uprooting three-hundred-year-old olive trees and Jewish soldiers restraining Palestinian villagers crying hysterically over the destruction of their groves. I traveled to the West

Bank—Israeli-occupied Palestinian land—and saw the hillsides denuded of trees to build Jewish-only settlement cities. I saw Palestinian homes demolished and orchards uprooted to make way for a twenty-five-foot-high concrete wall cutting through Palestinian cities, villages, and fields. I didn't buy the story that this was for defense. What I saw convinced me that this was not what the wall was for.

What Peace Process?

The Israel-Palestine conflict pulls all who try to solve it into a quicksand of contradiction and enmity. Sputtering efforts at a "peace process" to resolve the conflict between Israel and its Palestinian subjects appear increasingly futile to a growing number of stakeholders on all sides, despite the efforts of American presidents, European leaders, and broad coalitions of Arab governments. Indeed, the entire effort to achieve a "settlement" appears to be based on a collective self-deception: while appearing to hold Israel to account, world powers give Israel free rein to pursue policies that breed popular resistance among Palestinians and promise to prolong the conflict. At the same time, we hear criticism of Palestinian terrorism and failure to self-govern effectively, while failing to see that the growth of a healthy society and the capacity for development of competent structures of government are sabotaged politically by our unqualified support of Israel's policies of control and annexation on the one hand and economically by the effective creation of third-world dependency on the other. Although there is increasing recognition of and sympathy for Palestinian strivings for self-determination and political autonomy, acts of popular resistance by an increasingly impoverished and frustrated populace continue to be tarred with the brush of 9/11 and dismissed as terrorism. Nonviolent activism on the part of Palestinians, Israelis, internationals, and joint Palestinian-Israeli organizations is ignored by the media.

Meanwhile, a civil war has erupted between those American Jews who staunchly defend the Jewish state against all critics and those who fear for its very soul. A powerful, well-organized system of American Jewish institutions—synagogues, Jewish philanthropic federations, political lobbying organizations—move quickly to suppress or neutralize any possible criticism of the Jewish state or threat to the financial and political support flowing to Israel from the United States. The pastor who opens his or her church to a conference on Palestinian human rights faces protests and editorials from Jewish organizations charging anti-Semitism. Christian Zionist fundamentalists join with the pro-Israel lobby to support saber rattling toward Iran. Indeed, in the discourse on the conflict, reality is turned on its head: the victorious and empowered seen as victims, the dispossessed as oppressors.

Looking for the Truth

In this climate of denial and political obstruction, little progress can be made toward addressing the root causes of the conflict and bringing peace to the region. As the deadlock continues, the Israeli government and the Palestinian Authority (the administrative body established in 1994 to govern parts of the Palestinian territories in the West Bank and Gaza) are becoming increasingly desperate and politically weak, reduced to the repetition of demonstrably failed policies. At the same time, the last five years in particular have produced groundbreaking writing that focuses on the key issues underlying the present situation. Much of this work takes direct aim at the myths, falsehoods, and denials that have been presented to the world at large and that help perpetuate the cycle of violence and political stalemate:

- In late 2006, former U.S. president Jimmy Carter published Palestine: Peace Not Apartheid. In the book, he described the occupation as illegal, in violation of human rights standards as well as numerous UN resolutions, and as the source of the current deadlock. Carter wrote, "In order to perpetuate the occupation, Israeli forces have deprived their unwilling subjects of basic human rights. No objective person could personally observe existing conditions in the West Bank and dispute these statements" (208–209).

- In the same year, professors Stephen Walt of Harvard and John Mearsheimer of the University of Chicago published *The Israel Lobby and U.S. Foreign Policy*. The article claimed that the excessive power of the political action committee and the associated coalition of organizations that promote America's massive support of Israel is keeping the United States on a foreign policy course that is contrary to its national interest. A longer form of the article appeared as a best-selling book in 2007.

- In a series of published writing and speaking appearances, Archbishop Tutu of South Africa, who along with President Carter compared Israel's policies to apartheid, called for a global movement to oppose Israel's violation of human rights in the occupied territories.

- Israeli historians (the so-called New Historians) have continued to mine newly-released primary sources that present a narrative contrary to the Zionist depiction of the birth of the state in 1948 simply as a war of self-defense against superior Arab armies. Ilan Pappe's 2006 *The Ethnic Cleansing of Palestine* revealed that a plan to rid large sections of Palestine of its indigenous Palestinian inhabitants was planned well in advance of the 1947 United Nations partition vote and was carried out deliberately by Jewish forces between 1947 and 1949. Pappe maintained that the subsequent policies of the state have continued to implement a program of ethnic cleansing.

- A growing chorus of Israeli journalists and social critics has exposed the abuses and illegality of the occupation and the political and social damage inflicted on the State of Israel itself by the subjugation of Palestinians in the West Bank and Gaza. Jewish Israeli journalists Gideon Levy and Amira Hass have filed weekly reports and opinion pieces in Israeli newspapers chronicling human rights abuses in the occupied territories. In *The Accidental Empire: Israel and the Birth of the Settlements, 1967–1977,* journalist Gershom Gorenberg showed how the power of the religious settler movement and the failure of political will on the part of the Israeli government resulted in the massive, ongoing, and illegal occupation. The book demonstrated how "moderate" left-wing Israeli governments allowed for and then supported the project of annexation and control that has been responsible for continued conflict and the failure of successive peace initiatives.

- Israeli public figures have begun to challenge the concept that Israel is a democracy. There is growing awareness that Israel's continuing efforts to maintain its Jewish majority is a major barrier to the establishment of a democratic society. Additionally, there have been legal challenges to laws regarding the ownership of land and real estate, which were designed in the pre-state colonization era to facilitate Jewish settlement and have been preserved in order to impose limits on the sale of land and housing to non-Jews. A July 30, 2007, article in *The New Yorker* about Avraham Burg, a prominent Israeli and former Speaker of the Knesset, quoted Burg's warning that Israel—"Holocaust-obsessed, militaristic, xenophobic, and, like Germany in the nineteen-thirties, vulnerable to an extremist minority"—was in danger of losing its status as a democracy.

- American and British journalists and former foreign service professionals have started to expose the myth of the United States as an "honest broker" to the peace process and the distortions underlying the concept of the "generous offers" purportedly rejected by the Palestinian leadership. In an influential 2001 *New York Review of Books* article, coauthors Professor Hussein Agha and political scientist and foreign policy advisor Robert Malley disputed the commonly-held opinion that Yasser Arafat and the Palestinian negotiating committee were solely responsible for the failure of the peace process in 2000.

- Public awareness has increased as the result of high-profile cases of attempts to silence critics of Israel in academia, religion, and public service. These have included attempts to deny tenure to academics critical of Israel, cancellation of appearances of public figures such as Archbishop Tutu, and harsh criticism of former president Jimmy Carter's 2006 book.

- The church establishment in the United States has demonstrated increasing awareness of human rights issues for Palestinians and has begun to initiate educational, global mission, and advocacy projects, including initiatives to divest from companies profiting from activities that violate human rights in the occupied territories.

The American public is becoming increasingly aware that the obstacles to peace are complex and that Israel, far from being an innocent victim, bears considerable responsibility and must be held accountable. We are emerging from a simplistic, David and Goliath perception of the conflict (in which, ironically, Israel has been seen as David even though it is far stronger militarily) into a nuanced discourse in which journalists, political scientists, theologians, historians, and public figures are participating. It is a discourse in which we as a society seem increasingly willing to examine the true nature of this conflict.

The Call

In the fall of 2006, I had just returned from Israel and the West Bank. I had traveled there with an interfaith delegation that included a number of progressive Christians active in several Protestant denominations. In the company of one of my fellow delegates, I delivered an address at a church in Washington, DC, well known for its active involvement in human rights and social justice causes. The pastor of the church introduced my colleague and me, and listened carefully to our presentations. We both spoke of our deep concern over Israel's violations of international law and the human rights of the West Bank Palestinians. For my part, I spoke candidly about my horror at the occupation, the damage done to Israeli society, and my heartbreak about and fear for my people. I charted my "conversion" from a Jew critical of some of Israel's policies but supportive of the Zionist vision to one who now questioned Israel's good faith in wanting to make peace with the Palestinians and who was now willing to cast fundamental doubt on the Zionist project as a whole. I said that I saw the dispossession of the Palestinians in 1948 and the occupation of Palestinian lands since 1967 as the root causes of Palestinian resistance, and that I was fully committed to seeking justice for the Palestinian people as the only path to peace.

After the presentation, the pastor approached me and said that while he agreed with much of what I had said and admired my passion, he felt that in talking about the Israel-Palestine conflict, we had to be sensitive to the feelings of Jews. I asked him what he meant by that. He answered like this: "I have studied Christian history, and I have to tell you that as a Christian I feel personally responsible for the evil of anti-Semitism and indeed for the Nazi Holocaust. I have been involved as a pastor in social justice work for my entire career, including years spent working with an interfaith group of Christian and Jewish clergy. Until recently, Israel and the Palestinians simply didn't come up. When, however, the issue of the Presbyterian Church's divestment from companies involved in the Israeli occupation was raised in 2004, I decided not to push the issue out of sensitivity for the rabbis in the group who were opposing divestment."

My Jewish pedigree must be impeccable; I looked at him and, with what can only be described as *chutzpah,*[1] replied, "Pastor, you need to do something else with your Christian guilt. The rabbis who will not engage with you in an honest discussion

---

1. Supreme self-confidence; nerve, gall. Yiddish, from the Hebrew.

about Israel and Zionism are not being friends of Israel. We Jews are in great peril, and Israel is in danger. We need your help as a Christian leader and as a worker for justice and peace. Allowing this discussion to be muzzled and holding back from engagement in this struggle is not what Jesus would want you to do." The pastor didn't flinch; he neither backed off from his position, nor dismissed my challenge. What began then has turned into an ongoing dialogue and a friendship I treasure. What also happened at that very moment was a call—the realization that I had been given a voice. My encounter with the pastor that day is the genesis of this book.

Parallel Crises

In his introduction to Rosemary Ruether's 1995 *Faith and Fratricide*, Catholic theologian Gregory Baum discusses the church's effort to reconcile with the Jewish people and rid itself of its deeply-rooted anti-Jewish biases. The problem, states Baum, is that "if the Church wants to clear itself of the anti-Jewish trends built into its teaching, a few marginal correctives won't do. It must examine the very center of its proclamation and reinterpret the meaning of the gospel for our times" (6–7). Baum, along with a preponderance of other writers, both Christian and Jewish, ties the need for this daunting project to the impact of the Nazi Holocaust:

> It was not until the holocaust of six million Jewish victims that some Christian theologians have been willing to face this question in a radical way. In his *Voice of Illness*, Aarne Siirala tells us that his visit to the death camps...overwhelmed him with shock and revealed to him that something was gravely sick at the very heart of our tradition...Auschwitz has a message that must be heard: it reveals an illness operative not on the margin of our civilization but at the heart of it, in the very best that we have inherited...It summons us to face up to the negative side of our religious and cultural heritage. (7)

The Crisis for Jews

This book emerges from one Jew's response to an experience similar to Siirala's. It is a mirror image: many Jews—academics, theologians, clergy, laypersons—particularly those who have traveled in the occupied Palestinian territories, have experienced what Baum calls a "moment of truth." It is the reaction of a now-triumphant, dominant group to the evidence of where their actions have led in the form of oppression, the trampling of human rights, and a fundamental abrogation of justice, differences in scale and (some) methods notwithstanding.

The reactions of those Jews who have opened themselves to an awareness of the grim consequences of the Zionist project are varied. They range from a tentative willingness to peek under the covers of the Zionist dream, to an experience of horror over Israel's human rights violations, to a full-fledged opposition to the very concept of a state created for and run by Jews. For me there is a bright line that separates those who, although critical of Israel's policies, continue to support the validity of a Jewish state in historic Palestine from those who see the Zionist idea as realized in the modern state as the root cause of the injustices of the current situation.

What often separates these two groups is the experience of actually seeing the occupation up close. This not only produces the crisis I experienced, but also opens one up to an awareness of the events surrounding the establishment of the state over sixty years ago, events officially denied until very recently by Israel and most of the rest of the world. Few who allow themselves to understand the occupation for what it is—the systematic project to undermine the autonomous and free existence of Palestinians in the West Bank and Gaza in the service of selective annexation and effectively full control of the territory by Israel—fail to see it as a continuation of the ethnic cleansing carried out between 1947 and 1949. Thus, the full realization of what political Zionism has done in Palestine comes home. It is not only the "mistake" of the occupation that is the problem; it is the very foundation of the state itself established through the dispossession and continuing denial of the rights of the indigenous inhabitants of the land.

What is uncanny and tragic is that in the current discourse, the roles of the combatants are turned upside down: the Jews are portrayed as the victims, and the Palestinians as the aggressors. In truth, it is the Palestinians who have been most victimized: dispossessed, powerless, and pained. In every way, Jews have been victorious and all-powerful in historic Palestine. The Jews of Israel are, to be sure, victimized by acts of violent resistance on the part of extremist Palestinian groups, and the terrorizing effect of these acts is not to be minimized. During its over sixty-year history of six wars, two insurrections, intermittent suicide attacks, and long periods of cross-border shellings, the citizens of Israel have lived under the cloud of a threat they have experienced as unending and, for many, imminent. But the impact on Israelis must be seen in the context of the catastrophic losses suffered by the Palestinian people at the birth of the state, the destruction caused by two wars on Lebanon, the ongoing effect of Israel's military occupation on Palestinian society, and most recently the devastation caused by the invasion and bombing of Gaza in early 2009. The attacks on Israel are to be understood, therefore, not as the expression of implacable anti-Jewish feeling, but as the responses of a deeply injured and increasingly desperate indigenous population.

At the same time, Palestinian resistance, fueled by the desperation and humiliation of a displaced and occupied people, has been amplified and exploited by political forces within and outside Palestine. Acts of resistance such as suicide bombings and shelling attacks are terrifying. But Israel's overall power and security are not threatened by these acts. Suicide bombings are horrible and shocking. But it is too easy and too convenient to tar an entire people with the brush of terrorism, which is precisely what has happened. The image of the Palestinians as a violent people bent on the destruction of Israel is not a true picture. The truth is that by and large the Palestinians are a peaceful, patient people. Their sin over the last sixty-plus years has been their relative lack of organization—set up effectively by the British during their thirty-year rule—in the face of the highly organized and effective Zionist colonial project. They are paying for this now as they face the ongoing dismantling of their economy and their infrastructure, and the continuing program to disable their leadership and ability to self-govern. Israel, with the assistance of the United States, has taken over where Britain left off, and with far greater efficiency and thoroughness. A growing number of Jews in Israel and outside the state see this, and for us the effect has been shattering; the shock, horror, and crisis of identity I experienced as a Jew witnessing the crimes being committed in my name are not unique.

The Crisis for Christians

This crisis for Jews stands in poignant parallel to the Christian confrontation with the Nazi Holocaust. Christians, in the very midst of a struggle to come to terms with their relationship to anti-Semitism, must now also confront the complex reality of a Jewish state. Ironically, political Zionism owes its success in part to the Nazi Holocaust, the same catastrophe that has spurred a radical reevaluation of the foundations of Christianity. Historians have noted the influence of a deeply-rooted Zionism in Christian Europe in the support for Jewish settlement in Palestine in the nineteenth and early twentieth centuries. So there are two strains within Christianity: one conservative (Christian Zionism) and one liberal/progressive (interfaith reconciliation). Both produce a tendency to support both the concept and the reality of the Jewish state. Both act powerfully to stifle criticism of Israel. This helps explain the reluctance—phobia might be a better word—of many Christians to call Israel to account for its human rights abuses and its denial of justice to Palestinians. We are presented with a daunting irony: Christians, attempting to atone for the crimes committed *against* the Jews, are by this very fact blocked from confronting the crimes committed *by* the Jews.

Where does this leave Jews who today find themselves torn between their commitment to religious and racial equality and their loyalty and attachment to the State of Israel? Where does this leave contemporary Christians, committed to social justice and to their communal endeavors as faith communities? The book will return, again and again, to these questions: in our own time, with the question of Israel/Palestine only increasing in urgency, what is the proper relationship of the rest of humankind to the Jewish people and to our national homeland project? And what must we do as a Jewish community as we struggle with the agony of our situation in historic Palestine? What is the future we want to create for ourselves?

Chapter 2

My Journey

Could we say that the healing of our historical traumas might come about when we see in the faces of the Palestinian people our own faces, bloodied, humiliated yet bearing a great hope?

—Marc Ellis, *Beyond Occupation*

I am the grandson of a fifth-generation Palestinian Jew. My grandfather, Joseph Back, was the direct descendant of one of the great Hasidic rabbis of Europe. His family, out of religious zeal, settled in the Jewish quarter of the Old City of Jerusalem in the early nineteenth century. Joseph was born in Jerusalem in the year 1900: an orthodox Jew, a Palestinian, and a subject of the Ottoman sultan. As a boy, he played in the narrow stone streets of the Old City with Jewish and Arab playmates, and prayed in a synagogue built in the shadow of the site of the Temple destroyed by the Romans in 70 CE. As a young man (by most accounts a bit of a misfit in this pious family), he seized the opportunity to leave the poverty of Jerusalem for the reputedly gold-paved streets of America. His marriage was arranged; my grandmother and her two sisters, first-generation Americans born to a strictly orthodox Jew, were taken to the Holy Land to find husbands with a suitably devout pedigree. My grandfather met the standard, and they were packed off to America. They settled in the bustling immigrant enclave of South Philadelphia; my mother, their first child, was born three months after their arrival in early 1921. In 1945, she married another first-generation American, the charming and handsome son of two of the over two million Jewish immigrants who had fled the pogroms of Russia between 1880 and 1924 before U.S. immigration quotas slammed the door shut.

I was born in 1948, a month before the declaration of the State of Israel. Zionism was mother's milk to me—a Zionism framed in religion. Despite the unusual family history, my experience was far from unique. Any practicing Jew born in America in the postwar years was raised in a religion that was a mixture of political Zionism and Rabbinic Judaism. In this quasi-messianic stew, love of the State of Israel was completely intertwined with faithfulness to the commandments. Maps of the new state and photographs of daily life on the collective farms (one hand on the plow, the other on the gun) took their place alongside Bible stories and Hebrew language study in the synagogue classrooms. Zionist folk songs and Israeli military ballads were sung in school assemblies and festival celebrations alongside traditional liturgical tunes. The mythologically tinged history of the Zionist settlement and the history of the State of Israel was as much a part of the curriculum of my Jewish day school education as was study of Jewish ritual and theology. In our prayers, we beseeched God three times a day to protect and bless the State of Israel—"the first flowering of our redemption." I was taught that a miracle, born of heroism and bravery, had blessed my generation. The State of Israel was not merely a historical event; *it was redemption.* In every generation, so goes the song we would sing every year at the Passover seder, tyrants—Pharaoh, Chmielnitzki, Hitler, and, of course, Gamal Nasser—rise up to oppress us, and the Lord stretches out his hand to redeem our people. Jewish history was a story of struggle, exile, oppression, and slaughter that had culminated in a homeland, again, and at last.

I Meet My Israeli Family

My grandfather may have left the Holy Land, but the heart of the family remained in Jerusalem. Two of Joseph's four children and several grandchildren have emigrated to Israel. My mother's younger sister Sylvia was the first, having left for Palestine in 1947 as part of the wave of American Jews committed to the realization of the Zionist dream that was unfolding in the wake of the Nazi Holocaust. For Sylvia, this journey was at least in part a ticket out of the family she never quite felt she belonged to: the older sister—my mother—prim and responsible (Sylvia was wild, artistic, messy, rebellious); the brothers, who got the resources and privileges; the stern father, religious and hardworking; the mother, emotionally warm but depleted from the privations of the Great Depression. Sylvia joined Hashomer Hadati, the religious Zionist organization, adopted her Hebrew name, Yaffa, and hopped on a boat to become, in Zionist parlance, a "halutza"—a pioneer. There she met and married a Czech refugee, one of the few from his family to escape Hitler's Holocaust, and settled down to build the Jewish homeland.

It was the summer of 1965. I was seventeen, sitting on my aunt Yaffa's back porch in K'far Haroeh, a religious agricultural village on a hill overlooking Israel's coastal plain. A huge domed *yeshiva* (house of Jewish study) situated at the highest point dominated the settlement dotted with citrus groves and simple stucco homes.

It was the Israel of the picture books and novels of my childhood. I had come to Israel on the summer youth tour sponsored by the United Synagogue of Conservative Judaism. I had spoken Hebrew with the children in the schoolyard, the shopkeeper in the town, and the farmer in the field. Travelling the mountain road up to Jerusalem, I had seen the burned-out jeeps from the 1948 "War of Liberation," still maintained as a monument to the battle for the capital, lying by the side of the road approaching the city. I had met my grandfather's brothers, who looked like him (and like me) and were warm and loving to the grandson of the renegade—I was the boy who had "come home." Seventeen years of religious training and education in language, history, and culture had clicked into place. Proud of the miracle of modern Israel, of what my people had done, creating this vibrant country out of the ashes of Auschwitz, I was in love—deeply, ecstatically.

We were sitting together eating a meal—Yaffa, her three children, and I. They were talking about the Arabs. I don't remember the context of the conversation. But I do remember the tone and the attitude: it was the way people talked about black people in the pre-civil rights Philadelphia in which I had grown up. I heard the racism, and I understood the fear that lay just under its surface. I knew there were Arabs in the land—we didn't talk about Palestinians then—but in the story I had been told, they figured only as the enemies who had been defeated in the war and who continued to threaten the security of the young state. And in that moment, I understood that there was more to the story. In that moment, in the midst of my flush of enchantment and delight at the miracle of the Jewish state, and in the midst of the warmest family love I had ever experienced, I knew that there was a problem, a fatal flaw in the Zionist dream. The dream that had produced the storybook land of kibbutzim and cities of white stone and black-hatted men free to recreate their Old World of spirit and study was built on a shaky foundation, a foundation of denial. There were other people here; they were here when we arrived from the shores of an inhospitable, murderous Europe. I knew this, and I also could see that, in this ingathering of my blood, these "others" didn't count. And I knew, somehow, even then, that this fundamental flaw would grow and ultimately overtake the dream of independence and security.

A seed of doubt had been planted, but my attachment to the land stayed strong. Back in the U.S., as a college freshman, I watched the drama of the Six-Day War unfold, and I rejoiced in Israel's victory. David had triumphed, again, over the Goliath of the Arab nations that sought our destruction: "Jerusalem is ours!" The romance of the Land was playing out, more powerfully than ever. After college, I lived for a year on a kibbutz in the Galilee, ignoring the implications of the pre-1948 Palestinian houses still in evidence on the kibbutz grounds and the ancient olive trees standing at the edges of its fields and byways. I could not ignore, however, a meeting with a Palestinian family living down the road, a family displaced when their village, which lay in sight of my kibbutz, was turned into a pile of rubble. They told me the story of their banishment in 1948. They told me that, following their expulsion by Jewish forces, they returned again and again to their homes, despite being told by the Israeli army that their being there was a "security risk." Finally, they told me, the village was dynamited—"Golda blew up our village!" was the way they put it. *Golda? My Golda Meir*, the hero of my people along with David Ben-Gurion? *My Golda* was throwing people out of their homes, stealing their farms, dynamiting their villages? Another seed had been planted.

Returning home, Israel took a backseat to graduate school, marriage, and raising children. My concerns about Israel increased in direct proportion to the pace of illegal settlement building. Still, I held to the Jewish narrative: the occupation, although lamentably abusive of human rights, was the price of security. The seeds of doubt lay dormant for almost forty years. Then I went to the West Bank.

The Other Israel

Traveling in Israel and the occupied territories in the summer of 2006, my defenses against the reality of Israel's crimes crumbled. I witnessed the Separation Wall grabbing huge swaths of Palestinian land, the checkpoints controlling the movement of Palestinians within their own territory and strangling farming, commerce, access to health care, education, and social intercourse. I saw the network of new roads restricted to Israelis; I learned about the assassinations, midnight raids, and collective punishment; I saw the massive, continuing construction of illegal Jewish settlements and towns; I heard firsthand about the vicious acts of ideological Jewish settlers, and words like apartheid and ethnic cleansing sprang to my mind, unbidden and undeniable. That summer, forty years after my first encounter with the land, I saw all this, and my relationship with Israel changed forever.

My last night in Palestine that summer fell on the ninth of Av, a Jewish day of fasting and mourning, the traditional date of the destruction of the Temple of Solomon and the beginning of the exile of the Jews two thousand years ago. The book of Lamentations, a source text for our liturgy of mourning, attributed by tradition to the prophet Jeremiah, is chanted that night. It is a harrowing description of a people fallen and traumatized.

> *Jerusalem has greatly sinned*
> *Therefore has she been made a mockery.*
> *All who admired her despise her*
> *For they have seen her disgraced.*
>
> *Panic and pitfall are our lot,*
> *Death and destruction.*
> *My eyes shed streams of water*
> *Over the brokenness of my poor people.* (Lam. 1:8, 4:46–48; author's translation)

On that night, I sat on a hill overlooking the Old City, in the company of congregations of praying Jews, mostly American émigrés worshiping, I felt, at the shrine of their Jerusalem—a Jerusalem "reclaimed" at the expense of the Palestinian people; a Jerusalem that for Palestinians is also a spiritual and political center; a Jerusalem that is being taken from them street by street, farm by farm, village by village. I stood on that hill and chanted the words as I had every year on this day, descriptions of starvation, rape, slaughter, destruction of homes, and banishment from the land, and, for the life of me, I could apply the words only to the Palestinians. In these words, I now felt *their* suffering. And my eyes shed streams of water for them, my Palestinian brothers and sisters, and yes, for the brokenness of my own people.

Two Worlds

I had travelled that summer as a delegate with Interfaith Peace Builders, an organization that began as a program of The Fellowship of Reconciliation. FOR is an old and fascinating organization. It was founded in 1914 at the outbreak of World War I by an English Quaker and a German Lutheran who, on a railway platform in Cologne, committed themselves to working for peace even as their countries embarked on war. FOR has continued to work for peace and reconciliation everywhere in the world where there is conflict. Interfaith Peace Builders is devoted to building relationships between Israeli, Palestinian, and North American peace activists by sending delegations of North Americans to Israel/Palestine. It was the journey I had been dreaming of for years, and I signed up.

That summer, I lived in two worlds. I woke up every morning in the home of my uncle Nate and aunt Toby in the German Colony section of Jerusalem, a neighborhood of stately homes that, until 1948, housed well-to-do Palestinian families, now displaced and living in the West Bank or abroad. The neighborhood is now one of the most fashionable in West Jerusalem, and it is peopled entirely by Jews. None of them ever venture into Arab East Jerusalem except for the occasional shopping excursion to the Arab marketplace or religious pilgrimage to the Western Wall, near the site of the Jewish Temple destroyed in 70 CE. Between 1948, when the Jewish forces retreated from the walled Old City and the eastern half of Jerusalem in the face of the Arab Legion, and 1967, when the Israeli Army recaptured the eastern side in the Six-Day War, a Berlin-type wall had divided the city.

The wall of wood and mortar that had bisected the city was now gone, but the ethnographic barrier remained. I left Jewish West Jerusalem in the morning and walked to the east side to rejoin my delegation for a day of touring and meetings with groups devoted to activism, education, and reconciliation. I crossed the street that once marked the boundary wall, and in a surreal, almost magical moment—like a cinematic special effect—I entered another world. With one step, I left Jewish West Jerusalem and entered Arab East Jerusalem. Walking down Saladin Street, I reveled in the sights, sounds, and feel of the place. In contrast to sedate, devout, manicured, and ordered West Jerusalem, East Jerusalem was riotous in color and tempestuous in emotion. Daily, I experienced the vivid contrast between the two cultures. On the one hand, there was the indigenous Palestinian culture: passionate, industrious, wise, connected deeply to the land. On the other was the new Israeli civilization: transplanted from Europe, carved into the ancient landscape, marvelously creative, hardworking, and hungry for life…and ignorant of the people it was displacing. I stopped a distinguished-looking man in traditional Arab dress to ask for directions, and almost began to address him in Hebrew. I had forgotten that I had crossed the invisible barrier that separates Jew from Palestinian.

For my first fifty-eight years, "Jerusalem" had been Jewish West Jerusalem. I had now discovered the whole city, and it was split in half. In this divided city, I would have to choose which side I would prefer to live in, which language I would prefer to speak. I made this crossing twice every day: eastward in the morning, back west at night. I realized that I was feeling increasingly at home on the east side. I was profoundly disturbed by this feeling. I felt torn apart. What did it mean now to be a Jew? Who was I?

The Theft of the Future

Our delegation traveled that day to the Bethlehem area, to the town of Beit Sahour, a splendid West Bank city of homes, small factories, shops, fine churches, and stately mosques, spilling up and down the sides of a valley in the hills south of Jerusalem. Along the northen edge of the valley where once a wooded hillside graced the highest ridge is Har Homah, an illegal Jewish settlement. Visually, it is an obscenity: a gray, sprawling concrete scar on the landscape. Dominating the valley and the restricted Jewish road linking Jerusalem to Bethlehem, Har Homah links the planned "Greater Jerusalem"[1] with the fertile area south of

---

1. Following the capture of the West Bank in 1967, Israel illegally annexed East Jerusalem. The ensuing years have seen a systematic and aggressive program of "Judaizing" the areas north, east, and south of Jewish West Jerusalem. This includes confiscation of Palestinian land for the construction of Jewish-only neighborhoods and suburbs, virtual elimination of all non-Jewish construction, demolition of Palestinian homes, and construction of the separation wall and a system of new, Jewish-only roads to create an enclosed Jewish megalopolis accessible only to Jews. The

Bethlehem that is essentially becoming Jewish Jerusalem's southern suburb. The road marks the boundary of free movement for the Palestinian residents of the valley. Those who cross this road, even by foot, are subject to fines and other punishments—or worse. The people of Beit Sahour—prisoners in their own land—sit. Their frustration and anger fester.

Our delegation spent the night as recipients of the hospitality of a number of Beit Sahour's families. When my fellow delegate and I arrived at our host's home, I was greeted by Najwa, a warm, gracious woman of about my age, widowed three years before our visit. She had a love of life, harvesting the olive grove and herb garden on the plot of land adjoining her home overlooking the city. "This is your home," she said as she greeted us. Awad, her twenty-one-year-old son, reminded me of my son Jacob: brown curly hair, wide, deep, intense eyes, a tall frame, powerful hands. He was completing a degree in accounting at Bethlehem University. Upon graduation, there would be virtually no chance for a job in occupied Palestine. He did not want to leave his family or his hometown, but "I have no future here," he said. That night, his friend George visited; George was also twenty-one, a handsome, bright young man, still full of fire and humor. But his mood changed when I ask him what his current pursuits were. George was a gifted computer programmer. When he was still in high school, he moved freely across the Israel-West Bank border to apprentice with Israeli software companies. He was accepted, appreciated, and on his way. After the outbreak of the Second Intifada[2] in 2000, everything changed. Suddenly, the Israelis pulled back; he was no longer welcome in the workplace. "They treated me as if I were a terrorist. They looked at me as if I had explosives strapped to my chest!" The pain in George's eyes was

government-sponsored and financed plan for Greater Jerusalem absorbs previously Palestinian areas of settlement north and south of the city, and urbanizes agricultural land to the east toward the Jordan valley, effectively bisecting what remains of the Palestinian West Bank into two separated areas.

2. Palestinian uprising

deep. He was hurt, deeply, and stalled. He was going to school to become an accountant, but the enthusiasm was gone. What is left for a twenty-one-year-old who has no sense of a future?

I was deeply upset by my conversations with Awad and George. At dinner with Najwa, her two children, and my fellow delegate Nicole, I turned to Najwa and said, "The Israelis are scared of you. They don't know you, and they don't want to." Najwa was silent, her eyes sad, acknowledging the truth of my words. Later I called my aunt in West Jerusalem—without knowing why, I felt I had to talk to her—and as I spoke to her, I was overtaken by the strength of my feelings: "Oh God, Toby," I said, "we are killing them! We are putting up walls to make them invisible. We are stifling their growth, thwarting their young men, and we just don't seem to care! It's horrible, horrible!" The telephone connection to West Jerusalem, fragile at best, cut off as these words left my lips, and as the tears, surprising and unbidden, spilled down my face.

But who was this "we"? I am not an Israeli, but as a Jew I felt responsible for the actions of this state. Certainly, I became responsible for any continued inaction on my part once I had seen what I had seen, knew what I knew, and felt what I felt. It was not yet clear to me, however, what I was supposed to do. I was deeply torn; wasn't this Israel, the land that was to keep us safe, the dream of millennia, the haven from anti-Semitism?

The call to witness, however, is powerful. As I write about the experience of that summer, I find myself thinking about Amira Hass, Israeli peace activist and journalist, a child of Holocaust survivors, who lives in Ramallah in the West Bank, sending weekly dispatches to the Israeli press to tell her fellow Jews the true story of the occupation. Hass credits her mother for showing her the way to her own course of action as a Jew and an Israeli. She tells the story of her mother on a day in 1944, herded from a cattle car into the Bergen-Belsen death camp. As she climbed down from the train, Hass's mother observed a group of German women on bicycles, slowing down to watch with indifferent curiosity on their faces. "For me," writes Hass, "these women became a loathsome symbol of watching from the sidelines, and at an early age I decided that my place was not with the bystanders" (Ellis 2004, 143).

The Mount of Memory

On a hilltop in the hills west of Jerusalem stands Mount Herzl, also known as Har Hazikaron, the Mount of Memory. At its highest point lies the grave of Theodore Herzl, the founder of political Zionism. Israeli heads of state and other national heroes are buried on Mount Herzl. On the northern slope is Israel's national military cemetery. And on the western slope is Yad Vashem, Israel's Holocaust museum. When our group arrived that morning, the parking lot was already full of cars and buses: school groups, soldiers in training, tour groups like ours.

As visitors approach the museum from the parking lot, they pass under a huge archway inscribed with the words of the prophet Ezekiel from the famous vision of the Dry Bones: "I will put my breath into you and you shall live again and I will set you upon your own soil" (Ezek. 37:14 [Jewish Publication Society 1985]). Contemplating this inscription, I was rooted to the spot. We had been in Jerusalem and the West Bank for four days. I was bursting with outrage at what I had seen. I was not feeling close to the redemptive Zionist dream. It had been six years since my last pilgrimage to this museum. Since my last visit, the museum had been rebuilt; this was the new and improved version, taking much from the original museum and housing it in a new architectural format and adding new exhibits, the first of which confronts you as soon as you enter:

I stood before a huge wall on which is projected a movie depicting the lost world of the Jews of Eastern Europe. Moving before me, across a map of Russia, Poland, and Germany, was a stunning, heartbreaking photographic record of the world that had been lost: artisans, musicians, laborers, teachers, villages, houses of study, children. All gone. The movie ended with a photograph of a choir of Jewish children, somewhere in Europe, and on the soundtrack they are singing *Hatikvah* ("The Hope"), the Zionist poem and the national anthem of the State of Israel.

I was shattered. A hand had reached into me, grabbed hold of my heart, and drawn me back into my past, into the collective memory of my people. How could I turn my back on this? How could I walk away from my history, from this incalculable, unfathomable loss, and, more so, from Israel, my deliverance? It had worked. I was hooked. What was I to do now? I had no choice. Emptied, numb, and confused, I turned and walked down the hall into the museum.

It's a brilliant exhibition. One walks *down, into* it. It is subterranean—no windows, no light, no escape. You are led through corridors and tunnels, with no control and no way out but through. One traverses the whole, familiar story: from the laws enacted in the thirties, the walls of isolation, privation, and degradation closing in, to the Final Solution: the ovens, the stacked bodies, the faces of the children. Darkness closes your heart—you feel you will never escape from this horror, this black hole of evil and despair. Then, turning a corner into the final gallery, on display are the blown-up photos of the ships bringing the refugees to the shores of Israel, faces shining with hope and gratitude. There is David Ben-Gurion reading from the Israeli Declaration of Independence. And then, suddenly, you emerge. Ascending a wide flight of stairs, you are outside, in the light and the open air, standing on a wide patio that looks out on the Jerusalem Hills. *It's the final exhibit.* And then it hit me. This was no mere museum. This was a lesson; this was indoctrination: from the biblical quote at the entrance, into the depths, and to this sight—The Land. The reward. Our destiny.

The fifty-eight-year spell was broken. I got it. And something let go, and it was okay.

Diane, a fellow delegate, turned to me as we walked out and asked if I had seen the part about how the Nazis acted to marginalize, dispossess, and banish the Jews, the part before the extermination camps and the ovens. She asked if I had seen that this was what we had witnessed over the last few days. Yes, I had seen. The spell was broken. I got it. And it was okay.

Treading, as I had so many times, the sacred ground of the Holocaust, I had, for the first time, broken The Rule: our Holocaust, *the Holocaust*, must not be compared to any other disaster, genocide, or crime. It has to stand as the ultimate humanitarian crime, *the* genocide. Not only that, I had also broken a rule so fundamental, so important that it is never even spoken: I had compared the Jews to the Nazis. And it was okay. Because, for the first time, I knew what I had to do; I knew how to understand and integrate the Holocaust. For one thing had not changed: the Nazi Holocaust would continue to be the formative historical event of my life. But now, from this day forward, finding the meaning of the Holocaust meant working for justice for Palestine. There were too many parallels, too many ways in which Israel was doing to the Palestinians what the Nazis did to us. No, we had not built death camps. But we were turning into beasts, into persecutors, and we were killing a civilization.

Here was the most terrible irony in this scenario: in enshrining our own memory, in living out our liturgy of destruction, to use theologian Marc Ellis's phrase, we have been erasing the history of another. It is a terrible irony that Yad Vashem, along with Har Herzl, is built on top of these hills west of Jerusalem, hills littered with the remains of Palestinian villages. Some have been turned into parks for the Jews of Jerusalem. Most are ruins, stones bleaching in the sun, standing guard over uncultivated terraces of olives and grapes, witnesses to shattered lives and a murdered civilization.

The Erasure of Memory, the Courage to Remember

"Culture, Leisure, and Opportunity!" So read the real estate advertising billboard in front of the ruined train station of Manshiyah at the southern tip of Tel Aviv, where today's skyscraper-filled municipality stretches out its metal and glass fingers to obliterate the last shreds of Palestinian society on Israel's coastal strip. The magnificent Hassan Bek Mosque has presided in silent witness over the wasteland stretching from beach to industrial zone, land that had once been part of the thriving Palestinian city of Jaffa.

Our delegation stood on the sandy soil and contemplated this train station that once linked the people of Palestine to Cairo, Beirut, and Damascus and to the wider world beyond. The mosque has witnessed the gradual destruction of the neighborhood it once served. Jaffa, once a hub of Palestinian commerce and culture, a city of stone-paved clustered streets rising from the harbor, now houses shops selling kiln-fired platters and religious-themed oil paintings for the Israeli tourist market, air-conditioned real estate offices, and fish restaurants. The transition of Manshiyah to urban mall is the final step, the erasure of the last sign of the society that once thrived here. Now, the shopping mall and condominiums will turn the once busy station into merchandise for Tel Aviv developers. Only the great mosque remains—not yet a ruin, not yet a synagogue, yet too substantial an edifice to be touched. But the skyscraper has triumphed. "The city is eating the mosque," our Israeli activist guide told us.

In 1948, the Palestinians of Jaffa were driven into the sea, a scene captured in a single photograph showing a desperate rush into the harbor's waters, men and women carrying their belongings and their children on their shoulders. Many drowned. The white-hot sun and unnamed photographer were the only eyewitnesses as the world looked away, silently approving this taking, this conquering, this erasure. Today, five hundred yards north on the beachfront, a museum honoring the heroes of the "Battle to Liberate Jaffa" has been built atop the ruins of a Palestinian home. It serves as a popular backdrop for formal wedding pictures. *Culture, leisure, opportunity.*

Amid this there were signs of hope. Under the surface of an Israeli society devoted to office towers, software development giants, hell-bent highway construction, land taking, and military might, the struggle for human dignity and peace continues. That day our delegation met with a number of extraordinary individuals and organizations confronting the madness and self-destruction brought by the conflict, people and organizations devoted to finding positive forms of creativity, connection, and power in the midst of conflict, fear, and war.

We visited Combatants for Peace, a joint Palestinian-Israeli group of former fighters, and met Bassam Aramin, imprisoned as a boy for raising the Palestinian flag with his schoolmates, now a passionate fighter for nonviolence and self-determination for the Palestinian people. Bassam, whose ten-year-old daughter was murdered by the Israeli army six months prior to our visit, has not wavered in his commitment to bridge the gap between the two societies. He meets with Israeli and Palestinian schoolchildren to tell his story along with his Israeli partners: men who refuse to put on the Israeli army uniform to serve in the occupied territories. We sat with Rami Elhanan, a Jewish Israeli and war veteran, who, after his daughter was killed by a Palestinian suicide bomber, established the Bereaved Families Circle with his wife, Nurit. This group of Israelis and Palestinians who have lost children to the conflict meet to cross the lines of grief and conflict. They refuse to be enemies.

We met with Zochrot ("We remember"), a group of Israelis devoted to education about the Nakba—the ethnic cleansing of over five hundred Palestinian villages, towns, and cities during the military campaign to establish the State of Israel in 1948. And we sat with the men and women of New Profile, an organization of Israelis working to create a society fit for their children in the face of the militarism that pervades their schools, media, and political process.

Our day ended standing in the hot sun of Tel Aviv, the sparkling Mediterranean at our backs, gazing at the ruined railway station, the garish real estate billboard, and the stately, lonely mosque. In the midst of the erasure of memory, we found a commitment to the preservation of wholeness, respect, and continuity. In the midst of destruction, loss, and despair, we witnessed the courage to hope and the stubborn determination to fight for peace and human dignity.

Three Teachers

Sometimes—rare and precious times—you encounter someone who speaks to your heart directly, without pretense or holding back, without the condition or caution of "I must not come on too strong and risk offending or preaching." Nora Carmi of Sabeel is such a person, and our delegation spent an inspiring and, for some of us, shattering hour and a half with her on our first full day in Jerusalem. Sabeel is an organization of Christian Palestinians committed to liberation theology. The people of Sabeel—the Arabic word means "the way," and also "source of life-giving water"—confront the severe challenges of life in Palestine today by emulating the mission and life of Jesus. Sabeel does this by embracing nonviolence. This includes supporting and collaborating with nonviolent activist groups of all three Abrahamic faiths in Israel/Palestine, creating and disseminating educational materials, organizing local and international conferences, and working with youth.

Nora has worked for Sabeel for years. She is a Jerusalemite, a refugee in her own land—her family lost their West Jerusalem home in 1948. The wars and troubles of the land have brought Nora—a mother and a grandmother—pain, loss, and fear. Yet she does not lose her faith and her commitment to the true meaning of Jesus's life and message. "Jesus was a Palestinian Jew who lived under Roman occupation," Nora pointed out. As we all know, faced with this situation, Jesus did not turn to hatred of his oppressors, nor to fomenting violent rebellion. On the contrary: he taught nonviolent resistance to the evils of empire.

Nora said to us, "We do not have the right to destroy this land." She challenged us with the question, "How do we bring justice to this country of Muslims, Jews, and Christians?" I asked Nora if she thought that the reality of a Jewish state had led to injustice. She paused and answered simply, "Yes." She said that for this reason, Sabeel supports the ideal of one state in which Jews and Palestinians could live together as equals, even though she is not optimistic about this coming to pass. Despite this pessimism, Nora has faith and is philosophical. Empires do not last, she pointed out.

It had been important for me to ask my question. It was a question I had been asking myself for a long time. I didn't feel that Nora's answer was anti-Israel, and certainly not anti-Semitic. Nora said, "I feel sorrow and compassion for the Jews of Israel, as I do for all of us suffering through this particular period of history." Her statement presaged, for me, what we would hear several hours later from Israeli Rami Elhanan of the Bereaved Parents Circle, a man devoted to nonviolence and to mutual understanding between Jews and Palestinians, who asked what was Jewish about systematically humiliating and dominating a people for decades. "There is nothing Jewish about this," he said.

As we were leaving, I turned to my fellow delegate Yolande and said, "I would stand with this woman." Yolande said nothing—we both knew what I meant. Nora had shown us what it means to stand firm: how to know yourself and your faith so surely and with such conviction, clarity, commitment, and love, that nothing can knock you down—nothing from outside yourself, and nothing from inside yourself. Leaving Sabeel, I took with me a copy of Naim Ateek's book, *Justice Only Justice: A Palestinian Theology of Liberation*. I would leave Palestine still torn, still unsure of where I stood with my Judaism, but the book contained the key.

Naim Ateek was eight years old in 1948, the year of my birth, the year that Zionist forces expelled his family from their home, their farm, their church, and their village. Father Ateek spoke to me from the pages of his book, a book that recounts how his experience of dispossession and occupation led him directly to his belief in the centrality of justice in his faith. It is a book that traces a direct line from the Old Testament prophets of my youth to Jesus of Nazareth. Did I believe in the prophets' call for justice? Had I been taught that the core of my identity as a Jew was a commitment to compassion for all people, and the prophetic charge to walk humbly with God? Had not my own father taught me this? I realized that to feel the outrage I felt toward the actions of my own people was as Jewish as I could get. The work for justice in Israel and Palestine that gradually took shape in the months following my return to the United States was to become my synagogue.

I have learned that when telling this story, I have to explain that I have not converted to Christianity. Yes, Naim Ateek had brought Jesus's message to me, and it was to my Jewish identity that his words spoke. I saw Jesus, in the words of theologian Marcus Borg, as "a social prophet like the great social prophets of Israel" (1999, 72). After my return from Palestine and Israel that summer, I returned home one Sunday afternoon following a presentation to a church group. It was one of a string of appearances and meetings that month in churches and with Christian groups. My wife turned to me, and, only half joking (after thirty years of marriage she has learned to expect the unexpected), asked, "Are you becoming Christian?" I had not been prepared for the question. But the answer was right there. I said, "No, I'm becoming Jewish."

Yad Vashem had broken the spell. Sabeel had helped open a pathway back to the prophets. But there were more teachers along the way.

One of them was Said Rabieh, our delegation's tour guide, a Palestinian man of erudition, humor, and integrity. On a Friday evening on the last weekend of our tour, the delegation attended a Jewish worship service. It was the traditional ushering in of the Jewish Sabbath, which, like all Jewish holy days, begins at sunset. It's a beautiful service, infused with a joyous, mystical spirit. The service opens with the singing of a series of psalms and medieval hymns extolling the divine activities of renewal and contemplation that we imitate in observing the commandment to rest, as God did, on the seventh day. This was a synagogue established in Jerusalem by the United Synagogue of Conservative Judaism, an American Jewish denomination observing a midpoint between the poles of Orthodox and Reform Judaism. This was the denomination in which I had been raised and educated. This particular synagogue, located in the heart of West Jerusalem, caters to American Jews visiting or living in Israel. I had mixed emotions about attending the worship service—it had been some time since I had been inside a synagogue—but as the service began, I felt myself drawn into the singing and the spirit.

At that point, a large group entered; I didn't know them personally, but I knew who they were. This was a group of Jewish teenagers on a summer tour sponsored by this same American

Jewish denomination—the one in which I had grown up. They took up a large section at the front of the room, and began to sing enthusiastically, and, very much in the spirit of the service, to dance. They lifted up their voices and their arms to heaven, ecstatically welcoming the Sabbath in the style of the medieval Kabbalists. My heart froze. I was looking at myself, forty years earlier, a seventeen-year-old on the same synagogue-sponsored tour. I turned to Maia, one of our delegation leaders, a Quaker woman who had worked for peace in Palestine for many years. I whispered to her, "I know this group. They are in love with their Judaism and they are in love with Jerusalem. The Palestinians don't exist for them. They would see them dead for the pleasure of celebrating their Judaism in their Jerusalem." Maia simply looked at me and nodded her head; she understood.

It was an emotionally violent response; I had surprised myself. Several members of our delegation who heard about what I said to Maia—apparently the story got around—were horrified, and angry at me. And certainly, my characterization of these kids was unfair: I didn't know them. This was "my stuff" talking, my own anger and shame, my own still-to-be-resolved feelings about having been religiously programmed as a child. I was close to certain that the teenagers I was watching had not seen what I had seen and had no awareness of what had happened and was still happening to the Palestinians of Jerusalem. But this was partly the point; they had been indoctrinated into the Zionist narrative, as I had been in my youth. Unaware of the cost paid for their "Jewish" Jerusalem by the Palestinian people, were they not complicit?

After the service, I sat with Said, who had come to bring us back to our hotel. I had to talk to him; I couldn't contain my feelings. I told him the story, explaining to him how intense it had been to look in the mirror in this way, and I repeated my statement, but now in the second person: "They would see you dead, Said, for the privilege of worshiping in their Jerusalem." Said was silent, taking this in calmly; he, too, understood. "These are my people," I said. "This is who I am returning to." He answered, "Then you know what you have to do."

The third teacher was Professor Marc Ellis. After my return home, I picked up his *Toward a Jewish Theology of Liberation* and could barely put it down until the last page was read. As the Quakers say, this man spoke my mind. Ellis was inviting me to join him in exile from mainstream, Constantinian Judaism, and I gratefully accepted the invitation. After all, I had felt myself to be in a kind of exile for years, but it was isolated and lonely; it was the experience of an absence with respect to my being Jewish. I was aware that I didn't feel at home in the synagogue anymore, that the liturgy no longer spoke for me or to me, and that I did not feel a part of the congregation. This had left an empty space in my identity. I was looking for how to be a Jew. Ellis, like me, was on a path, and it was a path that led to an uncertain but desperately needed change.

A New Ingathering

That summer in the West Bank and Israel was the beginning of a journey. Growing up, I had been part of a close-knit, highly insulated Jewish community. Everything revolved around the synagogue, including the fervent commitment to the new Jewish state. Returning home from the Middle East, I began to construct a new community. "Synagogue" in Hebrew is *Beit Knesset*—literally, a gathering place. Rapidly, I began to find a new *Beit Knesset*, and it was much, much broader than the narrowly bounded religious community of my childhood. Many in this new community were Christians, and some were Muslims. But there were also Jews. Some, like Marc Ellis, I met through their writing. And some were Israelis, many of whom we'll meet in the pages to follow: Jeff Halper of the Israeli Committee Against House Demolitions; Ilan Pappe, the historian who has chronicled the painful history of the ethnic cleansing of Palestine in the birth of the Jewish state; Rami Elhanan of the Bereaved Families Circle; Eitan Bronstein, Tal Dor, and Norma Musih of Zochrot. I picked up their books and listened to them tell their stories, and I didn't feel so alone. I read David Shulman, a professor at the Hebrew University in Jerusalem who, along with other Jewish Israelis, works alongside Palestinians in nonviolent resistance to the occupation. Shulman writes in his memoir, *Dark Hope: Working for Peace in Israel and Palestine*, about returning to his West Jerusalem neighborhood after participating in the rebuilding of a demolished Palestinian home in the West Bank. The similarity to my own experience was uncanny:

> By midafternoon I am home in Katamon.[3] The contrast shocks me; I am back in the first world, in a manicured suburban street with its elegant stone houses and cypress trees. No one seems to be outside—perhaps they are all having their Shabbat sleep—but the cars along the curb speak eloquently enough: many of them have an orange ribbon tied to the antenna, a sign of support for the settlers of Gush Katif,[4] a sign that their owners reject Sharon's plan for disengagement from Gaza. My neighbors—many, perhaps most of them—stand with the settlers and the right. They don't believe in peace and, what is worse, they are completely and utterly indifferent to the fate of, for example, Arafat Musa and his house. Arafat Musa is, after all, a Palestinian Arab...of little or no consequence. So why bother about his house? Suddenly, as so often, a terrible loneliness courses through me. I briefly consider turning around and driving back to Anata,[5] where I have friends. (2007, 101)

The Jewish liturgy speaks of the ingathering of the exiles. Traditionally, this has referred to the Return to the Holy Land. But I had joined the ranks of Jews experiencing a different exile, one that looks toward a different return, a different ingathering. One that looks, not back to our archaic past, but to a future as yet unknown.

---

3. Katamon is a neighborhood in Jewish West Jerusalem.

4. Gush Katif was a Jewish settlement in Gaza, forcibly evacuated in 2005 by the Israeli government.

5. Anata is a Palestinian village in the West Bank four kilometers west of Jerusalem, where many Palestinian houses have been demolished by the Israeli government. It has been the scene of nonviolent protests against these demolitions by Palestinian and Israeli peace groups.

Chapter 3

Anti-Semitism, Jewish Identity, and the State of Israel

Anti-Semitism was an overwhelming force and the Jews would have to either make use of it or be swallowed up by it. In his own words, anti-Semitism was the "propelling force" responsible for all Jewish suffering since the destruction of the Temple and it would make the Jews suffer until they learned to use it for their own advantage.
—Hannah Arendt, on Theodor Herzl, "The Jewish State"

When I was a child, my brother and I would sometimes spend the night at our grandparents' small row house in South Philadelphia. South Philly in the 1950s was an immigrant enclave; there lived the Jews, the Irish, and the Italians. It was a bustling, colorful, tightly packed community. There were outdoor markets and synagogues and churches in abundance, all built on the models of the Old Country. The neighborhood smelled of cooking and garbage. Homeless cats and dogs owned the maze of alleys that ran behind the densely packed streets of narrow, humble brownstones. My brother and I slept in a tiny back room. Leaning out the window, you looked right into the neighbors' shoebox of a backyard.

One summer night it was noisy. As we prepared for bed, my grandmother, in her soft Yiddish accent, called our attention to the scene just outside the window that looked out over the alley: "*Goyim,*" she said, using the Yiddish word for non-Jews and pointing out the window at a small gathering of people talking loudly,

49

laughing, and holding drinks. "They're *shikker*," she told us, and I knew without her saying that this meant that being drunk was their natural state, and that this convivial, noisy, and collective condition was a shameful thing. Continuing her lesson, my grandmother told us the story of the Jew and the *goy* who worked for the same employer. Over the years, the Jew advanced to foreman, while the *goy* remained a laborer. One day, the *goy* comes up to the Jew and says, "Chaim, why is it that we started here together, and now you're second in command and I'm still hauling bricks?" The Jew looks at him and, saying not a word, takes him to the *goy's* backyard and shows him the garbage can, which is full of empty liquor bottles. "That's the reason," says the Jew. The *goy's* response to this lesson is unknown. Presumably (and undoubtedly in my grandmother's mind), in his *goyish* condition he remained unreformed.

I remember the moment. The experience of shock for an eight-year-old is not a well-delineated emotion. It's a damp, heavy blanket that settles over the heart; the colors of the world and the sharp lines of wonder at everyday experience are dulled, suffocating underneath its weight. I asked no questions in response to her lesson, which was that the world surrounding our Jewish bubble was a drunken, ignorant (and thus dangerous) rabble. But—I know now—I didn't buy it.

It was 2006, and I was in a large room in the Carnegie Endowment outside of Dupont Circle in Washington, DC. I was attending a panel entitled "Politics and Diplomacy: Next Steps in Arab-Israeli Peacemaking." There were eight men sitting at the front of the room: four Palestinians and four Israelis. A Palestinian spoke first, calling for—in plaintive tones, there is no other way to describe it—a resumption of negotiations before it was too late. The economic embargo of the newly elected Palestinian government with its Hamas majority had been in effect for five months. "We don't have much time left!" he told us. I was brought almost to tears by the sadness of his presentation, and I was a bit shocked, truth to tell, at his restraint as he described the humiliation and desperation faced by his people.

"I am a member of the Palestinian Authority Legislative Counsel," he continued, "and I haven't been paid in four months. I am one of the privileged, and I don't know how I'll make ends meet in the coming year!" I felt the room darkening; there was a silence. I felt shame, embarrassment, and anger.

Then it was the Israeli's turn to speak. I held my breath: what would he say? How would he follow this? A journalist for a popular Israeli daily and now ensconced at the Brookings Institution nearby, the Israeli sat back, smiled—*and opened with a joke.* He was, for all the world, a man delivering an after-dinner speech; he would enlighten us in due time, but first he would entertain, warm us up. Clearly, we were in the presence of the conqueror, the man holding all the cards. "We'll talk to them when the violence stops," he pontificated once the jokes were told and it was time to talk about who was to blame and how it would be fixed. It was the standard line, the old story. But it wasn't the words; it was the arrogance. No—it wasn't even the arrogance; it was the blindness, the sweeping, crushing insensitivity to the feelings expressed by the previous speaker. The Palestinian sitting next to him was invisible; he simply didn't count. And on it went. The other Palestinian panelists, leaning forward in their chairs, protested weakly that time was running out, pleaded for a resumption of negotiations. The Israelis sat back, opining about how the Hamas[1] victory rendered the prospects for negotiations negligible, talking about unilateral actions, i.e., their intention to simply do what they wanted, take what they wanted. Among them was a former Israeli general who, in *this* context, on *this* panel, spoke about the Jews' right to the land. But, again, it wasn't the words, and it wasn't the policies, shocking as they were; it was the negation, the utter, shocking, arrogant negation of the Other.

---

1. Hamas is a Palestinian political party that won an overwhelming majority of seats in the January 2006 Palestinian legislative election. Hamas is considered a terrorist organization by Israel, the United States, and other countries. Its name comes from the Arabic acronym for "Islamic Resistance Movement."

Anti-Semitism, Old and New

The attitudes revealed in these two memories—experiences bracketing fifty years of modern Jewish history—begin to explain why we as contemporary Jews are confronting the agonizing moral and political dilemma embodied by the State of Israel. The fear, insularity, and brittle sense of superiority that my grandmother carried as the legacy of Europe are tied directly to the blindness and arrogance of the Israeli statesmen, policy-makers, and opinion shapers that I saw on display that day in Washington. They also lead to the rigid, strident attitude of institutional American Jewry toward Israel on display today, the position of hard-line support that has played such a powerful role in American policy in the Middle East and that has so riven the American Jewish community.

The American Jewish Committee is a case in point. According to its web site, the AJC is an international organization devoted to "defending the rights and interests of the Jewish people...here in America and around the world." The web site goes on to high-light the work of the AJC in advocating for the State of Israel as "America's partner in democracy and peace," specifying its role as an ally of Israel "in its fight against second-class treatment at the UN and the International Red Cross." The AJC anoints itself "the most responsible, influential and effective voice of the American Jewish community." Lately, however, the AJC has had to step up its efforts to defend Jewish interests. According to the AJC, anti-Semitism is on the rise, and the evidence of this is an increase in criticism of the State of Israel. What most shocks and disturbs the Committee is that these attacks originate from the ranks of the Jews themselves.

In 2006, the American Jewish Committee published "'Progressive' Jewish Thought and the New Anti-Semitism," an essay by Alvin Rosenfeld, professor of Jewish Studies at Indiana University. In this essay, Rosenfeld attacks a number of Jewish writers who have voiced opposition to the policies of the State of Israel and who have raised questions about the legitimacy of Zionism itself as a political ideology. Rosenfeld's piece was the latest salvo in the bitterly fought battle currently underway within the Jewish community on the subject of Israel. Rosenfeld's point, as his title suggests, is that these Jews are expressing an animus against their own people. The fundamental assumption is that anything less than total support for Israel as a Jewish state is anti-Semitic, opens the door to the destruction of the state, and indeed threatens the survival of the Jewish people itself. Rosenfeld writes, "some of the most impassioned charges leveled against the Jews today involve vicious accusations against the Jewish state. Anti-Zionism, in fact, is the form that much of today's anti-Semitism takes, so much so that some now see earlier attempts to rid the world of Jews finding a parallel in present day desires to get rid of the Jewish state" (8).

Rosenfeld's piece is an example of a school of thought among Jewish intellectuals that first appeared in the 1970s in reaction to criticism of Israel. These writers were clearly aligned with (and some might argue were leading) the American neo-conservative movement that gained momentum in the 1970s. In a book published in 1974 entitled *The New Anti-Semitism*, its authors, Forster and Epstein, argued that concerns among non-Jews about Israel's trampling of Arab rights in Palestine—Jewish sovereignty over Jerusalem, for example—were actually motivated by anti-Semitism related to the "Radical Left" (9). This new threat to world Jewry, according to these voices, expressed itself chiefly in opposition to the State of Israel and to Zionism as an ideology. In the present day, defenders of Israel and Zionism continue to respond to the criticisms of Israel and of political Zionism that are beginning to appear with increasing regularity and frequency in the academic, journalistic, and activist communities. Their arguments and tone range from the respectably academic to the strident, abusive, and even scatological. The American Jewish establishment, which, since the time of Harry Truman's endorsement of the state in 1948, has confidently kept the money flowing and effectively controlled the public image of Israel, now feels itself in the position of having to stamp out brush fires of protest. Rosenfeld's piece encapsulates the arguments and represents the mind set well.

The Power of Fear

Rosenfeld opens his paper in full fear-mongering mode by invoking the specter of world anti-Semitism. By his account, Europe is awash in a resurgence of Jew-hatred, and world Islam is hawking Arabic translations of *Mein Kampf* and *The Protocols of the Elders of Zion*[2] on every street corner from Cairo to Islamabad in order to rouse the masses to exterminate the Zionist intruders. Rosenfeld even serves up the rumors of Jewish responsibility for the 9/11 attacks, the South Asia tsunami, and the Kennedy assassination to make his point that anti-Semitism is *on the rise*. We must thus be vigilant, he implies, against any hint of anti-Jewish sentiment, in the present case as expressed in criticism of Israel. Having thus established who the enemy is, Rosenfeld then directs his ire against those fifth-column Jews who dare question Jewish moral superiority and entitlement. To question Israel is to remove the defenses against anti-Semitism and, in effect, to invite the destruction of the Jewish people.

Rosenfeld and those who agree with this philosophy are encountering strange bedfellows these days. At the opening dinner of the March 2007 conference of AIPAC (the American Israel Public Affairs Committee, the largest organization among the many that comprise the Israel Lobby) in Washington, DC, Pastor John Hagee, leading Christian Zionist and founder of Christians United for Israel, received a rousing reception. To thunderous applause from the conference attendees, Hagee played expertly to these deep-seated Jewish fears. Referring to the newest threat to Jewish survival, Iran, whose leader "promises nothing less than a nuclear Holocaust," Hagee claimed that the situation is like 1938, only "Iran is Germany and [President Mahmoud] Ahmedinejad is the new Hitler." To drive home his point to the AIPAC audience, Hagee concluded that "we must stop Iran's nuclear threat and stop it now and stand boldly [with] Israel, the only democracy in the Middle East."

---

2. A nineteenth-century anti-Semitic work of forgery purporting to be a document outlining a plan for world domination by a secret society of Jewish leaders.

By publishing Rosenfeld's piece, the American Jewish Committee is catering to the same appetite. Rosenfeld sets the stage by presenting a picture of anti-Semitism that will frighten Jewish readers and remind them of the need for vigilance against any threat to the Jewish state. This is blatant fear-mongering; we in the United States have recently learned only too well how effective this can be in shaping policy. In this way, Rosenfeld has set up a classic straw man. Of course anti-Semitism exists. Indeed it can be said that it is deeply rooted in Western civilization, with tragic consequences throughout modern history. But to use the accusation of anti-Semitism as a club to stifle legitimate criticism of Israel is short-sighted, misguided, and dangerous.

The Jewish Narrative

We must pay attention to the historical experience that has brought us to this pass. For this is the Jewish narrative, the story we tell ourselves: *We have survived through the ages by managing to protect ourselves from a world that seeks our destruction. We have preserved our dignity in the face of marginalization, disenfranchisement, and demonization by maintaining a fierce pride and sense of superiority over the ignorant, violent forces surrounding us.* For anti-Semitism, like all racist ideologies, is not simply an attack on the physical security or economic viability of a group. Rather, it assaults the dignity and the very humanity of its targets. Zionism was European Jewry's response to the devastating effects of anti-Semitism and in particular to the despair at the failure of the Enlightenment to confer rights and equality to the Jews of Europe. The Zionist national movement was driven as much by a fierce need for dignity and self-determination as by a feeling of physical vulnerability. Modern Israel is, more than anything, a source of pride for Jews: it is good to have survived, and Israel is the proof of our survival. As such, Israel embodies an ideal: the desert made to bloom; the "new Jew," tanned, proud, and strong; Jerusalem reclaimed. Challenge this image, and you strike at the very heart of the deep-rooted Jewish need for security and well-being. You mobilize in us a fear so deep, so thoroughly internalized, that we have forgotten how much it drives us.

Rosenfeld's attack on Jews who criticize Israel and question Zionism has its source in that fear. The Rosenfeld who takes his fellow Jews to task for their criticism of Israel is not only attacking *ideas* that he finds unacceptable or threatening to his worldview; for him, it's *personal*. The Jews he wants to discredit are threatening to break through a powerful form of denial; they are challenging the attitude, now commonplace among American Jews, of not wanting to see *anything*, not wanting to feel *anything*, that challenges the powerful symbol of Israel as a source of power, security, and goodness. Our wars are pure—acts of heroic self-defense against merciless enemies. Our project is noble and good for the world—we encountered a barren, primitive land and made the desert bloom. Our actions, therefore, are not only necessary, but partake of the righteousness of the Zionist project.

In Rosenfeld's strident call for a circling of the wagons—an attitude representative of the position of the majority of religious and secular Jewish leaders throughout the United States today—I see the tragedy of modern Jewry in its confrontation with the uncomfortable realities of Israel. To be sure, and as discussed above, there are historical reasons for this attitude, and we are doubtless not the only group to have been guilty of this willful blindness, this sense of entitlement and specialness. But this tendency among many Jews today is so powerful and pervasive that it reaches the level of outright denial. Nowhere to be found in Rosenfeld's piece is even a gratuitous nod to the suffering of the Palestinians—not even the minimizing, grudging, disingenuous acknowledgment of the "unfortunate abuses" suffered by the occupied Palestinians often heard from the more "liberal" elements of the "pro-Israel" camp. But even more important, and ultimately more disturbing and potentially tragic, is the absence of any consideration of the issue of justice. To be sure, Israel may be threatened—the future is uncertain and geopolitical alliances are unstable and fickle. In the global arena, what gives you birth and supports you one day can turn against you the next. And to be sure, anti-Semitism is alive, and where not active it is very likely dormant. But where is justice? What is the state of our conscience? Given our history of persecution, disenfranchisement, displacement, and humiliation, given the still-pulsating ache in our collective heart of the experience of genocide itself, where is the sadness, where is the pain, where is the horror at what is being done to another people in our name by the State of Israel? Where is the recognition of *our* violence?

Jewish History: Survival and Its Shadow

Zionism was the answer to the anti-Semitism of Christian Europe. The failure, despite the Enlightenment, to establish the Jews as an emancipated, fully enfranchised group in Europe in the eighteenth and nineteenth centuries and the rise of political anti-Semitism in the late nineteenth century gave birth to political Zionism under the leadership of Theodore Herzl. Zionism expressed the powerful drive of the Jewish people to establish themselves as a nation among other nations, with a land of their own and the ability to achieve self-determination. This is why, in sermons from synagogue pulpits, in lectures on Jewish history, in classroom lessons for small children, and in spirited discussions about the Israel-Palestine question, you will so often hear the preamble "throughout the centuries…" followed by a description of the suffering of the Jews at the hands of our oppressors. It's in our liturgy, notably in the Passover seder. The story of Jewish survival in the face of unending persecution is in many ways our theme song; it's in our DNA; it's the mantra of our peoplehood. It runs deep.

This unique Jewish quality is not the product of some cultural aberration or collective character flaw. The Nazis' campaign to eradicate world Jewry has become part of our uniquely Jewish "Liturgy of Destruction" (Ellis 2004, 103), the way we Jews throughout the ages have made sense of our suffering by turning to the broader context of Jewish history. Arising from this matrix of vulnerability and victimization comes the Zionist cry "Never again!" Developing this particular brand of "character armor" has been part of our survival throughout ages of persecution, marginalization, and demonization. We survived, in part, by creating rituals, habits, and attitudes of insularity, pride, and persistence that allowed us never to forget, never to let down our guard, and to always be proud of our stubborn vitality in the face of "those who sought to destroy us." When, in our modern liturgical idiom, we talk of the State of Israel as "the first flowering of our redemption," we are reflecting the reality of our survival, the meaning of the achievement of political self-determination in the context of Jewish history. It is good to have survived.

In chapter 1, we touched on the impact of the Nazi Holocaust on Christian theology. The Nazi era produced a similarly profound effect on Jewish thought. Irving Greenberg, an orthodox rabbi, has been a prime articulator of the modern orthodox viewpoint of the place of the State of Israel in contemporary Jewish history. His vision of the place of Israel in modern Jewish life is shot through with messianic meaning. Greenberg writes,

> If God did not stop the murder and torture, then what was the statement made by the infinitely suffering Divine Presence in Auschwitz? It was a cry for action, a call to humans to stop the Holocaust, a call to the people of Israel to rise to a new, unprecedented level of covenantal responsibility. It was as if God had said: "Enough, stop it, never again, bring redemption!" The world did not heed that call to stop the Holocaust. European Jews were unable to respond. World Jewry did not respond adequately. But the response finally did come with the creation of the State of Israel. The Jews took on enough power and responsibility to act. And this call was answered as much by the so-called secular Jews as by the so-called religious. Even as God was in Treblinka, so God went up with Israel to Jerusalem. (1981, 15, 18)

This vision is articulated here by a rabbi, but it is held across a wide spectrum of modern Jewry. The Holocaust and the subsequent establishment of the State of Israel have taken their places as the major events in modern Jewish history.

As Jews, we must understand the shadow that this history casts on us today. We have striven to be the masters of our fate, but, having achieved this, we must also realize that we are responsible for our actions and for the consequences of these actions. Being free, we have free choice. The tragedy of Jewish Diaspora history, in our own cultural narrative as well as in reality, is rooted in our history of powerlessness and passivity. Zionism came to correct this, and it has undeniably succeeded, far beyond the expectations of Jews and non-Jews alike. But if we now become slaves to the consequences of empowerment, then we are not free, and we are not truly powerful. The Jewish state, by using the Holocaust as justification for unjust actions, is betraying the meaning we should take from our history of persecution and marginalization. You cannot achieve your own deliverance, even from the most unspeakable evil, by the oppression of another people. Indeed, in this current era of power and self-determination for Jews in Israel, we face risks to our peoplehood that far exceed the physical perils brought by millennia of persecution.

American Jews: Asking the Unasked Questions

Jews must become willing to overcome our profound denial about the injustices committed in the name of Zionism. Walter Brueggemann writes about the prophetic call to grieve and to mourn. Only in this way, he explains, can we hope to move on to a new and better reality. In Brueggemann's view, only when we are able to cry, in the prophet Jeremiah's phrase, for our own brokenness, and to confront the implications of the suffering we have caused, can we be the beneficiaries of God's bounty. In other words, we must break through the denial about what we have done. The power structure, of course, is committed to the very opposite. The state turns the story on its head in order to paper over the truth: *We do what we do in the name of national security. These others are the terrorists, the obstacles to peace.*

One particularly "slippery" form of denial, and evidence of this failure to grieve, is how some Jews take issue with some of the actions of the Israeli government while still avoiding a confrontation with the fundamental issues of justice. This can take several forms. The first is the "pragmatic" approach, essentially an appeal to enlightened self-interest. The occupation, so this position goes, was a mistake. It's bad for Israel. Denying self-determination for Palestinians and subjecting them to the humiliation of a military administration breeds hatred and desperation, which is then visited upon Israelis in the form of violence. *We need to get out of the territories, for our own sake.* Some American Jewish organizations, hoping to avoid being marginalized by the mainstream community or labeled "pro-Palestinian," adopt this position. Israel, they say, should get smart and change its policies if it wants to live in peace and limit the economic drain of unending conflict. In informal conversations with some Jewish Americans who articulate this position, I have heard confessions that their position is really much more extreme with respect to their feelings about Israeli policy, but that they feel it important to hew to this line for strategic purposes, in order to maintain credibility with the Jewish establishment as well as with government legislators.

A second kind of denial, for me more disturbing, is to be found in the ranks of Jewish progressives. In his critique of this element of American Judaism, Jewish liberation theologian Marc Ellis notes that whereas Jews in this group recognize the validity of Palestinian aspirations and condemn the human rights abuses committed by Israel, they also accept the idea of Jewish ascendancy as a solution to Jewish history. This viewpoint acknowledges the issue of justice, but attempts to do this within the context of Jewish mainstream assumptions of entitlement with respect to the rights of the Jews to historic Palestine: The occupation is wrong, claims the progressive Jewish camp. It goes against our Jewish values. If we can just clean up that messy business, things will come out all right, and we will be able to enjoy the land with a clean conscience.

This viewpoint limits the discourse to actions post-1967; it denies the history of Palestinian displacement prior to that. Consistently, progressive Jewish organizations and individuals avoid discussion of the Nakba, the Arabic word meaning "catas-trophe"—referring to the ethnic cleansing of three-quarters of a million Muslim and Christian Palestinians from historic Palestine by Israeli forces between 1947 and 1949. Finally, it avoids the fundamental question: how can a Jewish state, founded as a haven and a homeland only for Jews, be a true democracy, providing jus-tice and fair treatment for its non-Jewish citizenry? It also avoids the related and equally fundamental question of demography: how do you maintain a Jewish majority in Israel when the major-ity of people who have legal claim to that land are not Jewish? This question, above all others, drives Israeli foreign policy and fuels the current political and military conflict. On the whole, Jews outside Israel across a wide spectrum from "establishment" to "progressive" want to avoid these questions—they are off limits.

This is denial. It is a fundamental failure to accept the conse-quences of Jewish actions in pre- and post-1948 Israel/Palestine, and thus a failure to grieve over the particularly Jewish tragedy of the displacement and persecution of the Palestinian people from which we as Jews suffer today. Returning to the pre-1967 bor-ders will not make everything better. It will not make Israel a just society with respect to the Palestinian citizens living within its borders. It will not erase what was done to the Palestinians who were driven out of their cities, towns, and villages in 1948. It does not place the issue of justice as primary. Rather, it places the interests of the Jews of Israel as primary, and promotes an enti-tled, supremacist stance with respect to non-Jewish inhabitants of historic Palestine, on whichever side of the final status border they may reside when a political settlement is finally achieved. It preempts our horror over the crimes we are committing and the suffering we have caused. It muffles our own cries of pain over our sins and our cruelties. It suppresses the agony of confronting the contradictions and the excruciating dilemmas. It blocks the discussion. It closes our hearts.

Here is Walter Brueggemann describing the necessity for pro-phetic consciousness if a people is to grow and survive: "I believe that the proper idiom for the prophet in cutting through the royal numbness and denial is *the language of grief*, the rhetoric that engages the community in mourning for a funeral they do not want to admit. It is indeed their own funeral" (2001, 46; emphasis in the original).

Although it is painful and deeply troubling, I see the ferocity and depth of the current splits within the Jewish community in the Diaspora as an opportunity for dialogue. This is an issue of crisis proportions for Jews, and we need to take it seriously. We must encourage this conversation—we stifle it at our great, great peril. It is our responsibility as Jews to examine our relationship to Israel, rather than to passively accept the story fed to us by the Jewish establishment: the synagogues, Jewish federations, lobbying organizations, and the rest of the apparatus devoted to maintaining the mighty stream of financial and policy support for Israel from the U.S. government and from private sources. We must examine our convictions and feelings about the meaning of the State to us personally, especially in relation to anti-Semitism. For example, do I, as a Jew living in America, believe that the State of Israel is important to me as a haven if I should feel unsafe or disadvantaged in my home country? Do I personally feel that the existence of a Jewish state is an essential part of my Jewishness, or of the religious values and beliefs that I hold as a Jew? Do I believe that the world owes a state to the Jews because of the centuries of violence against and persecution of the Jews, culminating in the Nazi Holocaust?

As Diaspora Jews, we need to question where we get our information about the history of the State of Israel and about the current political situation. What news services do we rely on, and what web sites do we visit? What do we know about the discussion going on inside Israel today, exemplified by the active dialogue found in the pages of the Israeli daily newspaper *Haaretz*, in the organizations voicing opposition to Israeli government policy, and in the accelerated pace of revisionist Zionist history being produced by Jewish Israeli historians?

Anti-Zionism Is Not Anti-Semitism

But this discussion is largely muzzled today in the United States. To be critical of Israel is to be, quite simply, anti-Jewish. "Anti-Zionism" is another of Rosenfeld's straw men. For Rosenfeld, to question Zionism is to be anti-Semitic. It is not only actual criticism of Israel but almost any discussion that questions Israel's present course that fails Rosenfeld's loyalty test. This accusation is the favorite of the "my Israel right or wrong" camp, and its members wield it like a club against Jews and non-Jews alike. But it is important to distinguish "anti-Zionism" from criticism of Israel stemming from horror, shame, and outrage at the illegal actions of the Jewish state. Zionism is an ideology, and as such it can be subscribed to and debated like any other. In contrast, the State of Israel is a political entity—a nation state, that, like any other, should be held to standards of human rights, international law, fairness, and common decency. One could argue that one can be an ardent Zionist and still feel horror at—or at least feel grave concern about—Israel's policies and actions, and thus be moved to voice these opinions or even to political activism. Does this point up the need for an updated definition of Zionism or the need to ask whether the term is even relevant any longer as we consider the future of Judaism? "Zionism," stated Avraham Burg, Israeli statesman, author, and well-known critic of Israeli society and politics, in a recent address at a Washington, DC, synagogue, "is not the Torah. It's a chapter in our history. Let us go on to the next chapter!" (2008).

Contemporary Jewish historians, social theorists, and theologians have begun to weigh in on the implications of statehood for the Jewish religion itself. Israeli professor of social psychology Benjamin Beit-Halahmi holds that for American Jews, Zionism has become a "'religion,' kept by the class of high priests in Jewish organizations" (1993, 198). But, he writes, it is a "passive" religion, "more of an abstract faith than a plan of action" (198). Beit-Halahmi argues that the actual actions of Israel as a state are irrelevant to the role played by Israel in providing ideological content to make up for the decline in religious traditions and for the growing hunger among American Jews for spiritual fulfillment. Marc Ellis has written that "mainstream Jewish life has evolved into a new form of Judaism, one that seeks and maintains empire, not unlike Constantinian Christianity" (2004, 206). Ellis also points out in his 2004 *Toward a Jewish Theology of Liberation* that prior to WWII the Reform movement of Judaism in America was deeply split over the question of the Jewish state, but that following the Holocaust all dissent was effectively silenced. Thus it was that for me, born in 1948, Zionism—meaning unqualified love for and support of the State of Israel—was inextricably intertwined with my religious education and practice. Once an ideology and a movement among some Jews, Zionism is now effectively inseparable from Judaism itself. What is striking is that the term is subject to use or misuse by extremists on both sides: by the uncritical "defenders" of Israel's expansionism and militarism, ever vigilant against a possible threat to Jewish survival and ever watchful for the signs of an approaching holocaust, as well as by outright anti-Semites.

The Loyalty Oath

Rosenfeld maintains that the goal of Israel's critics is not Israel's withdrawal from the occupied territories or a change in state policy toward its own Arab citizens, but to bring an end to the Jewish state itself. For some of Rosenfeld's targets, this is true, if by this one means their principled stand against the concept and reality of a state founded and maintained on the basis of an ethnic nationalist ideology. But is this anti-Semitism? By this logic Rosenfeld would have accused Rabbi Judah Magnes, chancellor of the Hebrew University until his death in 1948, and Martin Buber, the eminent Jewish philosopher, of being anti-Semitic. They both opposed the establishment of Israel as a Jewish state. But Rosenfeld is not interested in a principled discussion about the nature and future of the State of Israel. Rather, he requires a declaration of allegiance, not to the State of Israel, but to an ideology of which the State is the primary manifestation.[3] For him, loyalty to the State of Israel is a test of one's loyalty to the Jewish people. If you challenge the State and Zionism on a fundamental level, you are operating out of unalloyed anti-Semitism. Recall that the article begins with a cataloging of the rise of virulent anti-Semitism, especially in the Islamic world. Anti-Semitism and anti-Zionism are conflated.

The effect is to stifle—indeed to render totally impermissible—any criticism of Israel on political, philosophical, historical, or ethical grounds. It's a slippery slope, Rosenfeld would argue: anti-Israel equals anti-Semite, and anti-Semites want to bring an end to the Jewish people. Actually, Rosenfeld has set us on a slippery slope, but not the one he fears. What we see here, in full flower, is the tyranny of the ideologue: it's the kind of thinking that leads to oppression in the name of God or the Nation. For example, in his rant against any notion of economic sanctions or conditions that might be imposed on Israel, Rosenfeld lumps those who would hold Israel to human rights standards required by international law with those who call "into question Israel's legitimacy and moral standing...[and] those who demand an end to Jewish national existence altogether" (2006, 24). Again, the thrust is all too clear: *we are in the right, and if you are not with us you are against us.* Criticizing Israel is providing aid and comfort to the enemy. Even certain words are out of bounds: according to Rosenfeld, using words like "brutal...oppressive,

---

3. This issue has recently surfaced in Israeli politics. Following the national elections in early 2009, Avigdor Lieberman, head of the Yisrael Beiteinu ("Israel is Our Home") party, introduced a bill to require a loyalty oath to Israel as a "Jewish, Zionist and democratic state" ("Yisrael Beiteinu To Advance Bill on Loyalty Oath," *Haaretz*, May 29, 2009). Given the ultra-nationalist platform of his party, this bill is understood to target Palestinian citizens of Israel and move Israel toward transfer of non-Jews out of the state. In a recent interview, Daniel Levy, codirector of the Middle East Task Force of the New America Foundation, credited the "Lieberman phenomenon" with creating a "moment of truth" for Israel ("Israel's Loyalty Oath," *The Real News Network*, February 20, 2009, (http://therealnews.com/t/index. php?option=com_content&task=view&id=31&Itemid=74&jumival=3330).

or racist" to describe Israel's actions equals anti-Semitism and is simply not to be permitted (16).

This reasoning is not only logically flawed, it is dangerous. In Rosenfeld's argument, permission is not granted to hold any views outside of what is what is commonly termed "pro-Israel" by the mainstream. "Behavior"—to use Rosenfeld's word—such as identifying with the suffering of oppressed Palestinian people by wearing a pin of the Palestinian flag, or seeking to find a path to peace through an understanding of the root causes of the horror of suicide bombing, is "bizarre" and "grotesque" (24).

Easy Targets

Rosenfeld never directly discloses his right-wing leanings and how they condition his position on Israel. However, he repeatedly exposes his ideological bias, which in his case is expressed as an animus toward and outright vilification of any views or persons associated with the political Left. He discounts what he terms anti-Israel "hysteria" as "politically motivated"—clearly code for "left wing" (20). In other words, criticism of Israel is nothing more than adherence to a radical political viewpoint, one that requires opposition to the State of Israel as a kind of left-wing litmus test. In one passage, using author and professor Jacqueline Rose as his poster child for the leftist anti-Zionist camp, he submits that "there are many like Rose today. Some are probably no more than *ideological fellow travelers...*" (25; emphasis added). Having thus dismissed any writers who may fall into this class, Rosenfeld argues that anti-Zionism is simply one more way for these people to "establish their leftist credentials." Then, in another characteristic thousand-league leap of logic, Rosenfeld alleges that "anti-Zionism...shares common features with anti-Jewish ideologies of the past..." (25). What these ideologies are, or what the "common features" shared with anti-Zionism are, is never made clear. The fact that these benighted ideologues do not see this connection, and the mortal danger it poses to the Jewish people, is "more than just a pity—it is a betrayal," cries Rosenfeld (25).

Rose is only one of the high-profile critics of Israel identified with the political Left singled out by Rosenfeld, but she is one of his favorites. A British academic, Rose is best known for her work on the relationship between psychoanalysis, feminism, and literature. Rose's leftist credentials alone are enough to discount her entirely in Rosenfeld's view, but, again, he uses her simply to set up his argument. In her writing about Zionism, Rose has attempted, in her words, to "steer a clear path between an elated identification with the state's own discourse and a string of insults" (Rose 2005). But Rosenfeld will have nothing to do with nuance. He advances a shallow critique, taking aim at concepts like "messianism" that Rose introduces as part of a careful analysis but that Rosenfeld, incredibly and cynically, takes literally, charging that Rose believes the Zionists to have been inspired directly by Jewish Messianic madmen from medieval times. In like fashion, Rosenfeld seizes upon Rose's use of the word "catastrophe" to describe the current state of affairs in Israel and occupied Palestine. He, however, links it with the Arabic *Al* Nakba, the Palestinian term for the ethnic cleansing of Palestine between 1947 and 1949. He thus charges her with being "aligned...with this reading of history...[that] the creation of Israel led to a historic injustice against the Palestinians" (2006, 10). This is the damning charge? That she acknowledges that injustice has been done to the Palestinians? Here Rosenfeld again shows his true colors: flat-out denial of the injustices perpetrated by Israel. In other words, if you acknowledge this fact, you are his enemy and an enemy of the Jewish people, as well as a person who has abandoned all rational discourse. Jews do not have the right to criticize Israel, indeed to even entertain the notion that Israel is not perfect—or perfectly entitled to do as it wishes. Further on in his attack on Rose, Rosenfeld, in another fallacy-ridden argument, challenges her question, "How did one of the most persecuted peoples of the world come to embody some of the worst cruelties of the modern nation-state?" (Rose 2005, 115). To this he responds: "Compared to the truly horrendous crimes of...Sudan, Cambodia...Serbia...or Chile—

Israel's record actually looks relatively good" (2006, 11). By any standards of logical discourse and decency, this is a despicable argument and merits no further comment.

Muzzling Voices of Protest

Is Alvin Rosenfeld my "straw man"? Is it fair or accurate to use this obviously polemical article to represent the attitude of the American Jewish establishment toward criticism of Israel? Are there not moderate, more responsible voices? The answer is that Rosenfeld's piece is the tip of the iceberg of Jewish institutional opposition to all voices that challenge the status quo of unquestioned and unconditional American support of the State of Israel. Accusations of disloyalty, anti-Semitism, and left-wing leanings find expression in myriad ways throughout the Jewish religious and secular establishment in the United States today in response to individual Jews who challenge the prescribed allegiance to the policies of the Jewish state. This vigilance against threats to support for Israel is not limited to Jews and Jewish institutions. The Israel lobby—a "loose coalition of individuals and organizations who actively work to steer U.S. foreign policy in a pro-Israel direction," to use the definition advanced by Mearsheimer and Walt as well as Rabbi Michael Lerner of *Tikkun Magazine*—casts a wide net in its mission to muzzle "anti-Israel" speech and activism perceived as hostile to the Jewish state.[4] Mearsheimer and Walt's term "loose" does not accurately characterize the well-funded, well-organized, and highly strategic matrix of organizations that

---

4. Lerner's definition from a recent piece in *Tikkun Magazine* is worth quoting: "When I talk about the Israel Lobby I mean to refer not only to AIPAC or The Conference of Presidents, but to a range of organizations, including the American Jewish Congress, the American Jewish Committee, the World Jewish Congress, B'nai Brith, the Anti-Defamation League (ADL), Hadassah, the Wiesenthal Center, the Federation, and the United Jewish Appeal (UJA), the various Jewish Community Relations Councils, most of the local Hillel Foundations on college campuses, most of the Hebrew schools and day schools introducing their students to Judaism or Jewish culture, the array of Federation sponsored newspapers that are distributed in almost every Jewish community in America" (2007).

together monitor the press, the United States Congress, academic institutions, and the major Christian denominations. Well-publicized cases in recent years include the successful blocking of Professor Norman Finkelstein's tenure at DePaul University, the unsuccessful attempt to block the tenure appointment of Barnard professor Nadia Abu El-Haj, and the cancelling of Archbishop Tutu's appearance at St. Thomas University (the archbishop has become an outspoken critic of Israel's apartheid-like policies and of the blockade of Gaza). Mearsheimer and Walt's article on the Israel lobby, ultimately published in a British journal, had been commissioned by *The Atlantic Monthly* but was rejected for reasons that have not been revealed by any of the parties.

Meanwhile, our best thinkers and writers keep producing. In spite of himself, Alvin Rosenfeld in his piece on the new anti-Semitism has made an important contribution to the cause for justice and renewal: his "enemies list" provides those of us hungry for these courageous voices with a superb recommended reading list. One only wishes he had given more attention to the work of Sara Roy, Senior Research Scholar at the Center for Middle Eastern Studies at Harvard University, whom we must count as one of today's most courageous—and intensely Jewish—voices of conscience. Rosenfeld dispatches Roy in two short sentences, citing a passage in which she comments on the "heresy" within the Jewish community of comparing the actions and policies of Israel with those of the Nazis (in the next paragraph, he effectively demonstrates her point by characterizing any comparison between today's Jews and their former victimizers as "unseemly") (17).

Rosenfeld's attack on Roy for daring to address the similarities between the actions of Nazi Germany and those of Israel in its occupation of the West Bank and blockade of Gaza is perhaps the ultimate symbol of the frightening blindness of his perspective. Roy's powerful evocation of the central meaning of the Holocaust in her personal history is a cornerstone of her human rights work. Along with the work of other Jewish writers such as Norman Finkelstein, who have chronicled the distortion and misuse of the tragedy of the Holocaust, Roy calls on us to honestly confront our current predicament in the light of the incalculable significance of this chapter in our history, and, indeed, of two millennia of anti-Semitism. She calls on us to draw from it the very moral clarity required to see our way forward. In a moving 2007 essay, Roy, the daughter of a survivor of the Nazi Holocaust, writes:

> My mother and her sister had just been liberated from the concentration camp by the Russian army. After having captured all the Nazi officials and guards who ran the camp, the Russian soldiers told the Jewish survivors that they could do whatever they wanted to their German persecutors. Many survivors, themselves emaciated and barely alive, immediately fell on the Germans, ravaging them. My mother and my aunt, standing just yards from the terrible scene unfolding in front of them, fell into each other's arms weeping. My mother, who was the physically stronger of the two, embraced my aunt, holding her close and my aunt, who had difficulty standing, grabbed my mother as if she would never let go. She said to my mother, "We cannot do this. Our father and mother would say this is wrong. Even now, even after everything we have endured, we must seek justice, not revenge. There is no other way." My mother, still crying, kissed her sister and the two of them, still one, turned and walked away.
>
> What then is the source of our redemption, our salvation? It lies ultimately in our willingness to acknowledge the other—the victims we have created—Palestinian, Lebanese and also Jewish—and the injustice we have perpetrated as a grieving people. Perhaps then we can pursue a more just solution in which we seek to be ordinary rather than absolute, where we finally come to understand that our only hope is not to die peacefully in our homes as one Zionist official put it long ago but to live peacefully in those homes. (Roy, 2007)

Where Do We Go from Here?

Roy's powerful story points the way. Turning from our anger, sorrow, disappointment, and outrage at the evil we ourselves have experienced, we open ourselves to our membership in the larger human community. This impulse is deeply rooted in the Jewish psyche. We demonstrated it in the Jewish Left's opposition to the Iraq War, and in our synagogue-based campaigns to oppose the genocide in Darfur. We expressed it in our passionate involvement in the American civil rights movement from its beginnings in the 1950s. My earliest memories include accompanying my father to countless appearances at Philadelphia synagogues where he presented talks and workshops about what we then called "prejudice"—racism against black people. Dad was a member of The Anti-Defamation League of B'nai Brith, which in those days was at the forefront of the struggle for racial equality. For my father, as for the ADL, being Jewish could only mean actively working for human rights as a member of the society in which one lived.

I am a Jew born at the midpoint of the twentieth century. I don't need to be lectured about anti-Semitism. Psychically, as a Jew, I have a packed suitcase under my bed and an eye ever watchful for the anti-Semitism present in Western civilization that, under the right conditions, can turn from latent to virulent. But I am unwilling, on the chance that I might someday need a refuge from discrimination or outright physical danger, to support the continued building of a militarized, expansionist state that is doing more today to fuel anti-Semitism than to construct a solution to it.

But let us grant that anti-Semitism is on the rise on a global basis. Let us even set out that it is deep-seated anti-Jewishness, and not sixty years of dispossession and ethnic cleansing, that is the cause of outbreaks of violence against Israelis by Palestinians. Even if this were all true, is the solution to build a hideous wall that steals land, blocks commerce and agriculture, and cuts families and communities in half? Is the solution to train your sons and daughters to hate and fear an entire people and to order them to invade their cities, villages, and homes, to humiliate and debase them in front of their children, and to terrify those same children and rob them of a future in their own land? Can anyone believe that this is an *answer* to anti-Semitism?

History and Memory

Historian and author Tony Judt is a British Jew who has recently come under attack for his criticism of Israel's policies and, in particular, of the destructive effects of Zionism on Jewish life in the Diaspora. Rosenfeld does not miss the opportunity to excoriate Judt for raising the question of whether the Jewish state as it now exists is the best solution to anti-Semitism and whether, in fact, Israel's actions may be contributing to anti-Semitism around the world. In a recent *Washington Post/Newsweek* blog, Judt courageously placed the issue of Israel and American Jewish attitudes in the larger context of world affairs. He writes:

> I see the hysteria surrounding the "Israel issue" in American life—and the shameful silence about what actually happens in the territories Israel occupies—as one more symptom of the provincial ignorance and isolation of the U.S. in world affairs. We can continue assuring ourselves that the whole of the rest of the world is awash in inexplicable, atavistic, exterminationist anti-Semitism. Or—in this as in other matters—we can re-enter an international conversation and ask ourselves why (together with an Israeli political class recklessly embarked on the road to self-destruction) we alone see the world this way and whether we might be mistaken. (2007)

I agree with Judt that the need for American Jews to emerge from our historical attitudes of insularity and self-protection is all the more urgent because of the implications of these attitudes for our world at large. As Jews, we can no longer afford to think only of ourselves—seeing ourselves as victims, as a beleaguered minority. This attitude and the behavior it engenders has not only put us at great risk—it adds significantly to the peril of the entire world. If we are indeed to be a "light to the nations," we must make common cause with the forces of progressivism and the advancement of human rights. As Jews, we must be part of the solution. Sadly—and Rosenfeld's essay is but one indication of this fact—we are still learning how not to be part of the problem.

Sara Roy's recent book, *Failing Peace: Gaza and the Palestinian-Israeli Conflict*, is an impassioned plea for an awakening to the moral issues confronting the Jewish people at this juncture in our history.

> Why is it so difficult, even impossible to accommodate Palestinians into the Jewish understanding of history? Why is there so little perceived need to question our own narrative (for want of a better word) and the one we have given others, preferring instead to embrace beliefs and sentiments that remain inert? Why is it virtually mandatory among Jewish intellectuals to oppose racism, repression and injustice almost anywhere in the world and unacceptable, indeed, for some, an act of heresy—to oppose it when Israel is the oppressor? For many among us history and memory adhere to preclude reflection and tolerance, where "the enemy become(s) people to be defeated, but embodiments of an idea to be exterminated." (2007, xx–xxi)

Jews understand human rights issues—we feel the moral imperative in our bones. But we are human. We make mistakes; we require correction. This is what the prophets were telling us in ancient times, and this is what our modern prophets are telling us now. Despite the increasingly vigorous protest of the Jewish establishment against even a murmur of opposition to Israel's actions, the voices of conscience within the Jewish community are growing stronger. What we are being forced to see is that we have a distance to travel; we are at one of those historical turning points. We have a choice. For us as Jews, and for all Americans contemplating our relationship to the world at large and to the urgent human rights issues of our day, there can be no more important questions than the ones Roy asks here, and no more chilling conclusion that the one she articulates. The choice of the quote from Northrop Frye with which she closes the passage above is telling, the choice of the word "exterminated" pointed. As long as we allow our minds to be closed, our voices silenced, and our eyes shut before the injustices and horrors in plain view, there will be more conflict, more dispossession, and the deaths of countless more innocents. And there will be no peace—not in the Middle East, not in our own midst, and not in our hearts.

I loved my grandmother. She was a sweet woman with a big heart. She brought her large family through the Great Depression and struggled her whole life with the personal legacy of a tyrannical father and the denial of higher education that was her lot as a girl growing up in an ultra-orthodox household. Most of all, as illustrated by my opening story, she was very much a product of her time and our collective history. Among my many memories of her is a framed group portrait that hung in her house, a black and white photograph dating from the early 1950s. In it, my grandmother sits with perhaps sixty other women, in neat rows, wearing drab dresses and sensible shoes. Before them is a banner proclaiming the local chapter of Pioneer Women, an American women's Zionist Organization founded in the 1920s to promote Jewish culture and Zionist principles and to provide material support for the struggling *yishuv*, or Jewish settlement, in Palestine and, after 1948, for the State of Israel. My grandmother looks out from the front row, clearly proud of her affiliation and steadfast in her commitment to the survival and health of the young Jewish state. For her there were no Palestinians and there was no Nakba. There was only this precious reality of Israel, this wondrous repository of Jewish culture, this bulwark against the nations who seek to destroy us. She was a product of her upbringing and of her times—and for the Jews of America those *were* simpler times.

We don't have the luxury of that simplicity anymore. We are engaged in a struggle to confront the consequences of our current situation, and to undertake the difficult work of self-examination and necessary reform. But to do that, we need to reach an understanding of who we are. To continue to answer this question, we need to take a deeper look at how we have come to this pass. There are many facets to that question, but surely one crucial issue is the relationship of Judaism with Zionism. This is the subject of the next chapter.

Chapter 4

A Movement of Hope and Desire

The claim of the Jews to the land—tenuous historically, all the more ruthlessly claimed biblically—rests therefore on the unique quality of Jewish self-fashioning, its ability to carve fate into the soil.
—Jacqueline Rose, *The Question of Zion*

In the introduction, we met Daoud Nassar, the grandson of a Palestinian Christian who bought a one-hundred-acre plot in the fertile hill country south of Bethlehem in 1916. On this windy hilltop, the story of the Israeli occupation of Palestine is unfolding. The Nassar farm stands alone, the last holdout in a region earmarked for annexation by the Jewish state. In 1991, using one of its chief methods of taking land and exerting control of the occupied territories, Israel declared the Nassar property "state land." The burden was then on the family to prove ownership. Few Palestinians have been able to successfully prove land title to Israeli standards in the West Bank, a territory that has changed hands many times in the last two hundred years. Israel's campaign of displacement is working. Farm by farm, village by village, Palestinian farmers are retreating to the teeming urban enclaves intended for those Palestinians who will not or cannot emigrate, bantustans accessible only through the network of restricted roads controlled by Israel: Hebron, Bethlehem, Ramallah, Jenin, Nablus, Jericho. Daoud, however, has pursued the case to the Israeli Supreme Court, spending close to two hundred thousand dollars in legal fees and land surveys over an eighteen-year period, and the court has upheld his claim. Frustrated by this, Israel has attempted to gain the land by private means, i.e., buying it through questionable third-party arrangements—another common method of land acquisition. Daoud has been asked to name his price, but he remains steadfast. "We are not permitted to give up," he says. "This land is my mother. My mother is not for sale."

One day, Daoud was on his tractor cultivating a plot bordering the neighboring settlement. He was approached by a young man, perhaps no older than seventeen or eighteen, carrying a semi-automatic rifle—standard issue for an ideological Jewish settler in the West Bank. The boy approached Daoud, challenging him with the words, "What are you doing on our land?" Daoud answered him simply, "This is my land." "No, it is ours," said the boy, glaring at the Palestinian and nervously fingering his gun. Not a man to be intimidated, the farmer looked the boy directly in the eyes and said, "My grandfather bought this land. We have the papers to prove it." The young Jew, pointing to the sky, replied, "You have papers from here. We have papers from God."

Whose Land?

Like virtually every other location in the tiny strip of land between the Mediterranean Sea and the Jordan River known as Palestine, the land on which Daoud's farm sits is fraught with history. In this case the history is relatively recent. The Nassar land is located almost exactly in the center of today's Etzion settler bloc, an area charged with nationalist meaning for the State of Israel. In 1943, religious Jews founded Kfar Etzion near the road connecting Jerusalem to Hebron to the south. By 1947, there were 163 adults and 50 children living there. The kibbutz, together with three nearby kibbutzim established in that period, came to be called Gush Etzion (the Etzion bloc). The United Nations partition plan for Palestine of November 29, 1947, placed the Etzion bloc outside the borders of the proposed Jewish state. As the forces on the Jewish and Arab sides gathered for the battle for control of Palestine, the Etzion bloc's location on the important Jerusalem-Hebron road lent it great strategic importance.

Over the winter of 1947–48, as hostilities intensified, the situation for the Jews of Kfar Etzion became increasingly desperate as several relief convoys were attacked, suffered losses, and turned back to Jerusalem. In January, the women and children were evacuated. The final assault by Arab forces began on May 12, and on May 13 the defenders showed the white flag. What followed is known in Israel as the Kfar Etzion massacre. Some facts are in dispute, but it is generally agreed that 129 Jewish inhabitants were mowed down by Arab irregulars. It is not clear whether a command was given or if someone opened fire and others followed. By one report, Arab soldiers shouted "Deir Yassin!"—the name of a Palestinian village near Jerusalem where over one hundred men, women, and children had been murdered by Jewish forces the previous month.

Kfar Etzion became the symbol of the heroism and martyrdom of those who died to bring the state into existence. The dead of Kfar Etzion were buried on Mount Herzl in Jerusalem, Israel's military cemetery. The date of the massacre was later established as Israel's Memorial Day.

In 1967, the Etzion bloc was recaptured by Israel. The Israelis who, as children, had been evacuated from the kibbutz in 1948 led a public campaign for the site to be resettled, and Prime Minister Levi Eshkol gave his approval. Kfar Etzion was reestablished as a kibbutz in September 1967; as such, it was the first Israeli settlement in the West Bank.[1] The Etzion bloc is one of the three major settlement blocs in the West Bank,

---

1. The story of the return of the descendants of Kfar Etzion is powerful and helps us understand the emotions driving the impulse to settle the West Bank as a "return" to the land. Yet it's important to keep in mind that the Israeli government has never sanctioned a "return" for Palestinians currently living in the West Bank, Jordan, Lebanon, and other countries, who were once forced out of their own villages in present-day Israel. I am grateful to Anna Baltzer for this observation.

and it has been an area of intense development and expansion, with settlement by immigrants from abroad and Israel proper actively encouraged. The entire Etzion bloc is situated in Area C, which is under the civil and military control of Israel per the 1993 Oslo Accords. The separation wall encloses the entire bloc at its northern, eastern, and southern boundaries, isolating the approximately twenty-five thousand Palestinian villagers and townspeople living within it from Bethlehem, East Jerusalem, and the rest of the West Bank. Most Jewish settlements in the bloc are religious. Israel claims this section of the West Bank as part of King David's biblical kingdom.

Neve Daniel is one of these settlements. It is named after the relief convoy from Jerusalem that was turned back in March 1948, an event that marked the beginning of the end for the people of Kfar Etzion. The settlement of about fifteen hundred religious Jewish immigrants from the former Soviet Union, France, and North America borders the Nassar land to the east. In fact, recent Israeli maps of the area where the Nassar farm sits show not the Nassar property, but an area of pale blue that signifies an area of future expansion for the settlement.

Shaul Goldstein is the mayor of Neve Daniel. His father fought in the battle in which Israel reclaimed the area from Jordan in 1967. In 2007, Goldstein was interviewed for a feature article by *Los Angeles Times* reporter Richard Boudreaux, who visited the Nassar land in preparing the story. "In my view," Goldstein is quoted saying in the piece, "Israel from the Mediterranean to the Jordan Valley is a Jewish state. Its lands are earmarked first and foremost for Jewish citizens" ("A West Bank Struggle Rooted in Land," *Los Angeles Times*, December 27, 2007).

The newspaper article provides recent historical background for Goldstein's claim. Since 1967, when the land was occupied, it reads, Israel has pursued a program of seizing land from Palestinians and turning it over to Jewish settlement development. "Parcel by parcel," continues the piece, "Israel is taking control of farms, pastures and underground water sources to expand the Gush Etzion settlements for a growing population that now totals more than 55,000." Drawing the obvious conclusion about the future planned for the Palestinians of the Etzion bloc, Boudreaux writes, "Clearly, the plan does not include a thriving of these communities, or even their continuation. This land is for the Jews." The Palestinians of the area, he points out, quoting a local Palestinian lawyer, are "'severed from their places of work and education, their medical services, their extended families and, indeed, the rest of Palestine…I don't believe that these small communities could survive for long.'"

Lords of the Land

What was the impact of this story on the readers of the *Los Angeles Times* when they opened their newspapers over morning coffee on December 27, 2007? What does an American think when he hears about a colonialist project to take land from indigenous people out of a belief that the land belongs to the colonists by divine right?

The story should be painfully familiar to Americans, who may nevertheless be shocked to see it unfolding in our own time. Israelis, however, have been hearing about it for over two decades. Amira Hass, the Israeli reporter for Israel's daily *Haaretz*, has been telling Israelis the story of the occupation for over two decades. Hass lived in and reported from Gaza from 1993 to 1997, moving then to Ramallah in the West Bank, where she lives today. She files regular reports on the impact of the occupation on Palestinian society as settlement activity has progressed, adding over a quarter of a million Jewish settlers since the mid-1980s. Hass has chronicled the growing boldness of ideological settlers who disrupt Palestinian agricultural activity through armed harassment—behavior allowed and even protected by Israeli security forces. This pattern, maintained throughout the West Bank from Jenin in the north to Hebron in the south, complements the "official" state policies of roadblocks, house demolitions, segregated roads, and the expropriation of land and water sources in the inexorable process of displacement and dispossession that is the occupation. The settlers, Hass is saying, are doing the state's bidding.

Hass filed a story in August 2007, describing how she, another Israeli journalist, and three UN humanitarian workers were assaulted by Jewish settlers. The armed ideologues attacked the team's jeep, smashing the windshield and effectively holding them hostage. "They behaved like lords of the land," writes Hass, explaining how the laws applying in the occupied territories prohibit Israeli police or military from taking direct action against the settlers; on the contrary, such soldiers are officially there to "protect" settlers ("The Hebron Tactic," *Haaretz*, August 8, 2007). "The tactic," writes Hass, "is one that is well-known from Hebron, the same tactic that helped to cleanse the Old City of most of its Palestinian residents: Jews harass and bully and then threaten to lodge complaints against their victims with the Israeli police… they practice terrorizing Palestinians because Israeli authorities let them do so. In their own way, they do the same thing the 'legitimate' occupation authorities do: They drive the Palestinians off their land to make room for Jews. In other words, they are following orders."

These daily encounters are not accidents. They are not the random acts of a lunatic fringe of Israeli society. The settler boy who confronted Daoud Nassar in his field, the soldiers who observe from the sidelines or intervene only at times and only half-heartedly to prevent overt bloodshed from the violent actions of nationalist fanatics, the government agencies that facilitate the systematic dispossession of an indigenous population, the contractors who build the restricted roads and bulldoze houses and fields to construct the separation barrier—these are all part of a system that draws power from the same source.

Jews here and in Israel who present themselves as sympathetic to the "Palestinian cause" like to distance themselves from what they call the "extremist fringe" represented by the ideological settler movement. They claim that the criminal, racist actions of this violent minority are not the true face of the occupation. Not that the occupation does not, of necessity, compromise Palestinian rights, continues this argument. It does, but it should come to an end once Israel can reach a negotiated agreement with the Palestinians. It's the classic straw man: the settlers are bad, but we, who believe in human rights, fair play, and nonviolence are good. Hass's reports, and the witness of anyone who has seen firsthand the ongoing ethnic cleansing of the shepherds of the southern West Bank and the farmers of the fertile territory in the northern hilltops and valleys, gives the lie to this "moderate" position. Hass's analysis is unerringly, tragically accurate: the settlers are acting out the will and intent of the Israeli government.

The Dreaded Trait of the Past

How did we get here? This is the precise question posed by Jacqueline Rose, the same Rose singled out by the AJC's Alvin Rosenfeld as one of the "new anti-Semites" of the Left. Rose, who visited the West Bank in 2002 to make a documentary, was moved to write the brief and compelling *The Question of Zion* in an effort "to understand the force—at once compelling and dangerous—of Israel's dominant vision of itself as a nation" (Rose 2005, xi).

Rose opens her book with the recounting of the 2003 suicide bombing in Haifa that killed four children. "While Ariel Sharon sent his planes into Syria in response," she writes, Israeli radio broadcasted an interview with Golda Meir, recorded during the Yom Kippur War thirty years earlier, in which she said that "Israel had no responsibility for war 'because all the wars against Israel have nothing to do with Israel'" (xi). Rose pursues the questions that we, not only as Jews but as citizens of the world, must ask ourselves: What is the source of Israel's view of itself as a nation? What is it about our collective Jewish consciousness that allows us to see ourselves as innocent of the trouble in which we find ourselves? Who is this people that presents itself, in Rose's words, "as eternally on the defensive, as though weakness were a weapon, and vulnerability its greatest strength?" (xiii). What is it, asks Rose, "about the coming into being of this nation, and the movement out of which it was born, that allowed it—and still allows it—to shed the burdens of its own history, and so flagrantly to blind itself?" (xii).

Rose feels, as I do, a personal closeness to what she calls "the legitimate desire of a persecuted people for a homeland" (xii). But having experienced as I did the shock of seeing the occupation up close, she is asking the same question that arose for me: how did the Zionist dream come to so poison the soul of Judaism? Rose believes, however, that simply to distinguish Zionism from Judaism, to in effect discount or vilify it, is counterproductive. Her aim, rather, is to "enter the imaginative mind-set of Zionism in order to understand why it commands such passionate and seemingly intractable allegiance" (13).

Rose identifies Zionism as "one of the most potent movements of the twentieth century...As a movement, Zionism has the power, that is, to sacralize itself" (14). Zionism's very power comes from its ability to transcend reality, to challenge what is perceived as possible, an attitude typified in Herzl's famous statement of 1902, "If you will it, it is no dream." Despite the urgently felt need for a solution to the intolerable conditions under which the Jews of nineteenth-century eastern Europe found themselves, Zionism, Rose asserts, "always knew it was propelling itself into an imaginary and perhaps unrealizable space. Before anything else, Zionism presents itself as a movement of hope and desire..." (16). Zionism is a form of messianism, she claims, and messianism "flourishes in dark times. Like Zionism, it is the child of exile" (17). Rose boldly focuses this historical lens directly on the present situation: "Messianic redemption is therefore a form of historic revenge. To put it crudely, it is way of settling scores. The violence of a cruel history repeats itself as its own cure" (20).

For me, this connection, grim as it is, hits home. How else do we come to terms with the horror and the tragedy of what we are seeing enacted in Israel and Palestine, a bloody drama that has ground down both Jews and Palestinians so mercilessly? But it is not advocacy for the oppressed Palestinians that is the aim of Rose's analysis. It is to the Jews that she addresses herself in her book, a scant three chapters spanning 150 pages. "There is a paradox here," Rose explains. "It was misery that drew the Jewish people to the apocalyptic tradition and its message of catastrophe. But as they move forward to the dawn of a new history, the misery accompanies the vision, lodges itself inexorably inside the dream. The future that is meant to redeem you borrows the most dreaded trait of the past" (20).

Rose's unvarnished picture, informed by her psychoanalytic perspective, helps answer the question of what is driving the Jewish people in the Zionist project. And is not an exploration of these psychological issues critical for understanding the "question of Zion"? Are these not the questions that we as Jews need to ask ourselves as we attempt to understand the tragic dilemma in which we find ourselves? But how far back into our collective experience do we need to travel to discover the roots of our current behavior? Rose makes the point that this spirit of messianic fulfillment runs "to the heart of Zionism *even when, or perhaps especially when, it does not know it is there*" (53; emphasis in original). Our self-narrative and our liturgy are shot through with stories of and a preoccupation with victimhood and suffering. Rose's point is that it is this long-standing quality that colors the dream of redemption. "How on earth," she asks, "can you stop something whose meaning stretches back through the annals of history and forward to the ends of time?" (20). We have to understand this in order to escape from its thrall. One way to do this, Rose believes, is to look at the heroes.

The Architect of Israel

Theodore Herzl may have been the visionary who created political Zionism, but it was David Ben-Gurion, born David Grun in 1886 in Plonsk, Poland (then part of the Russian Empire), who was the architect of the State of Israel. According to Rose, Ben-Gurion was possessed by a messianic vision for the Jewish people, a vision expressed in political Zionism. As a devout Zionist, Ben-Gurion did not believe that the Jews should continue to be dispersed throughout the world. He envisioned a radically different future. From his memoirs: "The emancipation of the Jews led not to assimilation but to a new expression of their national uniqueness and Messianic longing" (Ben-Gurion 1972, 25–26). The uniqueness and specialness is a key component of this self-image. The Jews, in the words of the blessing of Balaam in Numbers (23:9), are "a people who dwell by themselves, who are not to be counted with the other nations." For Ben-Gurion it was not just any place that the Jews should live out their separateness—for him, the Land of Israel was the only place for this solitary, special people. He saw Israel as the only appropriate object of this longing: "Without a messianic, emotional, ideological impulse," he wrote, "without the vision of restoration and redemption, there is no earthly reason why even oppressed and underprivileged Jews…should wander off to Israel of all places…The immigrants were seized with an immortal vision of redemption which became the principal motivation of their lives" (1972, 25–26).

It is clear that the destinies of all the Jewish immigrants to Palestine—those driven by ideological fervor, those who were fleeing persecution, and those for whom it was a combination of both, as well as those Palestinians whose lands and fates lay in the path of the Zionist project—were in the hands of this brilliant, messianic, fanatical dreamer. Recall that this was a man who left Russia in 1906. The trajectory of his life was set in motion by the failure of the emancipation; the lens through which he viewed the world was his experience of the Jews as an isolated, oppressed group at the mercy of a failing, murderous, autocratic state. In his writing and pronouncements, Ben-Gurion was talking about the survival not of Judaism, but of the Jews themselves. Although Ben-Gurion was himself a non-observant, secular Jew, the language he used was religious. Rose quotes from an address Ben-Gurion delivered in 1950, two years after the declaration of the State: "The return to Zion and to the Bible is a supreme expression of the rebirth and resurgence of the Jewish people, and the more complete the return the nearer we will come to a full political and spiritual salvation" (Ben-Gurion 1950, 1). According to Ben-Gurion, therefore, there was only one place for Jews—the "return" must be "complete."

It is as if the voice of David Ben-Gurion is being channeled through the mouth of Shaul Goldstein, the mayor of Neve Daniel and our modern-day enactor of the "rebirth and resurgence of the Jewish people" through the "return to Zion." As one surveys the surrounding landscape from Daoud Nassar's land and travels by car through Gush Etzion, the evidence of the vitality and driving force of this project is apparent everywhere. Down the hill to the west of Daoud's farm, spreading through the valley and threatening to engulf the Palestinian village of Nahalin, is the "settlement" of Beitar Illit. To call this place a settlement is a misnomer, a term disclaimed by the inhabitants themselves. As one approaches Beitar Illit from the main road, a road restricted to Jews only, one encounters a huge sign at the entrance that reads: "Beitar Illit: A City of Torah and Devotion in the Hills of Judea."[2] The visitor to the city's web site is greeted by a real estate prospectus, an advertisement for a city that is, according to its own advertising, reclaiming a site that dates from Roman times when it was held and settled by Jewish zealots. The zealots have returned. This time, however, *they* have the army and *they* are erecting the fortifications to protect their colonies. Rose sees all this clearly, and understands the implications. "It is shocking," she writes, "to consider that a nation, apparently inspired, believing fervently in its own goodness in the world, might be devoted not only to the destruction of others but to sabotaging itself" (2005, 21).

---

2. Note not only the designation "city," but the use of the term "Hills of Judea." "Judea and Samaria" are the Biblical terms for the territory of today's West Bank. Jewish settlers always refer to this territory in this fashion, In their view, this land is being reclaimed as part of "Eretz Yisrael," the Biblical Land of Israel. Political boundaries, armistice lines, international agreements and laws are secondary, irrelevant to the power of these claims for these ideological pioneers. With the election of a right-wing government in February 2009, this usage has entered the Israeli political mainstream, with Prime Minister Benjamin Netanyahu referring in a June 2009 speech to Israel's "presence in Judea, Samaria, and Gaza." ("Netanyahu: How Judea and Samaria Can Become 'Palestine," *Jewish World Review*, June 14, 2009, www.jewishworldreview.com).

But is this so shocking? Does it not follow that a nation "believing fervently in its own goodness in the world" might, given the right set of circumstances, follow a path to its own destruction? In the final chapter of his 2006 *The Ethnic Cleansing of Palestine*, Israeli historian Ilan Pappe draws the unavoidable parallel between the modern Jewish state, building walls to enclose itself from the hostile "others" surrounding it, to the medieval crusaders, "whose Latin Kingdom of Jerusalem remained for nearly a century a fortified island as they shielded themselves behind the thick walls of their impenetrable castles against integration with their Muslim surroundings, prisoners of their own warped reality" (253).

Seemingly unable to stop itself, and enabled by considerable and unconditional financial and political support from the United States, Israel continues to pursue its colonial settler enterprise and to build the wall that expands and secures its acquisitions. Its Palestinian victims look on in a remarkable combination of seething frustration and philosophical calm. In the summer of 2006, our delegation went to see the wall on our first day in Jerusalem. The twenty-five-foot-high concrete barrier slices like a giant cleaver through the village of Al Azaria, once a neighborhood of Palestinian East Jerusalem and now an isolated enclave. We stood in what was once the main street, now—like so many other former urban thoroughfares in Palestine—an empty, trash-strewn ruin. Numb, we stood before this inexplicable horror, feeling dwarfed both physically and emotionally by its size and its ugliness. Still rooted to the spot, I looked to my left and observed, standing in the shadow of this wall, a small neighborhood grocery store, the kind you see everywhere in the world. It was, of course, devoid of customers, empty of the kind of activity you see in such places: shoppers coming and going, local people sitting for a spell talking with the man behind the counter. Several of us entered. "What do you do now?' I asked the man behind the counter. "What can I do?" he replied. Yes, he told us, once this store gave him a good life: he supported a family, travelled. Now—he gestured at the empty shop, the desolate street—"it's all gone." I groped for words. "How do you cope?" I asked. He smiled, looking directly into my eyes: "Life is a circle. The sun rises and it sets. Bad times follow good times, and the good times return."

We have to ask ourselves how we ended up here, in the role of oppressor, in violation of our own values of humanitarianism and justice, defending the unlikely reality of a Jewish state, a colonial project established against the protest and violent opposition of the indigenous Palestinian population and most of the Arab world. Everywhere you turn in Israel, you are confronted with this question. It is impossible to begin to answer without naming the Holocaust. "It was the horrors of the Second World War that gave the Jewish people an unanswerable case," explains Rose (118). She tells the story of a journalist who asked a Palestinian-Israeli filmmaker, "Can you tell me what reason there is for the State of Israel?" The filmmaker replied, "'The Holocaust'" (119).

The reality of the catastrophe pervades Israeli society. Israeli writer David Grossman, in a talk at American University in Washington, DC, in October 2008, spoke about how, for Israeli society, the Nazi Holocaust is experienced as a current reality rather than something that happened in the past. When we refer to the Holocaust, said Grossman, we always talk about what happened "over there." It is never referred to as what happened "then." Israeli writer Avraham Burg sees the Holocaust as the central reality for Israel—infecting every aspect of daily life and even driving government policy:

> In our eyes, we are still partisan fighters, ghetto rebels, shadows in the camps, no matter the nation, state, armed forces, gross domestic product, or international standing. The Shoah is our life, and we will not forget it and we will not let anyone forget us. We have pulled the Shoah out of its historic context and turned it into a plea and a generator for every deed. All is compared to the Shoah, dwarfed by the Shoah, and therefore all is allowed—be it fences, sieges,...curfews, food and water deprivation, or unexplained killings...Everything seems dangerous to us... (2008, 78)

Rose observes that this Jewish worldview stretches far back in history to medieval times, to the Jewish mystical tradition of the kabbalah. Citing scholar Gershom Scholem, Rose observes that the kabbalah arose as a response to the infamous Chmielnitzki massacres in eastern Europe of the seventeenth century, as a way to make "historic destitution supremely meaningful" (2005, 137). These were dark times, times of profound suffering and insecurity for the Jewish communities of eastern Europe. Kabbalistic writings that spoke to the people about a time in which they would not only be relieved from their suffering and insecurity, but elevated to a glorious, triumphant, and blessed state gained wide acceptance. In this way the exile and suffering of the Jewish people took on cosmic significance. Modern political Zionism, therefore, although purportedly a secular movement, was mystically tinged. This visionary character, submits Rose, fundamentally influenced the tenor and direction of political Zionism. Palestine was not so much a real place as an ideal framed in messianic terms. Modern Zionists, both religious and secular, adopted the language of kabbalah. Rose quotes Abraham Isaac Kook, the first chief rabbi of modern Palestine and spiritual mentor of today's religious right wing: "The anticipation of redemption is the force which keeps exilic Judaism alive, and the Judaism of the land of Israel is salvation itself" (Kook 1963).

Rose's analysis may seem radical—but it goes far to explain the madness being pursued today by the State of Israel in defiance of international law and ultimately against its own interests. Unfortunately, when one calls it messianism, as Rose does, one risks weakening the argument, since the word calls up images of extremism, religious frenzy, fanaticism, and the End of Days. Yet what do we have here but a fervent desire for redemption and relief from misery, fear, and helplessness? As Burg has pointed out, the messianically tinged need for rescue and redemption born from extreme persecution persists, regardless of historical reality and the present political context. It can be detected, as the fundamental principle, in virtually every argument for and defense of the existence of Israel as a Jewish state. It matters little whether the source is liberal-progressive or conservative. We will see in coming chapters how even Christian writers have come to endorse some of the flavor and meaning of this Jewish yearning for redemption.

Jewish Empowerment: A Liberal Defense

Rabbi Arthur Hertzberg epitomizes the postwar, Zionist liberal Jewish establishment. His work provides an important counterpoint to Rose's probing critique. Hertzberg's 1959 *The Zionist Idea* became a classic textbook for Jews and non-Jews alike. Although critical of Jewish triumphalism after the 1967 war, near the end of his life (he died in 2006), Hertzberg took on the task of defending Zionism against critics from the Jewish Left. In so doing he adopted the pose of neither polemicist nor apologist, but rather of a man offering a balanced, fair perspective, willing to criticize Israel and Zionism when criticism was deserved. Hertzberg also presented himself as a religious Jew who nevertheless repudiated a Zionism mixed with religion. The subtitle for his 2003 book *The Fate of Zionism: A Secular Future for Israel and Palestine* is an expression of this point of view. According to Hertzberg, if Israel is to survive and Zionism is to fulfill its purpose, Israel must take its place among the nations of the world, unfettered by religious underpinnings or objectives. This, of course, meant that he had to mount an argument against the viewpoint that Zionism is in any way messianic. In the book Hertzberg firmly repudiates any messianic belief or feeling in his commitment to Zionism: "I never believed," he writes, "that any version of Zionist ideology offered the Jews a radical, messianic solution to the long-standing misery of being a persecuted minority almost everywhere in the world" (179).

Yet, does not the same self-image of the Jew as eternally vulnerable and threatened that fueled Jewish messianism shine through in this statement? Hertzberg's liberal pronouncements, supported by his own well-informed and intelligent analysis of Zionist history and current Israeli politics, are not balanced. They paper over the same exceptionalist ideology exposed by Rose and others. Hertzberg, like other progressive Jewish thinkers, fervently wants to frame Zionism in a positive, humanitarian light. Hertzberg's work is probably the best example of an argument for Israel that approaches being convincing, because he works hard not to appear partisan or argumentatively "pro-Israel." But, as we will see, in his work the fundamentals of a Zionist ideology that grants supremacy to Jewish claims survive intact.

Hertzberg opens *The Fate of Zionism* with a recounting of David Ben-Gurion's startling 1967 speech to Israel's then-dominant Labor Party. It was several weeks after the conclusion of the Six-Day War, in which Israel took possession of the West Bank (including East Jerusalem), Gaza, the Sinai, and the Golan Heights. In that speech Ben-Gurion warned that if Israel did not *immediately* return all the territory it had gained in the war, it was headed for disaster. The reader is thus disarmed: here is a man, one might assume, who is prepared to take on Israel, and perhaps Zionism itself! This, however, would be incorrect. In fact, the book is a frontal attack on Israel's detractors—branding them as "leftist" intellectuals all too willing to condemn Israel while ignoring human rights abuses elsewhere in the world. Hertzberg then employs the tried-and-true straw man maneuver, presenting the radical fundamentalist fringe in Israel as the element that must be defeated in favor of the moderate, gentler Zionists. Under its progressive, "balanced" surface, Hertzberg's book offers up a defense of Jewish supremacy in historic Palestine.

Herzberg is attempting to criticize Jewish empowerment while justifying it at the same time. He stands by the standard Zionist narrative—that the state is the necessary answer to anti-Semitism and to the continuing reality of the Jews as an "embattled minority"—while posing as a critic of Israel at the same time. By taking us back to 1967, he's bringing into service the favorite argument of Jewish progressives: "It's the occupation, stupid." Ben-Gurion, he maintains, was prophetic in his dire warnings about holding on to territories captured in 1967. It would be the occupation, goes this argument, that would spoil the grand experiment and destroy the Zionist dream. Ben-Gurion, Hertzberg writes, "saw that the Zionism he had helped fashion in the early years of the twentieth century, a movement whose main goal was the creation and support of a Jewish national state in Palestine, was being overlaid after June 1967 with Israeli triumphalism and myths about the advent of a messianic age" (ix). Zionism, he feared, "was being replaced by a new—and false—religion" (xi).

These are important points, but Hertzberg is rewriting history here. Yes, it can be said that the lightning-fast, total victory of 1967 produced a euphoria and triumphalism that had not been widely apparent before. But it is becoming increasingly clear that these qualities of triumphalism and messianism were present and active in the envisioning and the actual establishment of the Jewish state long before the 1967 military victory. In 1967, these qualities surfaced with striking clarity and force, and have since dominated the political landscape. But the expansionism that was unleashed in 1967 was and continues to be the legitimate child of the settler colonial Zionist project. There is no recognition here that the occupation is the faithful continuation of the actions that helped give birth to the Jewish state. Like the violence and racism of the settler movement, the occupation is used by proponents of political Zionism as a straw man: *This is not us*, runs the argument. *This is not the real Israel, the good, democratic Israel, the humanitarian, prophetic Zionism. This is an unfortunate development that we moral Zionists repudiate.*

A Secular Messianism

In his argument for what he calls an approach that leaves religion out of the equation, Hertzberg sets up messianism as yet another straw man. The coming of the Jewish state, protests Hertzberg, would not herald an end of days or a radical transformation of Jewish life. "Only some Jews," he predicts, "would return to Zion [*sic*], and others would choose to remain in the Diaspora even as they would be thrilled for, supportive of, and identified with those who were rebuilding a homeland for the entire Jewish people" (179). Here is Diaspora Jewry having its cake and eating it too. Jews can continue their comfortable existence in the West, even while enjoying the quasi-messianic reality of the notion of a "homeland" for the "entire Jewish people." The existence of this "rebuilt" homeland changes the coloring of Jewish life everywhere. What Hertzberg gives us is a secular messianism: a solution to the Jew's "long-standing misery." Zionism and its realization in the State of Israel is, in his words, "an instrument of survival and regeneration in a tragic century" (180). Furthermore, this solution is not limited to a response to the Holocaust; rather, it projects into the future: "These were the purposes that it served throughout the twentieth century, and these are the purposes that Zionism continues to serve" (180). Apparently, therefore, the misery of being a persecuted minority is not over. In his concluding chapter, Hertzberg writes, "The state of Israel is the guarantee that Jews, indeed, will have somewhere to go" (180). It is also a matter of what he calls our "cultural survival: "If Israel were no more, the Jews, and the world as a whole, would lose the national home in which Jews wrestle on their own terms with the moral and spiritual problems of modern life" (180).

Hertzberg thus repudiates any notion of a messianic strain in Zionism, yet he endorses in an unqualified way the fact of Israel as a "homeland." But where is the differentiator between these concepts? The very notion of "homeland" is built on the conviction of a need for such a thing: this is the heart and the bedrock of Zionism. It is the solution to the Jewish problem—"the long-standing misery of being a persecuted minority almost everywhere in the world" (179). Thus the liberal argument for political Zionism takes us, tragically, not toward a future of security and coexistence, but circling back into our experience of helplessness and victimization. It resurrects the messianically tinged urge for a homeland. This, as documented by Rose and others, was a fundamental component of Zionism from its early days. We see it operating today in the colonialist policies of the state and in the support of world Jewry for these policies. An essential component of this core belief underlying Zionism is what Marc Ellis has identified as the myth of Jewish innocence. This is an essential element of Jewish sensibility, related to what Ellis calls our "liturgy of destruction"—the Jewish preoccupation with vulnerability and victimhood. It has the effect of making only our suffering important and erasing that of others, *even when the others' suffering is caused by us.* The interests of the Jews always occupy center stage; the experience or point of view of others is secondary. Ellis points out that even when Jewish theologians attempt to grapple directly with the question of Israel/Palestine, this theme emerges strongly, revealing the same ethnocentricity and willingness to put the responsibility for violence on the other, in this case the Palestinians. He quotes progressive orthodox Jewish theologian Irving Greenberg: "The Palestinians will have to earn their power by living peacefully and convincing Israel of their beneficence or by acquiescing to a situation in which Israel's strength guarantees that the Arabs cannot use their power to endanger Israel" (Greenberg 1981, 26).

Is it any wonder that peace is so elusive? Has this not been the position taken by Israel, supported fully by Israel's U.S. "broker" pursuing "negotiations" with Palestinian "partners"? Our worldview—our attitude toward the other—is so totally conditioned by our sense of our entitlement, undergirded by the *idée fixe* of our eternal victimhood, that we cannot see the other except as a threat that must be neutralized. We are ever vigilant. This is our lens. It even lets us fool ourselves into thinking that this very reality is otherwise, that we are the world's universalists *par excellence.*

Jewish suffering continues to trump all other considerations of justice, fairness, or universalism. Hertzberg is calling for a secularism and a universalism based, he claims, on biblical tradition, but his commitment to Zionism contradicts all that. He invokes the great Jewish sage Hillel, who taught that "what is hateful to you, you should not do to the other" (Hertzberg, 182). But in the same breath he calls for a Jewish state, which exists as a haven for Jews in case of some undetermined future Jewish emergency. These are incompatible goals. Any claim that Hertzberg could make that he is presenting a balanced perspective falls away midway through the book when he advances two of the favorite arguments of the "pro-Israel" camp. The first is that Palestinians are not a "real" people—that the designation and concept of "Palestinian" arose only as a reaction to the Jewish settlement in the mid-twentieth century. Any competing or prior claim to the land on the part of the so-called Palestinians, therefore, is not valid. It is Golda Meir's famous 1969 statement about the Palestinians as a people: "They never existed." The second argument implies that criticism of Israel's human rights record is but thinly disguised anti-Semitism; that such charges, although factually based, betray a pernicious bias against Israel. Why, goes this reasoning, is there such "near hysteria," to quote Hertzberg (2003, 110), about Israel, when Saddam Hussein of Iraq, Hafez Assad of Syria, and Omar Hassan Ahmad al-Bashir of Sudan are responsible for the massacre of tens of thousands of their own citizens?

These arguments reveal the true intent of Hertzberg's project, which is to invalidate and stifle any real dialogue about the future of Israel in the Middle East by dismissing criticism of Israel as anti-Semitic. Is it not foolish, even unforgivable, to reduce this discussion to a comparison of which conflict is bloodier or which dictator more appallingly cruel? The establishment of the State of Israel and the subsequent denial of equal rights to the Palestinians within and from 1948 Israel and, more recently, within the occupied West Bank and Gaza represent one of the most blatant, systematic violations of human rights by one government of an entire people in the world today. It began with a two-year campaign of ethnic cleansing still unacknowledged by the West. This was followed by a colonial project of dispossession and control that has continued for more than sixty years, financially and politically supported by the greatest power in the world.

Hertzberg's self-presentation as a scholar dedicated to a frank critique of Zionism and a return to a reasonable, "secular" approach to the Jewish state doesn't hold up. Here are his true colors: immediately following the "what about Saddam Hussein" argument, having now established that criticism of Israel is self-evidently biased, he presents us with this final judgment on the matter. "The source of Arab's anger," he concludes, "is that they are at war with the Jews. The source of the anger in the West is that the Western liberals and leftists are at war with themselves" (111).

"It's Us or Them"

Turning from Hertzberg's purportedly progressive stance, it is almost a relief to consider the blatantly partisan pronouncements of the "pro-Israel" Jewish organizations. Morton Klein is president of the Zionist Organization of America, one of the oldest and most vociferously and militantly Zionist organizations on the American scene. On October 23, 2008, the following editorial by Klein was published by JTA, "The Global News Service of the Jewish People." Entitled "Palestinian Statehood Not the Answer," Klein's piece states that "only when the Palestinians demonstrate acceptance of Israel as a Jewish state will negotiations produce peace, not bloodshed." Citing statistics that show thousands of Israelis killed and maimed since "negotiations" began in 1993, and polls showing a majority of Palestinians in support of terrorist and missile attacks on Israel, the article goes on to describe a "cult of suicide bombing and martyrdom" that has been inculcated in Palestinian youth since the Palestinian Authority was established in 1993 through the Oslo Accords. Klein then repeats the myth of the multiple Western and Israeli "offers" for Palestinian statehood, beginning with the Peel Commission in 1937, through the UN Partition Plan of 1947, and the Clinton-Barak offer of 2000, all "rejected" by the Palestinians. The conclusion, of course, is that the Palestinians have never been in favor of a state of their own alongside Israel. Rather, "more than their own state, Palestinians want victory in the form of Israel's demise."

It is difficult to understand how, in the fall of 2008—in the midst of the last-ditch effort of the Bush administration to broker peace, and in the wake of Israeli Prime Minister Olmert's astonishing warning that if hopes for a two-state solution were to collapse, Israel "is finished"—something like this could be published by an organization claiming to represent the interests of the Jewish people. How else can we understand this but in the following way: here we have, preserved and persistent, the core of Zionism—the preoccupation with Jewish vulnerability and suffering, and the sense of entitlement to the land. Key to the maintenance of this belief system is an insistence on blaming the other: the violence originates only from *their* hatred and hostility. We are under attack by an enemy that hates us and wants to annihilate us. Naturally, one cannot negotiate with or talk to such an enemy.

It is becoming increasingly clear to what extent Israel's leaders and their supporters in the West need these "enemies" in order to support the validity of this belief system. Here is David Harris, Executive Director of the American Jewish Committee, writing in the organization's e-zine on October 19, 2008:

> There are real-life dangers to the Jewish people. They're not concocted, as some would suggest, by fear-mongering organizations or elderly Jews who see anti-Semites everywhere they look. They exist and need to be exposed and confronted.
>
> How much clearer can Iran be in desiring a world without Israel? How many more times do Hamas and Hezbollah spokesmen have to refer to Jews as "the sons of monkeys and pigs" before they're taken seriously? How much more unfairly does Israel have to be treated in the UN to recognize that no other country in the world "enjoys" the same status? How many more conspiracy theories about Jews staying home on 9/11, Lehman Brothers' partners hoarding billions in Israel, or American Jews controlling U.S. foreign policy must be circulated to grasp that there are those who wish us ill?[3]

There are progressive Zionists who would protest that these examples are extreme and that in offering them I am presenting a biased picture of the current pro-Israel position. They will argue

---

3. It is interesting to consider that right-winger Benjamin Netanyahu came into power in the 2009 Israeli elections partially on the strength of this fear of Iran's threat to annihilate Israel through a nuclear attack.

that many American Jews are sympathetic to the Palestinians, who have without question suffered at our hands and deserve to have a state of their own. I would counter that the attitudes presented in these statements by American Zionist organizations accurately describe the core beliefs—one could even say principles—of Zionism. They persist, unmodified by those Jews who seek to soften or qualify them with appeals to considerations of justice, fairness, or the human rights of those we have wronged. They continue to determine the actions of the State of Israel and the financial and political support of those actions by the mainstream Jewish community in the United States.

The proof is in the policies. The proof is evident to anyone who sees the occupation. Israel does not want to share. Israel wants the Palestinians to go.

Joining the Human Family

Increasingly, voices are emerging from the Jewish community, voices raised in opposition, even protest, against the Zionist program. This is not new—in the years before the birth of the state, giants such as philosopher Martin Buber and Hebrew University chancellor Judah Magnes cried out against the idea of a Jewish state. But these voices were silenced in the aftermath of the Holocaust and with the victory of Jewish forces in defending the newly established state. In our day, however, these voices have reemerged in the statements and published writings of academics, journalists, and social critics. We would be hard-pressed to find a voice more uncompromising and direct than that of Professor Joel Kovel. Kovel's *Overcoming Zionism* came out in 2007 to a resounding lack of reviews except in the leftist press. His central premise was that Judaism's tribal core is responsible for Zionism, which he calls "the curse of Judaism." Kovel writes:

> The theological reflex of being a people apart is known as the Covenant, a kind of promise bestowed by Yahweh...Obedience to a peremptory or guilt-inducing inner voice is a distinctive aspect of Judaic being, both a product of apartness and a

reinforcement for apartness. It leads into a kind of moral universe where the dictates of the tribe and those of the universal deity can be conflated, especially under circumstances in which the larger society reinforces the separation of Jews from others by law or persecution. When that happens,...then being apart and being chosen as exceptional became one and the same; spiritual greatness and collective narcissism flow together...if one's ethical reference point is the tribal unit, then all others are devalued, and one no longer belongs to humanity but sets oneself over humanity. This dilemma is to haunt Zionism once its state is formed and its logic of conquest put Jews in the driver's seat. *But it is much older than Zionism.* (20; emphasis added)

In Kovel's view, if you sign on to the idea of Jewish state, "you are taking the particularism which is the potential bane of any state, mixing it with the exceptionalism which is the actual bane of Judaism, and giving racism an objective, enduring, institutionalized, and obdurate character" (165).

Kovel's analysis, uncompromising and, it must be said, merciless as it is, puts Zionism in its proper perspective. It is not comfortable. It makes us squirm. It doesn't let us off the hook. Kovel's unblinking look at Zionism and its relation to the tribal origins of Judaism also allows him to see the prophets in a realistic frame. He honors the power of their vision, but sees also the limitations, given the tribal framework in which they operated. Accordingly, he credits Christianity for taking the next step. When the reality of these tribal elements of Judaism is acknowledged, Judaism's discontinuity with Christianity is revealed in its simple clarity. Kovel is drawn back to the first century, to the actions of that Jewish prophet and social reformer of two thousand years ago: "Isaiah was the greatest Old Testament prophet; but the greatest prophet of all...was Jesus of Nazareth. Jesus was authentically Jewish and yet a breaking point in the history of Judaism, which becomes defined thereafter by those Jews who did not follow him. Jesus was that Jew who made the Covenant universal by dissolving its tribal shell and extending it to all humanity" (32).

In the coming chapters, we will return, in the company of contemporary Christian theologians and scholars, to Palestine of the first century. The political reality that drove the events of that time will provide the framework for understanding the challenges and opportunities facing us today.

Jewish liberation theologian Marc Ellis sets out what those challenges are. Like Jacqueline Rose, Ellis confronts the disturbing consequences of Jewish empowerment, and seeks to help us understand what drives us, what has brought us to this pass. Ellis is urgently concerned about Jewish survival. For him, however, the question is not how to preserve Jewish security in the face of a hostile world, but how Judaism in the twenty-first century can overcome the effects of having *succeeded* in achieving power and overcoming chronic victimization. Ellis echoes Walter Brueggemann and other Christian theologians who understand the role of prophecy as opposing oppressive social systems. Jews today, maintains Ellis, must find their prophetic voice in order to counteract the destructive effect of political and military success. "Will the Jewish prophetic voice survive Jewish empowerment?" he asks. "Will the prophetic word break through the numbness of the Jewish community? Can it transform the power of the Israeli state to the homeland vision of Judah Magnes and Hannah Arendt?" (2004, 205).

For Ellis, in contrast to proponents of Zionism like Hertzberg, the valence on the word "homeland" is not on the physical haven, but on the concept of coexistence in a Palestine shared with others in a pluralistic, truly democratic society. In support of this, Ellis cites the 1981 essay by Israeli journalist and author Boas Evron, "The Holocaust: Learning the Wrong Lessons." Evron takes issue with the notion that Israel exists to save Jews from another Holocaust, and that the lesson of "never again" somehow ties Israel and the necessity for a Jewish homeland to the Holocaust. He challenges the fundamental assumption, sometimes implicit and more often explicit, that the Holocaust gives meaning to Israel (i.e., protection from extermination), and Israel gives meaning (i.e., redemption) to the Holocaust.

We must learn a different lesson from the Holocaust, asserts Ellis, quoting Evron: "The true guarantee against ideologically-based extermination is not military power and sovereignty but the *eradication of ideologies which remove any human group from the family of humanity*" (Evron 1981, 18; emphasis added). For Evron, continues Ellis, "the solution lies in a common struggle aimed at overcoming national differences and barriers, rather than increasing and heightening them as strong trends within Israel and the Zionist movement demand" (2004, 54).

Ellis is adamantly opposed to any role for religion allied with power, what he terms—using the prototypical Christian example—Constantinian. He prescribes this for all religious groups, not only the Jews, and shares a vision for the future in which traditional boundaries will be secondary to a common cause for social justice:

> Constantinian Christianity has now been joined by Constantinian Judaism. Constantinian Islam is also a reality. Yet there are Christians, Jews, and Muslims who also oppose and suffer under Constantinianism. Could it be that those who participate in Constantinian religiosity—whether Jew, Christian or Muslim—are, in effect, practicing the same religion, albeit with different symbol structures and rituals? And that those who seek community are also practicing the same religion?...Movements of justice and compassion across community and religious boundaries may be the vehicles for a better understanding of commonalities in religiosity that can no longer be defined by traditional religious labels. (217)

Ellis makes a compelling and passionate case for a renewal of Jewish life and theology based on the best of our tradition. In the course of this, he challenges the idea of a Jewish state as central—even necessary—for Jewish survival, both physical and spiritual. He writes: "A practicing Jew within the liberationist perspective sees Israel as neither central nor peripheral, but rather as a necessary and flawed attempt to create an autonomous Jewish presence within the Middle East" (214). In Ellis's view, contemporary mainstream Judaism, having adopted as its credo and its mission staunch support for Israel as a political haven for Jews, is on the wrong course. Those, like Ellis, who oppose the Constantinian direction that Judaism has taken, have chosen to be "in exile from mainstream Jewish life" (206). I understand Ellis's evocation of the image of exile for the experience of contemporary Jews who choose to forgo allegiance to the Zionist doctrine—I feel the pain of this condition myself. But I also feel reluctant to embrace the notion of exile as a unifying concept or identity. Exile may describe well the loss of attachment or belonging to a location or previously held sense of self—but does not exile thrust one into a wider landscape of identity and place? Ellis himself lays out a picture of a possible future that beckons. It is a future toward which not only the Jewish people, but the whole of humankind must strive, "a broader tradition of faith...with other struggling communities in a common struggle for liberation" (207). For Ellis this life of community is what we must strive for, in which religious identities may be preserved, but where these boundaries and idioms are secondary. Zionism has led the Jewish people, and humankind with it, not toward but away from this vision of community.

PART 2

Beyond Atonement

The ministry of Jesus, like the ministry of Second Isaiah, happens in the space between the clinging and the yearning. If there is only clinging, then the words are only critical. If there is yearning, there is a chance that the words are energizing. The staggering works of Jesus—feeding, healing, casting out, forgiving—happened not to those who held on to the old order but to those you yearned because the old order had failed them or squeezed them out.

—Walter Brueggemann, *The Prophetic Imagination*

We cannot continue to pretend that we are the chosen and all other people are the unchosen… Jesus commissioned his disciples to go into all the world (Matt. 28:16–20). They were to go beyond the boundaries of their nation, their tribe and most specifically their religion.

—John Shelby Spong, *The Sins of Scripture*

Chapter 5

Undoing the Damage: Post-Holocaust Christian Theology

No longer is it a case for the legitimacy of Judaism. Unless they succeed in finding within the New Testament some area which is substantially free of anti-Judaism, the issue becomes the legitimacy of Christianity.
—John G. Gager, *The Origins of Anti-Semitism*

When I challenged the pastor that day in Washington about his reluctance to criticize the State of Israel, I hadn't yet realized how deeply rooted this attitude was among American Christians. In fact, the feelings that my friend expressed to me that day are grounded in a powerful revisionist movement in Christian theology that began after World War II. It is important to understand the profound transformation in the attitude toward the Jewish people that developed in American Christianity in the second half of the twentieth century. As a result of this change, Jews came to be regarded not as a people to be pitied or reviled, but to be admired; not to be converted, but emulated. Whereas this shift is sometimes explicitly acknowledged in the seminaries or in conferences, it is rarely if ever discussed openly, even among the clergy or the leadership of church denominations. However, these attitudes are now deeply embedded in our modern culture and in the mainstream of American Christianity. They affect the way Christians talk about Jews and the way they talk to Jews. They have had a profound impact on the interfaith dialogue about the State of

Israel. In the next two chapters, we'll look closely at a number of Protestant and Catholic writers who have influenced the way generations of American Christians think about and behave toward the Jewish people. The influence of these theologians and scholars has been felt not only among the clergy, who studied them in seminary and graduate school, but by the laity as well, who have absorbed these attitudes through attendance at worship, church education, and popular literature.

Paul van Buren: One Covenant

American theologian Paul van Buren is generally recognized, if not revered, in one contemporary writer's words, as "a pioneer among theologians committed to putting the church's relationship to the Jewish people on a new footing" (Soulen 2000). Van Buren, himself deeply influenced by the writing of the twentieth-century Jewish theologian and philosopher Franz Rosenzweig, exerted a powerful effect on subsequent progressive Christian thinkers concerned with the future of Christianity's relationship with the Jews. In 1997, James Wallis, the progressive Christian writer and political activist, published *Post-Holocaust Christianity: Paul van Buren's Theology of the Jewish-Christian Reality*. In Wallis's telling, van Buren believed that in order to repudiate the anti-Judaism of early Christianity, one had to accomplish nothing less than a radical redefinition of Christianity. Van Buren's work on formulating a "new revelation" was an attempt to reverse the destructive aspect of Christian anti-Judaism by bringing the two faiths together within the embrace of a single, continuous tradition. In order to undo what he felt were serious flaws in Christian theology and to promote Jewish-Christian dialogue and reconciliation, van Buren set out to frame God's covenant with the Jewish people as the basis for the Christian revelation.

This was a fundamental redefinition of a cornerstone of Christian faith. Van Buren's significant achievement was in calling attention to the ways in which Christianity had allowed itself to be built on a foundation of *anti-Judaism*. Like Catholic theologian

Gregory Baum, quoted in chapter 1, van Buren had found himself standing, psychologically and spiritually, before the ovens of Auschwitz. The revelation of what anti-Semitism had produced, in the very heart of twentieth-century Europe, shocked him, as it had other Christian thinkers, into focusing his attention on this aspect of his faith's history and to begin the work of building a bridge of understanding between the two faiths. For the theologians among them, the first step was to reexamine some of the fundamentals of Christian thought. For van Buren and those who have followed, this meant finding a way to integrate God's special relationship with the Jewish people into a theology that could honor and encompass both religions. Wallis writes, "For van Buren, the church was meant to exist alongside Israel, and to cooperate with Israel and with God for the sake of world redemption. That this is not what happened historically is due to a church error. The anti-Judaic church is not the church that God intended" (1997, 124). "Christianity must refer to Judaism in order to make sense of itself," writes van Buren. This is in the service of the "church's reversal of its position on Judaism from that of anti-Judaism to that of an acknowledgement of the eternal covenant between God and Israel" (1998, 85).

In van Buren's model, God's promise of the land to the Jewish people is the centerpiece of the covenant, a promise made exclusively to his chosen people. "The church," observes Wallis, "in order to direct this promise to itself, spiritualized the promise" (1997, 82). It appears, however, that van Buren, in response to the grim history of Christians' treatment of the Jews, has issued a clarification: we Christians may participate in the spiritual Jerusalem with the Jews, but the Jews hold the deed to the actual real estate. And this truth has been revealed in the return of the Jews to possess that very same Promised Land. It is not the spiritual guidance of Moses but the military leadership of Joshua in accomplishing that possession that captures van Buren's attention. In reading van Buren, one wonders if one is looking at a kind of Judeo-Christian triumphalism—a significant step backward, to my mind, from the spiritualization of the land that characterized the original Christian formulation. Consider the following passage from a contribution to a 1979 interfaith symposium, "The Jewish People in Christian Preaching." Why, asks van Buren, after eighteen centuries, should Christian leaders "turn Christian teaching on its head" with respect to the Jewish people?

> The Holocaust and the emergence of the state of Israel…are what impelled them to speak in a new way about Jews and Judaism. It is my judgment that the emergence of the state of Israel was the more powerful of the two, for, shameful as it is to confess it, more than one Christian leader was able to absorb the Holocaust into our traditional theology of the Jews as wandering, suffering, despised souls, paying forever for their stiff-necked rejection of Christ. What could not possibly fit into that mythical picture was the Israelis, holding out and winning their war of independence against the combined forces of five national armies. It is sobering to think that we have first begun to take the Jews seriously when they first started acting like us—picking up a gun and shooting. Nevertheless, the Israeli Defense Force sweeping over the Sinai and retaking East Jerusalem was what could not possibly fit our traditional myth of the passive suffering Jew. The result is that events in modern Jewish history, perhaps as staggering as any in its whole history, have begun to reorient the minds of increasing numbers of responsible Christians. (van Buren 1984)

It is not so much the jarring echo of the mythology of a "new Jew" that shocks me, nor the one-sided, triumphalist narrative of the 1948 and 1967 wars—it takes very little imagination to hear echoes of Abba Eban's vaunting David and Goliath speech at the UN in June 1967 in which he pictures Israel triumphing over implacable, overwhelmingly more powerful foes. What is more disturbing is the theological undertone, the biblical drumbeat, in the appearance of two words in this passage: *Sinai* and *Jerusalem*. And it is not that van Buren's primary intent is to glorify the resurgence of Jewish power and the Jewish vision of the Return to Zion. It is more. It is that now Christians, with theological support, can join in this triumph, and absorb this historical event into their own vision of what it means to be faithful to God's plan. These events of our time, continues van Buren, reflect "the will of the holy one of Israel, that the greatest of all love affairs of history between God and God's people continue, but that God provides also a way for Gentiles, as Gentiles, to enter along with the chosen people into the task of taking responsibility for moving this unfinished creation nearer to its completion" (1984, 25).

In van Buren's view, Christian identity is completely tied up with the Jewish people. "We are gentiles who worship the God of the Jews," he writes. "We Christians and Jews really do exist for the sake of the world, and that means also for the sake of the world that is coming" (1984, 26). And is there any doubt that the promise of the land is not an integral part, if not a sign, of the approach of this completion, and of the sacred bond that unites—or rather reunites—the two faiths? Furthermore, what is the implication of calling God the "God of Israel"? In van Buren's writing, and throughout much of the revisionist literature, the deity is referred to repeatedly in this manner. If the covenant has now expanded to include Christians, then what of the Muslims, the Hindus, the Buddhists? The point of this revision of Christian theology is to rehabilitate the Jewish people. But this project carries with it two critical messages: (1) it connects God directly to one people—his chosen—and (2) it carries with it the terms of the covenant. Are we not seeing here a version of Christian Zionism, minus the Rapture?

Repairing the Rift: Overturning Supersessionism

"The only Jesus whom the church has ever known, or whom anyone can know, is the Jesus who comes clothed in the garb of his people's ancient oracles. For this reason, van Buren holds that Christians can and should use the Old Testament to correct the New when the latter veers toward anti-Judaism. The New Testament is merely the church's first 'copybook,' while the Old is the indispensable matrix of the gospel itself" (Soulen 2008).

These are the words of R. Kendall Soulen, professor of Systematic Theology at Wesley Theological Seminary in Washington, DC, writing about van Buren's perspective on Christianity's debt to Judaism. My pastor friend had given me a copy of Soulen's 1997 *The God of Israel and Christian Theology* as part of our ongoing dialogue. The stated purpose of Soulen's book is to correct what he sees as errors in the way the Jewish people and Judaism itself have been perceived in Christian thought. In his first chapter, Soulen observes that, following the Nazi Holocaust, the church sought to fundamentally change its relationship to the Jewish people by reinterpreting those aspects of Christian doctrine that are seen as the roots of Western anti-Semitism. The most destructive of the teachings of the church came to be known as supersessionism. Here is Soulen's summary of this historical posture of the church toward the Jewish people:

> God chose the Jewish people after the fall of Adam in order to prepare the world for the coming of Jesus Christ. After Christ came, however, the special role of the Jewish people came to an end and was taken by the church, the new Israel. The church, unlike the Jewish people, is a spiritual community in which the carnal distinction between Jew and Gentile is overcome. Accordingly, the church holds that the preservation of Jewish identity within the new Israel is a matter of theological indifference at best, and a mortal sin at worst. Yet the Jews themselves failed to recognize Jesus as the promised Messiah and refused to enter the new spiritual Israel. God therefore rejected the Jews and scattered them over the earth, where God will preserve them until the end of time. (1996, 1)

In Soulen's view, "overcoming the theology of displacement is one of the main theological tasks facing the Christian church today. Many churches have already taken a first step in this direction by repudiating supersessionism and affirming God's fidelity to God's covenant with Israel" (13). The task, therefore, involves not only undoing the blatantly anti-Semitic aspects of Christian doctrine, but reaffirming the special relationship between God and the Jewish people. Christianity, maintains Soulen, jumped from the story of the Fall of Adam and Eve in the first two chapters of Genesis directly to the New Testament, thereby ignoring and effectively cancelling out the entirety of the Old Testament, which is the story of the initiation and unfolding of God's covenant with Israel. To correct this, Soulen focuses on a Christian narrative that presents a "theological unity of the Bible" (21). His goal is to "show that Christians can interpret the Canon as a coherent witness…in a manner that overcomes the logic of supersessionism and that coheres fully with the contemporary church's affirmation of God's irrevocable election of the people Israel" (21).

Soulen maintains that "Christian theology is immediately engaged in a fight for its life" because of its need to solve the "perplexities" of existing "alongside…the Jewish people, which also glorifies the God of Israel but which cannot hear the gospel tidings of the living God" (ix). He charts the history of this perplexity by identifying two crises in Christian history. The first was "the great trauma of the early church's separation from the Jewish people" (x). Paul grappled with it in Romans 9:11, but the issue was soon "foreclosed" through the adoption of the doctrine of supersessionism, which held that Christianity had replaced Judaism. Judaism was relegated to being the shadow, the darkness to Christianity's light. The second era is our own time, embodied in two events that "shattered" the self-satisfied comfort and triumphalism of centuries of supersessionism: "the Holocaust, in which Christians had to confess their own complicity, and the return of the Jewish people to the land God promised to Abraham" (x). Very much in the same spirit as van Buren and other post-Holocaust Christian theologians, Soulen seems to be saying that as a result of the Nazi Holocaust, Christianity is no longer able to live with the theological unacceptability and the horrible consequences of supersessionism. Therefore, a new theology is called for: one that neutralizes the evil of supersessionism, repairs Christian theology, and clears the way for Christians to have a positive, fulfilling relationship with the Jewish people. It is also notable that this new relationship appears to include the embrace of political Zionism on the part of Christians.

In support of this drive to reconcile with the Jews by join-ing story of Israel with that of the church, Soulen cites the work of Jewish theologian Michael Wyschogrod. Wyschogrod believes that there is a powerful continuity between the Old Testament concept of the holiness of the Jewish people and the Christian belief in the divinity of Christ. The notion of the incarnation, he writes, is a way to conceive of the indwelling of God, which is like the indwelling of God in the people of Israel. "Understood in this sense, the divinity of Jesus is not radically different—though per-haps more concentrated—than the holiness of the Jewish people" (1986, 79). Following Wyschogrod, Soulen states, "Jesus' resur-rection does not transcend the distinction between Israel and the nations but confirms and realizes it in a new way" (1996, 170). *The evil of supersessionism is thus corrected and atoned for by reaf-firming the specialness and chosenness of the Jewish people.* In this way the new covenant of Christianity, which in the traditional Christian vision came to replace the original, tribally based cov-enant between God and the Jews, can now be reconciled with the Israel that gave it birth.

Elevating "God's Beloved Child"

The problem with this formulation is that Soulen, in his effort to forge a theological bond between the two faiths, has embraced what is an exceptionalist and ultimately triumphalist Jewish position. Wyschogrod is an orthodox rabbi who believes that the election of the Jews is the core of Jewish identity. He writes: "The foundation of Judaism is the family identity of the Jewish people as the descendants of Abraham, Isaac, and Jacob. Whatever else is added to this must be seen as growing out of and related to the basic identity of the Jewish people as the seed of Abraham elected by God through descent from Abraham" (Wyschogrod 1989, 57). And this: "Israel is the carnal anchor that God has sunk into the soil of creation" (256). In a recent paper discussing Wyschogrod's work, Soulen, apparently aware of the exceptional-ist tone of this and similar statements establishing the primacy of

Judaism and the Jewish people, claims that "God did not choose Israel because it was superior to other peoples" (2004). Yet, in the same paper, Soulen speaks again and again of "God's special love for" Israel and of "Israel's election" by God for a special role in history. Indeed, the notion of superiority is hard to separate from that of election. If being elected for a special role in fulfilling God's plan for his creation does not confer special status, what else could possibly be required?

It is one step from Jewish specialness to Jewish superiority, if not in Soulen's mind, then certainly, one must imagine, in the minds of most Christians, and most certainly in the attitudes of many Jews. Consider this quote from Wyschogrod further on in Soulen's 2004 paper. Here, Soulen describes Wyschogrod's concept of the special nature of God's relationship with the Jewish people. It is the basis for God's election of Israel and his persistent fidelity to the Jews despite their rebelliousness: "For this reason, God's love is not undifferentiated, having the same quality toward all God's children. Precisely because God is so deeply concerned with human creation, God loves it with a differentiated love, and it comes about that there are those whom God loves especially, with whom, one can only say, God has fallen in love" (2004).

To this Jewish reader, if this is Christianity, then it is a faith that has swallowed an extremely problematic concept. Soulen's arguments endorse an outright Jewish triumphalism. What we have here is, actually, a kind of *reverse supersessionism*, a backward subsuming of Christianity into the original faith. To accept this is to invite the prospect not of a community of shared faith, but a concept in which all religions are worshiping God on the foundation established by God through his covenant with Israel. Israel's on top. Perhaps sensing the powerful implications of this theory, Soulen, quoting Wyschogrod, notes that this specialness does not come without responsibility: "Israel tends to forget that its election is for service, that it is a sign of the infinite and unwarranted gift of God rather than any inherent superiority of the people" (2004).

I know this argument. It is well known to any Jew who has undergone religious education: *we are the chosen people, but this status carries special responsibilities.* But far from mitigating the sense of specialness, doesn't this argument really serve to reinforce and strengthen it? What is usually brought into to this discussion is the often quoted "light to the nations" passage from Isaiah chapter 49. From election, to special love, to special responsibilities to bring God's message to the world, God's election of Israel leads to Jewish exceptionalism and ultimately to triumphalism. A theology that attempts to correct for Christian supersessionism by preserving or incorporating God's election of Israel ultimately replaces Christian supersessionism with Jewish exceptionalism. And if Christian triumphalism as expressed in supersessionism led to the ovens of Auschwitz, then Jewish triumphalism as expressed in political Zionism has led to the ethnic cleansing of Palestine.

If, as Soulen proposes, the problem with the church is that it "has failed to understand itself in light of God's fidelity to the people Israel" (1996, 11), I submit that we need to find another solution. It will be a solution that, if it does hark back to that original covenant, does so in a fashion that looks critically at the implications of that covenant and searchingly at the dynamics of the conflict between the parent faith and the revolutionary movement that arose out of it. Christianity came to reshape, if not revolutionize, the covenantal bond of God to Israel—a bond that was tribal and exceptionalist in nature. Soulen has introduced us to Wyschogrod in an effort to undo the damage of supersessionism. But Wyschogrod is doing to Christianity what Christianity did to Judaism through that original doctrine. Embracing Jewish election may be one way to resolve the Christian problem of responsibility for anti-Semitism. Ironically, however, the effect of this is to legitimize, indeed boost, Jewish triumphalism, separateness, and tribalism, which I have argued is a destructive force within Judaism. Ultimately—and this can already be observed in the reaction of the world to the human rights abuses of the Jewish state—this effort leads to an increase in anti-Semitism, by reinforcing and lending support to Jewish exceptionalism and the behaviors that flow from that attitude and self-image. If Christians really want to help, if they really want to undo the evils of anti-Semitism, they will do what they can to help us overcome this quality, rather than shoring it up. Wyschogrod's model has led us to helicopter gunships, a separation wall, the siege of Gaza, the flouting of international law, and the hatred, resentment, and mistrust of an increasingly broad sector of humankind.

Reconciling with the Jewish people by reaffirming their status as God's chosen is an attempt to resolve the traumatic parting by undoing the pain of that separation. But given early Christianity's doctrine, which challenged Judaism's fundamental tribalism, and the refusal of the Jews of the time to relinquish the core beliefs as well as the ritual trappings of their tribal specialness, was this parting not inevitable? If Christians want to find a way to reconcile with Judaism and to bring the faiths closer together, then let us together look forward and find a way to join in a universal family. If, however, progressive Christians lead with an affirmation of the Jewish people's specialness, refitting aspects of Christian theology to allow for this, they end up negating the very thing that Christianity was doing, which was superseding the tribal in favor of the universal.

And yet the drive to do just that appears to be quite powerful. Here is how Soulen puts it in his first chapter: "...the question of whether Israel can see in the church a sign that is congruent with Jewish faith depends upon the church's attitude toward the Jewish people. Are the nations prepared to receive God's blessing in the context of God's covenant with Israel? Or do they seek to do away with God's beloved child in order usurp its place in God's affection?" (11).

Soulen's question presents us with a false choice, based on false premises. The problem with this kind of revisionism is that it denies the fundamentally tribal origins of Judaism and the way that the exclusivist character of the faith has survived. It is a character, reinforced over two millennia of persecution, that is firmly grounded in our history, our theology, and, as Wyschogrod correctly points out, in our identity. Christianity had it right: Judaism *was* tribal and exclusivist. In the Old Testament narrative, God *did* elect the seed of Abraham as his special people, and assigned this group a special role in history. Christianity came to recast the

Old Testament narrative in the light of an emerging Christian theology, a theology that radically transformed the nature of the relationship between God and humankind from the tribal and exclusive to the universal. Christianity was not *built upon* Judaism in a developmental fashion. Rather, it *arose out of* Judaism in a transformative, revolutionary process.

What Soulen is proposing is a deeply conservative model. This model preserves the most archaic elements of Judaism. It is in direct conflict with the direction of Jesus's message and Paul's subsequent project to expand beyond the tribal boundaries and the cultic and legalistic strictures that came with and served to preserve and strengthen those boundaries. Far from having been the basis of a relationship with Christianity, these very qualities of Judaism were the break points. If the parting was drastic, if it was, in Soulen's description, traumatic, then so be it. Crises are necessary for human development, for great things to happen in human history.

We must consider how the effort to reformulate Christian theology to incorporate the original Abrahamic covenant in effect negates the revolutionary nature of Jesus's message. Jesus came to challenge the power of empire—the triumphalism of temporal rule—and to replace it with the triumph of the spirit. Christianity made a tragic wrong turn in the view of many when it threw in with Rome in the fourth century, a mistake that it continues to seek to correct as we leave the twentieth century behind. The Jewish people now face a similar choice as we confront the grim consequences of our own empowerment. In the light of current events, one must wonder if the unintended consequence of this effort at correction and atonement works not toward the expansion of Christianity but rather its contraction. While honoring the impulse to atone for its own historical sins, Christianity must take exceptional care not to enable the current sins of its parent.

James Carroll: Healing the Rift

"While Judaism exists without essential reference to Christianity, the reverse is not the case. The God of Jesus Christ, and therefore of the Church, is the God of Israel. The Jews remain the chosen people of God. And with this comes the Land" (Carroll 2001, 566).

These are not the words of a fundamentalist Jewish settler in the occupied West Bank or of a dispensationalist Christian Zionist, but of a liberal Catholic theologian.

James Carroll, in *Constantine's Sword: The Church and the Jews*, picks up the work of Christian atonement for anti-Semitism where some progressive Christian theologians leave off. Carroll borrows Catholic theologian Rosemary Ruether's term "the left hand of Christology" to describe how even the seemingly positive framing of the New Testament "fulfillment" of the Old Testament is an implicit and powerful degradation of the earlier faith and its scriptures. Christianity, he points out, established itself not as an outgrowth or continuation of Judaism, but in opposition to Judaism: Judaism, in fact, "was the shadow against which Christianity could be the light" (2001, 109). He maintains that the negative picture of the Judaism of Jesus's time was a distortion of the true nature of Judaism, a Judaism with which Jesus was in more harmony than the New Testament writers depicted. Carroll argues, unconvincingly in my view, that Jesus's very presence in Jerusalem as recounted in the Gospels was evidence of his feeling of attachment to the Temple and the sacrificial cult. In Carroll's work we see an attempt to reconcile with the Jews for the anti-Semitism of the Gospels and the millennia of persecution by washing out the rebellious, iconoclastic, intensely anti-cultic and anti-materialistic nature of Jesus's message.

The history of the early church and its relationship to Judaism and the Jewish communities of the time is just that—history. Carroll's argument is based on a *post facto* analysis of documents that were the products of those times and bear only indirectly on the nature of the Judaism and Jewish establishment that Jesus himself was confronting and to which he was speaking. What is more important, Carroll's solution to the problems caused by early Christianity's anti-Jewish polemic distorts the discussion of crucial political, religious, and sociological issues that bear directly on the current situation in the Middle East.

Carroll wants to tie Jesus back to the Temple, and, by extension, to the Land. Jesus was indeed Jewish, intensely so. But is it not so that at the core of Jesus's Jewishness was his prophetic voice, a voice that, in true prophetic idiom, cried out against the spiritual materialism of the day? Was not Jesus expressing, in Walter Brueggemann's terms, opposition to the royal consciousness that dominated the Jewish political and priestly establishment of his time? Was not Jesus's prophetic voice raised in fierce opposition to the tribal framework of the Jewish establishment and to its theology linked to the Temple and the Land? Having said this, might we not go on to say that what Jesus did leave behind was potentially such a fundamental challenge to the Judaism of his day that, what then grew from his teachings was something that ultimately could no longer be called Jewish? Would not the "trauma of separation," then, have been necessary? And if so, what is this drive to undo this separation, to somehow reattach Christianity to the very aspects of its Christian roots that are the most non-Christian?

Because this is precisely what Carroll has set out to do: reestablish the land as the center of Jewish spiritual life, and to then ask Christians to embrace this through their reimagining of Jesus himself. Carroll argues for this in an astonishing set of statements: "Christians take the ongoing Jewish attachment to the ideal of the Temple as a kind of idolatry, and, by extension, many Christians take modern Israeli attachment to the land around the Temple as rank imperialism" (108). This is a mistake, submits Carroll, just as it was wrong and ultimately disastrous for Christian belief to have driven a wedge between Jesus and the Temple and to purge from the faith any attachment to a physical place as the focus for worship. This is a misunderstanding of Jesus, he claims, and, ultimately, of the Jewish experience. Rather, "the Temple continues even now—if only the idea of it—as the solitary site of Jewish worship…the Jewish hope is rooted not in a mythic never-never land but in a place on earth. Its specificity is the point. The Temple, and by extension the land are tied to the unbreakable covenant God has made with his people" (108). In other words, Carroll argues, in order to neutralize the supersessionist dogma that is the source of the Jews' suffering, we must undo that poisonous falsehood, and reaffirm God's covenant with the Jewish people—and with it the land promise. We could frame this reasoning in this way: *You killed our Lord. In return, we killed you. To compensate you for millennia of murderousness, you can have the Temple back.*

Let Jesus Be Jesus

In Carroll's telling, Christianity arose out of Judaism in one continuous, developmental process. There was no discontinuity, no break, no parting. For Jesus, he submits, "there was only *one* covenant," which was one suffused with love (108). It was a relationship that, if not unconditional and not without its vicissitudes, was enduring and endures still. Carroll points out that the phrase "New Covenant," as it came to be used by Christianity to define its status as superseding Judaism, was first used by Jeremiah. He submits that Jeremiah's message in that passage was one of renewal and love, like Jesus's. But what is missing here, again, is the difference in context between the message of the Old Testament prophets and that of Jesus. What is missing is a recognition of what was *new* in Christianity. Jeremiah—whatever he meant by the image of a new covenant—was operating within the framework of God's relationship with the people of Israel. The prophet's grief at Israel's transgressions and his exhortations to return to the ways of the Lord are expressed in the context of God's grief at his people's betrayal. In other words, it is particularistic—Jeremiah's grief is expressed completely in the context of the Old Testament narrative and worldview. In contrast, what Jesus was talking about was a radical shift to a *universal* covenant, one that would be available to all of humankind, all of God's children. Yes, the prophets talk about love. But love of *whom*?

Carroll wants us to believe that Jesus took his message *to* Jerusalem, and not, as in the New Testament telling, against Jerusalem. Again, he is protesting against the anti-Semitism in the Christian narrative. That anti-Semitism is painfully apparent. But why should we reinvent Jesus in order to make up for this, as if we could undo that evil by recasting what is core in Jesus's message, which is that he was bringing something *new*? It was something so new, in fact, such a departure from the tribal, separatist nature of the Israel that he knew, that ultimately there was no turning back from a break with those Jews who would not relinquish that same quality of their peoplehood and their relationship with God.

To Carroll, therefore, and to those Christians who are, in good faith, attempting to heal the wound and to reconcile with the Jewish people, I put it to you this way: Say you're sorry. Affirm your sense of connection, even continuity, with the Jewish sources of your tradition and your history. Study and honor the treasure and majesty of the Hebrew Scriptures—but let Jesus be Jesus, and be willing to leave the original covenant behind! The path to reconciliation and coexistence with the Jewish people is not through embracing what was and continues to be most problematic about our tradition. For there is a problem with the movement among progressive Christians to reestablish a connection with the Old Testament and to affirm its validity as a sacred body of work on its own merits rather than as a proof text for Jesus's divinity. The problem is that, absent an honest confrontation with these aspects of the Old Testament theology and worldview, this effort brings with it an acceptance and ultimately a legitimization of God's exclusivist, tribal covenant with the Jews. And it is this *implicit* legitimization that is most dangerous in the current context of the behavior of the State of Israel. Ironically, this effort on the part of Christians sets out the parameters of the current, urgent crisis for the Jewish people. We have long struggled with the tension between the universalism inherent in our monotheistic creed and ethical code, and the particularism so deeply embedded in our own identity and historical experience, and at no time more so than today.

The implications of this reworking of Christian doctrine with respect to the Jewish people are profound. As Paul van Buren himself points out, the powerful spectacle of a triumphant State of Israel lent force and validation to the Jewish triumphalism articulated in the new theology. In the political as well as interfaith arenas, the stage was set to make common cause with those within the Jewish community seeking to establish a theological and historical basis for the modern-day Jewish nationalist project.

Chapter 6

Theological Urgency and the Promise of the Land

That it took the Holocaust to open an honorable and reciprocal dialogue between Jews and Christians is an outrage. But that the Holocaust requires us, personally as well as institutionally, to understand how such events were prepared for by other events is an absolute moral legacy. The question posed itself not to me but to history: How did the cross of Jesus Christ become the cross at Auschwitz?
—James Carroll, *Constantine's Sword: The Church and the Jews*

I paid a visit to a professor of theology at the seminary of a major Protestant denomination. He is the author of articles and books in the post-supersessionist tradition, in which he takes on the blatantly anti-Semitic aspects of Christian doctrine, as well as strongly reaffirming the special relationship between God and the Jewish people. I told him that I felt we had a lot in common: that as a Jew, I was committed, as was he as a Christian, to religious reform, to rooting out those elements in my religious tradition that required correction. Drawing on my reservoir of *chutzpah*, I turned then to my critique of his work. Without question, I said, confronting the anti-Semitism embedded in supersessionism was a good thing, but had early Christianity's bold challenge to some of Judaism's central tenets really been such a misguided project? I told him that I thought that the very elements of Judaism in most urgent need of reform were precisely those that Christianity had come to replace. I made it clear that my ideas arose out of my great distress about the negative outcomes of political Zionism and my sense that something deeply embedded in Judaism itself was at work in the abusive practices of the Jewish state. My concern was that in the rush to atone for anti-Semitism, progressive Christian theology was indirectly—and often quite directly—permitting and even validating these practices by establishing God's covenant with the Jewish people as fundamental and primary. I expressed to him my concern about the political implications of this stream in progressive Christian thought, and my concerns that it legitimated Israel's land grabs, suppressed criticism of Israel's human rights violations, and thwarted honest, productive interfaith dialogue about the Israel/Palestine situation.

The professor's response was swift: "That's an old story," he said to me. "It's the story of an archaic, tribal Judaism and an enlightened, universalist Christianity. We don't tell that story anymore." He stated that even if this "old story" had not been discredited by virtue of its blatant anti-Semitism and its responsibility for millennia of persecution of the Jews, it was passé, having been demonstrated to be theologically unsound.

I was stunned by this reaction. Yes, this may be an "old story": much of late twentieth-century Christian theology is devoted to correcting this theory as, in the words of James D. G. Dunn, "a parody of both second temple Judaism and Paul's debt to his Jewish heritage" (2003, 9). This simplistic and biased "black and white" picture fully deserved to be discredited, especially in view of its pernicious effects throughout Christian history. But I had expected more receptivity. The professor seemed closed to a discussion about the issue. Anything, apparently, that bore even the whiff of Christian anti-Jewishness had to be summarily discounted and barred from further discussion. What was required, rather, was vigilance about the appearance of such views. Although the professor had written extensively on this precise topic, there would be no nuanced theological discussion today, because the important issue was not the theological soundness of the original, discredited doctrine. What was important was the effect the doctrine had produced throughout history. Atoning for anti-Semitism trumped all other discussions.

The exchange with the professor that day is far from an isolated case. Vigilance against anti-Semitism underlies or explicitly characterizes most interfaith discussions today. In our current political climate, it seems acceptable for Christians to look critically at those elements of their own faith and their history that have caused harm, especially when these have been cornerstones of their doctrine. But it is not permissible to extend this conversation into any criticism of Judaism or into the examination of the behavior of Jews or their institutions that might deserve scrutiny or correction. While Christian sins are fair game, criticism of Judaism or things Jewish is simply out of bounds.

The Christian Sin

In the wave of horror and revulsion that overtook Christians in the wake of the Nazi Holocaust, combating anti-Judaism became a primary concern. "Anti-Jewishness," writes contemporary Protestant theologian Robert T. Osborne, "is the Christian sin" (1990, 214). Note that Osborne does not say that anti-Judaism is *a* sin. Rather, anti-Jewishness has taken first place as *the* Christian transgression. Correcting it would require a fundamental overhaul of the faith. According to theologian Paul van Buren, forging a positive relationship with Judaism and the Jewish people is nothing less than the reimagining of what it means to be Christian. "If the church stops thinking of the Jews as the rejected remnant of the people Israel," writes van Buren, "if it starts speaking of the continuing covenantal relationship between this people and God, then it will have to rethink its own identity" (1984, 23). In a real sense, revisionism turned this aspect of Christian theology on its head: Judaism would no longer be seen as Christianity's shadow, but rather would take its rightful place as the very foundation of Christian faith. A generation of pastors was raised on this new perspective as part of their seminary training. No longer would anti-Jewish sentiments be heard from the pulpits. Offending passages from the Gospels would increasingly be passed over or explained away.

The professor's reaction was not based simply on a disagreement on a matter of theology or the history of religion. He was saying that you simply cannot say these things about Judaism. But was he really listening? Apparently what he had understood me to say was that Judaism is an archaic religion and that it deserved to be replaced by the new, superior faith. That would be the old story, "the story we don't tell anymore." But that is not what I was saying. Rather, I was calling attention to exclusivist and exceptionalist elements of Judaism that had persisted, incubating over thousands of years. I was suggesting that these are the elements of our faith and our perception of ourselves that have become so devastatingly problematic in the modern context, having now been activated through Jewish empowerment. I was not saying that Judaism as a whole is archaic, or that these elements characterized the entire faith tradition or every Jewish attitude. Certainly, that would be one take on the Pauline anti-Jewish polemic, but that was not what I was proposing. My interlocutor was responding as if my suggestion that Judaism possessed elements in need of reform was damning the entire faith and by extension the Jewish people itself.

I wish I could have been as clear at that moment. What I did say was, "When I tell Christians they are not being anti-Semitic when they raise questions about Zionism or about the actions of the State of Israel, they are very appreciative. They appear very receptive, even hungry to hear this message!" Again, his response was sharp: "Of course they like to hear it," he said. "You are telling them that they are not anti-Semitic! How can you be so sure?" Once again, we were not communicating. His assumption was that this discourse is about assuring Christians that they are not anti-Semitic. It is nothing of the sort. It is about allowing a dialogue: it is about disabusing Christians of the notion, taught to them in the pews and in the seminaries, that it is not okay to challenge political Zionism or to criticize the policies of the State of Israel. The accusation of anti-Semitism is the club brandished to thwart open or critical discussion about the State of Israel. The unstated assumption, among Jews and Christians alike, is that Judaism is indistinguishable from Zionism, and that therefore to be critical of Zionism is to be anti-Semitic. But the issue has to be named. It is the elephant in the room.

A Guest in the House of Israel

The history of post-Holocaust revisionist theology is that of Christianity's attempt to reverse the effects of two millennia of anti-Semitism. To call this a project in systematic theology is a misnomer. This is more than a revision or "fix" of a doctrine seen as archaic, outmoded, embarrassing, or destructive. Rather, this project represents a fundamental reworking of how Christianity understands the relationship of God to humankind. Furthermore, it is not limited to rehabilitating Jews by exonerating them of the charge of deicide. Nor is it confined to a positive, no-cost statement about religious tolerance and the need for acceptance of multiple faiths and ways to God. No, this reformulation places God's original covenant with the Jews at the center of Christian belief, incorporating into Christian theology fundamental principles of Judaism such as election and promise—in van Buren's words, "...tak[ing] Judaism into Christian theology—really into it" (1984, 26). In a striking but apt phrase theologians in this tradition talk about the re-Judaization of Christianity. Furthermore, this is a theology that is very tied to practice—practice that stems from the Christian world's traumatic confrontation with the consequences of anti-Semitism in the twentieth century, practice focused on vigilance against anti-Semitism.

Clark M. Williamson's 1993 *A Guest in the House of Israel: Post-Holocaust Church Theology* is a scholarly, comprehensive treatment of the revisionist perspective. There has been, observes Williamson, a "profound theological urgency" to revisit the New Testament in order to correct the anti-Judaism so interwoven in the Gospel narratives and the epistolary writings (87). Williamson cautions against such urgency, noting that historical analyses motivated in this way often "tell us more about their authors than their subject" (88). Yet we will see how Williamson himself encounters this difficulty in his admirable effort to bring Christians and Jews together to build a better world.

In his opening chapter, Williamson presents three "rules" for what he terms a "Post-*Shoah*" theology.

- *Conversation with Jews:* "Christians," writes Williamson, "cannot give theological shape to their self-understanding as Christians without engaging in conversation with Jews" (9). Williamson advocates a reinterpretation of Jesus and of Paul with respect to their Jewishness and their relationship with the Judaism of their time.

- *The burning children:* Williamson asserts that any Christian theology must establish the *shoah*, i.e., the Nazi Holocaust, as a fundamental point of reference. He cites theologian and Rabbi Irving Greenberg's principle: "No statement, theological or otherwise, should be made that would not be credible in the presence of the burning children" (Greenberg 1977, 23). Any Christian theology, indeed any theology, writes Williamson, must "meet the test of Auschwitz" (1993, 13).

- *Discipleship:* Theology must lead to a way of life that is focused on repairing the world through good works. Williamson relates this directly to the first rule: Christians must now be guided in their relationship to humankind by the divine commandments to the Jewish people set down in the Jewish scriptures.

Williamson's adoption of the term *shoah* is noteworthy. The word, from the Hebrew word meaning "utter and sudden destruction," came into common use in the 1950s to refer to the near-total extermination of European Jewry by the Nazis. The use of this word implies that *this* disaster, *this* genocide, stands alone in the history of crimes against humanity. *Shoah* is another way of saying "*the* Holocaust." It's interesting to consider that the Nazi

Holocaust, alone in the long history of the persecution of the Jews in the West, has provoked this fundamental revision in Christian theology. Why is this so? Clearly, this is not the first historical instance that could have prompted Christian leaders to examine their theology with respect to the Jewish people. One possible explanation is that this is seen as no mere crime. The *shoah* was not an isolated paroxysm of violence, but the culmination of millennia of persecution. Christian theologians after WWII realized that the Holocaust had emerged directly out of Christian animus against the Jews. Williamson offers the chilling and compelling observation that the Nazi's Nuremberg Laws drew directly from Canon Law from medieval times that served to restrict Jews and marginalize them in society.

The confrontation with the Nazi Holocaust shook Christianity to its core—as well it should have. It necessitated a wholesale reevaluation of central articles of faith and of identity. Christians stood before the ovens and the bodies piled like cordwood and saw not only the present horror, but the millennia of demonization, expulsion, and massacres, and experienced shock, revulsion, and shame of catastrophic proportions. *This is not us,* they must have felt. *This is not what God intended. This is not what our faith in Jesus Christ leads us to.*

Theological Urgency

The reexamination of the historical Jesus's relationship with Judaism is a central concern of post-Holocaust Christian theology. Williamson takes direct aim at "a self-conscious Christian tradition that deliberately distanced itself from the historical Jewish context in which Jesus had lived and died" (49). Traditionally, Jesus is portrayed as being in conflict with the Judaism of his time, with his death on the cross as the inevitable outcome (with the resulting deicide charge). Doctrinally, the resurrection was presented as proof of God's rejection of the Jews. To combat this view and the theology it spawned, revisionism offered a new theology and a new picture of the historical Jesus, as well as a revised picture of Judaism itself. In this revision, Jesus is not portrayed as an iconoclast and social revolutionary in conflict with the Judaism of his time—a Judaism described in the traditional formulation as "decadent" and "degenerate." This was a Judaism, in Williamson's words, "that never existed" (49). Instead, Jesus is presented as having been primarily opposed to Rome and to the co-opting of the Temple structure into the oppressive imperial colonial system. Rome, therefore, was the problem, not Judaism. What Jesus wanted, in this view, was a purification and restoration of the Kingdom of God, now reinterpreted as a Jewish eschatology. In this revision, therefore, Jesus is a restorationist—or, depending on your perspective, a preservationist—of a landed Jewish polity based on Torah. A Jesus, in other words, promoting the old covenant.[1]

Williamson's book is an important contribution to the history of religion, and to the fascinating and important effort to understand the momentous events of the first century in Palestine. However, this is no dispassionate, neutral analysis. Rather, it is an argument driven by, to use Williamson's quoting of theologian John Gager's powerful phrase, the "theological urgency" to repudiate Christian anti-Judaism (Gager 1983, 202). But while the Judaism of Jesus's time may not have fit the later description of "decadent" and "degenerate," this characterization of Judaism functions in this argument as a straw man. Certainly, Judaism was disparaged in a grossly inaccurate and vicious way by Christianity through the ages. However, it is also likely that Jesus was confronting and speaking out against what he perceived to be real problems with the conservative and restoration-oriented

---

1. Progressive Christian interpreters such as Marcus Borg, John Shelby Spong, Dominic Crossan, Richard Horsley, and Neil Elliot share this view of Jesus's ministry as driven by an opposition to Roman oppression (and its Jewish client class) rather than as directed primarily against Judaism or Jewish practice per se. I will explore in later chapters how this view of Jesus and early Christianity takes these thinkers in an entirely different direction than that of the restorationist vision articulated by Williamson and the revisionist school.

nature of the Judaism of his time. The Pharisees were not the devil, but neither were they all good. This is an uncomfortable fact for Christian thinkers because of the virulent anti-Semitism that occupied a central place in Christian doctrine. According to Williamson, the error of Christianity was that it defined itself in relation to Judaism: "Every Christian doctrine can be and was interpreted through the lens of this anti-Jewish hermeneutic. God is the God who displaces the Jews and replaces them with Christians" (1993, 5). And he's right—Christianity should define itself in its own terms and according to its own values, rather than in opposition to or as an improvement on or replacement for Judaism or any other faith tradition. But what we have here is no mere correction.

What emerges from this drive to repudiate traditional Christian anti-Jewish thought is a stark reversal of the established doctrine, a *reverse supersessionism*, if you will. Ironically, Christianity is again seeking to define itself in relation to Judaism. But now, in place of accomplishing this in the negative—by invalidating the original covenant between God and the Jewish people—it *embraces* that original covenant, retaining the Jews' special status as the parent faith. Rather than establishing a new covenant as a replacement for the first, the Christian enters into the original covenant—per the title of Williamson's book—as "a guest in the house of Israel." Certainly, this formulation goes very far toward the elimination of official Christian anti-Jewishness. But it goes much further. It elevates Judaism to the level of an ideal. Christians are now saying: while once we saw ourselves as the light and you as the darkness, now you are the light, the light that we need to illuminate our own nature, to fully understand God's plan for the church.

Again, this is no mere exercise in systematic theology. In the current historical context, it has profound implications. Elevating Judaism to primary, privileged status on a theological basis carries real meaning for the present day. Christians are, to borrow from the biblical story, ceding the patriarchal blessing and the primogeniture—and with the original covenant comes the land promise. Much is made in Williamson's discussion about how much of Jesus's teachings of love springs from his Jewish tradition, the Pharisaic school that was the foundation of Rabbinic Judaism. Yes, Christianity did arise from Judaism, and the monotheistic revolution that was Judaism started it all—credit must be given. But that doesn't mean that Judaism is not in need of reform, of the "conversation" with other traditions that Williamson cites as one of the rules of a post-*shoah* theology. The question must be asked: what is the recipient of the blessing doing with the power that it confers?

The Christianization of Judaism: Election as Grace

The renunciation of supersessionism is the keystone of the revisionist program. But building a theology that expunges supersessionism is not easy, since Christian doctrine is based on the notion that God's promise to the Jews had been fulfilled in Jesus Christ, that, in fact, the new covenant that conferred forgiveness from sin had *superseded* the original covenant. Even if the revisionist project were to succeed in cleansing Christian theology and doctrine of the more explicit and blatant vilification of the Jews themselves, the problem remains: Christianity *was* a departure from Judaism in important ways. With respect to the relationship between God and humankind, it was a now a different kind of deal, setting out different terms. The covenant with the Jewish people, which is the story of the Old Testament, specified that God would make the people great and prosperous and give them the land of Canaan in exchange for accepting him as their God and obeying his commandments. It was an exclusive arrangement between God and the Jews.

The work of the followers of Jesus modified that arrangement in fundamental ways, with respect to both theology and worldview. The announcement of Jesus's resurrection as the sign of the fulfillment of the divine promise to bring about the End of Days was the basis of the work of the apostles from the earliest days after Jesus's death. It was directed first toward the Jews alone and then extended to the Gentiles. Logically, it meant that the old arrangement was gone. God's relationship to mankind was changed, in several ways. The old arrangement involved belief (the acceptance of God as the one God), but also it involved behavior (adherence to a code of civil and religious law). In Christian idiom, the latter was called *works*. And, early on in Christian doctrine as articulated by Paul, this became counterposed to *faith*. The big change in Christianity was that salvation came by faith, not by works. This became a major point of argument and polemic for Paul, and later for Martin Luther, who cleared up any lingering ambiguity about the relationship between faith and works for achieving salvation. The new arrangement meant that no longer would salvation be dependent on what you do, but rather on your acceptance of Jesus Christ as Savior of humankind—as, in Paul's words, the "free gift" of God. This is crystallized in the concept of grace. In early Christian doctrine, further articulated by Saint Augustine and later Protestant theologians, reliance on works was inferior, wrong, somehow thumbing our noses in the face of God's love of mankind in having sent Jesus to walk among us to wash away our sins and take away death. The Jews, by adhering to the old faith and rejecting the new one, became the despised of the earth until the end of days.

Herein lies the problem for the revisionist project. Supersessionism must be renounced—but everything is built on its assumptions! If you are to renounce supersessionism, you have to make the Jews okay with God again. You have to rehabilitate the original covenant. Over time, in the work of successive theologians building on one another's work, a compelling and simple solution evolved: take the cornerstone of the covenant with the Jews, which is God's election of the Jews as his people, *and establish that this is an expression of God's grace.* Thus is this key Christian construct called into service in order to reframe the Old Testament narrative. In this way, supersessionism is renounced—the Jews are no longer the ultimate foil, the darkness by which Christianity is the light. And at the same time—here is the power and the elegance of this formulation—a framework of redemption is created in which Judaism and Christianity can now coexist.

This is the view advanced by a number of writers representing the "New Perspective on Paul," a term coined by British New Testament scholar James D. G. Dunn (1990). A major focus of the New Perspective was to understand Paul's relationship with Judaism. This is a daunting task, given the twists and turns of Paul's arguments and polemics. The thrust, however, is to argue for a closeness of Paul to the Judaism of his time. This is a significant departure from the traditional view of Paul as having denigrated Judaism as a rigid, archaic, legalistic religion in contrast to Christianity's emphasis on God's freely given love. The New Perspective focuses on Paul's efforts to create a strong link between the followers of Christ and all other Jews, by virtue of their Jewish birth. In this view, what linked them was their lineage, regardless of any differences in belief. When Paul says in Galatians 2:15, "We ourselves are Jews by birth and not Gentile sinners; yet we know that a person is justified not by works of the law but by faith in Jesus Christ," this, according to Dunn, "is covenant language, the language of those conscious that they have been chosen as a people by God" (Dunn 1990,190). Here, Paul is asking Jews to understand that their faith in Jesus is not in contradiction to but is "an extension of their Jewish faith in a *graciously electing* and sustaining God" (190, emphasis added). The key here is in the phrase "graciously electing." The two concepts are bolted together, so that election becomes an act of—indeed a central function of—God's grace.

Quoting from Gerhard von Rad, Williamson further articulates this notion:

> In thinking anew about how to frame its understanding of covenant, the church must go up to Jerusalem to listen to the Jewish tradition. Here covenant making is a form of God's grace to which walking God's way (Torah, *halakah*) is Israel's proper response; its purpose is to teach Israel to order its life so that it may live justly and be a light to the Gentiles to whom God and God's name are to be made known. God's covenant with Israel at Sinai...is prefaced with these words: "I am the Lord your God,

who brought you out of the land of Egypt, out of the house of slavery" (Ex. 20:2)…This preamble states in the indicative mode what God has done for Israel. In a manner parallel to Paul's writing, the indicative of God's grace precedes the imperative…"The God who speaks here," declared Gerhard von Rad, "is the God of grace."…By honoring the commands of God, Israel affirms God's gracious gift to and rule over Israel. (1993, 123)

In one stroke, God's promise to the Jewish people, beginning with the Abrahamic promise, to the covenant at Sinai (prologue to the conquest of Canaan), has been connected, in an unbroken line, to Jesus's ministry and vision. But what has happened here? Grace is a Christian concept, perhaps the central, defining concept of the faith. Can it be equated with the election of the Jewish people as recounted in the Jewish scriptures? It's uncanny: in an effort to rehabilitate Judaism, revisionist Christian theology has Christianized it. Supersessionism may have been overcome, but here Christianity has made Judaism over in its own image. The transformation in Williamson's argument is nearly complete, adding the most fundamental elements of each religious system into a stew of equivalency that compromises the meaning and integrity of both. Take, for example, Williamson's gloss on *torah*, in Hebrew meaning "instruction" or "guidance." As much as is made of the term in Jewish life, and as much as the term is used broadly, it is never confused with anything else—*torah* is God's law, the manual for life as a Jew, covering both religious and civil life. But here is Williamson's take on the term: "The broadest meaning of *torah* is instruction in God's gracious will for a people who accept God's gift of grace. In the whole range of meanings that *torah* has in the scriptures of Israel, it is comparable to what Christians mean by 'gospel'" (125). Again—a neat solution, but it's simply inaccurate. It ignores and washes out essential, fundamental elements of Judaism, elements that play a major part in our modern history as a people.

Torah is not Gospel. Election is not grace. The Old Testament covenant is not the New Testament gifting of salvation.

Promise in Judaism is not about forgiveness from sin. Rather, it is about *blessing*, in the way the ancient world understood the term: peoplehood, progeny, prosperity, and, in the case of the Jewish people, land. The Hexateuch—the Five Books of Moses and the Book of Joshua—is the Jewish people's story of itself: the story of its peoplehood, its relationship with God. It begins, as Williamson correctly points out, with God's introduction of himself to Abraham, his instruction to Abraham to settle in Canaan, and the promise to make his seed into a great people. This initial promise becomes increasingly articulated in the Old Testament narrative—continuing right through into the prophetic literature—in the concept of election: I have chosen you, the people of Israel, for a special role in history, in exchange for your exclusive devotion to me and adherence to my laws. Yes, at times God talks about his love for Israel. This, as pointed out by a number of commentators, can be seen to balance the view of the God-Israel relationship as stern and legalistic, but *election is not grace.* It appears, however, that for Christians in the aftermath of the Holocaust, the theological urgency to reconcile with the Jewish people was so great, the drive to find a theological meeting ground purged of the conflict and enmity of the past so compelling, that this fundamental difference was wiped out. It is as if, by validating Jewish election and particularity by establishing it as a cornerstone of the Christian worldview, the horrors of the past could be undone.

Williamson cites what is perhaps the ultimate statement of the covenant between God and Israel: Moses's extended address to the people of Israel as presented in the book of Deuteronomy. Here, Moses reminds the people that "The Lord your God has chosen you out of all the peoples on earth to be his people, his treasured possession" (Deut. 7:6). Citing this verse, Williamson comments, "All the strata of tradition in the Pentateuch are cognizant that 'chosenness' has to do with God's freely offered love and the appropriate response of Israel to that love, which is Israel's service to God and the peoples of the earth" (125). Note how God's election of Israel is framed here within a description that matches the Christian concept of grace. First, the word "freely" is a clear allusion to Romans

6:23, "the free gift of God is eternal life." Second, note the addition of "and the peoples of the earth" to the description of Israel's divine obligation. This last phrase implies that explicit in God's covenant with the Jewish people is that this will be extended universally. But is this element part of the covenant with the Jewish people? Christians want to see it that way—but that doesn't make it so. This is not a concept found in the Pentateuch.[2]

The revisionist effort to blur the differences between Christianity and Judaism is basically two-pronged. First, the particularism inherent in election morphs into the universality of grace. Second, the charge to Israel to serve God expands into a responsibility to serve all of humankind. Williamson, like many others, interprets the famous "light to the nations" phrase from Second Isaiah in this way. The Jews are God's chosen, so goes this argument, but their specialness comes with conditions: Jews must bring God's message of justice to the world. The Jews are particular, according to Williamson, but not exceptional, because "chosenness did not entail an exclusive privilege" (125). As I commented in the previous chapter, this explanation, familiar to me from my religious education, never made sense to me. I knew that, despite the disclaimer, I was being taught that as a Jew I was special, that as Jew I had been elevated above "the nations." The "conditionality" of having a special responsibility in the world didn't mitigate the exceptionalism; in fact it amplified it: we're on a mission from God!

The citing of God's often-quoted promise to Abraham from Genesis 12, "In you all the families of the earth will be blessed," serves as another example of how this quality is superimposed on Judaism by Christian commentators seeking to emphasize the continuity between the traditions. This is accomplished not by interpretation or interpolation, but by outright mistranslation. This passage is usually translated as meaning that the Jews

---

2. The case is made, by some Christian and Jewish interpreters, that evidence for the extension of God's charge to the Jews into a mission to humankind at large is to be found in post-Pentateuch biblical texts, specifically Second Isaiah, Jonah, and Ruth. This argument will be taken up in later chapters.

will bring blessing to the world, in other words to refer to Israel's actions in or effects on the wider world—Williamson's "service to the peoples of the earth" referenced above. But that's not what the verse means. The Hebrew is clear: it means that your name is invoked in blessings, as in: "May you be like Israel; may you be blessed like the Jewish people." Rather than mitigating the exceptionalism, the passage underlines it: You are special—and all Creation is to know and acknowledge this.

Christians are free to reform, revise, and reformulate their doctrine, in conversation with history and in response to perceived problems. This is a good thing, an activity to be emulated by other faiths as we confront challenges to equally deeply held beliefs. But in their revisionist project, Christian thinkers have ventured into an outright reframing of fundamentals of Jewish theology and ethics. In Judaism, repentance is central, certainly. And, yes, God is described as having qualities of mercy. But in Judaism, repentance bears but a very superficial resemblance to the Christian doctrine of grace. Indeed, this theory turns the Jewish concept of repentance on its head. In the Jewish scriptures, and in Rabbinic Judaism, repentance is tied to behavior. Abraham famously beseeched God to spare Sodom, but he was not appealing to a categorical quality of forgiveness. Abraham's bargaining was not for the forgiveness of the sinners, but for the sake of any of the righteous people who might be found in the city. In his famous negotiation with God, Abraham brought the number down to ten, *but these ten had to be found* in order to reverse the divine decree—and we know how the story ends. In the quintessential story about repentance found in the book of Jonah, God spared Nineveh *because they repented*: besides declaring a fast, the king of Nineveh demanded that "every one turn from his evil way, and from the violence that is in their hands" (Jonah 3:8). That's Jewish repentance.

Validating the Election of the Jewish People

The reframing of Judaism to fit a revisionist Christian theology is driven by the "theological urgency" to reconcile a great wrong.

Williamson writes, quoting contemporary Finnish theologian H. Riasanen, "One result of Paul's strained negativity toward Judaism and the law is that his distorted portrayal of Judaism 'has, contrary to Paul's intentions to be sure, had a share in the tragic history of Jews at the mercy of Christians'" (93). Williamson goes on to argue that it was Paul's misunderstanding of Judaism that led him to "drive a wedge between law and grace, limiting 'grace' to the Christ event" (93). But in this argument, the "law" versus "grace" issue translates to the conflict between the particularism and conditionality of the old covenant and the universalism and non-conditionality of the new covenant. It was precisely that quality of Judaism—not the monotheism, not the ethical code, but the nationalism, particularism, and, ultimately, the exceptionalism—that Christianity came to change. Paul's vision was of a community that was open to Jew and Gentile alike. This principle of universality became fundamental to church doctrine and practice. Although it was not Paul's intention to found a new religion, that is what developed. Anti-Jewishness was a tragic by-product of this important element of Christianity—but does that merit a disavowal of this very quality of universalism? Is this not replacing one problematic theology with another? In the first, now discredited theology, Jews were set up as God's rejected, and this turned out to have huge and tragic consequences. But in this new, alternative formulation, Christians have glossed over the essential differences between the faiths, in the process conferring doctrinal status to God's election of the Jewish people. This last piece of the argument, the theological alchemy intended to resolve the problem of supersessionism by accepting, whole cloth, the terms of God's covenant with the Jews, has implications for human history similar to the negative consequences of the original, anti-Jewish Christian doctrine. When you assert that the election of the Jews was an act of grace, you step, with both feet, onto a steep and very slippery slope.

Those Christians who, in an effort to undo the evil of anti-Semitism, embrace this revised theology are endorsing a theology and view of history that goes like this: The Jews are special—

God's chosen—and remain so (God does not go back on his promises). The terms of the covenant are in force. With that comes the right to the land, the right to triumph over their enemies, and, fundamental to all these, the sense of apartness that comes with that specialness. Being a people apart means that the rules that apply to the rest of humanity don't apply. The covenant conferred and continues to confer an exclusive privilege. The rest of humanity plays no part in this arrangement, except in three supporting roles: (1) as people who have to be pushed aside (in biblical terms, exterminated) in order to make way for the conquest and occupation; (2) as nations pressed into service as God's agents of punishment of the Jews for disobedience; or (3) as witnesses—per the "light to the nations" concept—to God's oneness and glory through the example of the Jews' survival, triumph, and prospering, secure in the land and worshiping at the shrine of Jerusalem. Note: "the nations" are not to be converted or be brought inside the covenant. They are there as bystanders.[3] There is a role for Christians—and this notion drives the revisionist effort—through the mediation of Christ, to worship the God of the Jews and, in the words of Paul van Buren, "to enter along with the chosen people into the task...[of] moving... creation nearer to its completion" (1984, 25). James Carroll summarizes this position well: "While Judaism exists without

---

3. The term "nations" (Hebrew *goyim* and sometimes *amim*), as used by Isaiah and commonly in the Old Testament, is generally translated in the New Testament as "gentiles." But the concepts are far from identical. When Isaiah uses these words, he means *other* nations—the peoples surrounding us, the non-Jews, those who are different from us. But the concept of "nations" undergoes a transformation—signified by the shift in translation from "nations" to "gentiles"—in the New Testament. When Paul talks about "Gentiles" he is referring specifically to non-Jews who have become Christians, and, potentially, to the entire rest of the world, who can then be approached to be converted to be followers of Christ. The difference—it couldn't be more fundamental—is between making a clear demarcation between "us and them" (whether the intention be friendly or hostile) in the Old Testament context, and the thrust to find a way to include these "others" into the fold in that of the New Testament.

essential reference to Christianity, the reverse is not the case. The God of Jesus Christ, and therefore of the Church, is the God of Israel. The Jews remain the chosen people of God. And with this comes the Land" (2001, 566).

Reframing the Discourse

The writers of the Gospels and Paul in his letters quoted freely (in both senses of the word) from the Jewish scriptures in order to establish a basis for their new faith—in other words, to write their own story. In view of what we are observing about post-Holocaust revisionism, it seems that Christians can't seem to break the habit of reinterpreting Jewish material to fit a worldview and theology that may differ in important ways from that of the parent faith. In the case of the first century CE, the result, if not the intention, was to establish a counterposing theological structure and worldview. In our contemporary context, the intent seems to be to reverse the fundamental shift that was accomplished two thousand years ago, and to reestablish Judaism as the primary faith. In our present case—as in the first—Christianity, in doing so, is in danger of doing damage to both traditions. And when this is being done in the service of channeling or controlling the conversation about the current political situation in the Holy Land, we find ourselves involved in a game in which the stakes are unacceptably high.

A 2008 interfaith conference cosponsored by the American Jewish Committee and the Washington, DC Synod of the Evangelical Lutheran Church of America illustrates this point. Called "Land and Promise: Jewish and Lutheran Perspectives on Israel The Holy Land [sic]," the conference featured presentations by Rabbi David Rosen, director of the American Jewish Committee's Department for Interreligious Affairs, and the Rev. Dr. Peter Pettit, director of the Institute for Jewish-Christian Understanding at Muhlenberg College. Both men strongly support the primacy of Jewish claims to historic Palestine. Rabbi Rosen has urged Christians to join with Jews in opposing the forces of "Palestinian nationalism" that are, according to him, posing a barrier to peace and putting Palestinian Christians at risk in the Holy Land (Rosen 2004, 6). At this conference, he emphasized the threat to Jews from global anti-Semitism and the importance of the State of Israel for Jewish identity as well as security. Rev. Pettit advocates vociferously for Christian vigilance against anti-Semitism. He claims that in the current discourse on Israel/Palestine, it is anti-Jewish feeling that often underlies apparent support for the cause of Palestinian human rights (Pettit 2008). He promotes a theology in which the biblical promise of the land, having been erroneously "spiritualized" in Christian thinking, is reinstated as the gift to the Jewish people. In his address at this conference, Rev. Pettit called the land the "Jewish sacrament."

In short, this was no "interfaith dialogue" between Christians and Jews on the issue of the Holy Land in their respective traditions. Rather, it was a presentation of a single viewpoint in support of the superior right of the Jewish people to possess and control the land. Although advertised as jointly sponsored by Christian and Jewish organizations, the conference was initiated and in large part programmed by the American Jewish Committee, for whom Rosen and Pettit are regular speakers. This is an example of the trap that well-intentioned Christians can fall into in their interfaith efforts. In such encounters, the unwritten rules are to unquestioningly support Jewish striving for self-determination, and to avoid or downplay criticism of the State of Israel. Some local Lutherans were unhappy with the tone and substance of the conference. To its credit, the synod held a follow-up conference in early 2009 that presented voices from the Holy Land directly addressing the contemporary issues of justice affecting all peoples of the region.

Paul's Drive for Universalism

The modern effort to rid Christian theology of anti-Jew-ishness did not occur in a vacuum. It was and is, according to every proponent of the project, a theological project undertaken in direct response to a historical event. Does it not then follow that this revised theology must be considered with respect to *its* effect on historical events? Williamson himself makes this point when he establishes his three rules for a post-*shoah* theology. All three rules have to do with action in history: conversation with Jews, the burning children, and discipleship. It follows then that the theology that conforms to these rules should be evaluated in terms of its implications for and impact on the current urgent situation of the Israeli-Palestinian conflict. The conflict presents a crisis on many levels. For the world at large, it is a major threat to world peace. For the Jewish people, it is a spiritual crisis, as well as a threat to the security and well-being of the citizens of Israel.

We've seen that the doctrinal issue of *faith versus works* is central for the revisionists. The issue is important for their argument because in a theology that rehabilitates Judaism, God's election of the Jews must be seen an expression of his grace toward humankind. I would submit, however, that whatever one thinks of this formulation on a theological basis, *faith versus works* is not the important issue for our time. Rather, the issue that bears directly upon the historical and political situation we face today is that of *peoplehood and identity*. Dunn recognizes this, noting that "the new perspective sheds light on Paul's theology by allowing us to see that its polemical thrust was directed not against the idea of achieving God's acceptance by the merit of personal achievement (good works), but against the Jewish intention to safeguard the privilege of covenant status from being dissipated or contaminated by non-Jews. Paul was reacting primarily against the exclusivism which he himself had previously fought to maintain" (2003, 10).

Dunn has it right. Paul brought forward the doctrine of justification by faith in an attempt to overcome the exclusivism of election. He tried mightily to build his new belief system within the framework of Judaism, but Judaism could not bend that far. Election and exclusivity remained, and Paul and his heirs ultimately parted company from the Jews who would not relinquish the privileged and special status conferred by the original covenant. The revisionist argument is that Paul wanted to reform and expand Judaism, not break with it. He wanted to take Judaism beyond its exclusivist framework, to expand the story into a new future for all of humankind. In this new story, the promise to Abraham that "all the nations [Gentiles, for Paul] shall be blessed in you" was fulfilled in Christ. But Paul couldn't pull it off—his writing on this subject, doubling back on itself, contradictory, impassioned, and tortuous, is evidence of his frustration and struggle.

Ultimately, the Jewish establishment of Paul's time was not about to adopt this new concept of God's love as universal and unconditional. Judaism's theology was inseparable from its nationalism—the Jews' tie to God was framed in the covenant. Revisionist theology revisits this original parting of the ways. It attempts to reconcile the early, foundational work of Paul in establishing the grace of God received through faith in Jesus with Jewish concepts of nationhood and election. However, the olive tree metaphor of Romans 11 notwithstanding, this split, this discontinuity, did occur, as it had to. Modern attempts to reengraft the branch to the trunk will not change the reality that the split did occur—and over a fundamental issue: exclusivity versus universalism. Christian and Jewish realities with respect to this issue in Jesus and Paul's time were different—if this had not been so, there would not be two religions now called Christianity and Judaism.[4]

The Challenge for Judaism

The Jews' identity as God's chosen and as a people apart thus remained intact, reinforced and strengthened by the marginalization and persecution suffered by Jews over the millennia. In a very different fashion, Christian revisionism continues to reinforce these

---

4. Williamson also makes the point that in Paul's time the Jews were under enormous of pressure from Rome. The Macabbean revolt and its grisly aftermath were recent and vivid memories. So to ask the Jews to give up the "markers" of their nationhood was reminiscent of what occupiers had done in an effort to disempower and destroy them. Circumcision, the Sabbath, dietary laws, and other Jewish observances are not mere rituals but "identity badges." In that sense, what Paul was asking the Jews to do was to commit national suicide. Williamson acknowledges Dunn for this observation.

same qualities of particularism and exceptionalism. Revisionist theology holds that Christianity must fully rehabilitate Judaism by establishing the House of Israel as primary and taking up residence within it, but as a guest, at the pleasure of the Jews, who, as God's chosen, the preferred children and the recipients of the primogeniture, are the gatekeepers. But the world we Jews face today looks very different than the world in the aftermath of World War II. It is not Christian anti-Semitism that threatens Jewish survival today. Rather, the challenge facing the Jewish people now is what to do about the persistence of those very qualities in our makeup that are being elevated in this revised Christian theology. In its advancement of this "reverse supersessionism," Christian revisionism thwarts Jewish renewal by insulating us from the painful process of self-reflection about the effects of particularism and exceptionalism. As a Jew, therefore, I have this to say to those Christians who endorse and promote this revisionist view of Judaism: *we are not special.*

Yes, we have suffered. But we are not special. Jews are heir to a monumental religious, cultural, and literary tradition. But ours is no more special than any other faith tradition, and no less subject to the need for reform. Jewish tradition is built on deeply rooted and timeless beliefs and values that are its enduring bedrock, as well as elements in need of change in conversation with the rest of the world and in response to the flow of human history. In this way we are just like Christianity, Islam, or any other faith. Our continuation and health depend on our ability to change and grow, just as in those other traditions. But in his argument, Williamson sets up Judaism as the primary faith, with the implication that its values and traditions provide the standard and benchmark. Borrowing from a statement by Karl Barth, he has subtitled his book *A Guest in the House of Israel.* I agree that we should live in one house, but it is God's house, and it's a very big house, and we can have many families living in it. To call it Israel's house in order to overturn supersessionism is to substitute Jewish triumphalism for Christian triumphalism. The revisionist project exalts those very aspects of Judaism that need to be eclipsed: our exceptionalism and current attachment to ethnic nationalism are archaic and dangerous. Our current experience with political empowerment has presented us with the grim evidence of this truth.

Christians seem to believe that by elevating Judaism to an ideal status, and furthermore, in a paradoxical, backward twist of an argument, by reframing Judaism as the theological basis of a reformed Christianity, the sin of anti-Semitism can be expiated, the horror mitigated. But history cannot be undone. No more can Christians accomplish this than can the Jews undo the incalculable horror and loss of the *shoah* by establishing a messianically tinged romance of a Jewish state in historic Palestine. The State of Israel is a living, breathing political entity. To the extent that it continues to be seen by some as an answer to the Nazi genocide rather than as modern political reality, the State of Israel will continue to struggle—unsuccessfully—to take its place among the other nations of the world that are attempting to live according to principles of universal justice and human rights.

There are myths operating on both sides here. For Christians, it is the myth of a unity, a coherence with the Judaism of the first century, as if it were possible to undo the fateful parting that laid the foundations for anti-Semitism. For Jews, it is the myth of the possibility of a return to a mythical state of national unity and dominance, exemplified by the Davidic dynasty of Temple and political hegemony, as if this could somehow redeem the suffering of millennia, the burning of children. There is a profound denial of horror here for both groups—an attempt to make it all better. Christians can't undo two thousand years of persecution and the effects of Christian anti-Judaism on not only the Jews but on all of Western civilization. We Jews can't restore the Palestine of 1948, return seven hundred and fifty thousand Palestinians to their cities, villages, and farms, or reverse the effects of four generations of dispossession and refugee status—nor are we realistically expected to do so.

So don't do me the favor of making me special. I reject the status of God's chosen. I am part of humanity. I do not want to belong to a "people apart." As a Jew who loves my tradition and identifies proudly as a member of the Jewish people, I want to shed the exclusivism and nationalism that threatens the very soul of my people, as well as our physical security. Yes, we suffered at your hands, and this has affected our development and our character. As Jews, we are the ones who will have to deal with the consequences of the choices we have made in response to that painful history. Only we can change ourselves; only we can look honestly and critically at the consequences of holding on to our chosen status, to those aspects of the covenant that gave us birth and have in the past helped sustain us, but that now propel us toward a painful process of reform.

I do believe that one can "make it better," but by looking forward, not back. I welcome a conversation with you, a conversation in which we recognize our differences, our failings, our challenges, and what we have to teach one another—but standing side by side, and on a level field. In the direction it has taken, Christian revisionism sets up a very different conversation. It elevates those aspects of Judaism that are the most non-Christian, those aspects that, despite the effort of revisionism to deny this truth, were the basis of the separation of Christianity from its Jewish trunk. This effectively preempts discussion of the issues that are the most crucial in the current situation. I ask you to separate your own process of theological reform from your feelings of shame and horror about the tragic aspects of our shared history. If you can do that, then we can move on—indeed, we can help one another move on. We can make common cause to fight injustice and racism wherever it occurs, whether committed by Jew or non-Jew. We can have a new conversation.

The New Conversation

Professor Williamson's book is scholarly, thoughtful, cogent, and comprehensive. It provides an intelligent summary of the revisionist position and makes a passionate statement about the need for such a project. It is clearly Williamson's deep faith and his profound commitment to the doctrine of universal love undergirding

Christianity that motivates his work. It is the virtue of his work that is also its problem. Like van Buren, Williamson is simultaneously horrified by the burning children and drawn strongly to the power and romance of the biblical story of God and the Jewish people. These feelings create an urgency and drive the theology. It is this urgency, this tunnel vision, if you will, that causes Williamson to violate the spirit of those very rules for a post-*shoah* theology that he sets out in his first chapter. Williamson's application of his own rules subverts his goal of fixing the world. Instead of removing the conditions that lead to conflict, mistrust, and bloodshed, the revisionist project to atone for anti-Semitism now actually supports them. If there is to be, to use Williamson's word, a conversation that brings us closer to fixing the world, the terms of the conversation must change.

Let us identify what those new terms should be by revisiting Williamson's three rules:

- *Discipleship:* In Williamson's first rule, through conversation with Jews, Christians will be reminded that the primary function of theology is to fix the world. Williamson sets righting the wrongs done to the Jews as primary for Christians. This seems to me to be a very narrow approach to discipleship. Despite claims by some that anti-Semitism is on the rise, to make vigilance against anti-Semitism the primary focus of good works in today's world is self-evidently narrow and wrong.[5] This is perhaps the clearest indication of how the revisionist project is driven by theological urgency. Why this is problematic is more clearly demonstrated by the next rule.

- *The burning children:* This rule continues the theme of placing the sins against the Jews at the top of the list for Christians. But the rule of the burning children cannot apply exclusively to Jewish children. Clearly, in the light

---

5. See Appendix B for a recent example of how one Protestant denomination has struggled with this issue.

of the multiple genocidal catastrophes of the twentieth and early twenty-first centuries, the lessons of Auschwitz are placed in front of us again and again. Yet, in his articulation of this rule, Williamson refers only to the "teaching of contempt for Jews and Judaism...that made the *Shoah* possible" (13). When the suffering of one people upstages that of others, it can become the rationale for oppression and injustice. In the present historical context, we of all faiths must focus our vigilance above all on this lesson. Recently, Catholic theologian Rosemary Ruether courageously addressed this most sensitive of issues, specifically the use of the Holocaust as a justification for, in her words, "a claim to a unique entitlement of the Jewish people to a state built on Arab land." "Clearly," she writes, "what is needed is a breakthrough to a compassionate sense of co-humanity, in which Israelis and Palestinians can mourn each other's disasters and refuse to use one disaster to justify another" (2008).

- *Conversation with Jews:* The third rule states that Christians cannot understand themselves as Christians without "engaging in conversation with Jews" (Williamson 1993, 14). Having set out this condition for a post-*shoah* theology, however, Williamson proceeds to offer not a conversation but a confession, not a dialogue but a *mea culpa*, not an exchange but a treatise on Judaism redefined in his terms. There may be some Jews who will enthusiastically endorse if not the details then certainly the intent of his efforts, but Williamson's analysis does not reflect the range and variety of Jewish thought. At bottom, this project, as it currently stands, has little to do with the urgent issues facing the Jewish people. It is not the conversation that is required—not for Christians, and not for Jews.

Of Williamson's three rules, this last rule is the one that points us most urgently to the future. Therefore I say to Professor Williamson and to other proponents of and subscribers to the revisionist project: you are missing the point. Yes, the Christian denigration of us was wrong, and there is a need for an adjustment in your theology. But let us, together in conversation, work toward a new covenant that moves us into a future that will preserve our civilization, rather than risk pulling it back into exceptionalism, divisiveness, and endless conflict. The conversation that Jews need to have with Christians is one in which Christians are free to challenge us, rather than simply idealize and praise our tradition. If you would have a conversation with us, have it not with our scriptures, but with us, living today, in the realization that we Jews speak with a multiplicity of voices. And know that a growing chorus of these voices is expressing grave concern about some of the principles that you set out as the heart of Jewishness. There is a nuanced and spirited conversation going on within the Jewish community about Zionism, the State of Israel, and the place of the land of Israel in Jewish life. And yes, about being God's chosen people.

When you enter into this conversation with us, it can and will challenge your theology. You will then embark, with us, and with people of all faiths, on a process of reform that addresses the urgent issues facing us today. It is a process that requires a breaking down, rather than a reinforcing, of those nationalistic and triumphalist tendencies that go against God's will. To use Walter Brueggemann's terms, what we need now, more than ever, is the promotion of prophetic imagination in opposition to royal consciousness. This is not alien to Christianity—in fact the opposite is true. The postwar revisionist project itself is witness to Christianity's self-reforming capability. The ability of Christian theologians, clerics, and lay leaders to undertake this fundamental reassessment of Christian belief was remarkable and courageous. This achievement should serve as a model for all traditions for how faith can be in conversation with history. For, as discussed in chapter 1, this was no mere theological exercise—it was a wrenching response to a "moment of truth." Christians, Jews, and Muslims now face a similar challenge as we contemplate the suffering of all the peoples of the Holy Land—Jews, Christians, and Muslims; Israelis and

Palestinians—as the conflict continues to take lives and tear at the fabric of their societies.

Jews confronted the prospect of annihilation, and Christians confronted their culpability—but today, we are all in this together. The stakes for the future of humanity could not be higher. This, therefore, is a plea for care and thought about the purpose and nature of any interfaith project. Christians must move beyond atonement. Jews must move beyond redemption. Together, with Muslims and people from all the world's nations and faith communities, we must look forward and focus, above all, on social justice. As we search for concepts and models that can inform that search, we will do well to look to the prophets. In the next chapter we examine the work of a contemporary Bible scholar who has done just that.

Chapter 7

Walter Brueggemann and the Prophetic Imagination

The prophets do not offer reflections about ideas in general. Their words are onslaughts, scuttling illusions of false security, challenging evasions, calling faith to account, questioning prudence and impartiality.
—Abraham Joshua Heschel, *The Prophets*

Walter Brueggemann is one of the foremost Bible scholars of our day. He has written extensively on the Old Testament and Christian theology, focusing on their relevance to the critical issues of our times. Brueggemann has had a profound, wide-ranging, and enduring impact on generations of clergy, Bible scholars, and laypersons who love scripture and are seeking a path to faith in these complex times. His concept of the prophetic imagination provides a powerful model with which to understand the role of faith in bringing about justice in the social and political spheres, as well as a way to understand the process that must be undergone by groups and communities of faith in their own development as individuals, social groupings, and even political bodies. Brueggemann's seminal work on the prophetic imagination gives us a way to understand the tragic predicament facing today's Jewish people, a predicament strikingly and tragically parallel to that faced by the Jews of the Old Testament monarchies. His work also provides a road map for Christians struggling to navigate the minefield of the Israel-Palestine conflict. Indeed, Brueggemann's own grappling with the question of the Jewish people, the land, and the Palestinians provides a useful and inspiring example of such a journey.

The Prophetic Imagination

In *The Prophetic Imagination*, Brueggemann describes the Old Testament prophets as itinerant poets responding directly to the social and political injustice perpetrated by the power structures of their times. Brueggemann is very clear about the direct link between prophecy and politics: "We will not understand the meaning of prophetic imagination unless we see the connection between the *religion of static triumphalism* and the *politics of oppression and exploitation*" (2001, 7; emphasis in original).

In Brueggemann's analysis, prophetic imagination arises as an alternative to the sensibilities and worldview of the dominant culture, which he terms "royal consciousness." Royal consciousness is what drives the structures of political power—institutions that, devoted only to their own perpetuation, exploit and oppress the people they are charged with protecting and serving. Transposing the biblical context into our modern idiom, we could call it the "monarchical-priestly complex" of king and Temple. Royal consciousness is concerned only with maintaining the systems that increase power and wealth for the few. Moreover, this is not a cynical endeavor, carried out with full awareness of the ethical implications and consequences for society and the environment. Rather, the maintenance of royal consciousness depends on the suppression of a moral and ethical sense as well as the denial of a wide spectrum of experience, chief among them the emotions of fear and grief. "Royal consciousness," writes Brueggemann, "creates a subjective consciousness concerned only with self-satisfaction, including "the annulment of the neighbor" (37).

The reference to "neighbor" in the preceding quote—biblical shorthand for those others for whom one is responsible—is deliberate on Brueggemann's part. Prophetic ministry, in contrast to royal consciousness, is devoted to the imagining and creation of an alternative to the dominant culture of selfishness, greed, and insularity. It is a consciousness leading to an alternative community devoted not to the power of the few, but to the needs of the many. The prophets continually remind king and subject alike of the divine imperative for justice and mercy, particularly as expressed in the commandments related to social justice. True kingship—true leadership—requires never losing sight of the pain, grief, and hardship of everyday life. This, of course, runs counter to establishing and holding on to temporal power, an enterprise that involves "no mysteries to honor, only problems to be solved" (37). As long as the people can be fed (enough), and controlled so that they do not notice the "cries of the denied ones" (35), the management culture of royal consciousness can continue—even in the face of evidence of its own moral bankruptcy and imminent peril. Royal consciousness consists of and depends upon the denial of pain, fear, and suffering. It is "committed to numbness about death. It is unthinkable for the King to imagine or experience the end of his favorite historical arrangements" (42).

The modern prophets who rail against the injustice and brutality of the current Israeli regime can be situated firmly in this framework. I return, reading this description of Brueggemann's vision of the empire's tragic blindness, to the moment in Jerusalem on the ninth of Av, when I stood on the outskirts of Jerusalem, a Jerusalem I now saw marching to its own destruction. I felt, like the prophet Jeremiah and like Jesus eight centuries later, overcome with grief. I saw a people seemingly unable to emerge from the trauma of their holocaust and wedded to a self-destructive course of colonial conquest and militarism. I saw a people numb to the suffering of their neighbors, a people committed to the denial of a humanitarian crime perpetrated sixty years ago and continuing to this day. I saw, to use Marc Ellis's term, a communally accepted liturgy of destruction used as pretext and rationalization for capitulation to the demands of royal consciousness. Brueggemann points the way out of this tragically self-destructive trap: "I believe that the proper idiom for the prophet in cutting through the royal numbness and denial is *the language of grief*, the rhetoric that engages the community in mourning for a funeral they do not want to admit. It is indeed their own funeral" (46).

The prophets, of course, and for Brueggemann Jeremiah chief among them, mourn for the brokenness and imminent disaster awaiting their people. But the mourning is not about victimhood: it's about the self-inflicted nature of the disaster to come. Note this passage from Jeremiah, quoted by Brueggemann:

Your hurt is incurable,
and your wound is grievous.
There is none to uphold your cause,
no medicine for your wound,
no healing for you. (Jer. 30:12–13)

The word *shivraich* in verse 12, translated "hurt" in this version (New Revised Standard Version), is from the Hebrew root *shever*, which means "brokenness," "fragmentation," "disintegration." It is a theme familiar to the Jewish people. The following passage from Lamentations, attributed to Jeremiah, is recited every year by Jews on the day commemorating the destruction of the Temple in Jerusalem by Babylonia in 586 BCE and again by Rome in 70 CE. The same word for "broken" appears in both verses of this passage, and are translated here as "destruction" and "brokenness:"

Panic and pitfall are our lot,
Death and destruction.
My eyes shed streams of water
Over the brokenness of my poor people. (Lam. 3:47–48;
author's translation)

This was my experience witnessing the occupation of Palestine and learning about the dispossession of three-quarters of a million of the indigenous inhabitants of Palestine to make way for the Jewish state. Like Jeremiah, and like the thousands of Jewish and Christian pilgrims who visit the Holy Land every year expecting to be uplifted but instead find themselves cast down into grief and rage witnessing the abuses of power, I wept as I stood before Jerusalem. But the leadership of the State of Israel, locked into a destructive cycle of expansion, repression, and militarism, is numb to the pain it is causing for both peoples and deaf to today's prophetic voices. Here again is Brueggemann, on the situation in the kingdom of Judah of two thousand years ago:

> The covenant was frozen and there was no possibility of newness until the numbness was broken. Jeremiah understood that the criticism must be faced and embraced, for then comes liberation from incurable disease, from broken covenant, and from failed energy. The tradition of biblical faith knows that anguish is the door to historical existence, that embrace of ending permits beginning. Naturally kings think the door of anguish must not be opened, for it dismantles fraudulent kings…The riddle and insight of biblical faith is the awareness that only anguish leads to life, only grieving leads to joy, and only embraced endings permit new beginnings. (2001, 56)

The Land as Promise to the Landless

We've seen how Brueggemann's concept of the prophetic imagination provides a powerful model for understanding the situation in the Holy Land today. Brueggemann's work on the prophetic sets the stage for our consideration of his writing about the promised land. In *The Land*, first published in 1979, and appearing in a new and revised edition in 2002, Brueggemann delves deeply into the meaning of the land in the experience of the Jewish people. We will follow the development of Brueggemann's thinking over the period between these two publications. To do this is to trace his struggle to reconcile the profound importance of the land for the Jewish people with his growing awareness of the social justice issues that have arisen on the modern political stage. We turn first to Brueggemann's original vision of the land promise contained in the Old Testament.

In a profound way, writes Brueggemann in *The Land*, the promise of the land confers identity: "At the heart of the Jewish experience is a sense of homelessness and a yearning for home, and its history is the history of being on the way to being home. And this cements the relationship with God. Israel is a people on the way because of a promise, and the substance of all its promises from Yahweh is to be in the land, to be placed and secured where Yahweh is yet to lead it" (2002, 5). For Brueggemann, the land is a core metaphor for the drama of God's people struggling to come to terms with the divine imperative to live justly. Moreover, the land promise is a fundamental aspect of the covenant, from the moment of its initiation in the Abrahamic promise (Genesis 12:7). Brueggemann sees the people tied inextricably to the land—and it is at once the promise and the problem. The people in exile is a metaphor for a people punished and disinherited. Possession of the land is totally conditional on obedience to God's plan as expressed in the covenant.

The land, writes Brueggemann, is a powerful force for "wellbeing characterized by social coherence and personal ease in prosperity, security, and freedom" (2). It is rootlessness, not meaninglessness, he writes, that creates the crisis of faith for the people: "There is no meaning apart from roots" (4). For Brueggemann, the land is a vast metaphor about home, homelessness, loss, transgression, forgiveness, and redemption. The land is the place upon which history is enacted and takes on meaning. It is the way in which history transcends the individual, and the manner in which a community of faith experiences its communal history and identity. God's promise of land to Israel, therefore, beginning with his very first revelation to Abraham, is at the heart of the covenant.

To understand the Jews, not only then but now, Brueggemann is saying, one must understand this central relationship to the land:

> Christians cannot speak seriously to Jews unless we acknowledge land to be the central agenda. While the Arabs have rights and legitimate grievances, *the Jewish people are peculiarly the pained voice of the land in the history of humanity, grieved Rachel weeping.*

And unless we address the land question with Jews, we will not likely understand the locus of meaning or the issue of identity. The Jewish community—in all its long, tortuous history—has never forgotten that its roots and its hopes are in storied earth, and that is the central driving force of its uncompromising ethical faith... (202; emphasis added)

In this description, we have, it appears, gone beyond simple understanding: in Brueggemann's view, there is an *entitlement* that must be acknowledged. We must then ask, what is this conversation, in which Christians "address the land question" with Jews? Is it a conversation in which Christians acknowledge the importance of the land to the Jewish people? The Jews need little additional acknowledgement of that in light of the current sense of entitlement to an ever-expanding percentage of historic Palestine. Is it a conversation in which Christians lend political and material support to Jews by way of supporting them against apparent threats to their security and survival in the Middle East? Or, rather, might it not be a conversation in which Christians enter into a discussion with Jews about how, if the land is the force behind its "uncompromising ethical faith," one explains the need for land driving the egregious transgressions against God's law? What would the prophets say? And how exactly does Christian scripture figure into this? Brueggemann continues: "But we have not only new understandings to embrace. It may be that we have also an important role to play vis-à-vis the Jewish land question. It is clear that the question of land allotment in the 'Holy Land' is a deeply complex matter. Not only does the contemporary state of Israel appeal to old traditions as a basis of entitlement, but that appeal is, of course, reinforced by the abomination of the twentieth-century Shoah" (203).

In the space of two pages, Brueggemann has twice introduced the "Jewish land question." It appears, therefore, that the fulfillment of the land promise is not a foregone conclusion: there is an "appeal" to a "basis of entitlement." Brueggemann, quite rightly, introduces the historical event that is universally acknowledged to be at the root of this entitlement. And by virtue of his use of the term *shoah*, Brueggemann suggests that this appeal has special power: this is no ordinary holocaust; it is *the* Holocaust. But he continues: "That claim of entitlement, however, cannot now be permitted to go uncontested, and Christians who appeal to the same authoritative land traditions must now be deeply engaged in that contestation" (203). Which Christians might Brueggemann be talking about here? Dispensationalist Christian Zionists? Mainstream Christians who support the Jewish claim to the land? We have here the Protestant Old Testament scholar, a man who in his writing and teaching is passionately devoted to questions of ethics and justice, and who does not shy away from—indeed he embraces—the explicitly political in this teaching, a man who brings the eighth century BCE right up to the present in his interpretations of the Bible, whose concept of the prophetic imagination is all about direct opposition to the most extreme abuses of power. Here is this same man struggling with the reality of contemporary Jewish empowerment. And indeed, the resolution of this question lies at the very heart of Brueggemann's analysis: land is metaphor. Just like the cross, it is metaphor. Why do we then take the land of Palestine literally, and grant it to the Jews as an actual political entitlement?

Inasmuch as he is addressing Christians in this book, Brueggemann is urging them to embrace the symbolism of land. Christianity undertook a radical transformation of human experience, in which land was taken out of its physical and political context and completely spiritualized. Brueggemann sees the crucifixion as Jesus's "embrace of homelessness" that leads to "the awesome, amazing gift of home (resurrection)" (202). This is prophetic language, clearly in contrast to territorial landedness in the royal consciousness sense. This brings us to what may be the fundamental question: how does Brueggemann reconcile the apparent contradiction between the prophetic message, which is clearly against physical landedness, with the specialness of Israel in the covenantal framework? His own struggle with this question is illuminating.

Entitlement Leads to Occupation

Brueggemann's greatness lies in his drive to examine his own conclusions about the meaning of scripture. His work is based on the assumption that scripture can only be understood in the context of and as a response to human events. Thus, in the preface to the second edition of *The Land*, written twenty-three years after the book's original publication, Brueggemann is clearly questioning what the land promise can mean, in light, as he writes, of "the ideological import of the text as it impacted other people as a necessary cost of Israel's land claims" (xv). In Brueggemann's rethinking of the issue, the theology of promise is reframed as an ideology of entitlement, an ideology that must be questioned.[1] "This ideology of land entitlement," he points out, "serves the contemporary state of Israel" (xv). It is an ideology, he continues, that is "enacted in unrestrained violence against the Palestinian population...It is clear that the modern state of Israel has effectively merged old traditions of land entitlement and the most vigorous military capacity thinkable for a modern state" (xv). These are strong words from a theologian who two decades earlier had written about the centrality of the land for the identity and soul of the Jewish people (and, by extension, for Christians as the heirs to this Old Testament theology). This is not an isolated observation targeted at the Israeli regime; it is part of Brueggemann's overarching vision of how power corrupts and how land promise can become land entitlement in service to systems under the sway of royal consciousness. "It is clear," he writes, "that the same ideology of entitlement has served derivatively the Western powers that are grounded in that same ideological claim and that have used that claim as a rationale for colonization...The outcome of that merger of old

---

1. Rosemary and Herman Ruether have taken up this issue of Jewish identity and land. Along with other commentators, they hold that in the modern era, with the birth of the Jewish state and "as Judaism as the basis of religious community erodes for many Jews, activity for Zionism is used to replace Judaism as the basis for Jewish identity" (Ruether and Ruether 2002, 227).

traditional claim and contemporary military capacity becomes an intolerable commitment to violence that is justified by reason of state…That is, *land entitlement* leads to *land occupation*" (xv; emphasis in original).

Brueggemann has come full circle. These reflections are fully in line with the vision of prophetic ministry that constitutes both the ideological bedrock and the practical trajectory of his work. In this bold formulation, Brueggemann fulfills the prophetic requirement to identify royal consciousness, confront its consequences, and bring the people back to a faith grounded in social justice and right action. The land may be a central symbol, the source of joy and well-being, but as such it must be understood *on this same symbolic level.* When it becomes real—when, to paraphrase Jewish Liberation theologian Marc Ellis, Judaism becomes empowered—the result is intolerable.

Brueggemann is thus using the modern example of Israel as a cautionary tale. He is addressing the danger of religious fundamentalism in the pursuit of power in general. Yet, even as Brueggemann takes us down this path, he remains fully in a biblical framework, a framework that reaffirms the covenantal land promise. Using the word in a sense very close to its original meaning as "the way that is to be followed," Brueggemann invokes *Torah* as the force that will counter unbridled power and royal consciousness: "In the Old Testament itself that strand of violence intrinsic to the theme of land is relatively held in check by connection of land to the Torah" (xvi). The prophetic, as Brueggemann points out, draws directly on this theme of what he terms "Torah obedience." And what is Torah obedience? It is the heart of the covenant: the promise of the land in return for obedience to God and his law. He brings in the Deuteronomic admonition—devoting almost a full page to the famous passage from chapter 30 that sets out the terms of this covenantal tie:

> If you obey the commandments of the Lord your God that I am commanding you today, by loving the Lord your God, walking in his ways, and observing his commandments, decrees and

ordinances, then you shall live and become numerous, and the Lord your God will bless you in the land that you are entering to possess. But if your heart turns away and you do not hear, I declare to you today that you shall perish; you shall not live long in the land that you are crossing the Jordan to enter and possess. I call heaven and earth to witness against you today that I have set before you life and death, the blessing and the curse. Choose life! So that you and your descendants may live...so that you may live in the land, as the Lord swore to your ancestors, to Abraham, Isaac and to Jacob, to give it to them. (Deut. 30:15–20)

Thus in his warnings against the evil of royal power and the peril to which this subjects the State of Israel, Brueggemann appeals to tradition: "The tradition of Deuteronomy is repetitious and insistent in its connection between *land possession* and *Torah obedience*" (xvi; emphasis in original). Brueggemann is pointing out that the Bible that establishes the special relationship of Israel and the land is the same Bible that warns against the dangers of possession. In so doing, he has highlighted the contradiction between the prophetic demand for justice and the implications of the covenantal land promise. The Bible recognizes the perils of landedness, yes. But it issues the warning in an effort to bind the people to the covenant, to *reinforce and fulfill the land promise*. The traditional claim persists, and the contradiction deepens: *Getting the land is part of following Torah. Following Torah means getting the land.* Brueggemann has understood land as a powerful metaphor. As such, it transcends time, ethnicity, and location. But setting it squarely in the original biblical context as he has done places it firmly in the framework of the covenant. As such, the land is primary—transgressing against God's laws may get you dispossessed and exiled, but the promise of Return is always there. Dispossession and exile are temporary; possession is the ultimate and, essentially, persistent state.

In his 2002 preface, Brueggemann invokes the Deuteronomic admonition in the context of a *mea culpa*: "...land as theological theme is never to be taken as innocent and surely not as innocently as I had done in my book." But in so doing, in holding up Torah as the "force that will counter unbridled power and royal consciousness" (xvi), Brueggemann remains within the traditional framework that one page earlier he has faulted as leading to "an intolerable commitment to violence" (xv). Essentially this same claim is used to validate the land promise across the Jewish religious spectrum—from progressive Jewish thinkers, to mainstream Jews hewing to traditional Rabbinic Judaism, to Jewish fundamentalist settlers. The "merger of old traditional claims and contemporary military capacity" leads where it leads—unavoidably, inexorably.

Grieving and Letting Go

Where does this leave us?

We are looking at the need for nothing short of a transformation of the Jewish connection with the land—a new covenant. I suggest that this is precisely what early Christianity sought to accomplish. In the preceding chapters, we saw the effort on the part of Christian theologians after the Nazi Holocaust to undo this transformative act—to in effect deny the discontinuity between the Judaism of Jesus's time and the radical new worldview that had emerged from his ministry. This revised theology established instead an invented, single, shared covenant—a covenant in which the land connection is preserved. This revision, still in force today, serves two related functions: it legitimizes Zionism and it relieves Christians of their guilt through an attempt to atone for that period of Christian history in which Christianity defined itself through, to use van Buren's term, "anti-Judaism" (Wallis 1997, 53). The claim, therefore, is that this theology was a church error. But this is not so much a correction as an attempt to deny the shame and sadness over the sin and misery that happened as the result of the split from the parent faith. But, as Brueggemann reminds us with such passion, denial doesn't work. Christians, confronted with the horror of the Nazi Holocaust, have to grieve. Indeed, they have to experience the full depth of their horror and their sorrow about what Christianity has wrought, just as we Jews someday must come to recognize, deeply regret, and grieve what we have done to establish and maintain the Jewish state.

Brueggemann may be pointing us in this direction when, in this same preface, he raises the issue of exile. As one aspect of the land metaphor, Brueggemann writes, "exile, as either history or as ideology, has become definitional for Israel's self-discernment" (xvii). Exile, as the inescapable and darkness-filled experience of the consequences of overweening possessiveness, leads us—hopefully—to a realization of the evils of the royal and toward the embrace of the prophetic. Brueggemann writes, "Israel's royal history in the land moved inexorably toward exile. Kings tend to think about the next crisis rather than the general drift and destiny of their community. Kings in Israel refused or were unable to think that exile could be their ultimate end. But the prophets, the partners and challengers of kings, know where Israel was headed—to exile. It is the business of the prophets to discern what kings cannot see and to articulate what kings cannot bear...So they think unthinkable thoughts and speak unspeakable words that kings cannot tolerate or dare to face" (101).

For today's State of Israel, the unspeakable and unacceptable is the unsustainability and injustice of the colonization of the West Bank and the knowledge, now finally reaching the consciousness of the West and of Israel itself, of the crime of ethnic cleansing that was carried out in the period 1947–1949. These realities, rather than the real or inflated threat from Palestinian nationalism or the demagoguery of a regional power, represent the real challenge to the security and viability of a Jewish presence in historic Palestine and to the deeply felt commitment to the Zionist dream of a national homeland for the Jewish people. It is the fact that Israel's denial of its own past and its blind pursuit of its current course will destroy that dream. It is the realization that, indeed, this process is well underway.

Brueggemann has given us a powerful message about the power of scripture to shape our thinking and action in the world. In *The Land* he has placed the central meaning of the land in the Bible within the framework of his body of work. Brueggemann's evocation of "land as promise, land as challenge" serves to stimulate our thinking, especially at this point in history. But the ultimate relevance of his work for those concerned with the Israel-Palestine question today depends on how we take the metaphorical and symbolic and project it onto the real world. It can't work in the other direction—if it's metaphor, it can't also be an actual, physical location or political entity that can then be granted spiritual, religious, or metaphysical meaning. The land as it figures in the Bible must be understood on a symbolic level, and only on that level.

This perspective is gaining ground among theologians concerned with the future of the Holy Land.

In September 2008, Christian theologians from Palestine, Europe, and North America met to discuss the situation in the Holy Land from a theological perspective. From the report by Ecumenical News International:

> "The contemporary conflict in Palestine-Israel resounds with biblical metaphors," the 85 participants said in a statement agreed to at the end of the meeting in the Swiss capital of Bern. "However," the statement continued, "there was significant consensus in the conference that the Bible must not be utilised to justify oppression or supply simplistic commentary on contemporary events…A central issue for the conference was how the Bible is read," participants said. They noted that it is particularly important to differentiate between biblical history and biblical stories, and to distinguish between the Israel of the Bible and the modern State of Israel. (Brown 2008, 32)

American theologian Harvey Cox, professor at Harvard Divinity School and a longtime force in bringing theology to bear on the struggle for human rights, was at the conference and weighed in on this issue. "What do we really mean by 'promised land'?" asked Cox. "How has the term been hijacked and used for various political reasons, when maybe that is not the significance of the texts at all? Ancient Israel is often confused with modern Israel.

They are not the same. We can talk about an integral relationship which must be there theologically between Christians and the Jewish people. Jesus was Jewish; the whole background of Christianity comes from the Jewish people, but the Jewish people and the modern State of Israel, though they overlap in certain ways, are not the same, and therefore we have to be thoughtful and self-critical about how that theme is dealt with" (2008, 33).

Cox and other scholars thus join Walter Brueggemann in grappling with the theological questions raised by the reality of the modern Jewish state. We witness a similar process, spread across a canvas devoted specifically to the issues of anti-Semitism and the Israel-Palestine conflict, in the work of some of today's most courageous thinkers in progressive theology. We consider two of them in the next chapter.

Chapter 8

Progressive Christianity, Israel, and the Challenge of Reform

There is a tortured reasoning…which seems to suggest that Christians should not speak out in criticism of Israel until there are a substantial number of Israelis and western Jews doing so. This is an odd moral principle. Is it not mostly a strategy for saving oneself from attack as an "anti-Semite"?…Would one really wait to criticize American or white South African racism until there was a majority of white Americans or white South Africans doing so?
—Rosemary Ruether, "Beyond Anti-Semitism and Philo-Semitism"

The authors reviewed in chapters 5 and 6—progressive theologians all—promote an unvarnished Zionism. In their formulations, the Jewish people, restored to privileged status by a revisionist theology dedicated to undoing the two-thousand-year-old sin of anti-Semitism, are granted a superior right to the Land of Israel. It's a curious phenomenon, this endorsement of an ideology that grants theological justification to an exclusivist, nationalist movement in historic Palestine by thinkers who otherwise merit the label "progressive." As we will see when we look at their counterparts in progressive Jewish thought, this theologically based support of political Zionism appears to be a blind spot for these writers, a striking inconsistency in careers otherwise dedicated to human rights and a vision of universal justice. In fairness to them, the issue of the land and the topic of Zionism is not the primary focus of their work. The problems—

theological, political, sociological—posed by the Israel-Palestine conflict are not on their radar screens. In Walter Brueggemann we saw a transitional figure, his focus on the centrality of the land in the biblical narrative shaped by his commitment to uncovering the Bible's relevance to the urgent issues of contemporary life.

In contrast, there are scholars, religious leaders, and theologians who have taken up the issue directly—people deeply troubled by the situation in Israel/Palestine, individuals devoted actively in their work to the support of liberation struggles and social justice causes. In this chapter and the next we will consider their contributions. We will not find in them the complacency that characterizes the theological visions of the revisionists, the apparent lack of awareness of the human rights and justice issues raised by the enactment of the Zionist vision that they find it so easy to uplift. Rather, these writers have demonstrated an urgent concern for the agony on the ground in the actual, terrestrial Holy Land and a sharp focus on theological issues raised by the conflict. I will consider two of these writers in this chapter. The first is a Presbyterian minister and professor of theology, raised in an evangelical tradition and now involved deeply in the struggle for justice in Palestine. The second is a renowned Catholic feminist theologian and proponent of liberation theology. Both are heroes of mine, and so it is with some trepidation that I present a critique of their work with respect to the issue of Jewish exceptionalism. It is my hope—and belief—that my treatment of their work will help advance the conversation and the search for reconciliation in our increasingly complex world.

Donald Wagner: God Is Doing a New Thing

Reverend Donald Wagner is a Presbyterian minister, an associate professor of religion and Middle Eastern studies at North Park University in Chicago, and a longtime activist in the cause of human rights for Palestine. Wagner has written extensively about the modern-day Christian Zionist movement that grew out of nineteenth-century premillennial dispensationalism, an ideology that asserts the absolute right of the Jewish people to the Land of Israel as one of the necessary conditions for the second coming of Jesus. Wagner holds that this is a grievous misinterpretation and distortion of the scriptures, both in word and certainly in spirit, with respect to the modern-day struggle for justice in the territory of historic Palestine.

Wagner has worked to forge a progressive Christian theology in the service of justice for all the peoples of the land. To this end, he seeks to bring an understanding of the Old Testament into line with his theologically based case for justice for the Palestinian people. Wagner goes right to the source: God's promise to Abraham in Genesis 12 to give "all the land that you see...to you and your offspring forever." He advances the interpretation that the land does not belong to the people but to God, who grants the rights to the use of the land in exchange for devotion to God. The promise of the land, therefore, is conditional. This is amply supported, according to this argument, by the Deuteronomic warnings that the possession (Hebrew *horish*) of the land is highly conditional on obedience to God. Citing the teachings of Fr. Paul Tarazi, a leading Palestinian Eastern orthodox theologian, Wagner sums up the argument in this way: "The land is not an end to itself but an instrument or means by which the people fulfill their high calling. The Israelites were in effect God's tenant farmers or caretakers. The land is a derivative of the covenant and not the goal. Whenever land becomes a people's primary focus, they are guilty of idolatry" (1995, 63).

This is valid theology. But how true is it to the spirit of the Old Testament? And really, does not the interpretation itself argue against Wagner's point? In the story of God's promise and his covenant, which *is* the story of the Old Testament, the people of Israel are granted a privileged—indeed an exclusive—status. The conditions placed on this gift, even taking into consideration the social justice aspects of the civil laws found in the Old Testament, don't mitigate the specialness of the relationship. The Deuteronomic admonitions themselves underscore this fundamental feature of the covenant. Yes, there are strict conditions, but the land remains central: possession of the land is the primary element in this transaction, and it is never taken off the table, the fine print notwithstanding.[1] In this characterization of the special role of the Jews inherent in the Old Testament covenant, Wagner detracts from the very point he is trying to make. Note the language in the quote above: "fulfill their high calling" and "God's tenant farmers." The Jews' special, exclusive relationship with God is only emphasized in these arguments against the notion of a superior claim to the land.

Jonah: A Universalist Tract?

The book of Jonah is often held up in support of the argument for a universalist strain in the Old Testament. Wagner joins Rosemary Ruether and others in citing this text as evidence of a message of universal justice in the Jewish scriptures. "Your God is too small," writes Wagner in his free rephrasing of God's exhortation to Jonah under the withered desert bush. "God is doing a new thing in the world and you need to catch up with it" (1975, 68). And what is this new thing? "Only when you are faithful to your original calling of being a blessing to the nations will you truly be the people of God" (68). I fully agree with what I believe Wagner's message to be here: that the Jews will only be truly a people of God when they transcend tribalism and embrace a universal love of humankind in both their beliefs and their actions. But I question whether his reading of Genesis 12:3 is in line with the meaning of that passage. In fact, as noted in a previous chapter, the original Hebrew points to the opposite conclusion. A translation faithful to the original would be: "You (the people of Israel) will be invoked as a blessing." In other words: "When offering blessings, they will say, 'May you be as blessed (fortunate, successful, favored) as the People of Israel.'" Clearly, this is not the

---

1. The verb *horish*, employed in the Old Testament to denote the granting of the land to the Jewish people, is best translated as "to inherit." Few if any conditions would apply to this form of entitlement.

same as being a force for blessing or good in the world! Rather, the biblical blessing emphasizes Israel's difference, set-apartness, and specialness, rather than being an exhortation to bring benefit to the other nations. Furthermore, Wagner is arguing that God is calling on Jonah to promote a new universalism in the world through the example of his mission to Nineveh. In fact, what God has explicitly asked Jonah to do is to "take pity" on the people of Nineveh, and to have compassion for them. He is not requiring Jonah to include the people of Nineveh in the covenant with God. Where is the universal message there? Indeed, if God is as much the God of the people of Nineveh as he is the God of the Jews, why doesn't he talk to them himself? Or why doesn't he call on an Assyrian prophet to save "his" people from destruction?

Wagner's effort to advance a theology of universal justice based on a unified vision of the Jewish and Christian scriptures is part of his work for reconciliation between the faiths. He has earned the right to this territory. In his work here and in Israel/Palestine, Wagner has devoted himself to the support of Palestinian Christians struggling to survive under an oppressive Israeli regime and to the strengthening of bonds between Christian communities in Israel/Palestine and the rest of the world. Most impressively, he has urged Christians in the beleaguered communities of Palestine to "respond to the all-encompassing challenge of reconciliation with Jews" (166). And it must be granted that in his interpretation of Jonah he is appealing to our better nature as Jews.

I urge caution and realism, however, in ascribing a fully realized universalism to our tradition in the face of the evidence that it is lacking. Wagner, in my view, strays dangerously close to the revisionist project of merging the two religious traditions, of blunting the essential differences between the faiths, when, in his gloss on Jonah, he puts Paul's words from Corinthians 5:17 ("Everything has become new!") into God's mouth when he chastises Jonah for his lack of compassion for the people of Nineveh. In doing this, Wagner is inserting a worldview that is simply not to be found there. If we Jews are going to find our way to the reconciliation Wagner describes, our task is, to paraphrase Shakespeare, to find the fault in ourselves. I fully agree with Wagner that it is critical that the values of universalism and reconciliation be held out as the only path to peace. However, claiming that these values are espoused in the Old Testament, whether it be Genesis, Deuteronomy, or the Prophets, only dulls the challenge to my people to struggle with the particularism so deeply embedded in our identity. We already have voices from the Christian mainstream granting us the right to the land. Our common cause with exceptional people like Reverend Wagner must be based on a hard-nosed rejection of those elements in our own tradition that would support that same claim. Only then will we be truly able to join in the effort toward reconciliation and in the joint work of renewing creation.

Rosemary Reuther: Another Take on Jonah

Rosemary Ruether is a Catholic scholar and theologian, a pioneer in feminist theology, and an outspoken proponent of human rights and nonviolence. We will turn to a more thorough review of her work as it pertains to Israel/Palestine. But first, let's consider her discussion of Jonah. In it we see the assertion of an Old Testament universalism similar to what we noted in Wagner's writing. In the 2002 *The Wrath of Jonah: The Crisis of Religious Nationalism in the Israeli-Palestinian Conflict*, coauthored with her husband Herman, Ruether focuses directly on the issue at hand: "The perspective of the Hebrew Scripture varies from a tribal, militaristic view of conquest of the land to a critical ethical view of Israel's relation to the land. It also ranges from an ethnocentric to an increasingly universalistic view of the chosenness of Israel in relation to other peoples. The book of Jonah represents the high point of this universalist development. God creates, loves, and seeks to save the other peoples equally with Israel" (13).

Here again the book of Jonah is held up as the example for—might we say the evidence of?—a universalist ethic in the Old Testament. Reserving for a moment the question of where this "critical ethical view of Israel's relation to the land" is to be found, we must ask again, where is the universalist message in Jonah? Here are the Ruethers in the introduction to *The Wrath of Jonah*: "The book of Jonah was written in the post-Nehemiah period (fourth century BCE), after the return of Jewish leaders from the exile into which they had been cast by the Babylonian conquest of Palestine in the early sixth century. This book was meant to promote tolerance and coexistence of Jews with other communities within the Persian Empire after the return of Jewish religious leadership in Jerusalem. It was a gentle satire on a type of self-righteous Jewish religious exclusivism that had arisen after the return" (viii).

Whether or not we agree or not with the Ruethers' historical gloss on Jonah, we will likely be in sympathy with the anti-exclusivist sentiment they ascribe to the author. But this very interpretation raises questions about their characterization of the book's universalistic message. Just because the people of Nineveh are deserving of God's mercy, does that imply that they are as good as the Jews, who are God's people? Does the fact that the people of Nineveh are also God's creation really have bearing on the Jews' special relationship with God? Note, again, that it is a Jew whom God appoints to be his messenger to the people of Nineveh. The Ruethers' point is that the book is directed at the Jews: it's a homily, meant to chasten, to warn, to teach humility. But this humanitarian lesson directed at the Jews does not necessarily carry with it a message of universalism, or the removal, qualification, or diminution of an exclusive, favored relationship with God.

Is the Ruethers' slant on Jonah intended to soften the hard edges of their condemnation of Israel's actions to be found elsewhere their book? Or is it perhaps meant as a hopeful attempt to separate Judaism from Zionism, to bring out those elements in Judaism that may lead Jews to mend their ways and return to the justice-based core of their creed? We will see that, however valid the case against Christianity for the evils of anti-Semitism, however important the effort to rid Christianity of this burden and create optimal conditions for interfaith reconciliation, this argument leads the Ruethers to a virtual defense of Zionist aims that is in conflict with the universalist values they are promoting and attributing to Judaism. This conflict is to be found in Ruether's earlier work, in which she takes on the topic of anti-Semitism directly.

Anti-Semitism and the Right to a Homeland

In her 1995 *Faith and Fratricide: The Theological Roots of Anti-Semitism*, Ruether makes the case that Christians must acknowledge the fundamental anti-Judaism in their doctrine, rather than glossing it over. Ruether takes on early Christian anti-Judaism, citing its dire consequences in the abrogation of Jewish rights throughout European history. She takes direct aim at those doctrinal and polemical elements of the New Testament that are responsible for anti-Semitism. For example, Ruether points out that Paul's supersessionism is not conceived in a linear, historical frame, in which Christianity simply comes along to replace Judaism. Rather, for Paul, Christianity, coexisting with Judaism, was something completely different from and in opposition to the parent faith. In Ruether's terms, for Paul, the issues were clear cut: the carnal versus spiritual, the godly versus the outright rejection of God. Significantly, Ruether fully acknowledges the virulent anti-Judaism in the Gospel of John. The intentional attack against the Jews to be found in that Gospel, Ruether points out, cannot be interpreted away—as is increasingly being done—by claiming that it refers to class rather than ethnicity, or to a small group within the Jewish community, even to the extent of rendering "Jews" as "Jewish leaders"(as it is rendered inaccurately in some modern translations) (104).

In Ruether's view, this vilification of the Jews in the service of "Christian self-affirmation...has retarded Christian theological self-affirmation" (228). She argues that "rethinking anti-Judaism" is an urgent task of Christian "theological reconstruction" (228). From the viewpoint of the need to cleanse Christianity of this obvious blight, I agree with Ruether. However, with respect to the specific issue of Zionism and the State of Israel, I see a problematic by-product of this effort, and it is this: Ruether, in her identification of the evils of virulent, persistent Christian anti-Semitism, offers an antidote—an alternative, more advanced, balanced vision of Judaism. It is a vision that in its generosity and attempt at balance validates the Jewish yearning for a return to the homeland. It effectively legitimizes, on theological grounds, the notion of a political Jewish homeland. Thus, although Ruether is willing to take a painful, direct look at a dark side of Christianity, this is accompanied by a reluctance to shine a critical light on problematic aspects of Judaism—aspects that are very much at work in the violations of justice and human rights brought about by the Zionist project. Consider this passage from chapter 5:

> The end of Christendom means Christianity now must think of itself as a Diaspora religion. On the other hand, the Jewish people, shaken by the ultimate threat to Jewish survival posed by modern anti-Semitism, have taken a giant leap against all odds and...founded the state of Israel. The Return [sic] to the homeland has shimmered as a messianic horizon of redemption from the exile for the Jewish people for many centuries. But Christianity dogmatically denied the possibility of such a return, declaring that eternal exile was the historical expression of Jewish reprobation. *Now this Christian myth has been made obsolete by history*...When viewed from the perspective of oppression in exile, the Return to Israel is indeed a liberation movement and a salvitic event for the Jews. (227; emphasis added)

Here Ruether, like other progressive theologians, has stepped out on that slippery slope of Jewish exceptionalism. The "Return," in the form of political Zionism—albeit, as Ruether says, a messianism that is in difficulty—is granted legitimacy, replete with religious overtones. Anticipating the 2002 *Wrath of Jonah*, Ruether acknowledges that Zionism is a deeply flawed project, yet the tendency to bless the project is clearly detectable. In striking contrast to her position ten years later in *The Wrath of Jonah*, Ruether falls into the trap of presenting a "balanced" perspective on the conflict. She writes, "There are serious problems, of course, inherent in the taking of the land: Jewish nationalism vs. Palestinian nationalism, national security against equality and justice for all. This struggle takes place in a land with a heritage of communal and imperial conflicts, from ancient times to modern colonialism and neocolonialism" (227). In these words we can detect familiar themes in the current discourse about Israel, arguments heard in circles ranging from the staunch defenders of Israel to Jewish progressives guardedly critical of the state. The first is the often-heard call for "balance" in the discussion. This most often takes the form of a demand for an acknowledgment of the suffering of Israelis as a result of the conflict: "equal time'" must be given to the damages inflicted on both sides. We also hear this call in the implicit requirement to acknowledge the "conflicting" claims to the land. In other words, the issue is not first and foremost about identifying and addressing oppression and injustice, but rather about the need to mediate between two equally valid claims, between "two rights."

The second theme, evident in the above quote from *Faith and Fratricide*, is the notion of a never-ending history of conflict in the region. In this argument, the current conflict is normalized: the land has always been a battleground with nations and ethnic groups fighting over the same territory for years in an endless cycle of conquest, resistance, and suppression. This is simply the latest version. Such statements wash out the grim reality of a powerful, militarized state engaged in a long-term campaign of illegal land annexation and the displacement of an indigenous population, a campaign that has been effectively supported and winked at by the West. This is the very picture that Ruether would go on to present with such power and clarity in *Wrath of Jonah*, where in her commitment to moral and historical clarity, she is quite willing to dispense with this imposed requirement for "fairness" or "balance."

Here we see how progressive Christian thought, in setting up Christianity as responsible for the conditions that motivated its rise, returns repeatedly to this implicit defense of Zionism, and in so doing essentially works toward its legitimization. "Every criticism of Zionism," Ruether writes, "is not to be equated with anti-Semitism. Yet there is no doubt that anti-Zionism has become, for some, a way of reviving the myth of the 'perennial evil nature of the Jews,' to refuse to the Jewish people *the right to exist with a homeland of its own. The threat to Jewish survival, posed in ultimate terms by Nazism and never absent as long as anti-Semitism remains in the dominant culture of the Diaspora, lends urgency to the need for the Israeli state*" (227; emphasis added). Ruether recognizes the dangerous problems created, unavoidably, by this interpenetration of the religious, the theological, and, indeed, the messianic: "...the religious interpretation of Israel, as the Promised Land given by God and as a land whose restoration was regarded as a messianic event, impedes the search for that pluralism that is necessary for peaceful coexistence with indigenous Arab peoples, both Moslem and Christian. Stuck between a religious orthodoxy forged in the Diaspora and secular nationalism, Israel awaits the rebirth of that prophetic tradition that can transform Zionism into a language of self-criticism in the light of that ultimate Zion of justice and peace which is still to be achieved" (227).

Ruether has it right, of course: religious orthodoxy and messianism don't mix with democracy. Yet, unless we directly confront the implications of the messianic in Zionism—a powerful strain, as Jacqueline Rose demonstrates convincingly, deeply embedded in so-called secular Zionism—it will continue to exert its influence. Messianism is messianism: it does not give way to democratic reform; it does not yield to the evolution of a pluralism based on principles of justice and fairness. Here, Ruether invokes the prophets as the theological and ethical solvent that will eliminate the dilemma. Yet the notion that the "prophetic tradition" provides a model or blueprint to "transform Zionism into a language of self-criticism," an idea frequently advanced in progressive Jewish discourse and in interfaith discussions, bears scrutiny.

Ruether's analysis endorses the heart of the Zionist ethos. The overcoming of the Diaspora becomes the triumph over anti-Semitism. Zionism, even as it is critiqued in light of recent events, is elevated to "a salvific event." I do not believe, especially in view of her more recent writing, that Ruether thinks Israel has brought salvation to the Jews. Indeed, she has consistently and for decades maintained quite the opposite in the strongest terms. But there is a casting of the Zionist yearning in sympathetic terms that continues as a stream in her writing. The point has been made by others, Jacqueline Rose among them, that Zionism is not, nor has it ever been, a secular movement. In this realm where history, faith, and tradition merge, Zionism is a religious movement, and Ruether goes on to illustrate this point with stunning clarity. There is a contradiction, therefore, that emerges in Ruether's writing on this topic. Ruether has vividly exposed, in her words, "the left hand of Christology" in her effort to present a positive image of Judaism (103). In so doing, however, she has tied Christianity's *right* hand behind its back. For it was precisely the revolution that Christianity represented, the wrenching of God out of the tribal and into the universal, that was the essential and needed advance for civilization. And it is the persistence of the tribal in Judaism that has led to the present tragic dilemma wrought by Zionism—a situation that is, in the words of Professor Joel Kovel, "the curse of Judaism"—and to a desperate crisis for the Jews (2007, 8).

Judaism's Shadow

What seems to be happening here is that in their effort to undo the evil of the demonization of Jews and the establishment of the Jews as Christianity's—indeed humankind's—shadow, these thinkers journey all the way back to the "original parting" in an attempt to undo it. In so doing, they risk losing sight of what was important and essential in the revolution that was early Christianity. As Ruether rightly highlights in her treatment of Naim Ateek's work, the schism in Judaism that led to Christianity was not about the question of the divinity of Christ. Rather, it concerned the nature of God and his relation to humankind. Once we understand this, we see that what transpired in the first and second centuries CE was the lifting of God out of the tribal framework of the Old Testament narrative. The moment we face this squarely, the Jews lose their special status. In the Christian formulation, Christ made us all part of Israel in the metaphorical sense. Israel becomes not a tribe, and certainly no longer a nation, but a metaphor for all humankind joined in and through God's love.

However, in the current move toward what is sometimes called "interfaith reconciliation," we can see a disturbing tendency to find a way to preserve the Jews' special standing within the framework of an updated, progressive Christian theology. A theology that professes to place justice in the forefront but that also seeks to grant Jews privileged status raises serious political and moral questions for both Jews and Christians in the context of the current political situation. First, for the Jews: how will we ever achieve "repentance," in Ruether's use of the term, if we do not recognize the sense of entitlement and exclusivism in our collective makeup? No matter how many "Save Darfur" banners we display in front of our synagogues and Jewish Federation offices, it won't wash. We have no right to advertise our support for human rights while Israel proceeds with its campaign of ethnic cleansing in Palestine with our vocal support and with our money. Our claim to a universalist, justice-based tradition is tainted. Psychoanalyst Carl Jung named such unacknowledged, unexamined aspects of individual and group character "the shadow" (Abrams and Zweig 1990). Our Jewish shadow is the still-to-be-understood and flushed-out exceptionalism, the legacy of a tribal past amplified and perpetuated by millennia of persecution and marginalization. As long as traits such as these remain in the shadows they will drive behavior in an uncontrolled fashion. The policies of the State of Israel stand as evidence of that shadow in action: the militarism gone amok, the settlers acting out the will of an expansionist government, the people closing their eyes to it, accepting and ultimately sanctioning the injustice and the racism. Second, for Christians: if Christians collude in this fantasy and this denial, they are disempowered from taking the actions they ordinarily would take in their global mission and social justice work. We have seen this in the evisceration of the Presbyterian General Council's 2004 resolution to divest from companies profiting from the occupation of Palestine, largely as the result of enormous pressure from Jewish groups. We see it in the thwarting of dialogue and the attempt to block public appearances of speakers who are critical of Israel (even those of the stature of former U.S. presidents and South African archbishops!). Whenever that is allowed to happen, Christians are enabling the Jews in their self-destructive behavior.

Ruether Redux: The Sins of Zionism

Ruether and her husband Herman have devoted their professional lives to the cause of social justice. It is therefore not surprising that a considerable shift occurred in Ruether's thinking following a period of living and teaching in Palestine and witnessing first-hand the occupation and colonization of the West Bank and Gaza. At the height of the first Palestinian Intifada (or uprising) in 1988, the Ruethers published *The Wrath of Jonah: The Crisis of Religious Nationalism in the Israeli-Palestinian Conflict.* The book presents a comprehensive discussion of the religious, historical, and philosophical background of modern Zionism. It is also a clear-cut condemnation of the actions of Israel toward the Palestinians, challenging the very fundamentals of the political Zionist project. The Ruethers describe the powerful strains of messianism, utopianism, and nationalism to be found in modern political Zionism. *The Wrath of Jonah* is an impassioned plea for the self-inspection and self-criticism that is urgently required of Israel in order to escape the cycle of violence and enmity created by this tragic conflict.

In their analysis of Zionism, the Ruethers go directly to what is the key issue for Jews, namely, our perception of ourselves as a people special and apart, and therefore not subject to the same rules as other groups. The Ruethers go to the theological heart of the matter, taking on the issue of God's election of the Jewish people, disputing that it can be used to claim an innate superiority and special entitlement. This is a courageous position, given the prevailing tendency of progressive Christian theology to highlight those very elements of Old Testament theology often used to lend support to Jewish land entitlement.

In *The Wrath of Jonah*, the Ruethers draw the subtle and important distinction between the power of the homeland concept for Jewish identity and the right to use any means to realize it. They do not shy away from a consideration of the history of the conflict. They are particularly pointed about the need for a single, coherent story about what happened in 1948—taking issue with the now fashionable approach of offering two parallel narratives, one Jewish and one Palestinian. Rather, assert the authors, there is one story: that of the determined and indefatigable Zionist program to establish a Jewish state, and the cruel and tragic dispossession of the Palestinians to make way for it. The Ruethers look to the Israeli and Palestinian revisionist historians to establish that single story, urging that it "be communicated across the two communities" (2002, xxiii).

Finally, the Ruethers do not hesitate to wade into the political. They hold Israel to account for the sabotaging of the 1993 Oslo Peace Accords through the continued illegal settlement of the West Bank. The book takes direct aim at the shibboleth of "Israel's right to exist," naming it—correctly—as "Zionist rhetoric" that is in reality "a covert appeal to this religious myth that Jews have an a priori right to exist as a nation in a particular territory" (230). In short, *The Wrath of Jonah* takes on frontally the sacred cows of Zionism, issues almost always avoided by Christian as well as Jewish voices in the discourse out of concern that this will sabotage the chance for dialogue and a common meeting ground. One need only read the 2002 preface to the second edition of *The Wrath of Jonah*, running a mere three pages, for an analysis that is as penetrating and accurate today as it was at its writing over seven years ago. Here the Ruethers puncture the myth of the "peace process," summon up a picture of apartheid and ethnic cleansing, and, disputing that Arab anti-Semitism is at work in fomenting opposition to Israel, name the root cause of the conflict as the "Israeli scheme of colonial apartheid" (xiv). Although surely not ignorant of the failures of Palestinian leadership, the authors dispense with the obligatory nod to "balance" in the discourse, laying responsibility for the failure of peace directly at the feet of Israel and the United States. *The Wrath of Jonah* is a courageous book: it breaks the unwritten rules of our careful, polite interfaith dialogues on the topic—when these dialogues allow themselves to touch the topic at all.

The Ruethers take particular aim at the moral failures of Zionism, in particular the exploitation and even encouragement of Diaspora anti-Semitism by Zionist leaders, even to the extent of collaboration with anti-Semitic and genocidal regimes in an effort to increase Jewish immigration in the years before and after the founding of the state. As such, it's a severe and sometimes bitter indictment of the sins of Zionism. The Ruethers offer a historical overview that is highly critical of Zionism as an ideology, even before they address the specifics of Israel's acts against the indigenous Palestinians. In their 2002 preface and postscript, their outrage and anger at Israel are apparent. They take care to spell out the huge power imbalance between the parties to the conflict, putting the onus on Israel to make the necessary changes to bring an end to the conflict. The Ruethers are under no illusions about the willingness of Israel to relinquish its position of dominance and to open itself to fundamental changes in its pursuit of Jewish hegemony—economic, demographic, and political—in historic Palestine. Rather, they submit, it will be up to the rest of the world to make this happen. They advocate boycott and pariah-state status, invoking the case of apartheid South Africa. The book basically advocates a one-state solution, "dissolving the ethnic discrimination inherent in the idea and legal structures of a 'Jewish state'" (244). Here, the Ruethers all but utter the heretical thought: the reality, if not the idea, of a Jewish state is untenable and, ultimately, morally unsupportable. But there is one further step to be taken, and they do not take it.

The Jewish People Get a Pass

In their introductory chapter, the Ruethers provide an overview of nationalistic and exclusivist streams in all three Abrahamic faiths, pointing out that this is not an issue unique to Judaism.

This is true, but given the focus of the book, we need to pay attention to how this information is put to use. The sins and abuses of Christianity and Islam are not tolerated, whether in social, political, or frankly nationalist forms today. Why then is the Jewish version granted a pass? The Ruethers want to put all three faiths on equal footing in the service of finding a way for them all to "share" the Holy Land. That's a balanced position, but it runs the risk of glossing over the phenomenon of Jewish triumphalism as manifested in political Zionism and its enactment in the State of Israel—the ethnic cleansing of 1947 to 1948, the failure to enact a constitution in line with the democratic principles articulated in the 1948 Declaration of Independence, and the overtly colonial policies pursued after 1967 in the occupied territories. If Israel is to reverse its course and open the way for a settlement based on fairness for all parties to the conflict, whatever has been driving these actions and policies requires exploration and analysis. Here, the Ruethers' balanced, egalitarian approach tends to divert us from this analysis.

The Ruethers' discussion of the religious and secular roots of Zionism provides another window into this issue. In a brief, searching review, they show how modern political Zionism, spawned by the failure of the emancipation of the nineteenth century and by the social and political disintegration of Czarist Russia, was synthesized out of both modern and archaic roots: European nationalism and religious messianism. The Ruethers then describe how, curiously, three additional and very dissimilar strains fed into the creation of the Jewish state: Labor Zionism, Rabbi Abraham Isaac Kook's messianic Zionism, and Jabotinskian fascist revisionism. David Ben-Gurion, the genius architect of Israel, was happy to exploit all three in his fashioning of the modern state. The Ruethers take note of the fact that fundamentalist messianism and fascist nationalism were so seamlessly and effectively integrated into Labor Zionism, the purportedly secularist, universalist mainstream of the Zionist movement. The story is that Ben-Gurion justified his decision to accept the religious parties as political bedfellows by predicting that the success of

Zionism would eventually render obsolete the need for traditional Judaism: was not Rabbinic Judaism created, after all, to replace the Temple and the Jews' political autonomy? With the return of Jewish political self-determination, according to Ben-Gurion's reasoning, orthodox Judaism would atrophy and disappear.

We now know that the opposite has happened—in fact, the state has provided fertile soil for the luxuriant growth of a fundamentalist religious ideology, the proponents of which have served the state and have continued to be supported by it. This ideology continues to play a powerful role in the political process, and bears considerable responsibility for prolonging the current conflict. The Ruethers, in their 2002 postscript to *The Wrath of Jonah,* call for the development of an alternative consciousness on the part of Israeli Jews, uniting with World Christianity in a "critical mass that can midwife a change to a just peace" (247). I fully endorse this view. I see the churches, in alliance with the most progressive elements in the Jewish community here and in Israel, as our major hope for the achievement of this critical mass.[2] I would add, echoing statements that Ruether herself has made

---

2. Rosemary Ruether understood this and made this point as early as 1990 in a collection of essays co-edited with Marc Ellis entitled *Beyond Occupation*. Observing, with uncanny accuracy, that the Israeli government was "paralyzed" from acting to end the occupation, she noted that "American citizens—Christian, Jews, and a growing body of Arab-Americans, both Christian and Muslim, hold a major responsibility for mobilizing the collective will that can force the American government to act decisively in this matter." Notably, she then focuses on the American Christian community in this regard, observing that "The Christian Churches in America have been particularly silent on this issue. They have not taken the role of moral leadership that they have taken in other areas of international justice, such as Central America and South Africa. The reasons for this have been a combination of ignorance and misinformation about the actual situation, guilt for Christianity's evil history of abuse of the Jewish people, and an identification with Israel on grounds of a shared Biblical and Western culture" (193). American churches can no longer plead ignorance, but the barriers of guilt and identification with Jews on theological and cultural grounds remains. Happily, one can no longer level the charge of silence on a blanket basis. American churches, on an individual and denominational basis, have begun to embrace the cause of justice in Palestine in a variety of ways.

repeatedly, that in order for Christians to be fully free to do this, they must break out of the guilt trap. As for the Jews, we must take a long, hard look in the mirror.

In the 2002 postscript, the Ruethers write, "we believe that those who care about the Jewish people should support their liberation from a Zionist bondage to Israel as the supposed solution to anti-Semitism. The actual injustices of Israel, and the ideological cover-up of these mistakes, need to be clearly exposed to critical examination. At the same time, the negative energy of disappointment might be transformed into a positive energy of reform, of both Israel and world Jewish institutions" (223). But they continue with the following: "The break with Zionist ideology might create the new freedom and energy for a broad religious and social renewal of Judaism. It would provide the opportunity for restatements of what it means to be a religiously based and morally concerned global community. This does not mean a rejection but rather a new relationship of world Jewry to the State of Israel, as a political project of the Jewish people" (223).

These are admirable sentiments, but do they stand up to the hard reality of modern Israel? Why do Christians think we can—and should—have a "modern" yet "religiously based," and, what is more, *Jewish* nation state? I applaud the Ruethers' call for a renewal of Judaism, especially with regard to the future of the State of Israel, the continued existence of which they clearly support. Israel is a remarkable achievement. Its people deserve to live in peace and security with their neighbors. The question, however, remains: how can we continue to pursue our "political project," to use the Ruethers' term, of a Jewish state, while maintaining our commitment to human rights and democracy? How can we be liberated from Zionism, and still have our Jewish state? Are we, to use their words, a "religiously based and morally concerned community," or are we a modern nation state? It is *the* challenge facing us as a people and as a faith tradition. Moreover, it is a challenge that we face together with our Christian sisters and brothers, who have been and are the witnesses to our struggle for survival. In view of the political as well as religious crisis wrought by the reality of today's Israel, the future of Judaism and the Jewish people is as much an issue for Christians as it is for the Jews. It's challenging enough to try to deal with this contradiction in talking to Jewish progressives who think we can have our cake and eat it too—a morally just, democratic, Jewish Israel. For this reason, it is increasingly important to confront the willingness of Christians—even the most progressive among them—to give us this ethical, political, and theological slack. Distinctions must be made, and bright lines must be drawn—as agonizing a process as that may be.

For it *is* agonizing: Christians have worked hard for over sixty years, since the confrontation with the ovens, to establish ties of understanding and reconciliation with the Jewish people. Entering into honest dialogue about the failure of the State of Israel to live up to its human rights obligations as a member of the community of nations threatens to disrupt, if not destroy, the results of that hard work. And what makes the situation all the more difficult for Christian laity, clergy, and leadership is the willingness of the organized Jewish community to exploit this reluctance among Christians to tamper with the real gains in interfaith communication that have been achieved. The sad reality now is that more often than not, because of the unwritten rule to keep the issue of Israel off-limits, what once may have been a vibrant, productive enterprise in mutual sharing and respect has become an empty exercise—a careful, brittle détente. Marc Ellis originated the term "the ecumenical deal" to describe how Christians, out of repentance for the Holocaust, "sensitivity" to the feelings of Jews, and fear of being labeled anti-Semitic have—to paraphrase Rosemary Ruether—sold out the Palestinian people. What is even more problematic is that the terms of this deal have been upheld, not only by the most ardent and staunch defenders of Israel, exemplified by the American Zionist organizations, religious denominations, and lobbying groups (we met some of them in chapter 4), but in subtler forms by the Jewish progressive camp in the United States and Israel.

The final section of the book opens with a look at some of those Jewish thinkers.

PART 3

Beyond Interfaith

If we cannot find ways of peace and understanding, if the only way of establishing the Jewish National Home is upon the bayonets of some Empire, our whole enterprise is not worthwhile…It is one of the great civilizing tasks before the Jewish people to enter the promised land, not in the Joshua way, but bringing peace and culture, hard work and sacrifice and love, and a determination to do nothing that cannot be justified before the conscience of the world.

—Judah Magnes

Our rejection of "the other" will undo us. We must incorporate Palestinians and other Arab peoples into the Jewish understanding of history, because they are a part of that history.

—Sara Roy, "Israel's 'Victories' in Gaza Come at a Steep Price"

For centuries, and in the United States until a few decades ago, there was a conventional expectation that everybody would be a member of a church (and perhaps this applied in synagogues too)…This expectation no longer exists…The "good news" in this decline is that, very soon, the only people left in mainline congregations will be the ones who are there for intentional and not conventional reasons. This creates the possibility for

the church once again to become an alternative community rather than a conventional community...
—Marcus Borg, *Jesus: Uncovering the Life, Teachings and Relevance of a Religious Revolutionary*

While a Christian congregation in the prosperous United States is not at all parallel to subcommunities of resistance and alternative in more manifestly brutal societies, the church as a subcommunity in the United States is a thinkable mode of ministry.
—Walter Brueggemann, *The Prophetic Imagination*

Chapter 9

Except Thou Bless Me: Jewish Progressives Wrestle with Israel

> People bring tragedy on themselves, after all, not with malice but with fidelity—not by doing the wrong thing but by doing the right thing for too long…I hope to tell a heartbreaking tragedy of this sort, how Israelis who could not surrender the romance of Zionism harmed—and may yet wreck—their country's chance to survive as a democracy.
>
> —Bernard Avishai, *The Tragedy of Zionism*

In previous chapters, we've explored how Christian thinkers have grappled with the complexities of land, covenant, and interfaith reconciliation as related to the Israel-Palestine conflict. But it must be said that Jews face even bigger challenges as we search for a compassionate, honest way out of the tragic dilemma in which we find ourselves. Nowhere is this struggle more apparent than among the most progressive elements in the Jewish community, both in the United States and in Israel. Israeli statesman and writer Avraham Burg is a striking example. Burg was the chairman of the Jewish Agency for Israel and former Speaker of the Knesset. He is now an outspoken and, in some circles, notorious Israeli social critic. Burg was born in Jerusalem in 1955 into the Israeli "aristocracy" of the immigrant German-Jewish community—a community rich in intellectual lineage and holding a privileged place in Israeli society. Burg, until his abrupt resignation from Israeli politics and his emergence as an outspoken critic of Israeli policy in 2004, exemplified the typical Israeli: born after statehood, fiercely patriotic, firmly grounded in Jewish history and his place in it as one privileged to see the end of exile and the building of a new Jewish society.

Burg's 2008 book *The Holocaust Is Over: We Must Rise From Its Ashes* is a courageous piece of writing. In the book, Burg sets himself to accomplish nothing less than the uncovering of what in his view have been the myths and deceptions that political Zionism has inflicted upon the citizens of Israel. Burg's central theme is the persistent effect of the Holocaust. What is the result, asks Burg, of our never-ending belief that the world is against us? What happens when we turn the Arabs into the Nazis and see every act of violence or conflict as an imminent threat to our very existence? Burg credits the preoccupation with the Holocaust for the poisoning of Israeli society, politically and morally: "The centrality of the armed forces in our lives, the role of language in legitimizing the illegitimate, the infiltration of a right-wing narrative into the mainstream and the indifference of the passive majority—these are the major players that allow racism to contaminate our world" (66).

Israeli society is paying a high cost for this preoccupation with the past, contends Burg. He opens his book with a powerful image. Burg tells the story of the day he visited the zoo with his son:

> I found myself sitting and watching the captive monkeys. All of them jumped energetically and playfully from one branch to another. Holding on with one hand, the other stretched in the air toward the next branch, up they went. But one monkey sat alone and did not mingle. I asked a passing staff member what was wrong. "He is different," replied the veterinarian. "He can't climb because he is afraid to let go of the branch. If you hold a branch with both hands, you cannot move up. This is his fate," he commented sadly. "He sits on the floor all day like a person in mourning, isolated from the life around him." (9)

Burg does not hold back from expressing his sorrow and outrage, and his fear for Israel's current, self-inflicted peril. He does not refrain from employing "hot-button" words (e.g., "genocide") and raising inflammatory subjects (e.g., the threat of another Holocaust justifies all actions). Even though these are the very arguments that in the current discourse are used as ammunition by those who seek to invalidate all criticism of Israel, Burg calls it as he sees it: "Israel today does not stand at the gates of the gas chambers. It is reasonable to assume that if the values of the Palestinians' transfer and Torah-style genocide will be on our government's agenda, I and many of my friends will no longer be free citizens of this state. We will struggle with all the legitimate means at our disposal to prevent our state from committing moral suicide" (64).

A New Judaism

In a chapter titled "A New Judaism," Burg lays out the tragic dilemma in which modern Zionists find themselves. He traces how deeply ingrained attitudes of grandeur and superiority developed during different periods of Jewish history as a way of managing the effects of near-continual oppression by the majority culture. This, writes Burg, was an adaptation to severe and sustained stress. He explains that to preserve hope and the sense of a future, we had to maintain ourselves as separate and aloof. Burg invokes the unavoidable analogy of the abused child who becomes the abusive parent, the battered who becomes the batterer. "In the same way," writes Burg, "a humiliated and persecuted people can become similar to the worst of its tormentors" (189). He is prepared to go all the way on this point:

> It would be wrong for us to whitewash the truth and say that we are immune and that it will not happen to us. It happened to the Germany of Schiller, Goethe and Mendelssohn, and also to us. In Israel of Agnon, Oz and Rabbi Ginzburg, bad things happened. The source of some is the trauma, and source of others is the groundwater of Jewish identity and the segregationist,

confrontational nature of our national existence for ages. I fear certain rabbis and their overt and covert theories, and I also fear there are some thugs among us. There is a built-in element of discrimination, arrogance, and preference for anything that comes from Jewish genes. It is much more present than deniers wish to see. (190)

Burg displays a commendable and in some ways astonishing capacity for honest self-scrutiny. Yet we can also observe a curious ambivalence in his position. On the one hand, Burg seems completely willing to acknowledge that there is a fundamental problem with modern Jewish identity, a fatal flaw in how we see ourselves in relation to the world. Yet there is also a holding back. Note the use of the passive voice in his reference to the abusive treatment of the Palestinians by Israel: "bad things happened." But Burg's distancing from the sins of Israel that he has so courageously exposed is actually much more profound than an excusable use of the passive voice. In fact, Burg goes on to effectively disown the violence by attributing the crimes against Palestinians in the occupied territories to "certain rabbis" and "thugs." Even as he describes the fatal flaw in modern Jewish identity with rare brilliance and razor-sharp accuracy, Burg neutralizes the power of his critique in a straw man maneuver. The more he exposes the dangerousness and ugliness of these "thugs," the more he distances himself—and the government system that nurtures them—from their activities and their ideology.

Burg opens his chapter exposing what he calls the "great darkness" that threatens Israel—racist, fundamentalist Jewish supremacists. They are represented by Rabbi Yitzchak Ginzburg, a leader of "the new religious and spiritual radicalism in Israel" typified by the West Bank Hills youth and their parents, described by Burg as a "rabble of dangerous fanatics" (182). Ginzburg believes that by virtue of their election by God and by their inherent superiority the Jews are entitled to possess the entire Land of Israel. Quoting from a privately published book by Ginzburg entitled *Kingdom of Israel*, Burg gives us a taste of Ginzburg's credo: "The land," writes Ginzburg, "should be settled by those who chose to become the people of God…the [people who] gave morality and intelligence to all the peoples" (182). "Ginzburg is just one of many," writes Burg (182). These are the Jews, he tells us, who are the perpetrators of the violence against Palestinians in the West Bank, who represent the vanguard of the settler movement, going back to the early days of the occupation.

Burg mercilessly exposes the ugliness of the extremist ideology underlying the settler movement: fundamentalist Jews committed out of religious fervor to the colonization of all of historic Palestine. He cites Rabbi Ovadiah Yosef, the current spiritual leader of the ultra-orthodox Shas political party in the Israeli Knesset. In a weekly address after Hurricane Katrina devastated New Orleans, Yosef declared that the natural disaster was visited upon the "negroes" of New Orleans because they were unbelievers—literally because they do not study Torah.

Rabbi Yosef is the Jewish version of Pastor John Hagee, the hugely influential American Christian evangelist who famously explained Hurricane Katrina as God's punishment of the people of New Orleans for fostering homosexuality. Ginzburg and Yosef are only two of many such people infecting our society, writes Burg. The results, he says, are predictable: "Eventually there is hooliganism, violence, and lethal incidents. All these connect to a clear and present threat to the modern Jewish identity of the state and its current form" (182).

A close look at this last statement reveals how Burg uses the settlers to distance Israel from responsibility for the occupation. To make his point, Burg has chosen the most egregious examples, those sure to shock. Then he effectively disowns the evil with the passive voice: "there is hooliganism." In so doing, Burg has failed to address the most important issue: What causes this criminal behavior? Who is responsible? Who is steering the ship? Are the "rabble of fanatics" the ones who are constructing the land grab wall, erecting the checkpoints, demolishing the eight thousand homes to clear East Jerusalem for Jewish settlement, and building the network of restricted roads? Did these pathological fringe groups exist in 1947 and 1948 when Jewish forces systematically expelled three-quarters of a million men, women, and children from their cities and villages in the Galilee, coastal plain, Negev, and Jerusalem corridor? Are Gush Emunim and the West Bank Hills youth responsible for the continuing dispossession of the remaining Bedouins in the Negev and the hills around Jerusalem to make way for continued Jewish expansion? Radical fundamentalists may support the project, but are they the architects of the government-supported plan to cleanse the Old City basin of its remaining non-Jewish inhabitants?

Rabbi Ginzburg is a decoy in this argument. He is not the architect of the occupation. He did not plan the ethnic cleansing of Palestine in the years leading up to the establishment of the state. No, the enemy here, to quote the comic strip character Pogo, is us. The clear and present danger is to be found in the policies of the state itself, a political power structure of largely secular people, a corps of generals and bureaucrats who don't study Torah and don't go to synagogue. Burg is ready to acknowledge this, but alongside his demonization of the radical fringe is a striking minimization of the official actions of the state itself. In the following passage, for example, Burg argues that we have become like our ignorant, racist tormentors in Europe. He maintains that this no longer makes sense, since "the State of Israel is meant to be the cure for all Exilic illnesses. Yet the separatists carry on the past's inferiority complex and convert it into an obsession of absolute superiority. Its practical outcome is discrimination in many areas and a hint of racism that taints our government's decisions" (190).

A *hint* of racism? Discrimination in *many areas*? After setting up this bigger-than-life enemy, this stain on the conscience of the state, Burg's striking act of minimizing tells the tale: it's not us; it's *them*. They—the fanatical rabble—are the ones who present the danger to our national well-being. The state, says Burg, was supposed to fix our collective character problem, make us into a new people, and end the ills that come from a "harsh and painful exile." And, he appears to be saying, if it were not for "the separatists," this would all be working out.

This is, therefore, a sad book, and an instructive one. For here is our fundamental challenge: as long as we insist on locating the problem in those "others," we won't be able to fix it. We will not be able to follow through with the necessary, painful work of change and reform. The Jewish state—Burg has this right—rather than curing the ills of exile, will enact it in the hideous fashion that only empowerment can bring. As Israeli journalist Amira Hass pointed out in her story on the violent Hebron settlers quoted in an earlier chapter, *we* created these people, and we continue to allow them, in fact empower them, to carry out their vicious deeds.

Searching for a Future, Trapped in the Past

Burg's book is written to inform the future, but in fact it looks back in an effort to provide Burg with a link to his past. It is a past to which he is profoundly connected but that he also wants to leave behind, a past that he feels has trapped Israel in the Holocaust. The State of Israel, says Burg, provided a rebirth for the Jewish people—a people of wanderers, dreamers, fighters, pragmatists, and holy men. But can it be reborn into community, into humankind? This is what Burg claims he wants, but I fear that his brand of reform will not get us there. In his penultimate chapter, Burg provides us with another demonstration of this problem. Here, Burg undertakes a discussion of Israel's national days of commemoration. These rituals, he maintains, demonstrate Israel's self-absorption and fixation on suffering. Burg catalogs them and offers alternatives. For example, he objects to *Yom Hashoah*—Israel's Holocaust Memorial Day—because it is designed to coincide with the date of the Warsaw Ghetto uprising, which Burg associates with Jewish hero worship, self-absorption, glorification of the military, and Zionist myth making. Instead, Burg wants to change the date to January 27, the day of the liberation of Auschwitz. In this way, he suggests, Jews can join with the other peoples who suffered in the war and who were symbolically liberated from Nazism on that day. On that day, he writes, "we will study other people's holocausts...We will convert our personal wounds into a cure for all humanity" (233). Burg proposes that a second Holo-caust Day be observed on May 9, in solidarity with the Soviets over their victory over Nazi Germany. Finally, he suggests that there be a *third* day to commemorate the *shoah,* to be observed on the ninth day of Av in the Jewish calendar, the traditional day of mourning for the destruction of the Temple in Jerusalem. "This day," Burg writes, "will be a time for our own private memorial, a family gathering, ours alone" (234). This day will be just for Jews—our Temple, our national catastrophe.

As I read this, I feel that, beyond the oddness of this set of suggestions, something is wrong. Then it comes to me: *something is missing.* In this catalog, there is no mention of the Nakba. The Palestinians' catastrophe is absent from Burg's reflections and his search for days of memorial that we can share with humankind. His alternative days of commemoration and mourning, for all the talk of joining with humanity, are examples of yet more self-absorption. In his stated effort to be emancipated from a tribal, self-protective past, Burg misses the urgent, pressing need for reconciliation with those *we have wronged.* Burg's suggested revisions of Israel's national myths are just another version of "light to the nations." He has succeeded only in creating another national myth, a myth in which we, of course, are the center.

There is more. In the book Burg discusses three fundamentals of Israeli life that need to be repaired. He first sets his sights on the Law of Return. I am immediately interested. This law, one of the very first enacted by the State of Israel, is the cornerstone of political Zionism and the state's raison d'être. It specifies that all Jews have the automatic right to Israeli citizenship. In what fashion, I wonder, will Burg take issue with it? Burg explains that he doesn't like the Law of Return because, to his mind, it is a mirror image of the Nuremberg Laws of Nazi Germany that condemned all Jews to death. For him, therefore, the Law of Return is problematic because it means that Hitler is still defining what it means to be a Jew! Here, Burg shows himself to be stuck in the very past that he claims he so desperately wants to escape. What is most sad—most tragically ironic—about his argument is that the most pressing issue for Israel's future is not the *Law* of Return but the *Right* of Return. It is the right claimed by the descendants of the eight hundred thousand Palestinians, displaced to make way for Israel, to return to their homes in what is now the State of Israel. Burg is so preoccupied with the past that he can't see the elephant in the room, *the* issue upon which hangs the future of his country: the fate of the people dispossessed by his father's generation.

Burg does devote four pages to a discussion of the Palestinian refugee issue, in which he acknowledges that the State of Israel bears responsibility for the refugees. He laments that the government of Israel has never acknowledged this fact. But he can't confront the problem directly, resorting instead to excuses and arguments that are more properly the province of staunch defenders of Israel "right or wrong." Burg hauls out the false equivalency of comparing the Palestinians displaced and dispossessed by Israel to the Jewish refugees from Hebron, Ramallah, Cairo, and Kurdistan.[1] We Jews solved our "refugee problem," he argues, gathering Jews from all over the world into Israel; why can't the Arabs do the same? Finally, he plays the victim by complaining that "the heirs and descendants of our old European persecutors, who had slaughtered us and expelled us from Europe beaten and injured… use the refugee problem to denounce our leadership and try to undermine the moral basis of the Jewish people's state (84).

Burg can't seem to confront the real issue underlying the refugee problem for Israel—that acknowledging Israel's responsibility for the plight of Palestinian refugees presents a grave threat to the Jewish character of the state. This is the dilemma of the Jewish progressive: On the one hand, he clings to the dream of a

---

1. During the twentieth century and at an accelerated pace after 1947, hundreds of thousands of Jews left Arab lands to settle in Israel and other countries. According to the World Organization of Jews from Arab Countries, this migration was the result of anti-Jewish violence and the systematic policies of the governments of these countries. Claims have been made of Zionist involvement in prompting these emigrations. The issue is complex and controversial. Jews also were displaced from Palestinian cities such as Ramallah and Hebron as the result of anti-Jewish violence in the early decades of the century.

Jewish state in the belief that it is a necessary bulwark against the repetition of the trauma of Europe. On the other hand, he can't face the present situation squarely and see that the Palestinian people are an inescapable part of his reality. Burg can't allow himself to see that without reconciliation with the Palestinian people there is no future for Israel. Certainly it will not be a future that conforms to his dream of a better Jewish people, a Jewish people who repudiate the paranoia, exceptionalism, and racism of the fundamentalist settler rabbis he excoriates, a Jewish people who can join humanity and play by a single set of rules. Where, for example, in Burg's discussion of Israel's future—in which he invokes Marx, Trotsky, Heine, Spinoza, Freud, and Heschel, and asks, "Can the State of Israel best herself to the level of those individuals and serve the world as collective and universalist Jews?" (218)—is there any mention of Israel's continued and flagrant violation of international law in colonizing occupied territory? The issue simply does not arise. This makes Burg's follow up question—"Can Israel help free the world of its hostility block and blaze new trails to the venue of peacemaking, reconciliation, and acceptance?" (218)—merely rhetorical. It sounds nice, but it is just a new brand of Jewish exceptionalism. It is the latest version of "light to the nations," left-wing Zionist style.

Except Thou Bless Me

Jews do not have a monopoly on the very human qualities of grandiosity and self-delusion. But we come by these failings honestly. The biblical narrative of the lives of the patriarchs records these very human struggles dramatically and with sensitivity and nuance. Genesis chapter 32 tells the story of the patriarch Jacob at midlife. A wealthy man with two wives, eleven children, and herds of livestock, he is facing his greatest crisis: a confrontation with his brother Esau, from whom he had stolen their father's blessing twenty years earlier. Jacob learns that Esau is approaching his camp, "four hundred men with him" (Gen. 32:6 [KJV]). Terrified that Esau has come to kill him, Jacob divides his camp, hoping to save half his family, servants, and herds. He also sends gifts ahead, thinking to appease his brother and earn his forgiveness. Night falls and Jacob, according the biblical narrative, "was left alone; and there wrestled a man with him until the breaking of the day" (32:24). It is the dark night of the soul for the patriarch. His past has caught up with him, and he is afraid. Stubbornly and with remarkable endurance, Jacob struggles with this mysterious adversary throughout the night. At daybreak, the man begs Jacob to release him. But Jacob says to him, "I will not let thee go, except thou bless me" (32:26).

Jacob has won; he has demonstrated that he can prevail through perseverance and determination. But this is not enough—he must exact a blessing. Jacob believes that it is God with whom he has been wrestling, and that his own fortitude and agency has earned him legitimacy and power. "I have seen God face to face," proclaims Jacob, as he limps off to meet his brother and his fate.

Burg has struggled with his demons long and hard, and he has survived the night. His insight into the Jewish pathology of victimhood and our cultural servitude to a heroic, supremacist ideology is deep, on target, courageous, and compassionate. He is willing to look in the mirror, and what he sees are the deep flaws in the Zionist dream and the destructive effect of the Zionist myths. But he cannot or will not take the next step. He cannot or will not look directly at the Zionist enterprise itself and ask: What if? What if the concept and reality of the Jewish state is unsustainable and, in view of our experience and our current perspective, an error? In speeches Burg talks about leaving Zionism behind, consigning it to history—but can that translate into leaving behind the Jewish state itself, the real-life creation of that same eclipsed ideology? Burg loves the Jewish people, but it appears that this love includes a clinging to its modern-day child, the State of Israel. Like a loving parent not yet ready or able to acknowledge the truth about his child, Burg is not yet ready or able to let go. We are reminded of Burg's own analogy of the zoo monkey who, unable to let go of the branch to which he is clinging, is unable to participate in the wider society. We must be able to ask, what if? What would the future of the Jewish people be without Israel as it is currently constituted, as a state for Jews and only Jews? Burg, a religious Jew and Israeli statesman, cannot ask that question, at least not in public or in writing. His critique of Zionism and of the state itself, searing and damning as it is, arrives at the following conclusion, which appears to be its final destination: we can make it work. We must make it work. Burg is asking for a blessing. Like Jacob's ultimatum to the visitor in the night, this request is really a demand—you *must* bless this project; you must grace it with success.

Of course this tactic, while common enough, doesn't work in the end. You cannot force success from a flawed project by dint of perseverance and brute strength. And here is the final lesson to be learned from the story of Jacob's night of struggle: when, the next day, he meets Esau, it is a joyful reunion. Esau tearfully embraces him—all is forgiven. They are brothers, after all. And then Jacob says an astonishing thing to Esau: "I have seen thy face, as though I had seen the face of God" (33:10).[2] Jacob had thought that he had encountered God the previous night—encountered God and prevailed. The next day, he realized that it was himself who he had met during the night: his own fears, his own self-involvement. The face of God that he had sought was waiting for him across the river. It was the face of his brother, whom he had wronged and who had already forgiven him. The answer to our dilemma is waiting, across the river, across the boundary of walls and defenses that we have built to protect ourselves from our own fears. Our brothers (and sisters) await us.

A Sacred Duty from a Perfect Grievance

Burg's struggle exemplifies the conflict experienced by many progressive Jews. It is the profound contradiction between opposition to exclusivist and racist elements of Israeli society, politics, and culture and a fundamental commitment to the goals of the

---

2. I am grateful to Rabbi Brian Walt for pointing out this text.

Zionist project. This conflict is evident in the work of Rabbis for Human Rights, an Israeli human rights organization. According to its web site, Rabbis for Human Rights "was founded in 1988, in response to serious abuses of human rights by the Israeli military authorities in the suppression of the Intifada."[3] Over the years, Rabbis for Human Rights has expanded its mission, taking on a range of human rights issues in Israel, including abuse of foreign workers, abuse of women, and availability of health care. Most visibly, however, the organization operates in the occupied territories, acting alongside Palestinians in nonviolently resisting the taking of land and the violent harassment of Palestinians by Jewish settlers in the West Bank.

In December 2008, Rabbis for Human Rights and its American arm, Rabbis for Human Rights North America, held the second North American Conference on Judaism and Human Rights in Washington, DC. The last day of the conference featured an address by Rabbi Arthur Green, a prominent Jewish scholar and rector of the Rabbinical School of Hebrew College. Rabbi Green, who identified himself in the title of his address as a "religious Jew and secular Zionist," described himself in his address as one who "for more than four decades now [has] stood on the critical left flank of Israel's supporters, urging peace with the Palestinians, negotiated return of territories, and a viable two-state solution to the problems of the Middle East" (Green 2008).

---

3. "Intifada" here refers to The First Intifada (1987–1991). It was a largely nonviolent Palestinian uprising against Israeli rule in the territories captured by Israel in the 1967 war. The uprising (literally, "shaking off" in Arabic) began in the Jabalia refugee camp and quickly spread through Gaza, the West Bank, and East Jerusalem. The widespread nature and persistence of the Intifada is generally explained by the deep sense of frustration among Palestinians who were living under the Israeli occupation, which was characterized by brutal treatment, taking of land, intensive building of Jewish settlements, and a increasing disappointment and anger at the Palestinian Liberation Organization for failing to effectively protect Palestinian rights and bring about an improvement in their situation.

In his address, Green grapples with the problem that "we co-exist as Yisra'el [Jews, the people of Israel], with another entity, Medinat Yisra'el [the State of Israel]—one that has citizens, Jewish and non-Jewish, borders, customs officials, and all the rest, and to which we are …of course closely related by sympathy, pride, and deep if agonized involvement. How do we begin to sort it all out?" As a rabbi, Green searches for the answer in the texts and traditions of Judaism. He is firmly attached to the idea of Israel as a *Jewish place*, a place inextricably connected to the Jews' relationship with God. Quoting in Hebrew from the Jewish prayer for peace, in which Jews self-identify as *Yisrael amekha*, translated as "Israel Your [God's] people," Green describes Jerusalem as "the place where many of us have most fully experienced the sense of Yisrael amekha, and the undisputed heart of Jewish love and longing, alongside lots of pain and agony."

Green acknowledges that the wording of this prayer, which emphasizes the Jewish people's specialness, must now be reconciled with the modern world's "borderless" and universal quality. But in the context of this modern age, he asks, "What is left of our distinctiveness? In what way do we want to go forward as a people?" Green claims that "we post-Holocaust Jews have abandoned the ancient claim that we stand at the center of human history." But Green, although granting that we may not be at the center, seems unwilling to relinquish the notion that we are special. He continues:

> …does anything remain of the uniquely Jewish vision of messiah bringing a more glorious human future? And is there any special place for the survival of the people Israel, as such, within it? Is our legitimacy as a distinctive human group just like any other, that of the Roma, the Tutsi, or the Lao, except that it is our own? Do we still have something we want to offer to the world, or are we just exercising our "normalized," as Zionists once said, natural right and struggle for self-preservation, along with everybody else? In what sense can that be sacred to us believers in a single universal God?

Reading Green's words, I find myself asking, as I have asked myself repeatedly: what is this Jewish desire for specialness? And further, does this uniqueness, this specialness, confer special rights? Does this specialness make us, to use Green's words, *unlike* "any other," conferring rights, entitlements, liberties not allowed to "everyone else"? For example, if another one of these "everybody else[s]" were to occupy and by military force maintain control over land belonging to others, proceed to colonize it, and then pursue a program of ethnically cleansing those others, what would be the response to this behavior?

To follow the logic of Green's argument, if the Jewish people are "just" exercising our "normalized" right to self preservation in establishing the State of Israel, could we be doing this in a way that does not create these terrible problems? What if, in the course of claiming the right to establish a modern Jewish homeland in historic Palestine, we were to follow the rules required for the rest of humankind? To bring in the often-repeated plea that Israel is simply claiming the "right to exist"—this is not about Israel's right to exist. The issue at hand is whether Israel is playing by the rules required of all other nation states. Israel does exist—the issue is what kind of Israel is viable and sustainable in a post-colonial world.

A Unique Tale of Suffering

Like Green, as a Jew I feel the agony of my involvement with the State of Israel. The question is: what do we do with these feelings? I wonder what Green means when he asks, "How do we begin to sort it out?" Does he mean let us find a way to make Zionism work? Or does he mean let us find a way to resolve the "complicated" reality of a place that some Jews regard—to use Israeli historian Avi Shlaim's blunt term—as a "rogue" state (2009), and that for others is the center of their spiritual lives? I share Green's feelings of sympathy with and pride for Israel; we come from the same background, were raised in the same mix of postwar Rabbinic Judaism and modern political Zionism. But I fear that by "sort it out" Green means "make it better," or "make it work." And this earnest desire to hold on to the idea of a Jewish state, a state maintained by and for Jews, flies in the face of facts, facts that are becoming more and more visible in the harsh light of current affairs.

Zionism, as is so clear from Green's words, is an idea—an idea rooted in Jewish history, Jewish experience, and Jewish yearnings. But, as Bernard Avishai in his 2002 *The Tragedy of Zionism* observes, "Zionism's central ideas, while sound in their time, were never meant to serve as the organizing principles of a democratic state." Avishai continues, "Three generations after the Zionist revolution succeeded, Zionist ideas had become wrong. Their persistence in Israeli political life was unforeseen and, in retrospect, unfortunate; the Utopian improvisations that had given priority to inventing the nation—collective, exclusive land tenure, for example—became the justification for serious acts of discrimination against individuals. A post-World War II Zionist consensus emerged by 1948, according to which Hebrew settlement was not only a way of restoring Hebrew culture in the ancient Biblical land but, more important, rebuilding a decrepit Jewish people…Nationalism seems a sacred duty, derived from a perfect grievance" (xvi).

Here is the crux of the matter: Jewish nationalism as expressed in the State of Israel is in conflict with our modern values of fairness, universalism, and commitment to human rights. As Jews who are citizens of the world, we need to separate our commitment to these values from any religiously or culturally based attachment to the Zionist ideas Avishai talks about in the above passage. And that, to use Green's term, is agonizing. Green names the agony, but I wonder if he is prepared to feel it completely, to reach down and experience the bottom of it. The paradox here, and it is an agonizing paradox, is the fact that in order for Israel to survive, it must, in true prophetic fashion, fathom how it has strayed from the path of righteousness. It must be able to see how it has put its survival in jeopardy by claiming, to use Avishai's words, a right to commit "serious acts of discrimination." We are in the territory of Walter Brueggemann's warnings against the fatal habit of empire, or, to use theologian Walter Wink's term, the myth of "redemptive violence" (1992, 13). This grievous risk, which I fear the project of political Zionism has taken, will not be sorted out without facing the requirement to confront its myths and attachments. It is a kind of death that must be confronted. Royal consciousness, Brueggemann reminds us, "is committed to numbness about death. It is unthinkable for the King to imagine or experience the end of his favorite historical arrangements. Royal consciousness consists of and depends upon the denial of pain, fear, suffering. The empire will endure forever—this is the message of numbness and self-deception" (2001, 42).

Part of the agony in letting go of the Zionist dream of a national Jewish homeland is the fear of what may replace it. What will Israel become? We would prefer to cling to the relative certainty of the future we had planned. But without being prepared to imagine a different future, we are lost. We will continue to pursue a catastrophically flawed project.

Is the answer, then, as defenders of Israel might ask, to abandon Israel, disassemble its impressive infrastructure, pack up its culture, and, most frighteningly, forsake the security of its citizens? Are we to, as the pre-Israel, "decrepit" ghetto Jew would do in the classic Zionist imagery, passively offer our throats to the slaughterers? Hardly. Again, the question is not whether or not to be emancipated from a condition of helplessness and passivity, but by what means that emancipation is to be achieved. Here again we must look with clarity at Zionism itself, rather than through the distorting lens of sentiment and mythology. Avishai reminds us that, at its inception, nothing was certain about where the Zionist movement was going. "Nor," he writes, "can we assume Zionism to be the intention behind apparent political consequences. Today it is taken for granted, for example, that Zionism aimed to create a 'Jewish state.' But most competing streams in the Zionist movement were, from the start, never quite sure what a Jew was, and were even less certain what political structures would make sense: bi-nationalism, federation, or statehood" (2002, xvi).

What appears to have happened, now that the Jewish state has become a reality, is that Jewish identity and belief has shaped itself within the parameters and requirements of the state, making the preservation of the concept of a Jewish national project in Palestine a primary goal for Jewish life. This effort converges with a stream in Jewish identity that connects powerfully to the myth of the autonomous, proud, triumphant, and—perhaps most significantly—redemptive kingdom of the biblical narrative. This narrative contains two fundamental features. The first is our emancipation from slavery: in the biblical idiom, we were "brought out" of Egypt. And in that very phrase is contained the second feature—it was God who so redeemed us. The Exodus and the coming into the land (as one "comes into" an inheritance) were a continuation and fulfillment of the covenant. Political Zionism tapped into this feature of Jewish identity. It is as if two thousand years of Jewish participation in world civilization had ceased to be relevant, as if the emancipation—tragically incomplete as it was—had not occurred and did not matter. The Jewish people, although living and fully participating in the contemporary world, were, in much of their reality as well as in their core identity, still a people apart, their separateness confirmed by a history of oppression and suffering. This appears to be the implicit assumption in Rabbi Green's argument. In his formulation, it is the experience of suffering and the longing for protection at the core of our experience and self-perception that ties us forever to the idea of the ingathering in Zion. How then are we ever to let go of the Zionist dream, however much it crashes against the realities, requirements, and even the benefits of living in the modern world? The answer, implies Green, is that we must not let go, for to be Jewish is different, and here is why:

> The Jewish people to which I belong was forged in what Scripture (Deut. 4:20) already call the "iron furnace" of Egypt, the place of our shared suffering and enslavement…It is there that Israel became a people, one bearing a shared burden; it is there to which God looked down and "knew." At Sinai, we are told,

Moses, Aaron, and the elders beheld "the God of Israel," under whose feet was "something like a sapphire brick, bright as the very sky" (Ex. 24:10). We are told that this brick was brought by an angel from Egypt. When Pharaoh declared the Israelites had to make their own straw, the work hours became unbearable. Women tried to help their husbands by bringing their meals to the field. A pregnant woman miscarried in the heat and her baby fell into the mixer that was used to make bricks from the straw. An angel, seeing the tragedy, brought the brick to heaven and placed it under God's feet, so that Israel's suffering not be forgotten.

This is a parable of formation, the creation story of a people. It is, Green continues, "a tale of oppression and human suffering…It could be told of any suffering, that of black slaves in the American South or child slaves in today's Southeast Asia. *But it is also uniquely a tale of Jewish suffering,* one with which we identify as offspring of a people long oppressed, living in an age when survivors of the Holocaust are still in our midst. The people Israel is the people that lived through Egypt together, was redeemed together, sang together at the shore of the Red Sea, and *has not forgotten*" (2008; emphasis added).

If it is true that we were "forged" in the furnace of slavery, what would it mean to come up from there, to emerge as a people who do not define ourselves, at least in part, by our history of being oppressed? Could our true redemption, our true emancipation from Marc Ellis's "liturgy of destruction" begin with the recognition of how this "unique tale of Jewish suffering" is now manifesting in the darkness of ethnic cleansing, occupation, and the enabling of the fundamentalist racism that has gained ascendancy in Israeli politics? If Green is going to take us to the shores of the Red Sea, then let us listen to the song we sang there:

I will sing to the Lord, for He has triumphed gloriously;
Horse and driver He has hurled into the sea.
The Lord is my strength and my might;
He is become my deliverance. (Exod. 15:1–2)

This is a triumphalist anthem, a hymn of praise to a warrior God. Certainly, the solution for all that suffering, the desired outcome of our history of having been enslaved and then redeemed, is not to become a warrior state, a nation that through its official government policies steals the land and violates the human rights of a subject population in direct contravention of international law. This is not a good solution. Rather, to "sort it out," to find our way through, we must find a way out of our specialness, our attachment to our suffering. And precisely because this is a problem that stems from self-absorption, we can't do it ourselves. In the Bible story, we had Moses, backed up by God himself, to arrange our deliverance. The Egyptians were a side story—their only role was to provide a stubborn pharaoh and to die by the thousands at the hands of the deity. Today, the rules have changed. Today, if we are to leave Egypt, we must first come to terms with the Egyptians. This means we must take responsibility for what we have done and actively reconcile and join with those with whom we have been embattled. Marc Ellis, having named for us the liturgy of destruction, calls on us to recognize that we are not alone in history.

> The liturgy of destruction heard from the Palestinian side confirms the initial and ongoing Jewish intuition that Palestinians are as intimate to Jewish history as Jews are to Christian history…The search begins for a way back to the community vocation that affirms rather than destroys…paradoxically, the critical thought necessary to break through the ideologies and theologies that legitimate power rest with the defeated and marginalized.
>
> What is startling for Jews, as it was at first for Christians, is that today Palestinians call the Jewish community to account. For they have lived on the other side of Jewish power and see through the ideological and theological justifications of their oppression. The German Catholic theologian Johann Baptist Metz wrote, "We Christians can never go back behind Auschwitz; to go beyond Auschwitz if we see clearly, is impossible by us for ourselves. It is possible only together with the victims of Auschwitz." For Jews today it might be said, "We Jews can never go back behind empowerment;

to go beyond empowerment, if we see clearly, is impossible for us by ourselves. It is possible only together with the victims of our empowerment, the Palestinian people." (2004, 162–163)

This was not the vision presented by Rabbi Green at the Rabbis for Human Rights conference. For Green is looking back, not forward. Jewish identity is still about our suffering and how to meet the threat to our survival, and the answer is Zionism: "After Hitler came to power and the world avoided responsibility for the gathering storm, it became clear that we Jews needed both the protection and the pride offered by having a state of our own. *The political Zionists were made right by the history we all dreaded.* Israel as a place of refuge and the ingathering of exiles became a necessity after the war, and it is still unthinkable to me not to have Israel as a Jewish state" (Green 2008; emphasis added).

But Green goes further: the need for physical or political refuge, compelling as that may be, is still not enough of a reason for the state. Israel provides *meaning*—it is not merely a state; it is *Zion*, the dwelling place for the Jewish spirit and its ethos: "The Jewish people's return to Zion and the creation of a Jewish state in the aftermath of the Holocaust and at the very moment of the breakup of the colonial era in world history surely calls upon us to think about its meaning, all the more so as we hear undeniable echoes of ancient prophecies in the return of Israel to our ancient land. The coming together of these events first tells us that a society created by Jews in what we believe to be a holy place needs to be built on the universal values of Judaism" (2008).

A Humanitarian Zionism?

It is certain that not all the members of Rabbis for Human Rights would subscribe to each of the points Rabbi Green makes in this address. But what he expresses here is in line with the group's fundamental beliefs. According to its web site, "Rabbis for Human Rights reflects a Zionist commitment to the values of justice and equality, as expressed in Israel's Declaration of Independence. It also demonstrates its understanding of a Jewish responsibility to defy silent complicity, to bring specific human rights grievances to the attention of the Israeli public, and to pressure the appropriate authorities for their redress…Rabbis for Human Rights gives voice to the tradition's concern for the stranger and others vulnerable within society."[4]

Translation: We are a light to the nations.

The human rights work of Rabbis for Human Rights is rooted in an exceptionalist ground of being—"a sacred duty derived from a perfect grievance": *We are victims and need this protection, this army, this land. We are good and so we can make this project of ethnic nationalism good. And even in the face of evidence that we don't always act with goodness, our specialness can mitigate this evil. We help Palestinians harvest their olives by defying settler violence. We put our bodies on the line opposing house demolitions and other forms of ethnic cleansing. We work for a more just society inside Israel.*

And these *are* good, righteous acts! But do they cancel out the fundamental sin of creating and maintaining a Jewish state on the ruins of an entire people? Do they wash it away? Do they confront the root cause of the evil?

And certainly, Green is cognizant of the urgency and seriousness of the problem. He writes, "Our faith and the legacy of our history cannot permit a Jewish society to act as a colonial society, one in which a self-defined 'superior' population imposes itself upon, and appropriates the resources, including the land, of a 'native' human group, whom it then deprives of freedom. If it sounds to our ears as though Israel's founding might be too close for comfort to that description, it is our job, as *Yisra'el 'amekha*, to make sure that is not the whole story. Perhaps we did not fully realize how deeply we would be put to the test…" (2008).

---

4. This is a reference to one of the several passages in the Old Testament in which God commands the people of Israel to deal compassionately and equitably with non-Israelites living in their midst. Leviticus 19:33–34 reads: "When a stranger resides with you in your land, you shall not wrong him. The stranger who resides with you shall be to you as one of your citizens; you shall love him as yourself, for you were strangers in the land of Egypt" (Jewish Publication Society).

If, as Rabbi Green is suggesting, the test of the Jewish people's specialness and worthiness is the outcome of this experiment of an ethnic nationalist homeland in Palestine, then I submit that this test is ill-advised. It is a setup for failure. Again, the assumption is that as a Jewish state *we can do this:* we can become a just society. And perhaps we might achieve that, if we were to pursue the establishment of a truly democratic, pluralistic society in historic Palestine. Green, however, is advocating operating within the framework of Judaism as he sees it as the foundation for the State of Israel. No fundamental revision is required. In this vision, there is no examination of what it means to base the founding and perpetuation of the State of Israel on our self-image as a special people with a special claim to the land. But coming to the realization of what that self-image has brought us to in the reality of Israel today is precisely what is required. Citing examples of human rights principles from the Jewish scriptures and the principles of universalism and respect for human dignity to be found in the Talmud[5] will not get us there. The reality before us is more existential, more fundamental.

And Rabbi Green acknowledges the failure. But he still doesn't get it. "So far," he observes, "we are not doing too well. Arab intransigence and the horrors of the intifada years have weakened the vision of a humanitarian Zionism" (2008). Here it is again: the fixed belief in the righteousness of our cause. By blaming the victim—implicit in the reference to "Arab intransigence"—and choosing to focus on the Palestinian resistance uprisings known as the *intifadas* (Why are they horrible? For the violent suppression they engendered? Can we Jews ever forgive the Palestinians for what we have done to them?), Green distances the Zionist enterprise from the violence it has spawned. The very notion of a "humanitarian Zionism" lays bare the problem. The concept

---

5. A record of Rabbinical discussions and decisions, the Talmud was written between the third and sixth centuries CE, when it was codified. Although subject to continued interpretation, the Talmud remains the central body and source of Jewish religious and civil law, ethics, and customs.

belongs in the same category as the early Zionist myth of "a land without people for a people without a land." "Humanitarian Zionism" is a fantasy. It is an example of our stubborn, uncanny ability to deny the dark side of our nature. As Avraham Burg has argued, this trait has become woven into the fabric of the state itself, and it has become more pronounced as we become increasingly committed to defending the actions of the state. We heard it in a Washington, DC, press conference at the height of the bombardment of Gaza in the winter of 2009 in Israeli Foreign Minister Tzipi Livni's claim that Israel does not use phosphorus bombs and does not target civilians. We heard it in her insistence that Israel simply had to defend itself against the onslaught of "the rockets." Translation: it's all their fault—they started it.

What is a humanitarian Zionism? Rabbi Green has the answer ready: "...to have a Jewish existence that carries us forward under banners of caring, responsibility, and compassion for the world and for humanity hardly feels like a betrayal of our mission. In some deep and perhaps mysterious way—*dos pintele yid* ["the very core of Judaism"; "the Jewish spark"]—Jews still want to be a kingdom of priests and a holy nation, even those who cannot let themselves say those words" (2008).

"A kingdom of priests and a holy nation." I am one of those Jews who cannot say those words. The phrase conveys the source and the heart of Jewish exceptionalism. It is found in the book of Exodus, chapter 19. The children of Israel, just three months after their escape from Egypt, are camped at the foot of Mt. Sinai. Moses, knowing that something of monumental importance is going to happen, approaches the mountain to receive God's instructions. "The Lord called to him from the mountain, saying: 'You yourselves have seen what I did to the Egyptians, and how I bore you on eagles' wings and brought you to myself. Now therefore, if you will indeed obey my voice and keep my covenant, you shall be my treasured possession among all peoples, for all the earth is mine; and you shall be to me a kingdom of priests and a holy nation. These are the words that you shall speak to the people of Israel" (Exodus 19:3–6, Jewish Publication Society).

What does it mean to invoke such a concept in a discussion of Zionism and the problem of the Israel-Palestine conflict? It is clear from Rabbi Green's words that Jewish tradition is the source of the principles that guide the social justice work of Rabbis for Human Rights. This is consistent with the mission of the organization as presented on the web site. That's fine. But these very principles are grounded in Jewish exceptionalism. Citing universalistic elements to be found in the Jewish tradition do not mitigate that core reality. Green's references to the other genocides and the other liberation movements do not make up for the unwillingness to acknowledge the fundamentally exceptionalist bedrock of political Zionism.

We are standing on the same slippery slope as those Christian progressives who are attempting to fashion a justification for modern political Zionism out of a revised theology. We have entered the space of Christian Zionism through the door of Jewish exceptionalism.

Here is an example of Christian Zionism in its purest form, written by Reverend Malcolm Hedding on the web site of the International Christian Embassy Jerusalem (www.christian-zionism.org): "Israel has always been God's vehicle of world redemption (Romans 9:1–5). In a way, she is God's microphone, the means by which He speaks to a lost world. Moreover, she has birthed all God's covenants into the world and has now come back to her ancient homeland, by the promise of the Abrahamic covenant, to birth the final great covenant of history, the Davidic covenant. Herein lies the ultimate purpose of her modern-day restoration. Jesus will return to Zion as the root and offspring of David (Revelation 22:1–6; Psalm 2:1–12; Psalm 72:5–11)."

But one does not need to go to the dispensationalists to find an eschatology that casts the Jews in the starring role as God's chosen. In fact, there is an equally powerful vision of the Jews' mission to be found within the Christian mainstream. It is gentler, perhaps, and framed in more contemporary terms, but none the less pointed: the Jews, God's chosen people, are here to advance the work of making a more perfect world. God chose the Jews for this role—and the land promise is part of that covenant. The Jewish people are supposed to be in the Land of Israel: it is our destiny and our mission as God's "special treasure among all the peoples, for all the earth is Mine." Recall the discussion in chapter 5 of American theologian Paul van Buren, whose work exerted such an important influence on a generation of theologians and pastors in the post-WWII period and who led a widespread and ongoing Christian effort of reconciliation with the Jewish people. It was van Buren who, describing the relationship between God and the Jewish people as "the greatest of all love affairs in history" (van Buren 1984, 25), assigned to Christians the job—also planned by God—of helping the Jews move Creation nearer to its completion.

Religious Jewish progressives like Rabbi Green, even as they cast a critical eye on Israel in its failure to live up to the humanitarian ideals of Judaism, participate in this vision. We travel a very short way, if any distance at all, to find an exceptionalism very similar to that of mainstream Christian Zionism in the Zionism of those Jews who seek to hold Israel to their standard of "caring, responsibility and compassion for the world and for humanity" (Green 2008). In this progressive, ultimately forgiving analysis, the "abuses" of the Jewish state are unfortunate by-products of our larger effort to fulfill the divine charge to create a better world for all humankind. Yes, the abuses of Israel must be corrected, but they are not to be used to call into question the validity of the Zionist enterprise itself.

For Jews like me who, like Rabbi Green, are deeply concerned about Israel's future but who disagree with him about Zionism, such ideological differences create a dilemma. The men and women of Rabbis for Human Rights are doing good and courageous work. They are on the front lines in Israel on a wide range of human rights issues. You will find Executive Director Rabbi Arik Ascherman and his colleagues confronting Jewish settlers and Israeli Army forces in the West Bank when Palestinian farmers are being harassed or when Palestinian homes are threatened with demolition. Rabbis for Human Rights has taken on the issue of the Judaization of the Silwan section of East Jerusalem, where a Jewish settler organization in collusion with the government of Israel is attempting to cleanse the area of Palestinians who have inhabited it for generations. Rabbis for Human Rights champions an impressive range of human rights causes in Israel and the West Bank, including protecting foreign workers, opposing torture, and battling human trafficking.

So why the critique? Can't I embrace their actions even though I may disagree with the organization on some fundamentals?

I would argue that a just political settlement cannot be achieved as long as the Jews of Israel and their supporters in North America are operating from a position of being the light to the nations, God's special treasure, and a nation of priests. The natural outcome of such an attitude is that Jews will feel they deserve the land more than the Palestinians. They already have taken an unfair portion. The Palestinians already have compromised repeatedly, at each pass giving up more territory, more control, and more resources. The facts on the ground today represent a stupendous set of losses for the Palestinians: forested hilltops and fertile valleys have been replaced with cities of stone (for Jews only). Restricted roads now crisscross Palestinian byways. Checkpoints are destroying their commerce, hampering their opportunities for education, and disrupting their personal lives. The separation wall has turned Palestine into a giant prison. Do the humanitarian acts of rabbis confronting violent settlers fix that? Yes, Rabbis for Human Rights fights one battle at a time, and these battles are important: saving this olive harvest here, this home loss there, this theft of an orchard here. Going to jail for their acts of civil disobedience challenges the system that allows these violations to occur. All of these acts have value. But do they attack the root cause, which is the Zionist project to establish Jewish sovereignty over Palestine? This is the fundamental fact that created the settlers, that built the wall, and that drives the conflict. This is the fact that underlies the whole project that has put 100 years of Jewish settlement at risk, created 4.25 million regional refugees, and subjugates 4 million Palestinians today.

Confronting the Root Cause

The requirement for Jewish demographic and political dominance drives policy and perpetuates the conflict. The conflict
poisons Israeli society. Israeli historian Meron Benvenisti, writing
in *Haaretz* ("Woe to the Victors," January 26, 2009) in the wake
of the 2008–2009 invasion of Gaza, spells out this grim truth:
"Despite the revulsion from the operation, one cannot ignore the
fact that Israel scored a victory and demonstrated the futility of
continuing the Palestinian resistance. Now the Israelis will have to
wrestle with the spoils of this victory, with millions of beaten and
mourning Palestinians living under a totalitarian, discriminatory
regime and with a world that does not reconcile itself to insane
violence. A small minority of ashamed Israelis sadly contemplate
that stage of the national movement, the one that at its inception
embodied so many lofty ideals. A pyrrhic victory indeed."

The root cause of the violence against Israel's citizens and the
wars fought in its defense over the years is the same that has caused
those abuses of Palestinian human rights opposed by Rabbis for
Human Rights: the establishment of a Jewish state on Palestinian
land. Philosophy professor Michael Neumann addresses this issue
with a clarity and outspokenness that demands our attention. In
his 2005 *The Case Against Israel*, he wrote, "Zionism always was,
despite strategically motivated denials to the contrary and brief
flirtations with other objectives, an attempt to establish Jewish
sovereignty over Palestine. This project was illegitimate. Neither
history nor religion, not the sufferings of the Jews in the Nazi era,
sufficed to justify it. It posed a mortal threat to Palestinians, and it
left no room for meaningful compromise. Given that the Palestinians had no way to overcome Zionism peacefully, it also justified
some form of violent resistance" (86).

I am certain that Neumann, a moral philosopher, is not
approving of or rejoicing over the violence that has resulted from
that resistance. He is simply asking us to understand it as a response
to the structural, if not outright, violence of the dispossession of
the Palestinian people. And it does not matter, Neumann points

out, that some of that Palestinian land—from the early years of settlement to our present day—has been purchased by Jews: "The Israel/Palestine conflict is not about mere land ownership but about its use to establish the sovereignty of one group over another...It does not matter if the Zionists achieved wonderful things or 'turned the desert green.' That I do wonderful things while acquiring the power of life or death over you hardly legitimates my venture" (87).

Mitigating the impact of the occupation is not enough. Activism, on the part of Jews and non-Jews alike, but especially of Jews, must confront on a fundamental basis the expansionism, continuing dispossession, and brutal control over the daily life of a subject population that are the direct outgrowth of the political project that is Zionism. And as Jews we must take one step further: we must acknowledge the deeply rooted religious and cultural elements that provide the foundation for Zionism. I am troubled when Jews committed to the survival and well-being of Israel quote from Exodus and from the Talmud in order to establish a moral platform from which to carry out their humanitarian work for the benefit of Palestinians. I am troubled because Exodus chapter 19, of all passages, carries with it the ideology of entitlement and supremacy that is the cause of the evils these same Jews are fighting against.

Where is the opposition to the system that, created and legitimated by that ideology, is driving the occupation enterprise itself? Why, when the occupation is mentioned, is the focus on the settlers who are the spawn of this enterprise, the Frankenstein monster not only created by the government of Israel, but fed and protected by that government? The Jewish religious establishment, and in that I include the rabbis who make up Rabbis for Human Rights who culturally and by birth are part of that establishment, appears to be unable to let go of the ideology that underlies Zionism. It is that ideology that supports the uncomfortable truth that Neumann sets before us—that "Zionism is the illegitimate child of ethnic nationalism" (187). This is the same truth that Avraham Burg acknowledges, and why he beseeches

Israel and Israel's supporters to be willing to accept Zionism as the scaffolding that gave birth to Israel, but to now let it fall away and be open to what comes to replace it. Exodus 19 is part of that scaffolding. It will take not a nation of priests and a holy people to end the madness, but precisely the opposite—a nation willing to be people just like any other. It will require our willingness to relinquish our privileged status and simply to share as equals.

The tragedy here is that the people who make up Rabbis for Human Rights are good and moral people, courageous people who are horrified by what the state is perpetrating and who have devoted their lives and often their safety to opposing that evil. Arik Ascherman and his fellow activists are heartbroken and outraged over what has happened, not only to their country and to their dream of the end of the harsh and painful exile, but of what has happened to their Judaism—because they come at this from a religious perspective. Rabbi Ascherman goes into the West Bank wearing his yarmulke (skullcap), which along with his full beard makes him curiously resemble the fundamentalist settlers he is going head to head with, and I believe that this is intentional. This Jew, he is saying, is defending the true meaning of Judaism. The irony is that with one hand he is hammering against the wall and standing down the bulldozers, and with the other he is holding on to the Jewish state that is the source of the evil he fights.

What, then, is the role of progressive Jewish thought and activism—people like Rabbi Green here in the United States and Avraham Burg and Arik Ascherman in Israel? Their voices are critically important in the discourse. But where will their actions take us with respect to a peaceful solution to the conflict? Despite the focus on the "two-state solution"—and these voices are unanimous in supporting this outcome—Burg himself cautioned in a December 2008 address to Rabbis for Human Rights in Washington, DC, that we should not regard "two states" as a wonderful, end-point solution. It will be, he says, a problematic, highly flawed arrangement. Two states, he points out, should be seen as step along the way to a regional arrangement in which Israel will take its place among the nations of the Middle East. It is part of a process, a series of steps, Burg emphasized, taken *away* from Zionism and from the exceptionalism that is supported by and breeds the militarism that plagues today's Israel. The work for justice for Palestinians is crucial, but it will not take us toward peace, not in our cities, along our borders, nor in our hearts, until we are prepared to let go of our past of exclusivism and sense of entitlement. The result of our efforts will depend on whether we continue to direct our efforts toward increasing our sense of power over real and imagined adversaries, or instead toward establishing trust and a sense of community with other nations and faith communities. To use Walter Brueggemann's terms, will it be royal consciousness or the prophetic imagination that guides us? Recall Brueggemann's dictum: "We will not understand the meaning of prophetic imagination unless we see the connection between the *religion of static triumphalism* and the *politics of oppression and exploitation*" (2001, 7). With respect to the political solution we seek, the success of that solution will depend on the nature of the human arrangements to which we commit ourselves. And the nature of those relationships—the story that they tell—will be a reflection of the story we tell about ourselves.

A New Narrative

The story we Jews tell ourselves and teach our children goes like this: Exiled from our land, our Temple destroyed, we adapted. The vast body of work in law and lore governing religious, civil, and everyday life that was compiled in the first half of the first millennium, which became known as Rabbinic Judaism, became the core of Judaism and has sustained our people over the centuries. In other words, we underwent a fundamental change, making the transition from a tribal, Temple-based cult to a universalist faith no longer tied to place.

This is the prevailing Jewish narrative. Faced with the destructive scenario unfolding in the Holy Land today, in which we Jews appear to be anything but universalist and justice-based, Jews continue to evoke this narrative as if calling on it loudly enough will make it true. I believe that it has the potential to be true—we can realize the universalist and justice-based elements in our tradition. But this can only happen if and when we are able to overcome our denial about how much our current actions betray those elements, and to understand where we currently stand in our own history. Ironically, it is an emerging school of Christian writers that can help us to see Judaism more clearly. Retired Episcopal bishop and theologian John Shelby Spong describes the appearance of a universal vision in Judaism as a developmental process. According to Spong, Judaism's original focus on specialness and particularity, reflected in the national "epic" of the Old Testament, was first concretized in the sixth century BCE as a result of the national trauma of the Babylonian exile. In the post-exile restoration, the prophet Ezekiel and the priests who returned with him to Palestine from Babylonia reformulated the "defining epic" of the people with the addition of the so-called Priestly document that completed the Torah, or the first five books of the Hebrew scriptures. "The survival of the Jews' identity was the first priority of these priestly writers. In order to survive as a separate people…the Jewish people had to be distinct and different" (Spong 2005, 263). The Sabbath observances, kashruth (dietary laws), and ritual circumcision were established to reinforce the sense and experience of separateness.

Spong sees this hardening of what some have called the "tribal" character of Judaism as not essential to the faith but as a reaction to historical events, namely, the stress of exile and the loss of political autonomy. The universal aspects of Judaism were articulated by the prophets in the centuries preceding exile in reaction to the spiritual and ethical failures of the monarchy-priestly complex. These aspects of Judaism did not disappear. Spong, like others, sees Jesus as the heir to that prophetic tradition.

Spong, Marcus Borg, and others who we will consider in greater depth in the next chapter have been engaged in developing an understanding of early Christianity in the light of the Jewish experience of Roman occupation. Theirs is no academic exercise in church history. They are working on breaking down sectarian and religious barriers toward a realization of the values of social justice that can guide us today.

This work is very different from the effort to construct what I consider to be a false, if wished for, picture of a fully realized universalistic Judaism. For all its good intentions, this effort, elements of which we have seen in the work of both Christian and Jewish thinkers, serves to reinforce the myth of the Jewish state as a democracy committed to social justice and equal rights for all its citizens.

In a tragic irony, the narrative that presents the Jewish people as having fully made the transition from tribal to universal is belied by the actions of the State of Israel. Tribal Judaism is being enacted there. Progressive Jewish voices evoke the Old Testament prophets' message of justice as evidence of Judaism's universalism. But it is the ethnocentric element of Isaiah's message—not the lion lying down with the lamb but the smiting of the Philistines—that has now become dominant with the arrival of Jewish political empowerment. Isaiah's soaring vision of universal peace is not completely lost; there are voices, prophetic voices that are invoking these values, but we have gone very far indeed in the other direction. We brought to the world the concept of a universal God, a God who seizes us by the arm, binds us to his covenant, and demands justice. But we have handed power over to a political system that is enacting the creed of a tribal God who commands conquest.

For a way forward, therefore, we will review the work of several contemporary thinkers whose perspective stands in vivid contrast to the Christian revisionist school that we considered in chapters 5 and 6. It also provides a counterpoint to the exclusivist tone that persists in the writing of the progressive Jewish thinkers I have discussed. Theologians Marcus Borg, John Shelby Spong, and others invite us—Jews and Christians—to reclaim that precious part of our shared tradition. They urge us to overcome sectarian barriers and claims of exclusivity and privilege. Consider this passage from John Spong's 2005 *The Sins of Scripture*:

Jesus was shaped by the epic that produced the tribal religion of the Jews, who understood themselves to be God's favorite ones, God's chosen, who assumed that their enemies were God's enemies, who portrayed God rejoicing over the Egyptians who drowned in the Red Sea. But he was also part of the growth of that tribal God through Exile as reflected in the demands for love and justice that the prophets added to the epic of the Jews...Jesus seemed to understand that no one can finally fit the holy God into his or her creeds or doctrines. That is idolatry...We cannot continue to pretend that we are the chosen and all other people are the unchosen...Jesus commissioned his disciples to go into all the world (Matt. 28:16–20). They were to go beyond the boundaries of their nation, their tribe and most specifically their religion. (294–295)

Contrast this vision with the Christian theologians we considered in earlier chapters, who validate the exclusivity of the original covenant between the Jewish people and God, elevate it to primary status, and strive to have Christians join the Jews in this privileged status. It's useful to consider the historical contexts in which these widely different perspectives arise. In the aftermath of World War II, van Buren and his heirs in the Christian revisionist tradition were reacting to the horror of Nazism. Anti-Semitism became *the* sin of the church to correct. In the geopolitical arena, the West was fighting the evils of fascism and totalitarianism. As the Cold War intensified in the postwar years, we accepted a worldview in which a bright line was drawn between the evils of authoritarian communism and the virtues of Western democracy.

That was then. Today, we have become painfully aware of the sins of the West in its abuse of power on a global scale. Today, the system that threatens the future of humanity and challenges the fundamentals of our justice-based faith traditions is not fascism but empire as expressed in aspects of global capitalism. Today, Rome of the year 30—not Berlin of 1938 or Moscow of 1954—is the model of the evil to be overcome.

Walter Wink reminds us that it is precisely this system, this political and social order to which Jesus was referring when he said to the Pharisees, "You are of this world, I am not of this world" (John 8:23). Wink translates the Greek *kosmos* as "system," rather than "world," and, more specifically, as the "Domination system" (1992, 52). Jesus—when he made this declaration or when he preached about the Kingdom of God—was not picturing a heavenly "World to Come." Rather, he was talking about the transformation of the current world of oppression and injustice, the *kosmos* of the Domination system of Rome—including its Judean client rulers—into a just society. As a nation-state, Israel is involved in and implicated in the present-day global economic and political nexus. Its involvement can be for good or bad. And this is where some progressives, be they Christian or Jewish, fail to take the next necessary step. They call for a "just," "compassionate," or "democratic" Israel, but fail to call Israel to account for its blatant abuses of human rights. It's striking: many of these are men and women who have evidenced strong commitment to social justice for a range of causes, domestically and on a global stage. Yet Israel gets a pass from them.

There are other voices, however—compassionate and reconciling, but not as forgiving. One of these belongs to a Palestinian priest.

Zionism as Regression: A Palestinian Perspective

Naim Ateek is a Palestinian Anglican priest. He was eight years old in 1948 when his family was expelled from their village in the southern Galilee by Jewish forces. Ateek is the founder and director of Sabeel, the Center for Palestinian Liberation Theology in Jerusalem. He is a man of deep faith who has articulated a theology that responds directly to the historic and present suffering of the Palestinian people. In his first book *Justice and Only Justice: A Palestinian Theology of Liberation,* Ateek makes his case for a justice-based approach to the Israel-Palestine conflict. His work is characterized by (1) a direct identification with the experience of Jesus Christ as a Palestinian Jew who lived under Roman occupation, (2) an unflinching critique of those aspects of Old Testament theology that can be used to justify the dispossession of one people by another, and (3) a raising up of the prophetic tradition that places social justice above all other values. For Ateek, the issue of the particularist versus universalist nature of God is fundamental to the articulation of a liberation theology. He maintains that the Old Testament, through the prophetic and post-exilic period, never resolves the tension between the particularistic and the universalistic conception of God: "...the emergence of the Zionist movement in the twentieth century is a retrogression of the Jewish community into the history of its very distant past with its most elementary and primitive forms of the concept of God" (1989, 101).

Zionism, in Ateek's formulation, represents a backsliding into those archaic aspects of Old Testament theology. He cites the book of Joshua, a text typically passed over by apologists for Israel, in its description of the destruction of Jericho: "The city and all that is within shall be devoted to the Lord for destruction" (Joshua 6:17). Ateek notes that in the text, the Ark of the Covenant followed the priests blowing on the rams' horns, circling the city prior to the destruction. "Is such a passage," asks Ateek, "...consistent with how God is revealed in Jesus Christ? If not we must say that it only reveals a human understanding of God's nature and purpose that was superseded or corrected by the revelation of Christ. In other words, such passages are revelatory of a stage of development of the human understanding of God that we must regard, in light of Christ's revelation, as inadequate and incomplete" (83).

Clearly, Ateek in his citing of the Old Testament's more archaic passages is not constrained by the need to avoid the appearance of anti-Jewish attitudes that we have observed among some American theologians. He is even willing to be so politically incorrect as to use the word "superseded" to describe the relationship between Christianity and Judaism with respect to the warlike idiom that can be found in the Old Testament. This has subjected Ateek to the charge of anti-Semitism by both Jews and Christians. This charge is unfounded. The focus of Ateek's critique is political Zionism, not Judaism; it is aspects of Old Testament theology, not the Jewish faith itself, that he holds responsible for the victimization of his people. Even in the face of his unsparing critique of political Zionism, Ateek seeks to build a bridge between the two faiths. Like Bishop Spong, he posits the existence of a universalist stream in Judaism. In a formulation evocative of the viewpoint cherished by many progressive Jews, Ateek holds that Judaism was able to evolve out of its tribal exclusivism and into a more universal, ethically based social justice creed as a response to the loss of the Temple and political power.

Jonah: Searching for the Universal in Judaism

In his second book, *A Palestinian Christian Cry for Reconciliation*, Ateek, like the Ruethers and Wagner, turns to the book of Jonah as an example of the universalism to be found in Judaism. Like the Ruethers, Ateek understands the book to have been directed at the Jews returning from the Babylonian exile. It was intended to spur them to adopt a more open and tolerant attitude toward the non-Jews they would encounter in the pluralistic society of Palestine to which they were returning. "Thank God for Jonah!" exclaims Ateek at the conclusion of his discussion of Jonah (2008, 77). The book "refutes all narrow, restrictive, and exclusive theologies" maintains Ateek (77). Theologically, he argues, Jonah is in line with other Old Testament depictions of God, such as those found in Second Isaiah and the Psalms, which describe God in universal terms (i.e., creator and master of all of creation).

I think that Ateek's thesis is an overstatement, driven by his desire to find a basis in the Jewish scriptures for a post-tribal universalism in Judaism. Yes, the author of Jonah is critiquing the prophet's narrow worldview. Yes, the story is a homily, a lesson about seeing all people as God's children, equally deserving of his love and forgiveness. But the description of God as supreme over all creation does not cancel out or even mitigate his special relationship with the Jewish people. According to the Old Testament, God is Lord of all creation. As such, he has chosen Israel as his special people. He has laid out the terms of that relationship—namely, the covenant itself. Indeed, in the theology of the Old Testament, monotheism and the election of Israel are intertwined—the election and special blessing of Israel could only have been accomplished by the One God. Election, as articulated in the Bible, could not have been envisioned in a system in which each people had its special god and, conversely, each god his special people. Election and the Abrahamic covenant are essential components of Israelite monotheism.

Just because God is the God of all and, as such, chastises Jonah for his selfishness and lack of compassion for God's creations, does not mean that he is changing the terms of the covenant. What is the message to the people of Nineveh as told in the book of Jonah? God sends a Jewish prophet to save them—what might they understand from that? More to the point, what is the Jewish reader—in the fourth century BCE as well as the twenty-first century CE—to take from this story? Yes, the readers of the book of Jonah are being instructed in justice. I would dispute, however, that this humanitarian lesson carries with it a push from the particularistic to the universal. One can hold on to the land promise and to election in the Old Testament sense and still subscribe to the message of Jonah.

The book of Jonah points *in the direction* of the truly universalistic worldview and theology that Ateek is advocating. But Ateek is clear that this is a *Christian* theology and worldview. It is faulty logic to maintain that because Jonah (or Second Isaiah, or Amos) points toward a universalist worldview that this changes the fundamentals of the covenant, i.e., Israel's election and the land promise. This argument will not compel Jews to relinquish our superior claim to the land and energetically champion equal rights for Palestinians. Actually, what this line of argument achieves is the opposite—it soothes Jews into a false sense that we can hold on to our special status and, drawing on our tradition of dealing justly with "the stranger who resides with you" continue to enjoy the rights of being God's chosen. And, make no mistake, this carries with it the right of the inheritor and the conqueror.

A Jewish Reformation

Perhaps this is why the book of Jonah ends so abruptly. It leaves us hanging: what happens to Jonah now? Where, spiritually, does he go from here? This is the condition of the Jewish people today. Like Jonah, we are looking into the unknown. We can choose to withdraw into stubborn denial, believing that we can make this nationalist project work, that, in fact, this is what our God or our tradition wants us to do. Or we can recognize how truly uncomfortable—and ultimately unworkable—this position is. And from there we can continue the wrenching work of repentance. In the Jewish tradition, this is the work of deep reflection and self-awareness. This same tradition instructs us that this work of reflection is meaningless unless it leads directly to change in behavior.

Those of us, here and in Israel, who point to the savagery of the ideological settlers as the problem are fooling ourselves. We are indulging in a dangerous and sinful delusion. The settlers are doing our bidding, acting out what we have created and continue to support. We are looking in the mirror. This is where the book of Jonah leaves us: like Jonah, sitting under the blazing sun of God's disapproval. But this burning beam of truth is not saying, "Take pity on the people of Nineveh." It is saying, "Look at yourselves; change your ways." This is why Jews read the book of Jonah every year on the most solemn day of the year—Yom Kippur, the Day of Atonement. The subject of Jonah, of course, is not the people of Nineveh: it is Jonah himself. And this is why this book has captivated thinkers like Ateek, the Ruethers, and Wagner, theologians who, faced with the shocking, saddening reality of a modern Judaism pursuing a triumphalist, nationalist project, seek a biblical toehold from which to begin a quest for a conversation and some kind of reconciliation with the parent faith.

But it will take more than an appeal to our scriptures to turn us around. I do not believe that we Jews can join with our Christian sisters and brothers in the work of repentance and a mutual embrace of our shared scriptures as long as we are led by those archaic aspects of our theology that validate a superior claim to the land. By the same token, we are not relieved of our responsibility to regard our tradition critically simply because some (even most) Christians reassure us that these aspects of our tradition are sound. Rather it will take a wrenching, radical reformation in which we look at our tradition and say, *this over here we treasure and hold to, and this over here we honor as part of our history but are ready to relinquish.* Certainly, this process is not unfamiliar to Jews. We have consigned major chunks of Old Testament law and ritual to history—the sacrificial cult is one obvious example. Jews today practice our religion across a broad continuum of observance and embrace wide divergences in theology. We have demonstrated the ability to adapt in response to experience and to circumstances. It is time to apply this same ability to the question of what the land of Israel means to us. This process may—I emphasize *may*—take us some of the distance. But I think that we will have to take the rest of the journey without the support of scripture or tradition. In fact, we will have to do it *despite* some aspects of our tradition and long-standing features of our worldview. It means having the courage to change and to grow, not unlike Christianity did through its own reformation. This will come not from admonitions from the pulpit to obey God's commands to do justly, but from an honest and full confrontation with the injustice that we have perpetrated in historic Palestine.

Progressive Jews—good people—are buying the story that the State of Israel as currently constructed can be a society that can live peacefully with its neighbors and deal justly with its non-Jewish citizens; that if we only clean up this messiness of an occupation—if, in other words, we "deal justly with the stranger in our midst"—we can have a just state, a "humanitarian Zionism." To seal the deal, we can even draw on our scriptures to support this comfortable position: *see, ours is a tradition of justice—God, therefore, is telling us we can do this.* Like Jacob, we demand and expect that our work will be blessed. The evidence points in another direction.

Chapter 10

The Myth of Redemptive Violence

I live on the ruins of Palestine.
—Rachel Tzvia Back, *On Ruins & Return: Poems 1999–2005*

In the summer of 2004, I visited Israel for the bar mitzvah of my cousin Rachel's oldest son. Rachel emigrated to Israel at the age of twenty. She became a citizen, completed her military service, finished her education, and married the son of Jewish South African immigrants. They settled in Jerusalem, later moving to the Galilee. I'm fairly certain that Rachel and her husband, Yonatan, would agree to be described as belonging to the Israeli Left. They work hard to connect with their Palestinian neighbors in the villages and towns surrounding their Jewish village in the Galilee.[1] In her work as a poet, translator, and critic, Rachel has both embraced and advanced the movement among Jewish Israeli writers devoted to grappling with the psychological and ethical consequences of statehood. Many of Rachel and Yonatan's Jewish Israeli friends are on the left as well. At this family gathering, I struck up a conversation with one of them.

Oded is a man in his forties, Israeli-born of European stock. We got around to talking about politics. Oded wasted no time in

---

1. In 1948 when armistice lines were drawn setting the borders of Israel, most of most of the Galilee became part of the new state. Although many Jews live in the Galilee, it remains predominantly populated by Palestinians, who are citizens of Israel.

confronting me about my government's unconditional support of Israel's militarist and colonialist policies. "Why are you doing this?" he demanded, adding, using Israeli street language, *"Atem dofkim otanu!"*—a Hebrew expression that translates (somewhat delicately) into English as, "You're screwing us!"

At the time, I only vaguely perceived what he was talking about. But Oded's challenge helped wake me up, not only to a reality that I needed to understand, but to the fact that there were Israelis with whom we needed to make common cause. We, the citizens of the United States of America, were a big part of the problem.

Looking back on this conversation, I recall a similar encounter that took place two years later. It was the summer of 2006. Events, Oded's outburst perhaps among them, had brought me, in the company of a group of Americans, to the tiny Palestinian village of Tuwani in the hill country of the southern West Bank. Tuwani is a village of 150 souls, farmers, and shepherds who draw their water from wells and graze their sheep in the surrounding pastures. This village is centuries old. Its inhabitants are now beset by the occupying Israeli army that blocks their access to pasture land by concrete blocks, citing "military necessity," and by constant harassment from the residents of the nearby Jewish settlement of Maon.

Since 1982, more than fifteen hundred dunams (one dunam is equivalent to one-quarter of an acre) of land have been confiscated from the village by the settlers of Maon, at the rate of approximately seventy to one hundred dunams per year. While the people of Maon are equipped with plentiful water and electrical power from newly installed water pipes and power lines, all such services are denied to the villagers. The taking of land and denial of services has been only the prelude to the systematic campaign to rid the land of its historic inhabitants. Tuwani's flocks have been sickened and their milk spoiled by rat poison spread in their pastures by the Maon settlers. Tuwani's wells have been fouled by carcasses. Tuwani's children have been forced to take a circuitous route to the regional school, escorted by international peace workers and a reluctant Israeli army presence, because the settlers have physically assaulted them on the way to school.

Arriving in Tuwani, we visited with the villagers, drinking tea with them, listening to their stories, and meeting the international peace activists who live there as a constant presence to protect the human rights of the people. As we prepared to leave, the villagers thanked us for coming and witnessing their situation. One man, however, stepped up and said to us, "It's fine to come and visit, but you must do something, you must speak up. Go home and tell your president to stop killing our children." I was struck by this statement. He did not tell us to call on the *Israeli government* to let his people live in peace. He directed us to *our* government, which he understood to be the source of the evil he was experiencing. Indeed, the rest of the world, with the exception of the great majority of the American people, understands this.

We in the United States are called to make common cause with these Palestinians and the Israelis and internationals who support the rights of these villagers to live, farm, and raise their children free of harassment and the confiscation of their land. We need them to see us as not only courageous bands of peace activists and the occasional delegation of visitors—although these activities are crucial. Rather, those in the villages and cities of Israel and Palestine who seek a peace based on justice and coexistence must come to know us as part of a broad-based movement of Americans who are committed to changing the central role that our government has played in prolonging the conflict. We in America are called because it is our government, through its unconditional political and financial support of Israel's policies, that is enabling the violations of human rights and international law that are the root cause of the conflict.

God's Sword Cuts Both Ways

That we respond to this call is a matter of urgent political necessity, but there is an equally urgent religious and spiritual dimension to this as well. There is a fundamental transition in religious life underway. It is the transition from religious belief and practice devoted to the preservation of group boundaries and differences to a religious life that emphasizes community life across these boundaries and a commitment to common values and shared mission. It is the transition from religion based on ideological certainty to belief open to change and responsive to the challenges of current events. It is, above all, a transition from religion allied with, in Walter Wink's term, "The Powers"—the forces of conquest and empire—to religion that fosters a community of believers committed to working for social justice.

Contemporary religious thinkers liken this transition to the reformist revolution undertaken by the early followers of Jesus in the first century CE. They urge a return to the fundamental principles of social justice and community-based faith, a faith that was subverted by the Constantinian "takeover" of Christianity. Bishop John Shelby Spong has announced his own liberation from the exclusivist claims made by Christianity and has called for the barriers between the faiths to come down (Spong 2005). For over two decades, Jewish liberation theologian Marc Ellis has invited his fellow Jews to join him in exile from the Constantinian creed that has taken control of the Jewish establishment of our day, and into the evolution of a shared faith based on community. Palestinian liberation theologian Naim Ateek gives voice to this same need in emphasizing the connection between the universal messages of the Old Testament prophets and the struggle for human dignity and freedom articulated by Jesus. Ateek calls on Jew and Christian alike to share in a vision of justice based on the prophetic tradition stretching from the Jewish into the Christian scriptures.

The key to peace is discovering what is contained in our shared traditions that will unite us in the cause of universal justice. Theologian Walter Wink joins other progressive theologians in pointing out that the roots of such a movement are to be found in the early biblical tradition, articulated first by the Old Testament prophets. In his description of Jesus's "Third Way" of nonviolence, Wink observes that Jesus's mission of nonviolent resistance to oppression and his championing of social justice was a "logical development" of the early Israelite concept of God's "holy war" against injustice (Wink 1992, 188). In his formulation, Israel's liberation from slavery and its conquest of Canaan was achieved not by military might but by the hand of God. During the ensuing period of the monarchy, however, Israel became confused, demanding human warrior-kings and alliances with imperial powers. In this way, the survival and welfare of the nation became the ultimate good, justifying all acts of conquest and violence. It was out of this social and political context that the powerful reformist vision of the prophets arose.

> With its defection to monarchy Israel began waging political wars that the false prophets tried to legitimate as holy. Israel came to trust in military might rather than God (Hosea 10:13)…The unique contribution of the true prophets was their refusal to turn holy war into political war. This led them at times to declare that God was waging holy war *against* faithless Israel. They recognized the impossibility of maintaining a standing army and concluding treaties with foreign powers while still preserving Israel's utter reliance on God alone to fight for them. The prophets turned to a kind of "prophetic pacifism." Holy war came to be seen as a contest fought not with the sword but with the divine word: truth against power. In a new twist on the warrior asceticism of old, *the Hebrew prophets waged solitary moral combat against virtually an entire people who were convinced that wars of national defense, liberation, or conquest were their only hope of salvation. Israel had succumbed to the myth of redemptive violence, but the prophets had discovered that the word of God was a mighty sword that cut both ways, for and against God's people* (cf. Hebrews 4:12). (1992, 188–189; emphasis added)

God's sword cuts both ways. The imperative for justice will not be denied. And the true prophets are not silent. Here is Israeli journalist Gideon Levy, reporting in *Haaretz,* the Israeli daily newspaper, on December 19, 2008:

> The Israeli national flag flies high, defiant and arrogant over the Palestinian home in the Sheikh Jarrah neighborhood of East Jerusalem. This flag has never looked as repulsive as it does in the heart of this Palestinian neighborhood, above the home of a

Palestinian family that suddenly lost everything. The head of the house, Mohammed al-Kurd, died 11 days after the eviction. Now his widow lives in a tent. The house is reached via a narrow alley: Here Moshe and Avital Shoham and Emanuel and Yiska Dagan live happily. They are the settlers who managed to expel the Palestinian tenants and take over another outpost, in the heart of East Jerusalem.

Israeli greed knows no bounds: It sends its tentacles into the homes of refugees who already experienced, in 1948, the taste of expulsion and evacuation and being left with nothing. Now they are refugees for a second time. Another 27 families here can expect a similar fate, and all under the aegis of the Israeli court system, the lighthouse of justice and the beacon of law, which approves, whitewashes and purifies deceptive and distorted ways of evicting these children of refugees from their homes for the second time. The family keeps, as an eternal souvenir, the keys to the house in Talbieh that was stolen from them and the banana warehouse in Musrara that was taken from them. Now they have another key that opens nothing: the key to the home in Sheikh Jarrah, which they received decades ago from the Jordanian government and the United Nations as compensation for their lost home.

The right of return: The original owners of those houses, the Sephardic Community Committee, has this right forever. There is no judge in Jerusalem who can explain this double standard, this racist right of return for Jews only. Why is the Sephardic Community Committee allowed, and the committee of Palestinians not? What are the tycoons and the politicians who stand behind this hostile takeover thinking to themselves? What is going through the minds of the judges who permitted it? And what about the policemen who violently evicted a sickly man in a wheelchair in the middle of the night, without even letting him remove the contents of his house? And what are the Jews now living in these stolen houses feeling?

The drive to possess all of Jerusalem through the theft of Palestinian neighborhoods and the construction of the land grab wall will result in unending war. It will destroy any hope of a

Jewish homeland shared with the other peoples of the land. If Israel is to survive, it must change. And, because Israel's birth and its sixty-year history as a state is so tied to the history of the Jewish people and its relationship with the Christian world, we outside of Israel who are locked in this embrace with the Holy Land must change also. The path to that change is articulated in the Gospel of Mark: "Whoever does the will of God is my brother and sister." This powerful principle is echoed by Israeli peace activist Nurit Peled-Elhanan: "My people are those who seek peace." If Israel is to survive—if, indeed, the Jewish people itself is to survive—we must decide to join the community of humankind, because this is where our future lies. Placing ourselves squarely in our prophetic tradition, we must do this, not reluctantly out of fear for our survival, but joyfully, knowing that it is God's sword of truth that comes to cut away our bonds of insularity and separateness.

We must take a hard look at the history of our struggle for survival over the 110 years since the First Zionist Congress and realize that the drive to legitimize and intensify our separation from humankind has led—so predictably!—to the building of a wall. It is a wall that is destroying, for both peoples, the land they are meant to share. It is a wall that is destroying, with the setting in of each concrete section, the chances for peace.

I appeal to my Christian brothers and sisters: do not enable us in this self-destructive behavior. Help us tear down this wall.

By joining us in community, by tearing down not only the wall that separates our communities—you have already travelled far down that path—you help us tear down the walls that separate us from the rest of humankind. As Christians, you understand too well the damage that results from religious exceptionalism. Bishop Spong lists it as one of the Christian "sins of scripture." He terms it "religious imperialism," relating it to fundamentalism and the concept of the "one true God" (2005, 237). Clearly, it is our version of this sin that plagues us now as Jews. The original covenant bestowed upon the Jews enormous benefit and enormous privilege—albeit conditional on obedience to God. But it also powerfully conveyed the identity of being a "people dwelling apart" (Num. 23:9). The implications of this for Jewish identity have been profound. Author Joel Kovel has cautioned us that "being apart and being chosen as exceptional became one and the same...if one's ethical reference point is the tribal unit, then all others are devalued, and one no longer belongs to humanity but sets oneself over humanity" (2007, 21).

Help us tear down this wall.

Although Kovel is one of the fiercest contemporary Jewish critics of Zionism and those elements of Judaism that, in his view, have given birth to and nourished the movement, his is not a blanket condemnation of Jewish tradition. Judaism, asserts Kovel, was always headed in the direction of universalism. It has within it the potential to overcome the human tendency to seek certainty, exclusivism, and privilege. Along with virtually every other commentator, Kovel credits this quality to the Old Testament prophets: "Judaic being can conduce to universality and bring forth emancipation. We should regard this as its priceless potential...However, emancipation has always, indeed necessarily, occurred in reference to a critique of, and a standing away from, the established order, including the order of Judaism itself...The prophet is of the people but stands outside the city and reminds it of its falling away from the universal that is God's true being" (22).

Jesus stands in that prophetic tradition. We find in both the Christian and Jewish prophetic traditions the impulse to gather together "outside the city"—outside the walls and boundaries of national, religious, and ethnic identities, in solidarity with those who struggle for justice. Doing so was Jesus's own revolutionary—and intensely Jewish—way of calling for fundamental change in the face of a brutal and dehumanizing sociopolitical order.

The Myth of Redemptive Violence

Walter Wink, citing activist Saul Alinsky's principles for nonviolent community action, reminds us of the importance of presenting a "constructive alternative" when one opposes an oppressive system: "Jesus' constructive alternative was, of course, the Reign of

God...long-term structural and spiritual change requires an alternative vision...Jesus established a new community that developed universalistic tendencies, erupting out of his own Jewish context and finally beyond the Roman Empire" (1992, 45). This alternative, according to Wink, this Reign of God—as urgently required now as it was in Jesus's time—is nonviolence. It is the alternative to war, including the "just wars" of our times: "In his nonviolent teaching, life, and death, Jesus revealed a God of nonviolence. The God who delivered an enslaved people in the exodus was now seen as the deliverer of all humanity from oppression. The violence associated with God in the exodus was centrifuged away, leaving as its precipitate the image of God as loving parent. The violence of the Powers was exposed, along with their blasphemous misappropriation of God as legitimator of their oppression" (217).

How sad it is for me to read these words in these early days of 2009, as the violence of the Powers stands so clearly exposed. How heartbreaking and prophetic are Wink's words as the State of Israel, in its ruthless and self-defeating invasion of besieged and suffering Gaza, calls down the rage and horror of the entire world. Tens of thousands demonstrating in the capitals of Europe and Asia and mounting calls for the isolation of Israel in the world community appear to have no effect on the stubborn will of Israel's leadership in pursuing this course.

Palestinians wonder what will become of an entire population of Gazans for whom this war has been the continuation of years of trauma. Their leaders, international aid workers, and observers throughout the world contemplate the loss of an entire generation who have known only horror, terror, and despair. They fear for what this means for the dream of coexistence in a historic Palestine shared with the Jewish people.

Meanwhile, the citizens of Israel consume a sanitized version of a heroic war of defense. Its sons are sent into a battlefield where the civilian population is the enemy and the objective is the destruction of a society. We in America, who grew up with the Vietnam War and are now living through the occupation of Iraq, understand the impact of such a war on soldiers, who return home deeply scarred, some beyond repair. This is the calamity that the State of Israel has brought upon itself, with the full support of our government in Washington. This is what has been brought about by the unexamined myths that underlie the birth of the state and the continuation of its militarist policies.

"We trust violence," writes Wink in his appeal for its alternative. "Violence 'saves.' It is 'redemptive.' All we have to do is make survival the highest goal, and death the greatest evil, and we have handed ourselves over to the gods of the Domination System. We trust violence because we are afraid. And we will not relinquish our fears until we are able to imagine a better alternative. What if we were attacked by muggers? What if robbers break into our house?... What if another nation threatens our very existence?" (231).

Do We Have a Choice?

This cry of fear, victimhood, vulnerability, and justification for war has been both the mantra and the rallying cry of Israel. The outrage of the world over the Gaza invasion mobilized those institutional Jewish voices in America that defend and uplift Israel's commitment to redemptive violence. As ever, Israel is the victim, and only violence will save. In typical fashion, these same voices invoked the specter of the Enemy that Seeks to Destroy Us. On January 9, 2009, at the height of the Israeli invasion of Gaza and as the death toll of Palestinians was approaching nine hundred, an estimated half of whom were women and children, David Harris of the American Jewish Committee decried the comparisons of Gaza to the Warsaw Ghetto and the displays of swastikas in demonstrations against Israel's invasion of Gaza.

> Shame! Israel seeks to defend itself in a highly complex environment, where the adversary, Hamas, cravenly uses civilians as shields and mosques as armories. For that right to protect its citizens, which any sovereign nation would exercise under similar circumstances, it is labeled as the successor to the demonic force that wiped out two-thirds of European Jewry, including 1.5 million children.
>
> How many times does it need to be said?

Israel left Gaza in 2005. Israel has repeatedly renounced any territorial ambitions there. Israel gave Gazans the first chance in their history to govern themselves.

Israel has a vested interest in a peaceful, prosperous, and developing Gaza. This point cannot be stressed enough. After all, the two are destined to share a common border.

Israel has only one overarching concern in Gaza: Does it pose a security threat to neighboring Israel? The answer, tragically, is clear. That was the result of a decision taken in Gaza, not Israel. Hamas was chosen to rule, and choices have consequences. After all, Hamas denies Israel's right to exist. (Harris 2009)

Here, neatly listed, are Israel's myths: We, the seekers of peace, are a nation besieged, the victims of eternal hatred. We bear no responsibility for the violence directed against us. Above all, we must fight if we are to survive; *we have no choice.* Translation: there is a forced choice between victimhood—which we experienced for millennia and which culminated in the Holocaust—and being warlike conquerors. There is no other way. We cannot be weak. Furthermore, our taking up of arms is unlike that of other nations or resistance groups. Our wars are pure: *Israel has the most moral army in the world.*

Harris raises the key issues with stunning accuracy: "...there is such a thing as a just war," he feels compelled to assert. "War should be the last option, but there are times when it must remain an option." According to Harris, it is not war that is the problem when we are talking about Jewish survival, but its absence: "Defenselessness is no strategy. Jews were defenseless against the Nazi onslaught. They had no army, no recourse to weapons, and few who sought to defend them. Jews learned, at high cost, never to permit such vulnerability again. So, as January 27th approaches, and we recall the six million, spare us the lip service and the crocodile tears from those who would accuse Israel of Nazi-like crimes" (2009).

But the issue is not whether Israel is like Nazi Germany. To react in horror to the comparison is a comfortable tactic, one designed to demonize and invalidate critics by branding them as either openly anti-Semitic or naively foolish enough to once again offer the Jews' throats to the slaughterer. But why are we bound to this comparison? Why not compare Israel to the forces in the world today who feed on fear, who support the escalation of violence across the globe, who sold the invasion of Iraq to the American people in 2003? Rather than living in the past, and looking always for the next mortal enemy, why not gaze into the mirror instead?

A January 11, 2009, *Washington Post* article reported on how the Gaza invasion was covered by Israel's news media. The article presented an Israeli media industry resolutely dedicated to delivering a sanitized, heroic version of the war. It showed how Israel's victimhood and "right to defend itself" were emphasized, with the heroism and humanity of its armed forces held up as an example to the world of Israel's righteousness. Post reporter Grif Witte described how the Guernica of Gaza was removed from view. Panoramic photos of bomb plumes replaced the close-up shots of grieving mothers and the burned and shattered bodies of children, which regularly appeared in newspapers and video throughout the Arab world and other non-U.S. media. The article quoted from Gideon Levy, an Israeli journalist and a minority voice in Israel's press, a voice raised up in prophetic protest against Israel's glorification of war and the damage done to Israeli society. Witte quoted from an article by Levy in *Haaretz:* "There was a massacre of dozens of officers during their graduation ceremony from the police academy? Acceptable. Five little sisters? Allowed. Palestinians are dying in hospitals that lack medical equipment? Peanuts," he wrote. "Our hearts have turned hard and our eyes have become dull. All of Israel has worn military fatigues, uniforms that are opaque and stained with blood and which enable us to carry out any crime" (Levy 2009).

"But Levy's view is in the minority here," the *Post* article commented, "where polls show that 80 to 90 percent of Israeli Jews support the war. Far more common is the sentiment expressed by columnist Guy Bechor, writing in *Yedioth*

Ahronoth, Israel's largest daily, who declared a few days ago that 'we have won. No one in the Arab world will now be able to say that Israel is weak and begging for its life. The images of the past two weeks have been imprinted for years, and Hamas's bravado and arrogance have gone into the tunnels along with their frightened leaders.'"

That week, I wrote a letter to the *Post* editor in praise of the article. "The story of the coverage in Israel is the untold story, and highlights the real, ongoing damage to Israel and the deeper tragedy for Israeli society" I wrote, "far worse to my mind than the issue of terror from the Hamas shelling." Indeed, in the *Haaretz* piece quoted in the *Post*, Levy exposed what is really happening to Israel and issues a call for change:

> In this war, as in every war, an evil spirit has descended on the land. A supposedly enlightened columnist describes the terrible black smoke billowing out of Gaza as a "spectacular picture"; the deputy defense minister says that the many funerals in Gaza are proof of Israel's "achievements"; a banner headline, "Wounds in Gaza," refers only to the wounded Israeli soldiers and shamefully ignores the thousands of wounded Palestinians, whose wounds cannot be alleviated in the overflowing Gaza hospitals...
>
> This is precisely the time for criticism; there is no time more appropriate. This is exactly the time for the big questions, the fateful questions, the decisive questions. We should not just ask whether this or that move in the war is right or not, not just wonder whether we are progressing "according to plan." We also need to ask what is good about these plans. To ask whether Israel's very launching of the war is good for the Jews, good for Israel and whether the other side deserves it. Yes, to ask about the other side is permissible even in war, perhaps above all in war. (Levy 2009)

Levy points to the Third Way: negotiation, inclusiveness, sharing, and equality, as opposed to self-centeredness, privilege, and force. He calls for openness to what can be different as opposed to stubbornly hewing to the policies of the past.

A Future for Israel

What do we say, then, to the Jewish claim for a state of our own? We have before us the established fact of the State of Israel: indomitable and growing, a vibrant, complex society, full of people hungry for life and suffering from over half a century of conflict. If Israel is to survive, if it is to end the conflict that ultimately will bring about its own end, it must acknowledge its original sin. It must become the state of all its people. I agree with Avraham Burg when he says, leave Zionism behind! Let us move on to the next chapter, which is a state in and of the Middle East, living with its Arab neighbors and embracing its Arab citizens. Would it then be a Jewish state? Perhaps, depending on how you define such a thing. A state that exemplifies the Jewish values of justice and human rights would be a state that perhaps would deserve the name "Jewish." A state that commits itself to those principles is a state that would *earn* its "right to exist." But if this is to be so, Israel will have to change. Burg has given us a big piece of the blueprint: the ideology of redemptive violence and the clinging to the suffering of the past must be transcended.

Even Michael Neumann, the philosopher who in *The Case Against Israel* advances perhaps the most unqualifiedly negative verdict on Zionism's legitimacy, argues that Zionism's sins, past and present, have no bearing on the question of Israel's right to exist. States exist, Neumann reminds us, regardless of their actions, right or wrong—could this not be said, for example, about England, France, Sudan, China, Zimbabwe, and the United States? "Israel's existence is to all appearances an indelibly accomplished fact," he writes. "No one ought to try to wipe Israel off the face of the earth" (2005, 89). Debates about Israel's existence are pointless, argues Neumann. I agree. Rather, the question is, now that it is here, where is Israel headed? What is to be the next chapter? Our Jewish history of suffering is clear and is well documented. For that we have museums and books. But reenacting this history, as Avraham Burg has pointed out, in cultural rituals, school indoctrination, and the creation of a cult of military heroism is destroying Israeli culture and sickening the society. The manifest results of this sickness confront us at every turn: in the refugee camps of Bethlehem and Beirut, the roadblocks of Ramallah and Nablus, the blackened olive trees of Bil'in, the poisoned wells of Tuwani, the desolation of Hebron's Old City, the starvation of Gaza.

Yossi Klein Halevi, an American-born Israeli author and commentator, advocates interfaith dialogue within a multicultural Israel. Yet he is wedded to the Zionist dream and to the myths of Jewish vulnerability. He is trapped in Jewish history. As the Israeli invasion of Gaza began in the early days of 2009, the *Washington Post* published an opinion piece by Klein Halevi, entitled "As My Son Goes to War, I Am Fully Israeli At Last" *(Washington Post,* January 9, 2009). In it, Klein Halevi describes how it felt to receive a text message from his son serving in the Israeli army informing his parents that he had been mobilized to go into Gaza. Is this what I raised my son for? Klein Halevi asks himself. Having served in Gaza himself years before, he knew well the horror and folly of being an occupier. How did we come to this, he wonders, and when will it end?

But instead of using the stark evidence of the present as a springboard to, in Neil Elliot's words, "a different future" (2008, 115), Klein Halevi is drawn back into the past, into a reaffirmation of the beliefs, distortions, and myths that are the root causes of the current catastrophe: Gaza is not a starved prison of Israel's making—rather, we withdrew from Gaza in 2005 to give the Palestinians an opportunity to self-govern, but we got rockets in return. Conflict and occupation continue, not because of our illegal colonization of territory captured in war, but because of Arab intransigence: "Israel was ready to make the ultimate sacrifice for peace, uprooting thousands of its citizens from their homes and endorsing a Palestinian state. Israel," he claims, "was even prepared to share its most cherished national asset, Jerusalem, with its worst enemy, Arafat, for the sake of preventing this war." There is here no ability or willingness to see Israel's responsibility for the failure of peace. There is only one story, and it is *all about us*: about our righteousness, about how we, always the victims, always threatened with annihilation, are forced to go to war. The title of the piece is telling: "As My Son Goes to War, I Am Fully Israeli At Last." For this is our comfort zone, this is the trap we find ourselves in. "Even now," writes Klein Halevi, "perhaps especially now, I feel that our family is privileged to belong to the Israeli story. Gavriel, grandson of a Holocaust survivor, is part of an army defending the Jewish people in its land. This is one of those moments when our old ideals are tested anew and found to be still vital. That provides some comfort as Sarah and I wait for the next text message."

There are signs, however, that the defensive façade is cracking. The 2008–2009 Gaza invasion provoked increasingly direct and urgent confrontations by Israelis about what had become of the Zionist dream. Avi Shlaim, one of Israel's "New Historians," reviewing Israel's record toward the Palestinians in the occupied territories over the previous four decades, finds it "difficult to resist the conclusion that it has become a rogue state with an utterly unscrupulous set of leaders. A rogue state habitually violates international law, possesses weapons of mass destruction and practices terrorism—the use of violence against civilians for political purposes. Israel fulfils all of these three criteria…Israel's real aim is not peaceful coexistence with its Palestinian neighbours but military domination" (Shlaim 2009). Shlaim looks in the mirror and sees the reality with a chilling starkness. He quotes an Israeli fighter pilot:

> I name them (Palestinians) a people—although I do not see them as such. A people is fighting another people. Civilians are fighting civilians. I tell you that we, as sons of Holocaust survivors, must know that this is the essence of our lives, coming from there: no one throws a stone at us. I'm not talking about missiles. No one will throw a stone at us for being Jews. And Yonatan [Yonatan Shapira, a former officer who has refused to serve and founded an organization devoted to nonviolence] is one of the people who have lost their survival instinct. As simple as that. He does not understand that a war of cultures is being waged here between the likes of him and the likes of myself. (2009)

Help us tear down this wall. Join us in a new covenant.

Illusory Threats, Illusory Safety

In the previous chapter, I discussed how Jewish progressives stop short of relinquishing their attachment to a notion of Jewish exclusivism, privilege, and mission with respect to the Zionist project. Hannah Arendt, one of the twentieth century's preeminent political theorists, was a keen observer of the Zionist movement. Arendt grew up as a German Jewish intellectual in the mid-twentieth century. She had already written extensively about anti-Semitism when she escaped from Nazi-occupied Europe in 1941. Given her own experience, Arendt was very capable of understanding Zionism in the context of Jewish history. Here is her profoundly wise insight, dated 1946: "Herzl's picture of the Jewish people as surrounded and forced together by a world of enemies has in our day conquered the Zionist movement and become the common sentiment of the Jewish masses…" (Arendt 2007, 385).

Arendt saw this as a problem. Writing in 1946, she realized that Herzl's dream of a haven for Jews was an illusion—Palestine, she observed, is a real place, and "not a place where Jews can live in isolation" (385). The Jews share the land with the Palestinians, and must maintain themselves, with or without a state of their own, in the community of humankind. Zionism must guard against a dangerous set of illusions: "Some of the Zionist leaders pretend to believe that the Jews can maintain themselves in Palestine against the whole world and that they themselves can persevere in claiming everything or nothing against everybody and everything" (386). Of course, this cannot work; it is a prescription for disaster: "If we actually are faced with open or concealed enemies on every side, if the whole world is ultimately against us, then we are lost" (385).

Sadly, the tendency that Arendt saw and mourned in 1946 appears to be true and even gaining in strength in our time. What she describes is precisely how Israel behaves today. This behavior is based on a tragic illusion: that we can achieve safety and certainty in an unsafe world. It is easy to understand why this illusion persists. Israel is suffering from a form of collective post-traumatic stress disorder: the trauma remaining unresolved, the victim seeks continually—and fruitlessly—to achieve a sense of safety and certainty. The second result of the unresolved trauma—and a hallmark symptom—is the loss of the ability to trust. The trauma survivor lives in a frozen psychological reality in which the world is always dangerous and disaster continually looms. Palestinian-American literary theorist, cultural critic, and political activist Edward Said, arguably one of our time's most eloquent spokespersons for and interpreters of the Palestinian cause, understood this about the Jewish people. It is interesting to put his observations, those of a dispossessed Jerusalem-born Palestinian Christian and New York intellectual writing in 2002, alongside those of Arendt, a Berlin-born dispossessed German Jew and New York intellectual writing in 1946. Although looking through different lenses, they see the same thing. Said writes:

> The problem at bottom is that as human beings the Palestinians do not exist, that is as human beings with history, traditions, society, sufferings, and ambitions like other people. Why this should be so for most but by no means all American Jewish supporters of Israel is something worth looking into. It goes back to the knowledge that there was an indigenous people in Palestine—all the Zionist leaders knew it and spoke about it—but the fact, as a fact that might prevent colonization, could never be admitted.
>
> What is so astonishing is that notions of coexistence between peoples play no part in this kind of distortion. Whereas American Jews want to be recognized as Jews and Americans in America, they are unwilling to accord a similar status as Arabs and Palestinians to another people that has been oppressed by Israel since the beginning.
>
> The intellectual suppression of the Palestinians that has occurred because of Zionist education has produced an unreflecting, dangerously skewed sense of reality in which whatever Israel does, it does as a victim…American Jews in crisis by extension therefore feel the same thing as the most right-wing of Israeli Jews, that they are at risk and their survival is at stake. This has nothing to do with reality, obviously enough, but rather with a

kind of hallucinatory state that overrides history and facts with a supremely unthinking narcissism. (Said 2004, 179)

Said's use of a clinical term here—narcissism—appears judgmental, even damning, but it's a simple concept: in psychology, it means self-absorption and, by extension, an inability to consider the experience, point of view, and needs of others. Arendt was describing the same phenomenon in her analysis, linking it directly to the result of the historical Jewish experience of marginalization and denial of rights. She and Said have both astutely honed in on the same core phenomenon: the persistent experience of the Jew as victim, and the forms in which this self-image manifests in attitudes and behaviors.

We can't seem to work ourselves out of this, and if the analogy to post-traumatic stress disorder holds, this is not surprising. We need help. This to me is not a problem, but is in fact very good news. It is good news because an essential curative element for the condition is the support of others in escaping the hardened shell of the injured self. It is good news because it points us to the answer: community. This is the subject of the next chapter.

Chapter 11

A New Covenant

Both in the period of settlement and in the Revolutionary War, the colonists and rebels understood themselves as a biblical people, the new Israel establishing a new democratic covenant. In the excitement of independence, however, political leaders reached for a more grandiose sense of what they were about. The new nation was a new Rome, practicing republican virtue. They soon pretended, however, that building an empire would not corrupt that virtue.

—Richard Horsley, *Jesus and Empire*

Dream, Jan 19, 2008: It is Yom Kippur, the Jewish Day of Atonement. I am the cantor, the person who, standing on the pulpit and facing the *Aron Kodesh*—the cabinet containing the holy scrolls of the Torah—leads the congregation in chanting the sacred prayers. It is the holiest day in the Jewish calendar, and it is the climax of the day: the time to chant the *Aleinu* prayer. The Yom Kippur service takes us back to the time of the Temple in Jerusalem. The cantor assumes the role of the High Priest, reenacting the one time in the entire year when he was permitted to enter the innermost chamber, the place where the Ark of the Covenant containing the stone tablets of the Ten Commandments was housed. As described in Leviticus, this was an elaborate ritual, emphasizing the centrality of cult, priest, and Temple. In modern times, during the chanting of the adoration and commitment prayer of *Aleinu*, the cantor prostrates himself completely before the *Aron Kodesh*, lying completely prone and touching his head to the floor. This is the one time in the liturgical year that this happens. The *Aleinu* prayer itself, however, is chanted by Jews every day three times a day in the Jewish worship service. As we chant, we bend our knees and bow at the waist as we affirm our devotion to God and our commitment to the covenant that binds both parties.

In my waking life, I had performed this solemn Yom Kippur ritual, as the cantor entreating on behalf of the congregation, on perhaps six occasions. As a worshipper, I have chanted it thousands of times, from childhood through adulthood. In my dream, however, I can't do it. I am standing before the *Aron Kodesh*, about to perform this act, and instead of lowering myself to the floor, I am saying to myself, what am I doing? How can I be prostrating myself in this ritual, and saying these words?

> *It is our duty to praise the Master of All*
> *to acclaim the greatness of the One who*
> *forms all creation:*
> *He who did not make us like the nations of*
> *other lands,*
> *and did not make us the same as other*
> *families of the Earth.*
> *Who did not make our lot like theirs,*
> *but assigned us a destiny different from all the others.*
> *And we bend our knees, and bow down,*
> *and give thanks,*
> *before the King, the King of Kings,*
> *the Holy One, Blessed is He.*

Two nights later I have a second dream. In this dream, I am with a group of Christians. We are standing together in a church. I am translating the *Aleinu* prayer for them. It's a kind of "full disclosure" of how we Jews do in fact regard ourselves as the chosen—how we continue to hold ourselves apart and see ourselves as, well, superior. I tell them that for some time I have chosen not to recite this prayer when in synagogue (this is true). Someone remarks humorously that this Jew—me—is now "in" the Presbyterian Church. In the dream, I feel a vague discomfort about exposing this prayer to non-Jews. What am I doing, I ask myself, revealing this "secret clan" information to people outside the faith? Won't this contribute to Jew-hatred? Aha, they will say, what we've been told is true! The Jews are an exclusive club; they do feel superior to the rest of us, and all along they have been plotting to take over the world!

As dreams go, these two seem easy to interpret. They came to me while I was deep into the writing of this book. At first glance, they each seem to express different ways in which I was struggling with the personal crisis that had begun with my visit to Israel and the West Bank. In the first, to use the Freudian term, it is my "ego" that is speaking. In other words, I am involved in a healthy process of self-examination in a mature, adult fashion. The second is a more classic anxiety dream: the Freudian "super-ego," an internalized, scolding voice of authority, is punishing me for my disloyal, independent thoughts and actions. It's telling me to stop this childish rebellion and start following the rules: be faithful to the clan, keep the family secrets, and trust no one from the outside. The second dream is drawing me back into the fold of *Aleinu*.

But there is more here than the dramatization of a personal crisis. The function of dreams is to deepen one's experience and, sometimes, to help point the way to future behavior. The first dream put me back in the Holy Land, standing before Jerusalem, as we do symbolically at worship, facing in the direction of the Temple site. In the summer of 2006, witnessing the ethnic cleansing being carried out in my name and navigating between the two worlds of West and East Jerusalem, it was as if I were standing before my maker on Yom Kippur, with, as the liturgy goes, "a heart torn and seething." I felt myself hurled to the ground in sorrow, despair, and humility before the enormity of what I was experiencing. I was asking myself, as one is enjoined to do on the Day of Atonement, "How have I acted toward my fellow human beings? What do I see when, the veil of illusion and self-deception having been ripped away, stripped of my everyday routine and comforts, I look in the mirror? When I confront my sins of greed, lust, arrogance, and selfishness, what must I do in order to make myself whole with my fellow men and women and with my God, so that I may be inscribed for life in the coming year in the divine book of judgment? That was my existential state that summer.

For me, it was Yom Kippur. On this one day of the Jewish liturgical year, late in the afternoon when the fasting has done its work and the endless repetition of the confessional prayers has worn through our defenses, we read the book of Jonah. Without question, during that summer I lay in the belly of the fish. How was I going to find my way back to solid ground? What was the lesson I was supposed to learn? And—this was the question I was asking myself most of all—what was I to do now?

My second dream set me down here in my present life, and pointed to the future. In dreams, jokes speak the truth. No, I was not converting and becoming a Presbyterian. But in the dream, I am in the church, a location that had been "off limits" to me as a child. In my dream, I had stepped outside of the tribal frame and into the rest of the world. I was, finally, joining the community from which, according to the *Aleinu* prayer, I was supposed to hold myself apart. This would be my future—the work of repentance and renewal, throwing off the old prayer and joining, in community, with "the families of the earth."

Dreams rip away the veil. If *Aleinu* contains the secrets of the clan, then it is this very secret that needs to be exposed—not to the others but to our very selves—and transcended. As Jews, we have taken tentative steps in that direction. You can still find *Aleinu* in the prayer book of the Reconstructionist movement, the most reformist of the Jewish denominations, but the line "who did not make us like the nations of other lands" has been replaced with "who gave us teachings of truth and planted eternal life within us." It's a start, but it is not enough. We must guard against complacency and denial. This sensitivity to the exclusivism of the prayer could lead in a positive direction, but it could also serve to sweep the issue under the rug. For example, Christians, for their part, have retranslated, ignored, or simply omitted from worship the anti-Semitic passages in the New Testament. But is this act the beginning of a discussion about how we can begin to come together as faith communities, or simply a way to make amends and "smooth out" the historically rough edges of Christian-Jewish relations? Jews can edit out the triumphalism and separatism in *Aleinu*. Christians can excise or try to explain away the anti-Judaism of John 3 and Matthew 27. But is this scriptural sanitation activity "interfaith window dressing" or a genuine clearing away of the old triumphalism in the search for (or return to) a model of a universal human community? Do Jews really want to join the wider community as equals and to let go of our sense of entitlement and our preoccupation with our suffering?

A Prophecy of Surprise and Hope

We turn again to Walter Brueggemann to provide a vision for a new spiritual direction. In a 2008 article entitled "Prophetic Ministry in the National Security State," Brueggemann writes about "the core of preaching," namely, the meaning of the Gospel narrative of Christ crucified and risen. "That Friday turn of the world," he writes, "was the exposure of the vulnerability of God to the violence of the Empire" (286). In this piece, Brueggemann calls for a prophecy of surprise and hope, a vision that can help overcome society's propensity toward denial and dread. Prophetic ministry, in Brueggemann's view, invites us to accept our sense of vulnerability. He challenges us to feel discomfort, even agony, about what is happening in our world, and to face a future that, although uncertain, is committed to the creation of something new. This is in contrast to the comfortable refuge sought in the certainty of scriptural authority devoted to the support of our political beliefs, or to the equally comfortable refuge of a shallow humanitarianism. Brueggemann issues a challenge to Christian and Jewish theologians alike who articulate a "theology of certainty that supports empire-building" (311). Thus, in Brueggemann's vision, "prophetic ministry is neither prediction, as some conservatives would have it, nor social action as some liberals would have it. Prophetic ministry is to talk in ways that move past denial and that move past despair into the walk of vulnerability and surprise, there to find the gift of God and the possibility of genuine humanness" (295).

My people need to hear this message. It has become a matter of life and death for us to overcome our denial about the seriousness of our situation. It is urgent that we hear the truth spoken by our modern-day Israeli prophets—the Jeff Halpers and Rami Elhanans and Checkpoint Watch Women and Israel Army refusniks who are crying that there is no peace and demanding justice in Israel and in the territories. The time is now—we can't wait any longer—to expose distortions like "peace process" and "security wall" that disguise land theft and ethnic cleansing. We need to listen to Israelis Uri Avnery and Avraham Burg's warnings about the growth of, in Avnery's words, the "violent Israeli Fascism" of the settler movement that has taken control of Israel's policies in such a profound and destructive way. We need to hear President Jimmy Carter calling the world powers to account when he writes, "In order to perpetuate the occupation, Israeli forces have deprived their unwilling subjects of basic human rights. No objective person could personally observe existing conditions in the West Bank and dispute these statements" (2006, 208–209).

We also need to listen to our Old Testament prophets, whose message is particularly relevant to us today. Like the prophets, we must call for Jewish reform. We must call for a truly "new" covenant, one that will be shared and universal, one that transcends theological or religious categories. Leaving behind fundamental aspects of our covenant will require of Jews nothing less than a reformation—but do this we must. This will not make us Christians—as much as I think that we need to look to Jesus's ministry for prophetic guidance. Rather, we must make common cause with Christians who seek to join us in this same spirit of community.

Catholic theologian Richard Gaillardetz, in his 2008 *Ecclesiology for a Global Church*, referring to the reforming spirit of the Second Vatican Council of 1962 to 1965, observed that the willingness to open up the conversation about church doctrine was the result of "a new and positive engagement with the contemporary world" (xviii). This requirement to actively engage is precisely the point. It was true for the imperial context of first-century Palestine, and it is true for twenty-first-century Palestine and the geopolitical context in which it exists. It is in times of sociopolitical crisis that openness to change and to voices of resistance are most needed, and it is also in these periods that these voices are most likely to be silenced. Brueggemann points out that when an oppressive system feels itself threatened it enlists religion in the service of self-preservation (2008). Therefore, it is in those times that prophetic ministry is most urgently required. Gaillardetz asserts that it is prophecy's function to challenge "a communal vision numb to the gap between what is and what ought to be. It is a community bereft of a 'prophetic imagination,' incapable of mourning its failure to live up to the demands of the covenant and incapable as well of hoping for a new and different future" (6).

A New Family

The Gospel narrative provides vivid illustrations. In the prologue to this book, we encountered Jesus in the earliest days of his ministry. The Gospel recounts, "Then his mother and his brothers came: and standing outside, they sent for him and called him. A crowd was sitting around him; and they said to him, 'Your mother and your brothers and sisters are outside, asking for you.' And he replied, 'Who are my mother and my brothers?' And looking at those who sat around him, he said, 'Here are my mother and my brothers! Whoever does the will of God is my brother and sister and mother'" (Mark 3:31–35 [NRSV]).

In 30 CE, the people of the Galilee and Judea were suffering horribly under the heel of Rome. Popular revolts during Jesus's childhood against Rome and its client rulers were brutally suppressed (Horsley 2008, 81). Villages were burned, people killed or enslaved, and thousands of insurgents crucified. Jesus's ministry can be seen as a direct response to the cruelty of imperial rule. The

Gospel narratives attest to this suffering in metaphorical fashion: Jesus's exorcisms signify the driving out of the forces of evil that had taken control of Judean society. His healing of illnesses refers to the social consequences of the crushing inequities of imperial subjugation in the form of malnutrition and weakened immunities. The Kingdom of God proclaimed by Jesus in his earliest pronouncements was thus a *political* statement, referring to the replacement of oppressive Roman domination with a just society. Jesus, therefore, was building a new community based on commitment to universal values of justice: in his idiom, to commit to the coming Kingdom of God is to enter the discipleship of social and political transformation (Horsley 2008). Walter Wink, commenting on the above passage from Mark, observes that here Jesus "offers an alternative: a new family, made up of those whose delusions have been shattered, who are linked, not by that tightest of all bonds, the blood-tie, but by the doing of God's will" (1992, 119).

When experience shatters your assumptions, when crisis forces you to reassess your commitments or the comfort of your political beliefs, you must seek out new or expanded community and linkages. To fail to do so is to lose your moral compass. It also risks disintegration of that community or, worse, its organization around a destructive (and self-destructive) project. This is as true for individuals and families as it is for communities and even entire nations.

When Rami Elhanan and Nurit Peled-Elhanan lost their daughter to a Palestinian suicide bomber, they faced such a crisis. For them, their recovery as a family was inextricably tied to the responsibility they came to feel for their people. Nurit Elhanan spoke to an audience in Tel Aviv, Israel, in 2001:

> When my little girl was killed, a reporter asked me how I was willing to accept condolences from the other side. I replied without hesitation that I *had* refused to meet with the other side: when Ehud Olmert, then the mayor of Jerusalem came to offer his condolences I took my leave and would not sit with him. For me, the other side, the enemy, is not the Palestinian people. For

me the struggle is not between Palestinians and Israelis, nor between Jews and Arabs. The fight is between those who seek peace
and those who seek war. My people are those who seek peace.
My sisters are the bereaved mothers, Israeli and Palestinian, who
live in Israel and in Gaza and in the refugee camps. My brothers
are the fathers who try to defend their children from the cruel
occupation, and are, as I was, unsuccessful in doing so. Although
we were born into a different history and speak different tongues
there is more that unites us than that which divides us. (Peled-
Elhanan, 2001)

This lesson continues to be driven home in the starkest, most
agonizing way. At this writing, in early January 2009, during the
Israeli bombardment of Gaza, American Jewish academic and
peace activist Sara Roy published an article in the *Christian Science Monitor* entitled "Israel's 'Victories' in Gaza Come at a Steep
Price" (January 2, 2009). In it, she wrote:

I hear the voices of my friends in Gaza as clearly as if we were
still on the phone; their agony echoes inside me. They weep and
moan over the death of their children, some, little girls like mine,
taken, their bodies burned and destroyed so senselessly.

In nearly 25 years of involvement with Gaza and Palestinians, I have not had to confront the horrific image of burned
children—until today. What will happen to Jews as a people,
whether we live in Israel or not? Why have we been unable to accept the fundamental humanity of Palestinians and include them
within our moral boundaries? Rather, we reject any human connection with the people we are oppressing. Ultimately, our goal
is to tribalize pain, narrowing the scope of human suffering to
ourselves alone.

Our rejection of "the other" will undo us. We must incorporate Palestinians and other Arab peoples into the Jewish understanding of history, because they are a part of that history. We
must question our own narrative and the one we have given others, rather than continue to cherish beliefs and sentiments that
betray the Jewish ethical tradition. Israel's victories are pyrrhic

and reveal the limits of Israeli power and our own limitations as a people: our inability to live a life without barriers. Are these the boundaries of our rebirth after the Holocaust? As Jews in a post-Holocaust world empowered by a Jewish state, how do we as a people emerge from atrocity and abjection, empowered and also humane? How do we move beyond fear to envision something different, even if uncertain?

The answers will determine who we are and what, in the end, we become.

It's life or death. It's our choice between a commitment to empire or to our future as members of a human community. A persistent, steadfast focus on this choice must inform the activities of our faith communities if these religious traditions are going to not only "survive" but be a force for the survival of our species on this planet. Protestant cleric and theologian John Shelby Spong wrote that "Christianity must change or die" (1999). But it cannot be the task of one faith tradition to bring the others along. Christianity has begun to repudiate its doctrine of being the one true faith, and specifically the faith that superseded Judaism. The next step is to forge a community that transcends the barriers that separate one nationality, ethnicity, or faith community from another. In making sense out of the story of Jesus's death, Spong asserts that in Christian theology, Jesus's transformation into the Holy Spirit "became a sign of the intrinsic unity of all human life, creating a community beyond every human difference. The defining marks of the past—tribe, language, race, gender or even sexual orientation—faded. Inevitably, so will the most difficult and painful of all aspects of human behavior, namely, those barriers erected by the religious convictions of human beings" (223–224).

Gaillardetz credits the ancient Hebrew worship of the one God as the foundation for this "global church," a church that transcends faith community and national boundaries, and that establishes devotion to a universal, divine presence in history in opposition to the violence and divisiveness of empire. He cites Brueggemann's piercingly simple insight about the statement of

belief in Exodus 15:18—"The Lord will reign for ever and ever"—
as implying its opposite: "and not the pharaoh!" (Brueggemann
2001, 7).[1] In his recent collection *In the Shadow of Empire*, Richard Horsley writes about the theme of deliverance from imperial
oppression common to the foundational stories of both the Judaic
and Christian traditions. He notes that Passover commemorates
liberation from bondage, and Good Friday and Easter celebrate
"Jesus'…vindication by God as the true Lord and Savior, as
opposed to the imperial 'lord' and 'savior'" (2008, 7).

A New Framework for Peace

Sabeel founder Canon Naim Ateek advocates an ethos that
unites all faiths in a commitment to justice. With the story of his
expulsion as a child from his Galilee village as the backdrop, Ateek
turns to the Jewish people, challenging us to undertake the work
of reconciliation with the Palestinian people. In effect, he is asking
us to acknowledge the damage caused by our actions and to share
the land. In similar fashion, Ateek challenges his fellow Palestinians to achieve an understanding with the Jewish people based on
a common faith in a God of justice. Standing alongside Ateek in
this commitment to reconciliation, Marc Ellis also argues for the
importance of theology in building this communal future:

> Creating a framework for peace between Jewish Israelis and Pales-
> tinians demands…a new way of understanding Jewish life in the
> Middle East. Jewish theology and ethics come into play…If in fact
> the task of theology is to nurture the questions a people needs to

---

1. In Brueggemann's analysis, this is the beginning of the transformation of ancient
Israel into the justice-based and universalist creed that would lay the foundation for
the Judeo-Christian faith. The Song of Miriam is a paean to God's drowning of the
Egyptians in the sea. Brueggemann characterizes this song as the culmination of a
period in which the deity was seen in military terms, leading his chosen people into
conquest (2001, 16). Like Ateek, Brueggemann sees this as a developmental stage.
There would be a long way to go, with many twists and turns, to reach the point of
rejecting king and empire as the foundation of peoplehood and humanness. We stand
at one of those turns today.

ask about the history it is creating, then the task of Jewish theology is clear: to lay the theological groundwork for Jewish life beyond innocence, redemption, and the last stand. To look toward the end of Israel's sense of isolation and abandonment and toward a future of creative integration and independence is to propose what for most Jews seems to be the most paradoxical of options, that is, solidarity with the Palestinian people. (1990, 287)

But why should we view this option as "paradoxical"? There is no viable future for the Jewish people unless and until we can acknowledge the suffering that we have caused and open ourselves to sharing the land with the Palestinians. It is the path that beckons us if we are to escape from the prison of our separateness and self-absorption, from our attachment to an exclusionism and to an identity as God's elect. For the Jews, at this point in our history, the Palestinian people represent the other that we must join with in order to join humanity. Ellis continues, "a Jewish theology of liberation will be developed in a community that includes Jews and others who are not Jewish…In the new Diaspora, no one faith or tradition will predominate. Rather, carrying the fragments and brokenness of different traditions and cultures, those in the new Diaspora will share experiences and hopes, disappointments and possibilities" (287).

When theologian Marcus Borg wrote in 2006 about "the imperial captivity of much of the church in the United States," he was asking why, even though our reason for going to war violated Christian teachings, millions of Christians did not "throng the streets" in protest in the months leading up to the 2003 invasion of Iraq (298). In his call for an "emergent" versus a "conventional" church, Borg is advocating this same openness to introspection, self-criticism, and ideological ferment within the faith community itself. This is the value we saw articulated in Williamson's "rule" of conversation for a post-*shoah* theology, in which Christians, if their religion is to be vital and useful, must be free to reform, revise, and reformulate doctrine in direct response to the challenges raised by current events. With respect to the Israel-Palestine conflict, I suggest that we in the

Jewish community and in Israel must consider what a post-Nakba theology would require of us in order to achieve a true and lasting peace in historic Palestine.

The Church as a Force for Change

Borg is reaching for this same commonality of traditions in his depiction of Jesus as a "Spirit-filled Jewish mystic standing in the tradition of the Jewish prophets" (135). Borg is one of a group of contemporary New Testament interpreters that includes Dominic Crossan, Richard Horsley, Neil Elliot, and John Shelby Spong, who are formulating a new vision of Christianity. Like the post-Holocaust revisionists discussed in previous chapters, they seek to overcome the split with Judaism and find common ground in confronting the challenges of modern times. But, unlike the postwar revisionists, their focus is not on correcting the historical sins of Christianity, but on deepening our understanding of Jesus and the early church as a movement opposed to Roman imperial power. Crossan points out that the names for Jesus used in the New Testament were chosen to make very clear the distinction between Rome and the coming Kingdom of God: "Before Jesus the Christ ever existed and even if he had never existed, these were the titles of Caesar the Augustus: Divine, Son of God, God and God from God; Lord, Redeemer, Liberator, and Savior of the World" (2008, 73).

The story of early Christianity is the story of a movement of religious renewal in the quest for social justice in the Mediterranean basin of the first century. This is also our story today, playing out on a global basis. In his contribution to *In the Shadow of Empire*, Horsley points out that Jesus was leading an anti-imperial movement of Jewish renewal. In his chapter in the same collection, Walter Brueggemann emphasizes that the present "hope of the church" is to be found in the prophetic tradition that opposed the power of kings and their alliances with empire. The vision of the Old Testament prophets, asserts Brueggemann, is a peace that comes from a "just economy that is not based on force or exploitation" (2008, 39). The hope of the church is to be "a community that stands apart from and over against empire." Brueggemann enjoins the church to "recover its public voice that attests to an alternative rule in the world" (39).

What then is the role of the church to be? Current events require that we address this question on an urgent basis. Horsley questions the received wisdom that Jesus, in advocating nonviolence, was promoting passive nonresistance. The experience of the Iraq war—and has this event not been a "moment of truth" for Americans?—leads Horsley to conclude "that America has indeed been acting as an imperial power. Historians are reminding us how deeply the sense of being the New Rome, as well as God's New Israel, is embedded in 'America's collective identity.' These recent developments are now leading many Christians who feel uncomfortable about their role as the New Romans to inquire about the relation of the original Rome to the ancient Middle East and in particular about that figure whom the Romans hung on a cross as an insurgent" (Horsley 2008, 77). Neil Elliot, in his chapter in the same book, issues an urgent caution: "We must ask," he writes, "to what extent the inexorable logic of global capitalism, designed in the United States and enforced by its military power, determines the priorities of churches" (119). Sounding the theme of a return to community, Elliot asks us to recall the "tenement churches" that Paul assembled in contrast to and in defiance of the global imperialism of his time—and of ours.

In his contribution to this collection, Norman Gottwald, writing in the waning days of the administration of George W. Bush, takes aim at "the triumphalism of current American foreign policy" (23). In this regard Gottwald summons the voice of the ancient Hebrew prophets, who articulated a vision of "just community" deeply embedded in the life of ancient Israel. He writes, "the early communitarian life of Israel was responsible for shaping the subsequent course of the Israelite and Jewish people in profound ways...[lending] strength to the later prophetic movement...that sharply criticized the gross abuses of the monarchy and the ostentatious greed of the client classes of big landowners and merchants" (21). Using these "biblical criteria," he asserts that modern America has failed the test through its aggression toward relatively powerless countries in South America, Asia, and the Middle East. Gottwald brings his chapter to a close with a remarkable observation, as he trains his focus on one particularly critical spot in the global picture. The United States, he asserts, is very much like ancient Rome in its power and its aggressive stance—not, as some religious voices have wanted to maintain, like ancient Israel, which was in reality a "minor petty kingdom." It is, however, a "supreme irony" that "the Palestinians of the West Bank most nearly approximate the early Israelites since they occupy the same terrain, practice similar livelihoods, and long for deliverance from the 'Canaanite' state of Israel backed by the American Empire" (24).

Prophets state the obvious.

Toward Covenantal Community

As these interpreters make clear, this message is not limited to Christians—the Old Testament prophets took a clear stand against everything represented by empire. Just as it is a distortion of Christian values to use the Bible to support the unjust actions of any state—including the state of Israel—so is it a betrayal of Jewish values to justify collective crimes on the basis of Jewish scripture or Jewish history. Here is where Jews and Christians must make common cause. As Richard Horsley points out, Jesus was calling for a renewal of covenantal community. He points out that this was the covenant for social justice that was created when the Jewish people accepted God's law. In a previous chapter, we cited Jewish theologian Marc Ellis's warning that Constantinian Christianity, representing the yoking of imperial power to the religious establishment, has now been joined by Constantinian Judaism and Constantinian Islam. To counteract this, Ellis makes the powerful case for all religious traditions to join together in "movements of justice and compassion across community and religious boundaries" (2004, 217). Redeeming the current global situation, therefore, depends on the ability of the faith communities to achieve commonality of purpose. Indeed, transcending the group boundaries is part of the process that will help each achieve a true spirit of community within its own ranks.

This is the covenant that calls to us now. It is not the "one covenant" of van Buren and his heirs that links Christians to the exclusivist elements in Jewish tradition, the covenant that separates out—and elevates—one particular faith group from the rest of humankind and that, incidentally, supports Jewish land claims on theological grounds. Rather, it is the prophetic call for renewal and for a return to the community's support of social justice. In the final chapter, we will consider how this has already begun and identify specific directions and actions for the future of this movement. Before we turn to this, however, we will take a closer look at the social and political situation in Israel/Palestine today, a set of conditions hauntingly evocative of those experienced by the people of first-century Palestine. The Jews of that earlier time, to use Gottwald's words, "longed for deliverance" from the oppression of Rome. It was a time in which the call for justice was strong, a call that was answered by the rise of a movement of social renewal and resistance to oppression.

Chapter 12

Reenvisioning Israel and the Role of the Church

Neither Palestinians nor Jews will be saved, from one another or from themselves, if the ideology that still drives the Israeli policy toward the Palestinians is not correctly identified. The problem with Israel was never its Jewishness—Judaism has many faces and many of them provide a solid basis for peace and cohabitation; it is its ethnic Zionist character.
—Ilan Pappe, *The Ethnic Cleansing of Palestine*

In the YouTube clip, a stocky man with a white beard, bare head, and piercing eyes has chained himself to the door of a small house in a neighborhood on the outskirts of East Jerusalem. The house belongs to a Palestinian family, and the man is Jeff Halper of the Israeli Committee Against House Demolitions. The huge American-made, Israeli-operated model C9 Caterpillar bulldozer facing him is poised to pound the house into rubble. In the next scene, Halper, handcuffed and refusing to use his legs, is being dragged off by two soldiers to a waiting jeep. "Arrest that man!" cries Jeff to the soldiers, gesturing toward the Israeli official directing the demolition operation. "He is violating international law!"

Halper is an American-born Jew who emigrated to Israel as an adult and has devoted his life to nonviolent opposition to Israel's violation of Palestinian human rights. Halper's latest book, *An Israeli in Palestine: Resisting Dispossession, Redeeming Israel*, describes what he has termed the "matrix of control": the system of annexation and control of the occupied territories that is leading Israel down the road, if it has not already arrived at that destination, to becoming an apartheid state. Finding this unacceptable, Halper sets out a vision for Israel—a way out. I don't know if Halper would want to be called a Zionist—but he pointedly identifies himself as an *Israeli*. As such, he is looking for a way for Israel to continue to exist as a viable political entity.

Trapped in a Tribal Paradigm

Halper's political activism—and he is squarely in the nonviolent resistance tradition of Dr. Martin Luther King Jr. and Gandhi—is not simply oppositional, although the point is clearly to send a message of protest. Rather, as the situation worsens and options appear to be rapidly receding, his writing has become increasingly prescriptive. "We're trapped in a tribal paradigm," writes Halper, "that neither serves the interests of the Jews in Israel—most of whom have long since become Israelis with no need whatsoever for a 'Jewish' state—nor fits the global reality of the twenty-first century. There's got to be an alternative, an *Israeli* alternative" (2008, 268).

In his vision for Israel, Halper takes us back to early Zionists who, alarmed about the implications of nationalism for the future of Judaism, issued stern warnings about where they saw the Zionist program heading. Ahad Ha'am, Judah Magnes, and Martin Buber are the most well-known exemplars of this perspective, but Halper searches out other prophets from the early years of the Zionist movement and Jewish settlement in Palestine. One of these was Yitzhak Epstein, an early Zionist leader who had a deep understanding of Arab and specifically Palestinian society and culture. More than a century ago, records Halper, Epstein wrote, "we must rid ourselves of all thoughts of conquest and uprooting…How can we establish ourselves in the Land of Israel without sinning against justice and without harming anyone?" (Epstein 1905, 35–52) Epstein's answer to this question, from almost a century ago, echoes the central message of this book.

He articulates two principles "that must guide our actions when we settle amidst or near this [Arab] people: (1) The Hebrew people...respects not only the individual rights of every person, but also the national rights of every people and tribe. (2) The people Israel, as it aspires to rebirth, is a partner in thought and in deed to all the peoples who are stirring to life" (35–52).

Epstein's words are freighted with the worldview and idiom of nineteenth-century nationalism. And yet, given how nationalism has survived into our own time and continues to drive politics and human affairs, we would do well to heed Epstein's warnings against the dangers of Jewish exclusivism. Halper points out that everything Epstein warned of has come to pass in the form of violent conflict with the Palestinians, and might have been avoided if the Zionists had listened to Epstein' simple, prophetic message: "We must, therefore, enter into a covenant with the Arabs and conclude an agreement that will be of great value to both sides and to all humankind...because its outcome is the rebirth of two ancient Semitic peoples, talented and full of potential, who complement each other..." (35–52).

This is the vision that must guide us. It is the vision of community, of a new covenant. We must transcend the tribal barriers. It is not too late.

Halper is joined by others in Israel who understand this and are raising their voices in this simple truth. Furthermore, they understand that Israel has gone so far down the road of tribal conquest that it is unable to change course on its own.

A True Friend of Israel

As we saw in my encounter with the Israeli leftist in chapter 10, Israelis who are desperate about the state of their society and the course their nation has taken are looking to us for help. Indeed, their calls for help in recent months, particularly during and in the aftermath of the bombardment of Gaza, have become more insistent and desperate. And why not? How can the peace movement in Israel have any impact on its own government's policies as long as the United States continues to be the banker for Israeli expansionism and militarization? How can Israel possibly be held to account by its own citizens and by the world community as long as the United States blocks United Nations resolutions condemning Israel's actions? On December 3, 2008, an opinion piece titled "Obama Must Help Israel Break Its Territorial Addiction" appeared in the Israeli daily *Haaretz*, authored by Dr. Alex Sinclair, a lecturer in Jewish education at the Schechter Institute of Jewish Studies in Jerusalem. "For the past eight years," he wrote, "we have had an American president who was Israel's 'greatest friend'—a friend who stood by grinning feebly while we sank deeper and deeper into a mess. Israel is like an alcoholic, except we are addicted to territories, not to tequila." When, Sinclair asks, will America become a true friend to Israel? When will the United States stop supporting our habit by financing our government's illegal and self-destructive policies, and mouthing meaningless cautions about how "unhelpful" the policies are for peace? "If Obama wants to be a true friend," concluded the author, "he must put his hand on our shoulder and tell us to stop. He must take the bottle out of our hand."

Uri Avnery has been called the "grand old man" of the Israeli Left, a man deeply committed to Israel and an increasingly outspoken critic of Israeli politics. His biting, sardonic style is well known to Israelis: Avnery's social and political commentaries are regular features in the Israeli popular press. Avnery offered this piece in the December 22, 2008 edition of the left-wing e-zine *Counterpunch* at a time in which America, and with it the whole world, was holding its breath as the new American President prepared to take office and with elections for a new Israeli government pending:

> A man was asked about his sons. "I have three," he said, "but one of them is a complete idiot."
>
> "Which one?" they asked.
>
> "Take your pick," he replied.
>
> In 51 days, we shall vote for a new Knesset and a new government. Three big parties are competing for the prize: Kadima,

Likud and Labor. Is there a real choice? In other words, are there any real differences between the three parties?

Binyamin Netanyahu says that this is not the time for peace with the Palestinians. We have to wait until conditions are ripe. Not on our side, of course, but on the Palestinian side. And who is going to decide whether the conditions are ripe on the Palestinian side? Binyamin Netanyahu, of course. He or his successors, or the successors of his successors.

Tzipi Livni—or so it seems—is the very opposite. We have to talk with the Palestinians. What about? Not about Jerusalem, God forbid. And not about the refugees. So about what? About the weather, perhaps? Livni's plan, one has to conclude, is to go on talking and talking and talking, and never to reach any practical agreement.

Ehud Barak has not withdrawn his fateful pronouncement of eight years ago, when he came back from the failed (thanks to him) Camp David conference: "We have no partner for peace."

Not one of the three has stood up and told the public in simple words: I am going to make peace with the Palestinians in the course of 2009. This peace will include the establishment of a Palestinian state based on the pre-1967 borders, with agreed minor border changes on the basis of 1:1, turning Jerusalem into the capital of the two states and agreeing on a reasonable solution of the refugee problem, a solution Israel can live with.

Not one of the three has offered any peace plan at all. Only hollow words. Only spin.

Like the alternative offered by Netanyahu: to ameliorate the living conditions of the Palestinians. Living conditions under occupation? When 600 roadblocks in the West Bank prevent free movement? When every violent act of resistance leads to collective punishment? When death-squads go out in the night to liquidate "wanted men?" Only a madman would invest money in such a territory.

All the three are united in their view that Hamas must be eliminated. True, not one of them declares publicly that the Gaza Strip should be reoccupied. But all three support the tight blockade on the Gaza Strip, believing that if the population has no bread and the hospitals no medicaments or fuel, the Gaza public will rise up and overthrow the Hamas regime. Not one of the three has stood up and said: I shall talk with Hamas and bring them into the peace process. Neither did one of the three get up and say: I shall make peace with Syria in the course of 2009. The terms are known, I accept them, I intend to sign.

Perhaps all three of them secretly think so. But each of them tells himself/herself: "What, am I crazy? To take on the Golan settlers and their supporters in Israel?" Someone who is not prepared to remove even one miserable outpost in the West Bank, for fear of a clash with the fanatical settlers there, will not take any such risk on the Golan Heights either.

On the other hand, all three have the same emergency exit: the Iranian bomb. What would we do without it! "The main danger to the existence of Israel is the Iranian bomb!" declares Barak. Declares Tzipi. Declares Netanyahu. A finely attuned choir.

Since the beginnings of Zionism, it has been looking for ways to escape from the "Palestinian problem." Why? Because if the Zionist movement had admitted that there even exists a Palestinian people, it would have had to find a solution to the actual situation and to the moral problem. Therefore, a hundred different pretexts have been found, each in its time, to ignore the dilemma.

On February 11, 2009, the day after the coming elections, those who seek change must start to think anew. Those who long for a democratic, secular, progressive Israel, an Israel at peace with its neighbors and imbued with social justice within, must decide to take matters into their own hands. They must start a new intellectual and organizational effort to realize these important aims. No longer to be satisfied with voting for the "lesser evil" but finally to vote for the greater good, and—together with sectors that have not been partners up till now—to work out solutions that have not yet been tried in ways that have not yet been tried. To bring about an Obama-like miracle.

Instead of the three good-for-nothing sons, a fourth son must appear.

Who is the fourth son? It is us—Jews, Christians, Muslims, Americans, Israelis, people of conscience throughout the world, in solidarity with Israelis and Palestinians committed to coexistence and justice. Israel, trapped in a cycle of violence and conquest, is unable to accomplish this. Avnery's analysis of Israeli politics is tragically accurate. The history of the last forty years of lack of political will, even among so-called peace-seeking, moderate governments, supports this conclusion.

Observers of the political situation in Israel have begun to recognize how crippled Israeli leadership is with respect to moving toward peace. Those who allow themselves to get close enough realize that relying on Israel alone to take the necessary steps is a prescription for the continuation of conflict. Richard Falk, American professor of International Law and United Nations Special Rapporteur on the situation of human rights in the Palestinian territories, wrote in 2007, as the starvation and siege of Gaza was in full swing: "The truth is that there is no Israeli leadership with the vision or backing to negotiate such a solution, and so the struggle will continue with violence on both sides. The Israeli approach to the Palestinian challenge is based on isolating Gaza and cantonizing the West Bank, leaving the settlement blocs intact and appropriating the whole of Jerusalem as the capital of Israel. For years this sidestepping of diplomacy has dominated Israeli behavior, including during the Oslo peace process that was initiated on the White House lawn in 1993 by the famous handshake between Yitzhak Rabin and Yasir Arafat" (Falk 2007).

One wonders whether even Falk could have anticipated the ferocity of Israel's assault on defenseless Gaza one year after this piece appeared. Israel's action produced an uproar of horror and criticism from many quarters, not least of all from Israeli "New Historian" Ilan Pappe. In an opinion piece in *The Electronic Intifada* ("Israel's Righteous Fury and Its Victims in Gaza," January 2, 2009), at the height of the Israeli bombardment of Gaza, Pappe reminded us of the ideological source of and justification for Israel's action: "Israel presents itself to its own people as the righteous victim that defends itself against a great evil." In the piece, Pappe points out that "self-righteousness is a powerful act of self-denial and justification." Pappe is clear about what is needed in response to the actions of such a righteous victim: "Challenging by non-violent means a self-righteous ideological state that allows itself, aided by a mute world, to dispossess and destroy the indigenous people of Palestine, is a just and moral cause."

Taking Sides: The Role of the American Church

As a Jew, I was raised on justice. The story of the Exodus, the civil code of Leviticus, God's charge to the wandering people in Numbers and Deuteronomy, and of course the prophets—the imperative to act justly permeates the Old Testament. I was steeped in these texts from childhood, and I absorbed their messages. However, my contact with Christianity had been minimal. I first encountered the powerful social justice agenda of the American church when I returned to the United States from the West Bank in 2006. I learned that the Gospels build on the justice imperative of the prophets, and that this is expressed in the global mission of the church on denominational and local levels. Further reading in liberation theology underscored this theme for me. It helped me understand the strong response of Christians I was meeting to my message about the need for justice in the Holy Land. Pappe's direct, unvarnished statement quoted above resonates strongly. The American church hears it loud and clear. It is a call to action.

In *Jesus and Nonviolence: A Third Way*, Walter Wink spells out the critical difference between docility—which is the way Jesus's well-known injunction "resist not evil" from Matthew chapter 5 has been traditionally understood—and active, nonviolent resistance to oppression and wrongdoing. Not passivity or violent opposition, explains Wink, but "militant nonviolence" was what Jesus was advocating for the Jews of his time suffering under the tyranny of Rome. Wink's Third Way provides a road map for confronting the injustice in the Holy Land that is subjecting the peoples of both Palestine and Israel to unending conflict and loss.

I have remarked in this book about my impatience with "inter-faith" dialogues that avoid difficult discussions about the justice issues for Israel/Palestine. The church must engage this issue, not in the spirit of atonement for past sins, but rather in an active commitment to justice across denominations and with other faiths. There is an urgent need to engage in a dialogue that will lead to awareness and change. Wink reminds us that the pursuit of justice requires active involvement and often discomfort:

> Most Christians desire nonviolence, yes; but they are not talking about a non-violent struggle for justice. They mean simply the absence of conflict. They would like the system to change without having to be involved in changing it...When a church that has not lived out a costly identification with the oppressed offers to mediate between hostile parties, it merely adds to the total impression that it wants to stay above the conflict and not take sides. The church says to the lion and the lamb, "Here, let me negotiate a truce," to which the lion replies, "Fine, after I finish my lunch." (1992, 4)

Wink's admonition speaks directly to us as we witness the continued dispossession of the Palestinian people while the endless and so-called peace process continues. *One has to take sides.* Wink drives the point home when he says, "...when church leaders preach reconciliation without having unequivocally committed themselves to struggle on the side of the oppressed for justice, they are caught straddling a pseudo-neutrality made of nothing but thin air...Likewise, blanket denunciations of violence by churches place the counter-violence of the oppressed on the same level as the violence of the system that has driven the oppressed to such desperation. Are stones thrown by youth really commensurate with buckshot and real bullets fired by police?" (5).

One has to take sides.

Taking sides does not mean choosing the "side of Israel" or the "side of Palestine." Rather, it is to commit to justice, which alone will bring peace to those suffering from the conflict: Israeli, Palestinian, Muslim, Jew, Christian. Wink helps us to understand that it is the "Powers," as he names them, who are the enemies of peace. And nothing short of active engagement with the systems responsible for oppression will suffice. "The goal," he writes, "is not only our becoming free *from* the Powers, however, but *freeing* the Powers" (319).

Freeing the Powers: The Gospels as the Record of a Social Transformation Movement

Richard Horsley, in his 2003 *Jesus and Empire: The Kingdom of God and the New World Disorder*, draws a direct parallel between first-century Palestine and the current world situation. Characterizing the effect of global capitalism as *disorder* in its disorganizing and impoverishing effect on the great majority of humanity, Horsley points out that the intention and function of the Roman Empire was to exploit and oppress subject populations through military terrorism and economic control. He interprets the Gospels as a record of Jesus's movement against the forces of Rome and its destruction of the indigenous Palestinian (Judean and Galilean) society of his time.

Horsley points out that in the first century, our modern Western distinction between religion and politics did not exist. Over the centuries, however, and in the process of transforming Christianity into an established religion and then into the religion of the Empire, the Jesus of the Gospels has been depoliticized. The original, highly political thrust of his message has been removed or distorted. Horsley gives us a vivid description of the systematic domination of Rome over the Palestinian Jews in the centuries before and after Jesus's birth. He demonstrates, through an analysis of his sayings and ministry, that Jesus was resisting the abuses of the political system. Jesus grew up in the Galilee during a time of intense political unrest, resistance, and rebellion. His ministry must therefore be understood as the creation of a popular movement that was a response to the social and political reality of his time. The motivation for and thrust of Jesus's teachings was to support the peasants of the Galilee against the damage to their families, health, psyches, and communities caused by the terrorizing oppression of Rome and Rome's client rulers in Judea and Galilee. In fact, Jesus's struggle with the Jewish establishment of the time represented by the priests and the Temple was not over "religious" issues. Rather, his opposition to the Temple cult and its clerical power structure was based on its support of the Roman system of economic exploitation and political control of the people.

The Kingdom of God, according to Horsley, is a program for the renewal of Israel, meaning the establishment of a social and political order with "concrete economic, social and political" meanings (77). This vision of a renewal and of a new world order was advanced to directly address the crushing economic and political injustices of the times. Far from being about opposition to Judaism or an effort to "replace" Judaism with a new religion, Jesus's message was about a return to the core social justice principles of the Mosaic code, which was dedicated to the protection and preservation of a stable agrarian society based on family and village life. The parable of the tenants of the vineyard in Mark 12, for example, would have resonated powerfully with the Jews of Jesus's time. "Palestinian peasants," writes Horsley, "had firsthand knowledge of the slice of life portrayed in the parable of the tenants." It was the Roman program of exploitation based on legally sanctioned impoverishment and enforced by military terrorism (95). He points out that the farmers and villagers of the Palestine of Jesus's time "knew very well that that many of their number were being transformed from freeholders farming their own ancestral land into tenants of the wealthy rulers and their officers who had taken effective control (ownership?) of those lands" (94).

In bringing the example of the Palestine of Jesus's time directly into the present day, Horsley is calling for the "repoliticization" of the Gospels. "The Kingdom of God," he writes, "is somewhat analogous to the bipartite agenda of anti-colonial (or anti-imperial) movements in which the withdrawal (or defeat) of the colonizing power is the counterpart and condition of the colonized people's restoration to independence and self-determination" (14).

In other words, Jesus was leading a popular resistance movement. Its purpose was to support the agrarian, community-based society of first-century Palestine against the structure of control being imposed by Rome and its client rulers (king and Temple). It was a political system that was destroying the fabric of the society and the lives, families, and health of the people. His "prophecy" about the coming Kingdom of God was a call for change based on faith in God's love for the people and his intention to restore them. God's action in granting this renewal was dependent not on loyalty to God (Old Testament narrative) nor on faith in God's redeeming power (later Christian creed). Rather, Jesus called on the people to commit to a lifestyle centered in social justice and respect for human dignity, and for a social system based on interdependency, trust, and compassion.

Resistance to empire was a fundamental component of this vision, but not through violent insurrection. Under the circumstances, this would have been suicidal (Horsley speculates that Jesus would have witnessed the horrendous Roman suppression of the popular revolts in the early decades of the first century CE). Rather, Jesus's message was about shoring up and supporting the growth of the *ecclesia*—the small gatherings of the faithful, firmly based within the everyday life of the indigenous community. The model of *ecclesia* was, after all, the original model instituted by Paul throughout the Mediterranean during the early growth of Christianity. This is what is meant by the Kingdom of God. The references to food and to forgiveness in the Lord's Prayer, for example, are concerned not with duties to God, theological principles, or ritual observance. Rather, the prayer speaks directly to the relationship between people: forgiving indebtedness (indebtedness having been the chief mechanism, along with taxes, of forced impoverishment and land taking used by the Romans and their client rulers), feeding people, and social justice. Thy will be done *on earth* is the point of the prayer prescribed by Jesus to his followers.

What are the implications of this understanding of Jesus's ministry for the role of the church and, for that matter, the mosque and synagogue in our time? Wink's call to "free the powers" summons us to make our institutions into instruments of justice. Revisiting the situation of the first century calls us back to community, to the values of social justice and human dignity that are at the heart of religion.

In turning from his analysis of the Jesus movement to a critique of the modern church, Horsley echoes Wink's message. Horsley asks us to understand Jesus's utterances, as preserved in the Gospels, in the political context of the times. "The churches," writes Horsley, have, with some exceptions, "acquiesced to their own marginalization" (148). When we accept the modern depoliticizing of religion, we drift far from the original mission of the *ecclesia* formed around and devoted to the mission of social renewal and commitment to human dignity. When we see the "churches settled into their confinement to the religious sphere" (148), submits Horsley, we leave the empire "unchallenged" in its present incarnation of global corporations pursuing their goals of domination of subject populations with the support—willing or coerced—of governments. "It should be possible," advises Horsley, "to cut through the standard depoliticizing assumptions and approaches in order to listen afresh, with antennae attuned to imperial power relations, to the Gospel representations of a prophetic political leader of subject people" (149). This, according to Horsley, was the direction and meaning of the Jesus movement: to take "collective action to retake control of their lives under the conditions of the new world disorder that Rome had imposed upon them" (149).

How do we go about confronting the historical and ongoing injustice that has been the lot of the dispossessed, humiliated, and terrorized people of Palestine? How do we address the calamity visited upon the citizens of Israel, forced, as Ilan Pappe puts it, to live in "Fortress Israel," (2006, 253) subjected to sixty years of insecurity, militarization, and episodic terror attacks?

One State or Two States?

If Israel is to survive, it must reenvision itself. As we contemplate the disaster of stalemate and blindness that characterizes

Israeli politics today, and as the occupied territories continue to sink into a morass of violence and repression, denial begins to yield to the realization of the need for a radically new look at the fundamentals of the state. One way that this push for a new direction is manifesting itself is in the reemergence of the movement toward a "one-state solution." It is not a new idea, but it has resurfaced in an alliance of Palestinians who have had enough of the endless and fruitless "peace process" and Israelis—many in exile in the United Kingdom and the United States—who, with an increasing sense of urgency, have devoted their academic and political careers to saving their country. These Israelis, like peace activist Uri Avnery, have joined the ranks of Palestinians and others in declaring that the emperor has no clothes: that successive Israeli governments have been committed, not to progress toward a negotiated settlement, but to a policy of endless delay. Meron Benvenisti, the former deputy mayor of Jerusalem, stated the obvious in a recent article in *Haaretz*, "The Binationalism Vogue," appearing on April 30, 2009. In it, Benvenisti pointed out that the new Netanyahu government has no intention of moving toward the establishment of an autonomous Palestinian state. The government's use of the term "two states" can only be described as a "smokescreen of imagined progress toward a dead end."

The idea of a single state for Jews and Arabs emerged in the early twentieth century. It was championed by such Jewish luminaries as Martin Buber and Judah Magnes, who were joined in the 1920s by Albert Einstein and a number of Zionist organizations. The notion of one state for both peoples, always a minority position, suffered significant setbacks in the wake of Arab-Jewish violence in the late 1920s and the Arab revolt of 1936 to 1939. In 1937, the Peel Commission, appointed by the British Crown to recommend a political solution to the conflict between Jewish and Arab interests, concluded that the best solution lay in the separation of the two peoples through the partition of Palestine. Any further discussion about sharing the land was smothered in the ashes of Auschwitz-Birkenau and drowned out by the cheers of most of the Jewish and Western world that greeted the declaration of the State of Israel in 1948. Arab nationalist sentiment, faced with the reality of the Jewish state, similarly rejected the idea of binationality in the framework of a state so designated and so constructed. The concept only resurfaced in the aftermath of the 1967 war, in which Israel gained control of the West Bank and Gaza. It remained, however, the province of a small handful of Palestinian and non-Jewish Western analysts (e.g., Tilley, Abunimah) until recently.

Critics of the one-state solution say it's a dream, the obstacles too daunting. Those committed to keeping the idea in play counter that, with the colonization and fragmentation of the West Bank all but complete, the two-state option has already passed us by. For over half a century a discounted or frankly ignored concept, the idea of a single state for Jews and Arabs in Palestine is now receiving attention in the public forum.

In her review of a conference entitled "One State for Palestine-Israel" held in Boston, Massachusetts, in early 2009, analyst Nadia Hijab noted that "one of the few—perhaps only—Zionist speakers at the conference, former deputy mayor of Jerusalem Meron Benvenisti, came to bury Zionism not to praise it." Hijab quotes Benvenisti as saying, "As a Zionist, I wanted a Jewish state but that option is abrogated. The 'one state' is already here, the only question is what kind of state it will be." It's a false issue, continued Benvenisti, since it is not yet clear what kind of political settlement will be pursued, and in any case the final outcome is likely to be the result of a staged process. Ilan Pappe, who also spoke at the conference, suggested that given the extreme difficulty of the situation posed by the facts on the ground, we must at this point strive not for a "solution," but rather a process of continued dialogue in which the terms of the discourse are changed to acknowledge the rightful claims of the Palestinian people.

Stephen Walt, professor of International Relations at Harvard's Kennedy School of Government and coauthor of *The Israel Lobby*, weighed in on this issue in an article in the April 2009 issue of *Foreign Policy*. "So what are Israel's options?" he asks. "One alternative would be to make the West Bank and Gaza part of Israel, but allow the Palestinians who live there to have full political rights, thereby creating a binational liberal democracy. This idea has been promoted by a handful of Israeli Jews and a growing number of Palestinians, but the objections to it are compelling. It would mean abandoning the Zionist vision of a Jewish state, which makes it anathema to almost all Israeli Jews, who want to live in a Jewish state."

But what is it that is "compelling" about these objections to the idea of a liberal, pluralistic democracy in the territory of historic Palestine? Does the simple fact that some Jews do not want to accept the idea of a shared state render it somehow unacceptable or outside the bounds of allowable discourse? The question must be asked: do Jews want to live in a Jewish state or a secure and prosperous one? Can the vibrant Jewish society that has been created in Israel retain its Jewish character and also be part of something else, something more diverse, something that encompasses a vision bigger than the cherished right, granted by the Jews to themselves over one hundred years ago, to a national homeland in historic Palestine? Is it possible that those who insist on seeing the state as a prize awarded to a privileged, exclusive group might become a minority in Israel, much like the marginalized ultra-nationalists and ethnic supremacists that exist in the midst of other pluralistic, democratic societies the world over? Could it be that the Jews of Israel, and indeed the Jews of the world, find themselves on the cusp of accepting for consideration the concept of historic Palestine as "a country for all its citizens," as the subtitle of the Boston conference reads? Could we begin to understand that a solution fulfilling this simple description, whatever political form it may assume, is the one that might save Israel, whatever it becomes and whatever it is called?

Of one thing we can be certain, and Walt makes this very clear in his piece: time is running out for the two-state solution. It is increasingly clear that Israel's current government is not committed to the establishment of a viable, autonomous Palestinian state in the West Bank and Gaza. Walt appeals to Israel's supporters here in the U.S. to use every possible means to support the

Obama administration in taking a firm stance with the Netanyahu government. "If they don't," he warns, they may someday have to explain to their grandchildren why they watched Israel drive itself off a cliff and did nothing to stop it."[1]

What are the alternatives to the nondemocratic, apartheid reality which is rapidly coming to pass? There are two: In the first, Israel withdraws to the 1949 armistice lines, the de facto recognized border and the one that has now been accepted by the Arab League and several Arab governments, including Palestinian governments. It must dismantle the settlements; relinquish control of the roads, borders, and water resources of the West Bank; allow for the return or resettlement of Palestinian refugees; and cease and reverse the project to Judaize "greater Jerusalem," an expanded metropolis that effectively cuts the West Bank in half. The second alternative is to contemplate a unitary, multinational state, perhaps through a federated structure. Which scenario is more plausible?

It is not in the province of this book to answer that question. Qualified minds are studying this and working desperately hard to set the stage for the change that must come. What is important is that the conversation is happening. It is clear that, if the "one-state" option is rejected, a significant change must occur in the current political and military reality that exists now in historic Palestine. In both of the non-apartheid scenarios described above, Israel must undo forty years of occupation. If it fails to do this, it must be prepared to acknowledge that it has conquered

---

1. This same expression, "we are going over a cliff," was used by Daniel Levy, codirector of the Middle East Task Force of the New America Foundation, in an address at the annual conference of Churches for Middle East Peace in Washington, DC, in June 2009. Levy appealed to the audience of delegates from Christian denominations from across the U.S. to aggressively and urgently advocate for a strong U.S. role in brokering a peace agreement leading to a two-state solution. We are losing the battle for peace in Israel, said Levy, by "we" referring to the peace camp in Israel. The only hope, he stated, lies in the U.S., under the new Obama administration, stepping in and taking a firm stand with the Netanyahu government on critical issues such as the growth of Israeli West Bank settlements.

and now controls the entire territory, and that it is taking on the responsibilities of a colonial power. Israel would then face the prospect of continued ethnic cleansing and the strengthening of the apartheid system that is already in place. Only undoing the occupation, whether through partition or unification, brings with it the possibility of peace. The alternative will yield continuing popular resistance, unending conflict, and mounting isolation from the rest of the world.

The End of Israel?

The one-state concept serves to frame the issue. Fervent opposition to the notion of the single, shared state on the part of most of world Jewry is based on a notion that this will be the end of Israel. But is "one state" the end of Israel? As we know it, yes. But is that the end or a new beginning, reversing the mistakes that accompanied Israel's founding and that have led to this impasse? Is the end of Israel as a majority Jewish state the end of the Jewish people? Why should that be so? Because a "strong," Jewish Israel is needed to prevent the next Holocaust? What would Benjamin Netanyahu do without the threat of a nuclear Iran? Would he invent another mortal enemy? In a May 2009 piece, Stephen Walt names Netanyahu's approach to power "the treason of the hawks," using the term coined by Fred Iklé, Ronald Reagan's Undersecretary of Defense, describing "those tragic situations where hardliners stubbornly refuse to make peace and thereby lead their countries to disaster" (Walt 2009). As we contemplate the actions of successive Israeli governments, and now the rhetoric of Israel's present leadership, Walt's historic analogy is chillingly apt. We must reject the "treason of the hawks," those who would lead Israel into one disastrous war after another, and consider not the end, but the future of the Jewish people. Can we not be Jewish in the United States and the other countries of our so-called Diaspora? Could we not be Jewish in a new Israel, an Israel—whatever it is called and however it is politically fashioned—in which we live alongside and as equals with the other peoples of the land? Of course we can, if—to borrow Herzl's famous statement at the inauguration of the Zionist project over one hundred years ago—we really want it. We are facing a threat to our continuation that is as critical as that faced by the Jews in the inhospitable Europe of Herzl's time. But, unlike the situation in Europe at that time, the present threat is not external. It is, rather, our own inability to shift from the defensive position learned during centuries of persecution. What is required is not easy: we must recognize that the greatest threat to our survival today is not the existence of an external enemy. The threat, rather, is our unwillingness to embrace the other people in whose midst we live and with whom we are called to reconcile.

Christians faced a similar challenge when confronted with the consequences of their actions toward the Jewish people over the centuries. And the solution was reconciliation, dialogue, and mutual acceptance. Ilan Pappe, speaking at the March 2009 conference, indicated that the discussion prompted by the movement for one state involves much more than a political calculus. Rather, it requires the Jewish people to begin a discussion about the ways in which we have let our past experience determine our present choices. This discussion has begun at the grassroots level within American Jewry. In a recent blog, written on the occasion of Israel's celebration of its founding—a day called, curiously, *Yom Ha'atzmaut*, or "Independence Day"—Reconstructionist Rabbi Brant Rosen offered this declaration: "I didn't celebrate *Yom Ha'atzmaut* today. I don't think I can celebrate this holiday anymore." Yom Ha'atzmaut, it should be noted, is not just a holiday in Israel. It has entered the Jewish calendar throughout the world, with parades and festivals in our synagogues, schools, and community centers. Rosen goes on to explain his decision:

> That doesn't mean I'm not acknowledging the anniversary of Israel's independence—only that I can no longer view this milestone as a day for celebration. I've come to believe that for Jews, *Yom Ha'atzmaut* is more appropriately observed as an occasion for reckoning and honest soul searching. As a Jew, as someone

who has identified with Israel for his entire life, it is profoundly painful to me to admit the honest truth of this day: that Israel's founding is inextricably bound up with its dispossession of the indigenous inhabitants of the land. In the end, Yom Ha'atzmaut and what the Palestinian people refer to as the Nakba are two inseparable sides of the same coin. And I simply cannot separate these two realities any more....Many of us in the co-existence community speak of "dual narratives"—and how critical it is for each side to be open to hearing the other's "story." I now believe that it's not nearly enough…for us to be open to the narrative of the Nakba and all it represents for Palestinians. In the end, we must also be willing to own our role in this narrative. Until we do this, it seems to me, the very concept of coexistence will be nothing but a hollow cliche. (2009)

These statements of an Israeli historian and an American rabbi are examples of the "moment of truth" experience described in chapter 1. For the Jewish people, that moment of truth is now. For Christians, now witnessing the destruction of a society and the suffering of the oppressed, it is the call to return in their hearts to the Palestine of two thousand years ago, to a time when the prophet Isaiah's proclamation, recorded in the opening of all four gospels, was again sent out:

The voice of one crying out in the wilderness: "Prepare the way of the Lord, make his paths straight!" (Mark 1:3 [NRSV]).

The call to action is loud and clear.

Chapter 13

A Call to Action

Change the wind, transform the debate, recast the discussion, alter the political context in which decisions are being made, and you will change the outcomes. Move the conversation around a crucial issue to a whole new place, and you will open up possibilities for change never dreamed of before. And you will be surprised at how fast the politicians adjust to the change in the wind.

—Jim Wallis, *God's Politics*

Lana Abuhijleh is the country director of an international relief agency operating in the West Bank and Gaza. In February 2009, in the immediate aftermath of the bombardment of Gaza, I sat with Lana in her office in Ramallah, discussing, among other pressing issues, her inability to provide psychological assistance to her staff in Gaza because of Israel's continued blockade of the border crossings and the seaport. Like almost all Palestinians living under occupation, Lana has a story. At one point during our conversation, Lana told me about the morning her mother was gunned down by Israeli forces in front of her home in Nablus. Lana's father and brother were sitting beside her when it happened and were injured. "More tea?" she asked as she recounted this in a matter-of-fact way. These stories are not told for sympathy or to initiate further discussion. They are simply to record: this is our reality. I asked Lana about her present life. How did she live now? Did she have family? How did she manage to negotiate the restrictions on movement? Lana told me that she lived in Jerusalem now, commuting to Ramallah, a short drive if you don't consider the checkpoints. One day, she was making the trip with her eight-year-old daughter. The twenty-five-foot-high separation wall accompanies you on the six-mile journey, built right along the road, dividing the northern suburbs annexed by Israel that will comprise "Greater Jerusalem" from what will remain, presumably, as the Palestinian West Bank. Her daughter, sitting quietly for a time, turned to her and asked, "Mommy, why do they make the Jews live behind that wall?"

The wall had been built to keep this child out, but she saw the builders of the wall as the prisoners. Lana was telling me this to make that very point, and I agreed. My experience has been that the Palestinians, trapped in their ever-shrinking bantustans, cut off from their farmlands, markets, and families and forced to undergo humiliating and unpredictable delays at every turn, have not lost their dignity or even their hope. In contrast, the great majority of the Jewish citizens of Israel are the prisoners of their own fear, a fear buttressed by their failure to know their Palestinian neighbors for who they truly are. Both peoples, however, are trapped. Both peoples are crying for relief and for liberation. Palestinians are prisoners in their own land—dispossessed, powerless, contemplating the loss of their future as Israel's program of annexation and colonization continues. Israelis live behind a wall of fear, isolation, and a soul-killing racism toward a people with whom they share a history, common cultural elements, and the love of a single land. The political process has failed to bring down the walls and to liberate the people of the land. It is time to invoke Walter Wink's summons to "free the powers." Freeing the powers means taking power into our own hands. It is the purpose of this final chapter to outline how this can be done.

A Brief Review

Before we turn to specific ideas for action, it will be helpful to review the central arguments of this book:

This is a just, moral, and urgent cause. World peace depends on solving this conflict and bringing about a stable, lasting peace for the Holy Land.

Peace will not come without justice. Political arrangements and settlements must be informed by an awareness of the issues of justice and fairness. Political settlements that do not do this will not bring peace, but continued and worsening conflict.

Politics have failed to bring about such a resolution. What is needed is a broad social movement that will, in Jim Wallis's words, change the wind and drive the political process. This movement must consist of people in the United States working in collaboration with international peace groups and organizations operating in Israel/Palestine.

It is time to reframe the interfaith dialogue. There is a special role in this movement for the faith communities, who by their nature are called to work for social justice. The conflict challenges both the Jewish and Christian communities to examine deeply held beliefs and attitudes regarding the land and the relationship between the faiths. It challenges us to create the conversations that will help to bring about a lasting peace. In the process of these conversations, both groups must recognize the severity and the consequences of the historic and current injustice to the Palestinian people. For both groups, this will entail overcoming their reasons for avoiding, denying, or glossing over the facts of this injustice, the harm that it is causing for all peoples and faiths living in the Holy Land, and the insurmountable obstacle to peace that it constitutes. For both Christians and Jews, it means bringing courage and honesty to the interfaith activities that will be required for the work to come. It means ensuring that these activities are truly in the service of peace based on justice, and not merely a comfortable show of "peacemaking."

For the Jewish people, it means overcoming our legacy of using isolation and exceptionalism as a defense against persecution and marginalization. It means that we must leave behind, in both the theological and cultural realms, the image of ourselves as special and apart. It is only from this position that we will be able to enter into community with the Palestinians, with whom we share the land, and with the other faiths, with whom we must join in the struggle to bring about a world of justice and equality.

For Christians, it means honoring the continuing importance of atonement for Christianity's anti-Jewish past and vigilance against its future occurrence, while not confusing this with the imperative to recognize and fight injustice, whatever the source. In the current situation, this means confronting the fear that engendering the displeasure of the Jewish establishment will deal a fatal blow to the results of sixty years of interfaith reconciliation. It means being ready to grieve the disruption of relationships with Jewish friends and family members. And if, given the pain and discomfort of this process, patience is wanting, then perhaps there is a need to bring to mind the parable of the fig tree from the Gospel of Luke. Give the tree time to bear fruit.

The interfaith enterprise is a worthy and time-honored pursuit. But it must not be allowed to hold hostage the urgent requirement of witnessing and confronting the injustice taking place in the Holy Land. Christians have confessed their history of anti-Semitism and the anti-Jewish biases that can still be found among them. But fidelity to this confession must not be confused with or allowed to block the prophetic work that calls. Christians are called to this work by the social justice imperative of their faith that propels the work of global mission wherever in the world it is required. It would be wonderful if, as Christians respond to this call, they can do so in the company of the other faiths, and this is happening to some extent. But if some in the Jewish community decline to join in this work, this must not be seen as a barrier. If an organized portion of the Jewish community, claiming to speak for the whole, mounts official opposition to actions by American churches to address injustices suffered by the Palestinians, this must not impede or slow the work. If Christians allow opposition from some Jewish groups to thwart their work for justice and peace in the Holy Land, there may be a future confession that will have to be made: that the call to respond to the suffering of those in the Holy Land living under the boot of oppression was not heeded.

It's up to the United States to create the conditions for peace. We cannot rely on the parties to the conflict to reach resolution through a bilateral process. There is little to no possibility that the government of Israel and the Palestinian Authority will be able to reach a settlement. The Palestinian government has been incapacitated in various ways, most recently by the invalidation of its 2006 elections in which Hamas won a majority of seats.[1] Israel too is politically crippled by a system in which leadership must govern through a coalition of warring political parties. Israel is a state that, although it exercises total control over four million Palestinians, is itself out of control. Israel cannot save itself from its current headlong rush toward an apartheid system and a condition of permanent conflict. Left to itself, Israel will continue to build walls, conduct murderous assaults on defenseless civilian populations, and colonize territories captured in war, becoming more and more, in Ilan Pappe's powerful image, "fortress Israel." The United States, leading a coalition of international players, must intervene.

This will require an immediate, strong, and active stance—identifying the key components for peace and prevailing on both parties to reach an agreement through negotiation. The current U.S. administration appears willing and ready to assume this responsibility. However, there are significant political challenges

---

1. In the Palestinian legislative election of January 2006, Hamas (an Arabic acronym for "Islamic Resistance Movement") won an overwhelming majority of seats—seventy-six to the forty-three earned by Fatah, the then ruling party. Although the election was ruled free and fair by international observers, Israel and the United States combined efforts to block the formation of a government based on the results of the election. The U.S. shut off all financial aid to the Palestinian Authority. Israel jailed sixty-four of the elected Hamas representatives (they remain in jail at this writing, June 2009), as well as ten Hamas members proposed for the Palestinian cabinet. Other Hamas leaders went into exile. All efforts to form a unity government for the West Bank and Gaza failed. In June 2007, Hamas assumed control of Gaza. An interim government led by Fatah exercises control in areas of the West Bank.

facing the administration if it is to take on Israel/Palestine, an issue that has depleted political capital for previous presidents without producing a lasting peace between Israel and the Palestinians. This challenge is all the more daunting for a president who is now in the position of pushing back on a right-wing Israeli government that appears unwilling to stop settlement construction or embrace the idea of a Palestinian state. Therefore, it is urgent that we provide our government with the support it needs to take this on successfully. This then is the call to change the wind, as movements originating in the church have done in the past. And, because of the political realities of this particular issue, it is on the American church that this responsibility falls.

A settlement is not peace. At this writing, a new American administration has pledged to reverse the policy of noninvolvement of the previous administration and to move forward aggressively to reach a political settlement based on two states. But the question remains: what kind of settlement? Anyone who has seen the "facts on the ground" of the hugely developed infrastructure of the three settlement blocs penetrating deep into Palestinian territory and the network of restricted roads linking them with pre-1967 Israel wonders what a "return to the 1967 borders" can mean. There are those who are guardedly optimistic that the signals from the president regarding the Israel-Palestine conflict are an indication that a settlement will be reached in his first term, perhaps even within the first two years. We allow ourselves to imagine the end of the checkpoints and free movement for Palestinians to their markets, fields, and places of worship. We imagine an end to the humiliation of the Palestinians and the brutalizing of Israeli society. A political settlement is essential, and it is an urgent need. But it is only the beginning. Assuming that the issues of borders, Jerusalem, and refugees are resolved, the biggest questions that remain are: what will Palestinian society look like after this settlement, and what will be the relationship between the two peoples?

The faith community must be engaged. The Israel-Palestine conflict is not a struggle about religion. It is about land, water, demography, and human rights. That is not to say, however, that faith does not play a central role in determining the outcome of the conflict. What happens in Palestine is of compelling interest to people from the three Abrahamic faiths. As we've seen throughout this book, this interest is not limited to groups on the "extreme" edges: fundamentalist Jewish settlers, dispensationalist Christians, or fundamentalist Muslims. These groups wield influence, but as the minority. In contrast, the examples of Zionist beliefs within the liberal mainstream demonstrate the importance of engaging the major Christian denominations in the conversation about the future of the Holy Land. If a Lutheran theologian can say that the Land is the Jewish sacrament, and a liberal Catholic historian and a Protestant professor of theology can both hold up the covenant with Abraham, and with it the promise of the land, as the foundation for Christian belief, these must be considered as evidence of powerful Zionist sentiments to be found, hiding in plain sight, in the midst of mainstream American Christianity.

The beliefs that people hold about the meaning of the Holy Land are part of the problem, but they are also part of the solution. The beliefs that provide license for Jewish transgressions and that inhibit Christian actions to redress those sins are powerful, but they are not all-powerful. Brought out into the light of day, they yield to our better natures and our collective commitment to fairness and social justice. The majority of people of faith want to see the parties sharing the land equitably and coexisting in harmony and security. The drive for justice must be brought to bear in the framework of a new, shared covenant. Once the barriers to the forging of this new covenant are understood, the work of bringing it about can proceed.

Voices of Faith

Are we experiencing a "Great Awakening"? In his 2008 book by that name, Jim Wallis tells us that "something is happening. Faith is being applied to the work of social justice in ways that we might never have imagined just a few short years ago" (1). Wallis's thesis is that, when the times demand it, faith is the force that propels forward movements for political and societal change. Wallis further asserts that faith is a necessary adjunct to political activity—that in fact it is the driver—providing the guidance and the engine for change. As a prime example, Wallis describes how the black church's awakening in the fifties and sixties in the United States was an essential ingredient for the success of the struggle for civil rights led by Dr. Martin Luther King Jr. For King, it was his personal faith, tested in the crucible of failures, death threats, and frustration, that pulled him through. Faith, writes Wallis, provides the "fire, the passion, the strength, the perseverance, and the hope necessary for social movements to win, and to change politics" (21). But it was the church, with its powerful social justice agenda, that provided King with the structure and the platform for his movement. Let us recall how King closed the 1963 "Letter from a Birmingham Jail," his stirring call for nonviolent resistance to over three hundred years of institutionalized racism in America. Responding to the plea of his fellow clergymen for moderation and a delay until the time was right, King cried out in anguish, "Yes, I love the church...Yes, I see the church as the body of Christ. But, oh! How we have blemished and scarred that body through social neglect and through fear of being nonconformists." He continued:

> There was a time when the church was very powerful—in the time when the early Christians rejoiced at being deemed worthy to suffer for what they believed. In those days the church was not merely a thermometer that recorded the ideas and principles of popular opinion; it was a thermostat that transformed the mores of society. Whenever the early Christians entered a town, the people in power became disturbed and immediately sought to convict the Christians for being "disturbers of the peace" and "outside agitators." But the Christians pressed on, in the conviction that they were "a colony of heaven," called to obey God rather than man...the judgment of God is upon the church as never before. If today's church does not recapture the sacrificial spirit of the early church, it will lose its authenticity, forfeit the

loyalty of millions, and be dismissed as an irrelevant social club with no meaning for the twentieth century. (King 1963)

Like the power of prophecy, like Amos's mighty stream, the passion for justice cannot be forever held in check. This is why the impulse within the church to address the issue of justice in Palestine has begun to break through the barrier of the church's agenda of atonement for anti-Semitism. To borrow Richard Horsley's term, in order for this social movement to gain momentum, the depoliticization of religion must be overcome. The role of *ecclesia*, groups united by faith and rooted in community, must be reclaimed. Today, forty-six years after King's letter was penned in response to urgent human rights issues on a global scale, voices are being raised to reclaim that role for faith. Here are some of them:

Jim Wallis of Sojourners: What is needed is nothing less than a renovation of our souls and the soul of our politics…But this is not a spiritualized critique. It is instead grounded in the politics of the Bible, in what authentic faith/belief creates in terms of actions and lifestyle. Society and politics both shape and reflect our spiritual values, and those values are increasingly empty. How does a nation of endangered souls recover an authentic faith that is true to the gospel, the example of Jesus, the witness of the prophets, and the crushing needs of our times? What would such a recovery mean for evangelicals, mainline Protestants, Catholics, Jews, Muslims, seekers, and everyday people? (2005, 36)

Karin Armstrong, author of The History of God: I went to the United Nations recently and was told that this was the first time that they'd had a discussion of religion in the General Assembly. They've kept it out on grounds of principle. This is part of the reason we're in this kind of mess. Of course we value the separation of church and state, but religion is nevertheless a fact out there to be reckoned with. Whether the United Nations or the pundits or the politicians like it or not, fundamentalism worldwide has shown that people want religion reflected more clearly in their polity. This secularist disdain in government has got to end. It's just a matter of sheer common sense now to gain intelligence about religion; not just a quick crash course in fundamentalism or Islam, but a real understanding of the emotions, sensitivities, and aspirations that go along with faith. (2002)

Rabbi Michael Lerner, Network of Spiritual Progressives: We in the Tikkun Community use the word "spiritual" to include all those whose deepest values lead them to challenge the ethos of selfishness and materialism that has led people into a frantic search for money and power and away from a life that places love, kindness, generosity, peace, nonviolence, social justice, awe and wonder at the grandeur of creation, thanksgiving, humility and joy at the center of our lives. We believe that many of the secular movements that exist in the world today actually have deep spiritual underpinnings, but often they are themselves unaware of those foundations, unable or unwilling to articulate them and sometimes even holding a knee-jerk antagonism to explicit spiritual or religious language. (2002)

Changing the Wind

Momentum is growing—the ingredients are in place for the broad social movement required to change the politics of the Israel-Palestine conflict. A new American administration appears to be committed to changing the policies of the past. Through the Internet and a slow but steady shift in mainstream media coverage, the American public is becoming more aware of the true nature of the situation on the ground. Small but resilient groups in Israel and in the Palestinian territories carry out a wide range of nonviolent resistance activities on a daily basis—political protest, education, support groups, and services to provide assistance to groups engaged in nonviolent resistance and the provision of social services. Internationals, on the ground in the Holy Land and in their own countries, continue to provide support for these activist and civil society groups and for individuals and communities affected by the conflict and the ongoing occupation.

And the sleeping giant of the American church is waking up. No longer is support for and connection with the Holy Land the sole province of the humanitarian institutions, such as hospitals and schools, that the denominations have provided for generations, although these are important and vital projects. Congregations invite speakers from the region to talk about their experiences living under occupation or working for political change. Americans from all walks of life and political orientations are hungry for education on the history of the conflict. Increasingly, devotional pilgrimages to the Holy Land add visits with activist and peace groups to their tour itineraries. Christian and interfaith delegations visit places such as Hebron, Bethlehem, Gaza, and other locations where people are suffering from dispossession and from restrictions on commerce, worship, and family life. Israeli peace activists and military service resisters tour the United States to talk about the impact of their country's policies and their growing awareness of Israel's history of injustice to the Palestinians. Palestinians, sometimes in the company of Israeli Jews, visit churches, synagogues, mosques, and community centers to share their stories and forge critically important ties between our society and theirs. Experts equipped with maps and photographs visit churches and give lectures to warn that the time is near when a Jewish "Greater Jerusalem" will put an end to the possibility of a Palestinian state in the West Bank. They show in chilling detail how neighborhoods in East Jerusalem and historically Palestinian sections of Jerusalem's Old City are being systematically cleansed of their non-Jewish inhabitants through expulsions and home demolitions. Palestinian Christians are continuing their steady rate of emigration as their ability to make a living disappears and their children leave the country to pursue education and careers closed to them in their homeland. World Christians are contemplating the prospect of the virtual disappearance of the Christian population of the West Bank within two generations.

Americans at the grass roots are now seeing the true faces of the Holy Land: Palestinians who are farmers, not terrorists; Jews who are war resisters, not soldiers, and peacemakers, not wall-builders.

Denominations have taken the issue to a policy level at their national conferences, considering resolutions to divest from companies profiting from the military occupation and the illegal colonization of Palestinian lands. And, finally, the issue is being taken up at ecumenical and interfaith levels. These linkages, across denominations and faith communities, and between faith communities and secular organizations committed to peace, may ultimately prove to be the most important ingredient in the recipe for changing the wind. It is to these linkages—community writ large—that we must look as we turn to the work before us.

At this writing, the political landscape is shifting and unpredictable. Things may move quickly or persist for some time in their current state of simmering, slow decline. But whether a political settlement leading to a lasting peace is achieved within the next few years or the current situation of stalemate and intermittent conflict persists, the need will continue for the faith communities to be educated, mobilized, and increasingly active at two levels: support for civil society and direct political action. Under either scenario—that of a transition to a just political solution or a continuation of occupation—support for civil society in Israel/Palestine will be crucial. Maintaining the linkages between the three Abrahamic faith communities in the United States and those struggling to live a life of dignity in the Holy Land will continue to be paramount. However, in this time of growing awareness of the urgent situation coupled with the opportunity afforded by a new U.S. administration, the responsibility to act directly on the political level calls out the loudest.

This book opened with Jim Wallis's observation that when politics fail to bring about required change, great social movements emerge. We are facing such a time as we confront the situation of injustice and continuing conflict in the Holy Land. We identified two barriers to addressing this state of affairs: the Jewish clinging to a stance of self-protection and privilege, and the Christian focus on atonement for its role in Jewish suffering. For guidance on overcoming those barriers, we've looked to the example of Jesus's movement of social transformation in the face of conditions that bear uncanny similarity to the plight of Palestinians today. And we've considered that through a new covenantal community, one in which the barriers between faith communities and denominations can be overcome, a movement is being born that can truly bring about the transformation so urgently desired. We can change the wind—and the time is now.

A Prescription for Action

The following six categories summarize activities being pursued within the faith communities in the United States, by ecumenical and interfaith organizations, and on the part of secular groups working for peace. They are offered here as examples of work that has begun and that needs to continue. Among organized faith communities, the churches have the head start at this point. As these activities expand on local, regional, and national levels and are coordinated across congregations and denominations, and as the linkages with secular organizations grow, it is hoped that the Jewish and Muslim communities will increasingly participate. Appendix A provides a detailed list of organizations, web sites, and resources.

Local Actions

The church's social justice agenda is perhaps best exemplified in the global mission work being carried out on congregational levels. Committees devoted to identifying and pursuing global mission projects exist in most churches. Congregations often pursue these missions in partnership with "sister" churches in other communities in the United States or in foreign countries. In other examples, local committees support the hospitals, schools, or other humanitarian projects of their respective denominations, or create relationships with communities in need of long-term or emergency assistance as a result of natural disaster, conflict, or environmental degradation. Due to growing awareness of the situation in Palestine, congregations are adding Palestinian causes (in the occupied territories as well as in Israel) to their global mission activities.

Political Advocacy

There are a variety of ways to have an impact on U.S. policy through both the legislative and executive branches. As individual Americans have become more educated about the nature of U.S. policy toward Israel, they are beginning to make their voices heard on these policy issues through their elected representatives and through direct contact with the White House and the Department of State. Several developments provide hope that the near-absolute power of AIPAC, the American Israel Political Action Committee or so-called Israel lobby, over our national policy is beginning to weaken. A number of senators and congresspersons who visited Gaza in early 2009 in the aftermath of Israel's assault returned asking questions about the legitimacy and wisdom of Israel's actions and are calling for a fresh look at our policy toward Israel. J Street, the "other" pro-Israel lobby, advocates strongly for a more nuanced and effective stance toward Israel. Arguing that the U.S. must act swiftly to bring about a two-state solution before continued settlement activity brings us to a point of no return, J Street has made significant inroads in AIPAC's hold on both houses of Congress and has created ties with the White House. Individuals, organizations, and churches, in collaboration with advocacy organizations, have begun to engage legislators and members of the executive branch on specific policy issues and humanitarian and human rights cases. Appendix A provides a listing of denominational, ecumenical, and advocacy groups working specifically on peace in Israel/Palestine.

Grassroots Education

Congregations can provide education on local, regional, and national levels to raise awareness about human rights and civil society issues in Israel/Palestine. This can be accomplished through web-based campaigns, such as the "Peace Not Walls" program of the Evangelical Lutheran Church of America and the web site of the Israel Palestine Mission Network of the Presbyterian Church (USA). Congregational adult education can include invited speakers, and pilgrimages to the Holy Land organized at congregational and local levels can feature contact with and support of communities and organizations in the Holy Land working for justice and coexistence. Local, regional, and national conferences are not only a rich source of information and education, but an excellent way for individuals and congregations to establish connections with other congregations and with groups involved in education and activism. Finally, it is important that clergy in training at seminaries be provided with education on a range of topics related to the current conflict. These should include the political and cultural history of the Holy Land and a thorough, updated, and open treatment of the theological issues related to the land promise. See Appendix A for a listing of organizations that sponsor conferences and that are a source of materials and resources for information and connectivity.

Pilgrimages

Thousands of Christians visit the Holy Land every year on devotional pilgrimages through church and denomination-organized tours. Hundreds of seminary students do the same as part of their training. Traditionally, Holy Land pilgrimages are advertised as "walking where Jesus walked." The situation in the Holy Land today provides the opportunity to do just that. Jesus's ministry took place in the context of the devastating impact of power and militarism. He called for social and political transformation that would free the people of Palestine—not only the oppressed but the oppressors—from the soul-destroying effects of war, poverty, and injustice. For that reason, journeys to the Holy Land today, perhaps more than in any time in modern history, afford the opportunity to walk where he walked, see what he saw, and commit to the ministry he called on his followers to pursue. Visiting the "living stones" of the Holy Land—organizations, individuals, and communities that are working for peace and coexistence—is the most effective way of educating Americans of all faiths about the situation on the ground. Just as important, visiting Israelis and Palestinians who are courageously working for peace is essential to help keep their hope alive as they continue their work under difficult and frustrating conditions. Appendix A provides a comprehensive list of organizations sponsoring church-based, ecumenical, and interfaith journeys.

Support for Peace-building, Social Service, and Civil Society Efforts in Israel/Palestine

U.S.-based organizations can have a direct impact on a range of peace-building activities through partnerships with organizations and communities in Israel/Palestine. This can be accomplished by direct financial support through global mission initiatives; sponsorship of U.S. tours for speakers, exhibits, and performance artists; sale of local products; and other fund-raising activities. Appendix A lists many such organizations, the services they perform, and how to support them.

Advancing Denomination-level Activities

Recently, the Evangelical Lutheran Church of America inaugurated its "Peace Not Walls" campaign, providing educational and informational resources to increase awareness of the situation in the Holy Land and to provide avenues for direct involvement. The Presbyterian Church (USA) has an active Israel-Palestine Mission Network, established by action of the 2004 General Assembly. In the summer of 2009, IPMN began distributing a professionally-produced book and DVD entitled *Steadfast Hope: the Palestinian Quest for a Just Peace.* Information on how to obtain these materials is found in Appendix A. In addition to these educational programs and global mission activities in support of peace in the Holy Land, some denominations have undertaken consideration of resolutions and initiatives for positive investment/selective divestment. The Presbyterian and Methodist churches in the United States have initiated actions to engage constructively with companies identified as profiting from the Israeli occupation. These initiatives have provoked intense dialogue and controversy within these church bodies. Despite the discomfort that it engenders, this process is a sign of change and renewal. Indeed, the discomfort is to be welcomed, not avoided, as evidence of the presence of genuine reform.[2]

Ecumenical and Interfaith Activities

Ecumenical and interfaith discussions about bringing peace to the region are not new. However, until recently they have generally been characterized by carefully "balanced" statements about the need for peace for both peoples. They have avoided taking positions on specific policy issues or addressing the specific actions of parties to the conflict or of foreign governments with significant involvement. Statements by both ecumenical and interfaith conferences and signatories have been careful to avoid the appearance of being critical of either side, and in fact have tended to deplore violent resistance by Palestinian groups while ignoring Israeli state violence or violations of international law by Israel. More recently, however, dialogue and advocacy groups, increasingly frustrated with the failure of peace efforts, have begun to focus on real policy issues. They have become more willing to break the unwritten rules of "interfaith etiquette" in confronting those actions of Israel that have impeded progress toward a just settlement. In September 2008, the World Council of Churches convened a conference in Bern, Switzerland, as part of the WCC's Palestine Israel Ecumenical Forum Initiative. The conference of theologians, which included Palestinian Christians, reached a consensus that the "Bible must not be utilised to justify oppression or supply simplistic commentary on contemporary events" (Brown, 33). Harvard theologian Harvey Cox stated that although there was a need for "recompense" for the way the Bible had been used by Christians against the Jews, it had also been used in a way that favored "solidarity with Israel" but ignored the abridgement of the rights of Palestinians. In a strong statement, Cox argued against a theologically based rationale for Jewish claims on the Holy Land (2008).

---

2. Appendix B provides an example.

Among the most striking and inspiring examples of ecumenical-level activities by church and Christian organizations are teams that work on the ground in the Holy Land with Israelis and Palestinians to protect Palestinian human rights. These groups have become an important presence in those places in the Holy Land where the most severe human rights violations are occurring. Examples of these include the Ecumenical Accompaniment Program in Palestine and Israel (EAPPI) of the World Council of Churches, and the Christian Peacemaker Teams, initiated by Mennonites, Brethren, and Quakers (with broad ecumenical participation). Information on these groups can be found in Appendix A.

Churches for Middle East Peace is a coalition of twenty-two public policy offices of national churches and agencies—Orthodox, Catholic, and Protestant. CMEP has been vigilant and active in promoting a just resolution of the conflict. As the conflict has deepened, CMEP has consistently advocated for United States policy that is more aggressive in monitoring human rights abuses that impede progress toward a just resolution. The group issues regular dispatches to members, holds an annual conference, and conducts letter-writing campaigns to keep the issue at the forefront of the U.S. government's attention.

Linking with Secular Human Rights Organizations

The last three decades have seen the formation of numerous organizations devoted to the preservation and defense of human rights in Israel/Palestine. Many of these organizations are based in the United States, while many more operate in Israel/Palestine and provide direct advocacy and assistance to individuals and groups there. Although secular in nature, organizations in the U.S. are often linked to the Jewish, Muslim, or Christian communities, or the Arab (or specifically Palestinian) communities. Still others were formed to directly support a particular organization in the Holy Land. These organizations organize lectures and presentations, and provide information and opportunities for direct involvement in human rights causes and the support of civil society in the Holy Land. A list of these can be found in Appendix A.

A recent development on the ecumenical scene in the U.S. deserves mention. In May 2009, an unprecedentedly broad-based meeting of Christian leaders met at the Carter Center in Atlanta, Georgia. The meeting, titled "Towards a New Christian Consensus: Peace with Justice in the Holy Land," convened days before the planned visit of Benjamin Netanyahu, the newly elected prime minister of Israel, with U.S. president Barack Obama. The meeting combined a sense of urgency about the need for a just peace with mounting concern about Israeli intransigence with respect to key issues required for the creation of Palestinian state. Attendees included the top echelons from all of the Protestant denominations, leaders of evangelical movements and several evangelical churches, and ecumenical bodies including the World Council of Churches and Churches for Middle East Peace. Attendees were briefed by leading experts from Israel, the United States, and Palestine on the urgent human rights situation in the region and on the pressing political realities facing the new U.S. administration in its stated commitment to a resolution of the conflict. At the close of the meeting, the attendees approved and signed a brief letter to President Obama. The letter dispensed with the traditional language decrying violence from both sides. Instead, it focused on the need for a political resolution and called directly on our government to address human rights violations. It spoke, with one voice, as the American church, directly to the chief executive, and conveyed, above all, a message of urgency. Does a meeting such as this indicate a wind blowing? There is good reason to believe that it does.

A Shared Covenant

Christianity came to redefine the nature of God's relationship to humankind and to promote a faith grounded in love and a commitment to human dignity. As such, it builds directly on the monotheistic revolution of Judaism and the enduring ethical teachings that spring from God's covenant with the Jewish people. In a remarkable and courageous development, post-supersessionist Christian thinkers rejected the age-old dogma that set up Christianity as the superior faith with Judaism as, in James Carroll's words, "the shadow against which Christianity could be the light" (2001, 109). Judaism is the foundation upon which Christianity's fundamental concepts of faithfulness to God, commitment to community, and devotion to social justice are built. Today, however, Jews are in great peril because of where our nationalistic project has led us with respect to those same fundamental values. Certainly, the Jews are not the only religious group to be guilty of high crimes stemming from the blind, arrogant exceptionalism that religion can foster. But the urgency of our current situation requires that the Jewish people, in Israel and throughout the world, apply a laser-like focus on that very quality, a quality that now appears to be driving us. We must demand of ourselves the same humility, courage, and capacity for self-reflection that has been displayed by many Christians.

If, as contemporary Christian thinkers are suggesting, we are all of us—Christians, Jews, Muslims—called upon to revisit the momentous events of the first century CE, to this Jew it is clear what questions we must be asking ourselves: What was Jesus saying to the power structures of his time—priestly, monarchical, and imperial? What was the nature of the parting between the Jews of the time and those who came to be called Christians? Most important, what are the issues of faith and social justice that underlay the struggle between the parties to that historical drama that we must keep before us as we confront the urgent issues of our time? We must be very clear, therefore, about the purpose of the interfaith dialogue we undertake. We must call to account those Christian theologians who, in the service of "interfaith reconciliation," and in an effort to rehabilitate Judaism from Christian denigration, are supporting a superior Jewish claim to the land on theological grounds. It is not enough—in fact, it is dangerous—to be content with cautiously designed "mutual admiration" gatherings for appreciating differences and affirming common values, carefully steering clear of topics and issues that might create discomfort or conflict. The times do not permit us that luxury. Rather, in our dialogues we must ask: what can be the nature of the relationship between the faiths today that is true to the best in each and that can carry us forward in our shared commitment to justice? What actions—in our families, religious establishments, and halls of government—must we take in response to our consciences and to the prophetic voices that speak to us? In considering these questions, we will do well to keep in mind the recent words of Rosemary Ruether, who describes Jesus as a prophet espousing a "reversal of the social order...a new reality in which hierarchy and dominance are overcome as principles of social relations" (2008). If we are to have a new, shared covenant, it must be one that does not look backwards to the archaic and painful past but forward to a day when justice will reign.

Epilogue

Elias Khoury's 1998 *Gate of the Sun* is a novel of the Nakba. Its characters are the Palestinian villagers exiled from their homes in the Galilee between 1947 and 1949, who fled, mostly north to Lebanon, to live in the open and in temporary shelter in villages and towns. Until 1952, when the great majority of these refugees were settled permanently in refugee camps in Lebanon, many attempted to return to their homes in Palestine under threat of being captured or killed by Israeli forces.

Gate of the Sun is about identity, place, and history. It is about what happens to the sense of self and one's relationship to others when place is upended—what happens when the ground upon which you were nursed by your mother, raised your children, and brought bread and fruit from the earth is taken away by force. In the novel, the narrator, a young Palestinian, sits at the bedside of a Palestinian freedom fighter who will never regain consciousness. Is the dying man his father, his friend, his commander, his hero? As his feelings wash over him in waves of memory, the narrator himself does not know. Identities and relationships shift; nothing is clear in the erasure of history and obliteration of place that was the Nakba. Mothers call others' children by the names of their dead sons. "Victims of massacres," writes Khoury "disappear because they have no names...are reduced to numbers" (501). The narrator in vain tries to reconstruct the story of his own life—his family, his lover, his village, his people. Truth and legend blur—fantasies, dreams, memories, and desire swirl dizzyingly in the stories of the characters' search for their lives in the rubble of a camp, the makeshift home of a cave, or the shelter of a tree on the outskirts of a ravaged village. When history is taken away, the future becomes impossible to grasp and the sense of place disappears. Nahila, one of Khoury's characters, "no longer believed this world founded on destruction would last. 'We lived,'" she says, "'in expectation of something that would come, as though we weren't in a real place'" (400). Bab al-Shams—Gate of the Sun—the mythical village to which all look to return, is more real to Khoury's Palestinians than the temporary existence of Qana, the city in southern Lebanon where refugees huddled until the camps came.

Khoury tells the story of the Palestinian Nakba, but his tale is the story of any people uprooted, displaced, driven from their beds and homeland to be murdered or exiled. It is the story of what happens to identity, intimacy, the sense of generativity, fertility, the future. It is the Palestinian story, told as only a handful of other poets and novelists have done. But it is also the story of the Lakota, of Cambodia, of Sudan, of Armenia, and of the Jews. When do we begin to see that we together inhabit this place of searching, sit in mourning over the starved and murdered children, and dream of the treasured birthplaces—the village squares, the sun-filled rooms, and meals shared and seasoned with laughter and sorrow? That we all, together, yearn for return, for safety, for a place to love, give birth, and die knowing that our lives will go on in the seeding of our lands and our progeny? That we sit, brothers and sisters, refugees all, searching for community, and for the coming of the kingdom that we, only we, can bring?

> My grandmother didn't tell me much about Qana because she believed her exile only really began when they gathered everyone together in the camps around Tyre.
>
> Do you know what waiting, and the hope of return, meant to these people, Abu Salem? Of course you don't. However, the story of the buffalo of al-Khalsa astonished me. When my grandmother

told me the story, I thought she was telling me something like the stories grownups tell children that they don't expect them to believe. The story concerns a man called Abu Aref, a Bedouin of the village of al-Khalsa, belonging to the tribe of Heyb. He came to Qana along with everyone else and stayed there with his wife and five daughters. And he brought his buffalo. Seven buffalo cows, God protect them. "We all drank their milk, for the man used to give it away to everybody. He refused to sell it, saying the buffalo were an offering to al-Khalsa—'When we go back, we can buy and sell.' He was generous and stubborn, like all Bedouin. When spring came, the season when buffalo become fertile, people saw the man leading his herd toward the south. His wife said he was crazy because he believed the buffalo could only conceive in al-Khalsa, and he'd agreed with a cousin of his to hand the buffalo over to him at the Lebanese-Palestine border on the condition that he return them two weeks later. The man set off for the border, and his wife stood in the square at Qana to bid him farewell, mourning him and mourning the buffalo, but the man would have nothing to do with her. Then the buffalo disappeared from view, and everyone forgot about the matter."

My grandmother said Abu Alef returned alone, cowering, his spirit broken. He wouldn't speak. "He was bathed in tears, and we didn't dare ask him anything. He returned alone, without the buffalo."

"We've lost everything," said Abu Alef.

Abu Alef drove his buffalo to al-Khalsa because he was convinced the buffalo could only conceive on the land where they were raised, and, at the border post, the firing started. The buffalo sank to the ground, their blood splashing the sky, and Abu Alef stood there in the midst of the massacre.

He told his wife he was standing at the border making signs to his cousin when the firing started.

He said he ran from buffalo to buffalo. He said it was all blood. He said he raised his hands and screamed, but they were killed anyway.

He said his dog of a cousin never turned up. He said he'd taken off his white kufiyyeh and raised it as a sign of surrender, then started running with it from buffalo to buffalo, trying to staunch their wounds, the kufiyyeh becoming drenched in blood. He said he raised the stained kufiyyeh and shouted and begged, but they didn't stop. "The ground was covered in blood, the buffalo were dying, and I was weeping. Why didn't they kill me too? I wiped my face with the blood-soaked kufiyyeh and sat down among the buffalo."

The man returned to his wife cowering, frightened. He returned without his buffalo, carrying the blood-soaked kufiyyeh and the signs of despair.

That was Qana.

Acknowledgments

A man I met recently teaches what he calls the "Truths of Great Work." One of these truths is that "work is not a solo act. You need to draw on the wisdom, experience and compassion of those around you" (Stanier 2008). Since beginning the work that includes the writing of this book, I have been blessed with a wide community of friends and colleagues. I am grateful for the encouragement, assistance, and wisdom of these extraordinary people.

The nucleus of this book is a paper delivered at a 2007 conference titled "Interfaith Journeys on the Road to Liberation in the 21st Century" that was sponsored by the Center for Jewish Studies at Baylor University under the directorship of Dr. Marc Ellis. I am grateful to Marc for providing me with the opportunity to embark on the thinking and research that has led to this book. Beyond that, I am deeply indebted to Marc for his courageous and pioneering work in bringing a liberation theology perspective to this critical juncture in Jewish history. The reader will understand at the conclusion of the book how important his work has been to me.

I met Gabrielle Sutherland at the Center for Jewish Studies in her role as coordinator of the 2007 conference. Her expert advice in the early stages of conceiving this book and her encouragement and friendship throughout the writing process has been invaluable. Keren Batiyov, a passionate peace activist and poet, got me to the Baylor conference and introduced me to Marc Ellis. Keren's fierce devotion to justice is an inspiration to me. Our deep connection and Keren's ongoing support are a precious gift.

Joseph Groves, Mike Daly, and Jacob Pace of Interfaith Peace-builders (IFPB) created the opportunity for me to visit Israel/Palestine during two consecutive summers. Joe, Mike, and Jake continue to be friends and important supporters. My debt to them and to IFPB is incalculable.

Reverend Naim Ateek of the Sabeel Liberation Theology Center in Jerusalem is one of my teachers. Naim's work in liberation theology, along with his tireless activism, continues to inspire and challenge me. Naim's story, his spirit, and his cause are at the spiritual center of my own work. I am honored to call him my friend. My thanks go out to Naim, to the people of Sabeel, and to my friend and colleague Reverend Dick Toll of Friends of Sabeel North America for their friendship and support.

In early 2007, Greg and Susan Drinan of Abraham's Children invited me to deliver a series of lectures in Chicago with Father Elias Chacour, now Archbishop of the Melkite Greek Catholic Church of the Galilee and founder of the Mar Elias School. This experience counts as one of the great honors of my life. My brotherhood with Abuna Chacour, which was created the instant we met, is at the heart of this book. I owe much to Abuna, and to Greg and Susan. I treasure our friendship and our work together in the cause of justice for all the peoples of the Holy Land.

Pastor David Good of the First Congregational Church of Old Lyme, Connecticut, has and continues to make a central contribution to my thinking and to the development of my voice in reaching out to all the faith communities. David and the people of his congregation have walked the talk of social justice for a generation. David has given me the opportunity to preach from his pulpit, has powerfully demonstrated to me that our tradition is a shared one, and has guided me back to my love of Scripture. As chair of the Tree of Life Educational Fund, David has supported my work in many ways. It has been a privilege to know and to work alongside David, and I look forward to continuing our work for justice and reconciliation.

When Pastor Steve Hyde of the Ravensworth Baptist Church in Annandale, Virginia, and I met a few short years ago, we knew instantly that we were brothers. Steve and his congregation have welcomed me into their family and have actively supported the building of bridges between our society and the Holy Land. As a Jew sharing a prophetic tradition with Steve, I have preached alongside him, studied the Bible and talked theology with him, and basked, as have so many others, in the love given so generously by this man. I have learned from Steve what it means to bring your faith to the work for social justice. Ghassan and Kay Tarazi, members of Ravensworth, inspired activists and now good friends, have encouraged me and provided me with opportunities to reach others. I look forward to the work that awaits us.

After our return from the delegation to the Holy Land in 2006, Lee Porter, a dedicated peace activist and fabric artist, arranged for us to speak at the Friday Forum series at the New York Avenue Presbyterian Church in Washington, DC. This was a pivotal event for me. This was only the first of many important ways that Lee has supported my work over the past years. I am grateful to Lee and value our friendship. John Van Wagoner was another fellow traveler on that 2006 trip to the Holy Land. Our shared experience solidified our friendship, which continues to this day. I treasure John. He lives his faith. Ann Loikow is another Washingtonian and fellow delegate who has energetically continued the work for justice in Israel/Palestine. Ann and her husband John have been important supporters, and I am grateful to them.

The lecture at New York Avenue Presbyterian was the beginning of my friendship with Roger Gench, senior pastor of the church. My connection with Roger, a gifted pastor, champion of human rights, and student of theology, is one of the springboards for this book. Roger has supplied me with invaluable reading in contemporary theology, reading that has been critical in the writing of the book. Roger was also responsible for introducing me to Walter Brueggemann, who delivered a series of lectures at the church in late 2006.

Daoud and Jihan Nassar of Tent of Nations in Bethlehem have brought me into their family. They have demonstrated to me the meaning of the Arabic word *sumud*: steadfastness and devotion to what is precious and worth fighting for. It has been an honor to know them and to participate in some small measure in their work and in their struggle. Since beginning the work with Daoud, I have grown a second family here in Washington: Bill and Kay Plitt, Bill Mims, and Steve France are the steering committee of Friends of Tent of Nations North America. They have cheered me on in the work of writing, even as they have lovingly tolerated my distraction from the work of our organization. I hope that they know how special they are to me, and how honored I am to share this work with them.

The friendship and support of Hannah Schwarzchild of American Jews for a Just Peace is one of the wonderful new things to happen in my life. Hannah makes things happen, like cataloging terms for this book's index with forty-eight hours' notice. Hannah has provided superb advice on some of the book's toughest issues. I learn on a daily basis from Hannah's tireless—and lifelong—work for justice.

It is not surprising that Anna Baltzer, author of *Witness in Palestine* (Paradigm 2006), went above and beyond in her careful, incisive, and invaluable reading of the manuscript. In a few short years, Anna has made an unparalleled impact on the effort to bring an awareness of the Palestinian struggle for justice to the American public. Ours is another friendship—deep and unshakable—that was created at the moment of our first meeting. This book has benefited significantly from Anna's editorial suggestions and challenging comments on issues of activism, the view of the conflict, and the substance and meaning of justice.

Walter Brueggemann would be surprised to learn that he reintroduced me to my first love, but that is precisely what happened at the lectures he delivered in Washington, DC, in December 2006. Walter brought me back to my love for Scripture—especially the prophets—and helped send me back to my roots and onto this path. The lectures also sent me immediately to his writing, work that figures so importantly in these pages. When, not without trepidation, I sent him an early draft of my review—and critique—of his writing on the land promise, Walter read it, invited me to visit, told me the work was sound, and urged me to continue and to develop my voice. For me, one of the very good things that have come from this project has been his friendship. I am grateful for Walter's encouragement and for the gift of his wisdom.

The following colleagues and friends have all shared in some way and some measure in the thinking, experience, and commitment to justice that has gone into the conception and writing of this book. In the list to follow, I have certainly failed to include some people, and I apologize to them. Todd Deatherage, Rela Mazali, Shireen Khamis, Ghada Ageel, Dora Johnson, Alma Jadallah Abdel-Hadi, John Salzberg, Paul Verduin, Jerry and Gene Bird, Tal Dor, Amal Nassar, Mazin Qumsiyeh, Mai Abdul-Rahman, Dave and Betsy Sams, Suzanne Hoder, Grace Said, Philip Farah, Susan Wilder, Phil Anderson, Father Albert Scarioto, Tarek Abuata, Rachel Tzvia Back, Hythem and Beth Shadid, Fahed Abu-Akel, Canon John Peterson, Lisa and Mac Erlich, Billy Boardman, Bishop John Chane, Said Rabieh, Tala Abu Rahmeh, Joel Kovel, Kent Buduin and Carol Bullard-Bates, Reverend Catherine Alder, Brother Jack Curran, Reverend Conrad Braaten, Reverend Phil Anderson, R. Kendall Soulen, Jon Berquist, Walt Davis, Reverend Don Wagner, Hassan and Margaret Fouda, Jeff Halper, Harold Gorvine, Nina Mayorek, Robert Smith, Carol LaHurd, Joel Kovel, Nur Masalha, Bishop Richard Graham, Ray McGovern, Laila Liddy, Scott Munger, Sara Roy, Emily Siegel, Pastor Russ Siler, Bishop Allen Bartlett, Rabbi Arthur Green, Elizabeth and Peter Viering, Joan and Jerry Silberberg, Rabbi Brian Walt, Jim Wall, Neil Elliot, Jim Wallis, Sam Jones and Karin Ryan, Gregory Khalil, Jo and Bob Busser, Leila Sansour, Carol Salzman, Rabbi Brant Rosen, Rosemary Ruether, Richard Falk, Stephen Walt, Stephen Sizer, and Max Ticktin.

The staff at Synergy Books oversaw the production and editing of the book with wonderful attention to detail—and the process of managing the author with patience and grace. The final product is a testament to their skill and professionalism.

I am blessed with an exceptional family, and as always, their support has been paramount.

During the writing of an earlier book, my then thirteen-year-old son Jacob provided suggestions for style, substance, and, above all, clarity in thinking. Once again, Jacob, now a young man, has given me the gift of his prodigious skills in writing and critical thinking in his review of the manuscript. At that earlier writing, Jacob sent me off with, "Good job, Dad, but when are you going to write some fiction?" I have not followed through on that request, but I am once again in Jacob's debt for his encouragement and intellectual rigor, this time from two continents away. My other grown children, Noah Zuckerman and Leah Barcan, and their spouses, Marianne Zuckerman and Daniel Barcan, have stood by me and blessed me with their continued support on this journey. I do not believe that there is a greater sense of joy than that felt when one's children demonstrate that they are proud of you.

My parents are not alive to see the publication of this book, and I'm sad about that. I would have wanted to see how they stretched to take it in, because stretching is what they taught me. My mother loved Israel passionately—and she would have opened her mind and her heart to understand how this book is an expression of that same love that I share with her. My father's great gift to me was his skepticism and his inquiring mind: he never stood still. My parents' passion for knowledge, love of their people, and commitment to kindness and justice live in every page of this book.

This book is dedicated to my wife, Susan Braverman. I can cite Susan's tireless and highly skilled editing, her encouragement through the most frustrating periods, and the sacrifices in time, finances, and family life that were made to support this project. For all that, I am grateful. But that is not what the dedication is about. The dedication, "For Susie," is simply that. Like everything else, this is for her.

Bethesda, Maryland
July 2009

Appendix A

Resources for Information, Connection, and Further Study

Jewish, Christian, and Ecumenical Organizations and Programs

American Friends Service Committee (AFSC), founded in 1917, is affiliated with the Religious Society of Friends (Quakers). It provides humanitarian relief throughout the world and works for social justice, peace, and reconciliation. AFSC has a long-standing presence in Palestine. The Israel-Palestine section of its web site is an outstanding source of information on the history of the conflict, the effects of the occupation, and ways to work nonviolently for peace. Visit the web site for access to books, videos, and the excellent "Faces of Hope" program, featuring forty short biographies of Israeli and Palestinian peace-builders. AFSC also cosponsors delegations to the region with Interfaith Peacebuilders and features delegation reports on its web site.

www.afsc.org/Israel-Palestine/

American Jews for a Just Peace (AJJP) is an alliance of activists in the United States working to ensure equal rights, safety, and dignity for all the people of historic Palestine. AJJP is a predominantly Jewish organization, but welcomes the full participation of all people of good will. The web site is frequently updated and links to important peace initiatives, visiting lecturers, and news articles.

www.ajjp.org

Anna Baltzer is a Jewish-American award-winning lecturer, author, and activist for Palestinian rights. She documents human rights abuses and supports Palestinian-led nonviolent resistance to the occupation and to Zionism. Baltzer appears throughout the U.S. to educate communities about life in Palestine and to encourage audiences to take action. For more information about Anna's book *Witness in Palestine* or the DVD of her popular presentation "Life in Occupied Palestine: Eyewitness Stories & Photos," as well as her first-hand photos, maps, analysis, and tour details, visit her web site. The site is an excellent source for links to Palestinian, Israeli, and American organizations working for human rights in the Holy Land.

www.AnnaInTheMiddleEast.com

The mission of **Brit Tzedek v'Shalom**, the Jewish Alliance for Justice and Peace, is to educate and mobilize American Jews in support of a negotiated two-state resolution of the Israeli-Palestinian conflict.

www.btvshalom.org

Challenging Christian Zionism is a well-maintained web site focusing on education about Christian Zionism, from its historical roots to its influence on current events, politics, and culture. The site features book reviews, recent articles, videos, and a wealth of information on the religious, political, and theological issues related to Christianity and the Holy Land.

www.christianzionism.org

Friends of Sabeel-North America (FOSNA) works in the U.S. and Canada to support the vision of Sabeel, cultivating the support of American churches through cosponsored regional educational conferences, alternative pilgrimages, witness trips, and international gatherings in the Holy Land.

www.fosna.org

Global Ministries of the United Methodist Church The General Board of Global Ministries is the global mission agency of the United Methodist Church, its annual conferences, missionary conferences, and local congregations. Global Ministries has created strong ties with

Christian communities in the Holy Land and conducts active programs in support of religious freedom and human rights issues in Israel/Palestine.
gbgm-umc.org/global_news/full_article.cfm?articleid=3843

The Holy Land Education and Peace Project is dedicated to furthering the role of faith communities in the United States and Canada in the search for peace in Israel and Palestine. Holy Land Peace provides educational opportunities and resources. Through conferences, sponsorship of visits to the region, and web-based social networking, the organization creates connections between congregations, denominations, and faith communities regarding working for peace at home and in the region through education, support of human rights, civil society projects, and political action.
www.holylandpeace.org

The Interfaith Peace Initiative is a forum for dialogue and learning about the Israeli-Palestinian conflict and examining America's relationship to this region. This web site is an excellent source for information about U.S. and global companies involved in human rights violations in the West Bank and Gaza. It also contains an excellent presentation about the Palestinian village of Jayyous in the West Bank, as an example of how U.S. policy is allowing and funding the taking of land and the impoverishment of Palestinian villagers.
www.interfaithpeaceinitiative.com

The Israel/Palestine Mission Network of the Presbyterian Church (U.S.A.) (IPMN) was established in 2004 by the action of the General Assembly of the Presbyterian Church (USA). IPMN encourages congregations and presbytery mission committees, task groups, and other entities toward specific mission goals that will foster a deeper and wider understanding of the conflict and advance progress toward a just peace for all peoples of Israel/Palestine. IPMN has produced and distributes *Steadfast Hope: The Palestinian Quest for Just Peace,* a forty-eight-page bound booklet with a free companion DVD. *Steadfast Hope* challenges common myths and misperceptions about the Israeli-Palestinian conflict, presents a compelling picture of the current situation on the ground, and shows the work currently being undertaken by Muslim, Jewish, and Christian peacemakers. It also provides guidance on how individuals and congregations can get involved. The companion DVD is outstanding; if you can't get to the region, watching this DVD is the closest thing to being there and seeing for yourself. The voices of witness on this DVD will speak to you compellingly. You can order the booklet and companion DVD on the IPMN web site.

www.israelpalestinemissionnetwork.org

Jewish Voice for Peace (JVP) is a community of activists inspired by Jewish tradition to work together for peace, social justice, and human rights. JVP supports peace activists in Palestine and Israel, and works in broad coalition with other Jewish and Arab-American faith-based, peace, and social justice organizations. JVP features a unique blog, "Muzzlewatch," which monitors attempts to stifle criticism of Israel in the United States.

www.jvp.org

The Lutheran World Federation, a global communion of Christian churches in the Lutheran tradition, has a long-standing and strong presence in the Holy Land, and particularly in Jerusalem, through its Augusta Victoria Hospital and its ties with the Lutheran communities in Jerusalem and Bethlehem. LWF is a powerful force for social justice in Palestine.

www.lutheranworld.org

Methodist Federation for Social Action is an independent organization dedicated to mobilizing clergy and laity within The United Methodist Church to take action on issues of peace, poverty and people's rights within the church, the nation and the world. MFSA provides education to American Methodists on human rights issues in the Holy Land and supports initiatives for justice in Israel/Palestine within the Methodist Church.

www.mfsaweb.org

Peace Not Walls is a campaign of the Evangelical Lutheran Church of America dedicated to advancing the efforts toward a viable, contiguous

Palestinian state; a secure Israeli state at peace with its Arab neighbors; and a shared Jerusalem with equal access and rights for Jews, Christians, and Muslims. The Peace Not Walls web site is an excellent source of information about the Lutheran Church's "Strategy for Engagement in Israel and Palestine," accompaniment programs, travel, and advocacy.
www.elca.org/Our-Faith-In-Action/Justice/Peace-Not-Walls.aspx

Sabeel is an ecumenical grassroots liberation theology movement among Palestinian Christians. Inspired by the life and teaching of Jesus Christ, Sabeel seeks to deepen the faith of Palestinian Christians and to promote unity among them toward social action. Sabeel strives to develop a spirituality based on love, justice, peace, nonviolence, liberation, and reconciliation for the different national and faith communities. Sabeel hosts international conferences and maintains the Sabeel Center, which is located in Jerusalem and serves Bethlehem, Ramallah, and the surrounding areas, with a branch office in Nazareth.
www.sabeel.org

Political Advocacy and Lobbying Organizations

The American Association for Palestinian Equal Rights (AAPER) is a lobbying organization whose mission is to shape a U.S. foreign policy that recognizes the human and national rights of the Palestinian people by representing to elected officials the hundreds of American organizations and millions of American citizens that support peace and justice in Israel/Palestine, but have been without an organization to lobby Congress on their behalf.
www.aaper.org

The American Task Force on Palestine (ATFP) is a nonprofit organization based in Washington, DC. ATFP is dedicated to a negotiated agreement that provides for two states—Israel and Palestine—living side by side in peace and security. ATFP seeks to build strong working relationships with government departments and agencies, think tanks and NGOs, and the media.
www.americantaskforce.org

Churches For Middle East Peace (CMEP) is a coalition of twenty-two public policy offices of national churches and agencies—Orthodox, Catholic, and Protestant. CMEP maintains an ongoing dialogue with Congress, the White House, the Department of State, and the diplomatic community to advance concerns, assessments, and advocacy positions on the Israel-Palestine conflict, including human rights, arms control, foreign aid, and the unique nature of Jerusalem. CMEP helps its member organizations take action on their concerns about justice and peace for all people and countries in the region.

www.cmep.org

Friends Committee for National Legislation (FCNL), founded by the Religious Society of Friends (Quakers), is the oldest ecumenical lobby in Washington, DC. FCNL fields the largest team of religious peace lobbyists in the U.S. The Middle East section of the FCNL web site provides an excellent source of up-to-date information on legislative issues related to the Israel-Palestine conflict. Visitors to the site can sign up for regular newsletters and updates.

www.fcnl.org/middle_east/index.htm

J Street is the lobbying group established as an alternative to AIPAC, the American Israel Political Action Committee. It was founded to promote meaningful American leadership to end the Arab-Israeli and Palestinian-Israeli conflicts peacefully and diplomatically. J Street advocates a more nuanced stance toward Israel that better advances American interests. Arguing that that the U.S. must act swiftly to bring about a two-state solution before continued settlement activity brings us to a point of no return, J Street has made significant inroads in AIPAC's hold on both houses of Congress and has created ties with the White House.

www.jstreet.org

Human Rights and Activist Organizations

Adalah is an independent human rights organization, registered in Israel. It is a nonprofit, nongovernmental, and nonpartisan legal center. Adalah serves Arab citizens of Israel, numbering over one million people, or close to 20 percent of the population. Adalah ("justice" in Arabic) works to protect human rights in general, and the rights of the Arab minority in particular. Adalah's main goals are to achieve equal individual and collective rights for the Arab minority in Israel in different fields including land rights; civil and political rights; cultural, social, and economic rights; religious rights; and the rights of women and prisoners.

www.adalah.org

Al-Haq is an independent Palestinian nongovernmental human rights organization. Al-Haq documents violations of the individual and collective rights of Palestinians in the occupied territories and advocates before national and international bodies.

www.alhaq.org

The Badil Resource Center for Palestinian Residency & Refugee Rights takes a rights-based approach to the Palestinian refugee issue through research, advocacy, and support of community participation in the search for durable solutions.

www.badil.org

Breaking the Silence is an organization of veteran Israeli soldiers that collects testimonies of soldiers who have served in the occupied territories. Breaking the Silence voices the experiences of these soldiers in order to raise awareness in Israeli society about the impact of the occupation and military service. In 2009, Breaking the Silence collected and published testimonies of Israeli Defense Force soldiers about the conduct of the 2009 Gaza invasion that raised urgent concerns about war crimes committed against the civilian population.

www.breakingthesilence.org.il

B'tselem, the Israeli Information Center for Human Rights in the occupied territories, documents human rights violations in the occupied territories and helps create a human rights culture in Israel. B'tselem publishes reports covering torture, fatal shootings by security forces, restriction on movement, expropriation of land and discrimination in planning and building in East Jerusalem, administrative detention, and settler violence. This is one of the best sources for maps of Israel and the Palestinian territories. B'tselem recently opened an office in Washington, DC.

www.btselem.org

Christian Peacemaker Teams operates out of Hebron and works in villages in the southern hills of the West Bank, where inhabitants are subject to severe and continual harassment and violence by Jewish settlers. Under the motto of "getting in the way," these teams of internationals document abuses and human rights violations and, by their presence, effectively prevent or mitigate instances of violence and harassment.

www.cpt.org

Combatants for Peace was founded by Israeli Defense Force officers who decided to no longer serve in the occupied territories and who are devoted to combating the destructive effects of militarization and the occupation on Israel. They have joined with former Palestinian political prisoners who are equally devoted to nonviolent resistance and to the building of peace between the two peoples. Combatants for Peace presents lectures and educational programs for Israelis, Palestinians, and visitors to the region, and conducts international speaking tours.

www.combatantsforpeace.org

Ecumenical Accompaniment Program in Palestine and Israel (EAPPI) organizes teams of international peace workers to monitor and protect human rights in the occupied territories. Since the program was launched in 2002, EAPPI has sponsored volunteers from more than thirty churches and fourteen countries. Accompaniers serve in three-month terms in Jerusalem and West Bank villages. Activities include monitoring and reporting on violations of human rights, offering protection through nonviolent presence, supporting nonviolent resistance in cooperation with local Christian and Muslim Palestinians and Israeli peace activists, and engaging in public policy advocacy.

www.eappi-us.org

Friends of Tent of Nations North America (FOTONNA) is a nonprofit established to support peaceful coexistence between Palestinians and Jews in historic Palestine. FOTONNA sponsors education for youth and women, workshops and gatherings on nonviolence, and the preservations of human rights for Palestinians in the occupied territories, with a particular emphasis on land rights. Since 2007, FOTONNA has supported the work of Daoud Nassar, a Christian Palestinian farmer who is fighting for his land rights in the occupied West Bank. Daoud and his family have established a peace center on their farm that attracts over one thousand foreign visitors a year. FOTONNA sponsors U.S. speaking tours for Daoud and arranges for Americans to visit the farm and to volunteer for extended stays.

www.fotonna.org

Holy Land Trust is a nonprofit organization established in Bethlehem in 1998. The organization offers unique travel and encounter programs in Bethlehem and the surrounding areas as well as comprehensive media and news programs related to life in occupied Palestine.

www.holylandtrust.org

Interfaith Peace-Builders sends delegations of North Americans to Israel/Palestine. Participants have the opportunity to learn directly from Israeli and Palestinian nonviolent peace/human-rights activists, to spend time in Palestinian and Israeli homes, to experience the situation of Palestinians living under military occupation, and to interact directly with Israelis and Palestinians working to bring peace to the region. The program supports the work of participants on their return home to educate people in their communities and organizations about the conflict by writing and speaking about their experiences.

www.interfaithpeacebuilders.org

The Israeli Committee Against House Demolitions is a nonviolent, direct-action group originally established to oppose and resist Israeli demolition of Palestinian houses in the occupied territories. Since its founding, ICAHD's activities have extended to three interrelated spheres: resistance and protest actions in the occupied territories, efforts to bring the reality of the occupation to Israeli society, and mobilizing the international community for a just peace. ICAHD-USA (www.icahdusa.org) supports the work of ICAHD in Israel/Palestine by organizing U.S. tours and educating North Americans about ICAHD's work and human rights issues in Israel/Palestine.

www.icahd.org

Machsom Watch ("Checkpoint Watch") is an Israeli women's organization that monitors human rights in the occupied territories. Members of Machsom Watch are deployed at the over five hundred Israeli checkpoints that restrict movement of Palestinians on Palestinian land.

www.machsomwatch.org

The Mosawwa Center, the Advocacy Center for Arab Citizens in Israel, is a nonprofit, nongovernmental organization that works to promote equality for the Arab-Palestinian citizens of Israel. This organization publishes position papers and policy analysis and disseminates them to political and social activists. It also issues a regular "watch list" for developments related to human rights for Arab citizens of Israel.

www.mossawacenter.org

Open Bethlehem is an international campaign devoted to building awareness of the crisis facing the city of Bethlehem as a result of the Israeli occupation. The web site features excellent documentation of the urgent situation in Bethlehem, including slideshows that can be downloaded. Open Bethlehem arranges tours of the city and serves as a resource for information about the city and its people.

www.openbethlehem.org

Palestine Remembered provides extensive information and documentation on the Palestinian villages that were destroyed between 1947 and 1949. It is possible to search for specific villages on the site and to obtain historical and demographic data, as well as photographic records when available.

www.palestineremembered.com

Peace Now is one of Israel's oldest peace groups. Its web site describes broad-based peace activities going back to the 1980s. The organization offers a comprehensive analysis of Israel's illegal settlement activity in the occupied Palestinian territories. Americans for Peace Now [APN] supports the activities of Peace Now.

www.peacenow.org/il (Peace Now in Israel)

www.peacenow.org (Americans for Peace Now)

New Profile is an Israeli organization devoted to uncovering and combating the pervasive militarization of Israeli society. The organization advocates for people who do not want to serve in the military, working to establish a greater range of legal alternatives to army service and supporting those who are serving jail sentences for their refusal to serve. Besides their advocacy work, New Profile focuses on educating Israelis about human rights abuses in the occupied territories and the impact of the occupation on Israeli society.

www.newprofile.org

Rabbis for Human Rights (RHR) is the rabbinic voice of conscience in Israel. It was founded in 1988 in response to serious abuses of human rights by the Israeli military authorities in the suppression of the Intifada. Rabbis for Human Rights North America is an organization of rabbis in North America dedicated to supporting the work of RHR in Israel and to education and advocacy on human rights issues in North America.

www.rhr.israel.net (Rabbis for Human Rights)

www.rhr.na.org (Rabbis for Human Rights North America)

Yesh Din is a volunteer organization of Israeli human rights activists. It is composed of Israeli academics, lawyers, and former Israeli politicians, diplomats, and military officers. The organization documents human rights violations against Palestinians in the occupied territories, disseminates information in Israel/Palestine and abroad about human rights issues and cases, and works to change Israeli administration policy. Yesh Din is currently focusing on land issues and on Jewish settler violence in the West Bank.

www.yesh-din.org

Zochrot is an organization of Israeli citizens working to raise awareness of the destruction of more than five hundred Palestinian villages by Jewish forces in 1948 and the erasure of Palestinian culture that has continued since the founding of the State of Israel. Zochrot organizes tours and lectures for Israelis and international visitors and provides education on the history of the Nakba, including visits to the sites of destroyed Palestinian villages. The web site is an excellent source of information and resources on the ethnic cleansing of Palestine.

www.zochrot.org

Media

The Alternative Information Center (AIC) is a joint Palestinian-Israeli activist organization located in Bethlehem in the West Bank. AIC is supported by a number of international NGOs that have been involved in building Palestinian civil society and that oppose the Israeli occupation. AIC is engaged in the dissemination of information, political advocacy, grassroots activism, and critical analysis of the Palestinian and Israeli societies as well as the Palestinian-Israeli conflict.

www.alternativenews.org

The Electronic Intifada (EI) is a nonprofit, independent publication committed to comprehensive public education on the question of Palestine, the Israeli-Palestinian conflict, and the economic, political, legal, and human dimensions of Israel's forty-year occupation of Palestinian territories. EI provides a much visited and much valued alternative to mainstream commercial media representations of the Israeli-Palestinian conflict.

www.electronicintifada.net

Haaretz is Israel's premier left/center newspaper, in print and online.

www.haaretz.com

JTA, "the Global News Service of the Jewish People," provides a wide-ranging selection of articles related to Israel and to Jewish life in general. JTA claims to have no connection to any specific branch of Judaism or political viewpoint.

www.jta.org

Appendix B

Christian Vigilance Against Anti-Semitism: The Case of the Presbyterian Church

In the spring of 2008, I received an e-mail from the pastor of a Presbyterian church, alerting me to a short piece that had just been published on the web site of the Presbyterian Church (USA). The e-mail read simply, "Your thoughts on this?" My friend must have anticipated that I would have a reaction, but the strength (and length) of my reaction probably surprised me more than it did him. What follows is the original Presbyterian article, my response to it, a letter from three Jewish leaders, and my response to the revision of the original article and to the Jewish letter.

Because of how strong my words had been, I thought twice about including them in this book, but I was encouraged to do so by colleagues from the Presbyterian Church. "Who am I to publicly discuss internal church issues?" I said to them. "It's important," they answered. "This is the dialogue we need. This is the voice we need." And so I offer it here.

The circumstances behind the publication of the original Presbyterian statement and its replacement with a modified piece are not clear to me and I have not looked further, because the issues themselves are clear enough. The piece evoked considerable controversy within the church as well as reaction from outside. Did the church stumble in its handling of the affair? Perhaps. But I don't think that this reflects badly on the church. In fact, I feel the opposite: I admire the Presbyterian Church for the risks it has taken concerning the issue of Israel and human rights, and its willingness to step out onto this minefield. I'm sure it was painful for those in the center of the storm—the leadership in Louisville and the PC(USA)'s Office of Interfaith Relations—and confusing perhaps for the pastor or seminary professor witnessing the controversy. But this is not a bad thing. It would be a bad thing if the controversy were to cause the church to draw back from its engagement with the issue, like a hand from a hot stove.

I applaud all those in the church—on all sides of the issue—who have taken this issue on and who continue to grapple with it. I agree with those who encouraged me to write about this and to enter the conversation. Crises and difficult issues require open discussion, struggle, and correction. This is a positive story, a story about growth. It's about nurturing a new community, one that looks to the future.

May the conversation continue.

Vigilance Against Anti-Jewish Ideas and Bias
Original article published on the web site of the Presbyterian Church (U.S.A.)
May, 2008[1]

Since 2004, Presbyterians and Jews in many places across the United States have met to discuss reactions, concerns and differences regarding Presbyterian Church (U.S.A.) General Assembly policy decisions on Israeli-Palestinian peace and related issues. These conversations have been sometimes confrontational and heated, almost always open and frank and often productive of a deeper understanding of each other and of our concerns and commitments.

We Presbyterians aspire to build positive and respectful relations with our neighbors in the Jewish community, based on an honest exploration of the close ties between our two faith traditions and our shared concerns for peace and justice. One of the guideposts for Presbyterians in relation to Jews is a clear rejection of anti-Semitism and anti-Jewish teaching.

---

1. This original statement can be found at http://www.jcrelations.net/en/?item=2973.

- In 1990, affirming "our close spiritual ties with the Jewish people," the 202nd General Assembly of the Presbyterian Church (U.S.A.) stated "unequivocally that authentic Christianity can have no complicity in anti-Semitic attitudes or actions of any kind."

- In 1987, the Presbyterian Church (U.S.A.) acknowledged "in repentance the church's long and deep complicity in the proliferation of anti-Jewish attitudes and actions through its 'teaching of contempt' for the Jews." Our church repudiated such anti-Jewish teaching in the General Assembly document of that year, "A Theological Understanding of the Relationship between Christians and Jews." We pledged then "God helping us, never again to participate in, to contribute to, or (insofar as we are able) to allow the persecution or denigration of Jews or the belittling of Judaism."

We Presbyterians can celebrate the extent to which we have been able to rid our teaching, preaching and actions of such prejudice. We take these principles and commitments seriously and we believe that the official policies and statements of the General Assembly of the Presbyterian Church (U.S.A) live up to this standard.

However, we are aware and do confess that anti-Jewish attitudes can be found among us. Our conversations with Jews in the last several years have renewed our concern to guard against anti-Semitism and anti-Jewish motifs and stereotypes, particularly as these find expression in speech and writing about Israel, the Palestinian people, the Israeli-Palestinian conflict and steps toward peace. Once again, many Presbyterians have become aware that strains of an old anti-Jewish tradition are present in the way we ourselves sometimes speak and in the rhetoric and ideas of some writers that we may read regarding these matters.

Examples of such an anti-Jewish theology can unfortunately be found in connection with PC (USA) General Assembly overtures, such as the overture on Confronting Christian Zionism, adopted by the 216th General Assembly in 2004. Some of the authors cited in the rationale of that overture make use in their writings of arguments suggesting or declaring that the Jewish people are no longer in covenant with God, or make statements that echo the medieval Christian claim that the Jews are to blame for the crucifixion of Christ. The rationale and background sources cited in any overture are not General Assembly policy, but Presbyterians need to read such materials with awareness of these themes of classic anti-Jewish teaching.

When our analysis or critique of the Israeli-Palestinian situation employs language or draws on sources that have anti-Jewish overtones, or clearly makes use of classic Christian anti-Jewish ideas, we cloud complicated issues with the rhetoric of ignorance or subliminal attitudes, or the language of hate, and undermine our advocacy for peace and justice. Critical questions such as ending the occupation of Palestinian territory by Israel or the future of Jerusalem are complex and difficult. It does not help to import stereotypes, anti-Jewish motifs or classic ideas of Christian anti-Jewish theology into our discussions.

Similarly, in a few materials that have been circulated by Presbyterians, one finds characterizations of Zionism that distort that movement. They do not accurately present the history of the Zionist movement or acquaint readers with its internal debates and ethical concerns. Instead, Zionism is often presented as a monolithic force or merely as an extension of European colonialism and result of anti-Semitism, and nothing else. In such materials, the problems and suffering of the Palestinians are attributed solely—and inaccurately—to Zionism alone. The origins, development and practices of Zionism and its relationship to the realities of the Israeli-Palestinian situation are much more complex than such a picture presents.

Presbyterians who read writers speaking about Israel, Palestine, Israeli-Palestinian peace and related issues (such as Christian Zionism in its various manifestations) must always read with an especially critical eye, alert to any and all anti-Jewish ideas and bias. Despite problematic passages and ideas, much of what these writers say can be helpful in describing aspects of the Israeli-Palestinian situation. Nevertheless, it is our responsibility to read our sources thoroughly and not to accept anything in them that is anti-Jewish or anti-Semitic.

The voices of Palestinian theologians are of particular significance for us as American Presbyterians, because they are authentic voices of Christian brothers and sisters who speak not from the perspective of life in the United States, but out of life in the increasingly difficult conditions of the West Bank and Gaza. In what they write and say, they testify to how they understand their experience and God's relationship with them in the midst of contemporary events.

Nonetheless, writings of some Palestinian Christian theologians, and in particular those writing from the perspective of liberation theology, can raise especially difficult issues. Liberation theologians in many places—in carrying out their given task of explicating Scripture and applying it to the situations in which they live—typically claim that God has a special concern for the poor and oppressed, embrace the Exodus story as a story of God's liberation for all oppressed people and lift up Jesus' teachings against injustice and oppression. Such emphases express important theological insights. But they can easily resemble Christian supersessionism, for example, by seeming to replace the Jewish people in their own story, or by embracing only the universal application of God's gift of land in exclusion of God's particular gift of land to the Jewish people. Or they can seem to repeat classic denunciations of Judaism, for example, through polemic that identifies today's oppressors as Jewish authorities in the time of Jesus, and so forth.

When the perspectives of liberation theology are used to understand the situation of the Palestinian people, Christian theological ideas and metaphors are used to speak about the Palestinian people and their experience in relation to the policies of the state of Israel. So, for example, some Palestinian liberation theologians identify the Palestinian people with Jesus. Some liken the Palestinian experience to the passion of Jesus or describe the Palestinian people as being crucified as Jesus was crucified.

This is understandable, given the situation in which Palestinians are living. However, applying this reading of the passion narratives to the Israeli-Palestinian situation brings unique problems: moving beyond legitimate denunciation of injustices the state of Israel has committed or may commit, some writing from this theological perspective indict the state of Israel as a crucifying power. The introduction of such an emotionally and theologically "loaded" interpretation may vividly express and give meaning to the suffering of the Palestinian people, but it is troubling in its demonization of Israel and the Jewish people and its echoes of ancient Christian anti-Judaism.

Most Jewish readers feel that in theological statements such as this the Jews as a people are once again being charged with deicide. For Jews this is terrifying, because the narrative of the passion and crucifixion has been used as a theological basis for the ghettoization, denigration and killing of Jews for nearly twenty centuries. Especially when combined with sharply worded arguments that God's gift of land to ancient Israel is to be understood only as a universal gift to all peoples and not as a particular gift to a particular people (the Jews), this kind of statement raises the specter of the anti-Jewish tradition in Christian thought.

Again, what such Palestinian theologians say offers Presbyterians in the United States an important theological reflection on the Israeli-Palestinian situation from the perspective of Christians affected by it. Yet it remains our responsibility to critique—and not to accept—those statements or ideas within it that are anti-Jewish or anti-Semitic.

In the midst of ongoing tensions between us regarding issues and approaches to justice and peace in the Middle East, Presbyterians and Jews need to be vigilant in regard to our speech about and to one another. We can and should expect our Jewish colleagues to confront stereotypes and biases they may hold regarding the Palestinian people, to avoid stereotyping or demonizing us and to characterize our concerns and positions with accuracy and respect. Likewise, we Presbyterians can and should confront stereotypes and biases we may hold regarding Israel, characterize the concerns and positions of Jews accurately and avoid stereotyping or demonizing the Jewish people.

We Presbyterians need to increase our vigilance in this regard. We would do well to examine our own thinking, theology and advocacy to be sure that we do not accept or impart anti-Jewish ideas, but speak truthfully and without bias in our support of justice and peace.

Prepared by the Office of Interfaith Relations, Presbyterian Church (U.S.A.), May 2008

I penned the following response and sent it to my friend:

Response to "Vigilance Against Anti-Jewish Ideas and Bias"—A Jewish Witness

A Presbyterian pastor sent me an article, published on the PCUSA web site, entitled "Response to 'Vigilance Against Anti-Jewish Ideas and Bias.'" Intrigued by the title, and aware of the ferment of contro-versy about the Israel-Palestine issue within the Presbyterian Church in advance of the General Assembly that would convene later that month, I opened the document right away. I was immediately struck by the assertion, early in the piece, that, as Presbyterians "we are aware and do confess that anti-Jewish attitudes can be found among us." My curiosity was aroused. I wondered, "What is he talking about? Is anti-Semitism still so alive and visible in Christian circles?" Then it became clear: the writer was referring to "the strains of an old anti-Jewish tra-dition" that, he claimed, were present in the way some Christians were talking about Israel.

Of course, vigilance against anti-Semitism, as is true for all forms of racism or discrimination, is a good thing. In the case of anti-Semi-tism, one could say that it is overdue, in light of the suffering that Jews experienced over the millennia at the hands of the Christian West. But it is problematic when the rejection of and atonement for anti-Semitism is presented as the *key issue* in a discussion about a church's mission to pursue justice for the people of Israel and Palestine. Anti-Semitism is an evil and it has been responsible for great suffering. But in contemplating the situation in the Holy Land today, we are confronting a situation of a fundamentally different nature. To pose this in a different way: inter-faith dialogue is also a good thing—but we must always keep in mind the question: what is it for? If members of different religious groups are going to get together to talk to one another, we need to be mindful about the goals of that dialogue.

We need to look forward to what is required to create a world of peace, not backward to the sins of the past. But this piece is not looking forward—it is looking backward. The commitment of the Presbyterian Church to repudiate anti-Jewish attitudes and teachings of the past is accepted and firm. Now the church must move on as it confronts the Israel-Palestine situation. Of course, any discussion must be sensitive to the feelings of all involved groups and take into consideration the impact of history. But if the discussion is dominated by a preoccupation with this issue—if, as is indicated by the title of the piece, it is about being *vigilant* about *avoiding* something—then it will be distorted. And it will risk missing the point. That is the case here.

In its zeal to avoid even the appearance of anti-Jewish bias, this statement from the church reveals a bias of a different kind. Deeply embedded in the arguments offered is a profound confusion between a progressive theology that calls upon people of all faiths to embrace principles of universal justice, and regressive theologies that promote the supremacy of one people or one belief over another. There are deep issues here for Christians, and for progressive Christians in particular. If you have repudiated supersessionism—the doctrine that asserts that Christianity is the superior faith that came to replace Judaism—does it then follow that you must embrace the belief, as this article appears to be suggesting, in "God's particular gift of land to the Jewish people"? Does repudiating the idea that Christianity replaced the Jewish people in God's love require giving the Jewish people carte blanche to flout international law and principals of justice with respect to the Palestinian people? What some Christians are in fact advocating is the replacing of Christian supersessionism with Jewish exceptionalism—special rules for Jews. Where is the justice in that? How does this advance "interfaith" dialogue and reconciliation? What is driving this regressive push to elevate Jewish nationalism to the status of an article of faith? And, this Jew finds himself asking, how is this in line with Jesus's mission to expose the destructive power of king and priest and bring the people to a true knowledge of God? If the goal is for Christians and Jews to come together in common cause, if we are indeed to be vigilant, then let us rather speak out and act—Christian, Jew, Muslim, people of all faiths and persuasions—whenever we see ideology being abused in the service of oppression.

Presbyterians four years ago called upon themselves to divest from companies involved in the occupation of Palestine. They are doing so again this month, because the great injustice that was perpetrated on the Palestinian people in 1948 is continuing to the present day, supported by our own government. The resolutions being considered by the Presbyterian Church and those being proposed by other denominations represent an important way to bring effective pressure to bear on Israel and its ally, the U.S. to change a policy that denies basic human rights to Palestinians and continues the diabolically systematic process to dispossess them from what remains of their land. And the Presbyterian Church does not stand alone in this. Besides the actions of other Protestant denominations, the Presbyterians are joined by many, many Jews, in the U.S. and in Israel, who react with sorrow and horror at what is being perpetrated in their name. These are Jews who join with their Christian brothers and sisters across the globe in their outrage and their commitment to do something, out of their faith and out of their commitment to justice and fairness. What is more important, they do this in solidarity with Palestinians as well as Israelis in the Holy Land.

Given this, I am puzzled, saddened, and frankly shocked at the strength of the attack on Palestinian Liberation Theology to be found in this article. In it one finds the appalling and unfounded claim that because Palestinian Liberation Theology, like other liberation theology movements, makes a direct connection between Jesus's sacrifice and the political oppression today against Palestinians, and because the oppressors in this case are Jews, that this is tantamount to resurfacing the ancient, hateful charge of deicide. Nothing is farther from the spirit and practice of Palestinian Liberation Theology. The article, however, goes further. Following the assertion that this theology amounts to a "demonization of Israel" is the claim that "most Jewish readers feel that in theological statements such as this the Jews as a people are once again being charged with deicide." With all due respect to the authors and their intentions, this statement insults my intelligence and my sensibilities. There are, sadly, Jews who may believe this nonsense. These Jews fear that because of their history of oppression and victimhood, they must be "vigilant"—to use the word again—against even a hint of anti-Jewish sentiment that might possibly underlie criticism of the actions of the Jewish state. These Jews are as fear-driven as those Christians who will do anything to avoid being accused of anti-Semitism.

Yes, some Jews do cry anti-Semitism at the slightest hint of opposition to Israel's policies. They claim, with no small measure of hysteria, that criticism of Israel is tantamount to wanting to put an end to the Jewish people. But Christians must not participate in this dangerous notion, and must not be intimidated by Jews who use it to muzzle legitimate protest against injustice. Many, many Jews are heartbroken by what has developed out of the Zionist dream. We fear for our people. We do not desire the destruction of Israel. Rather, our actions are motivated by our realization that Israel's current course is unsupportable, destroys rather than creates security, and is eating away at the fabric of Israeli society. We have been called anti-Semitic and "self-hating" for identifying, as people who understand what it means to be marginalized, dispossessed, and oppressed, with the plight of the Palestinians in occupied Palestine today. Only by a twisted path of fear-driven reasoning can this sense of protest, sadness, and frank horror be characterized as self-hatred.

I reject, categorically, the article's unfounded and distorted characterization of Palestinian Liberation Theology. The article doesn't name its target, but I will. I know the people of Sabeel. They are dispossessed Palestinian Christians, some of them Israeli citizens, who have devoted themselves to the nonviolent pursuit of justice for their people. In this mission, their acts are informed by their Christian faith, in which they emulate Jesus's response to living as a Palestinian Jew under Roman occupation. They are hurt, but they do not hate. They build community, advocate for the rights of the oppressed, and teach nonviolence. Their strong faith enables them to persevere in the face of overwhelming frustration and continuing, increasing oppression without becoming bitter or resorting to violence. Sabeel is not anti-Jewish, nor is there a single word of anti-Jewish sentiment in its charter, its publications, or its actions. Sabeel does not call for the destruction or dismantling of Israel. What the article says, very simply, does not match the reality of Palestinian Liberation Theology. By linking the charge of deicide to the use of crucifixion imagery as a symbol of the suffering of the oppressed, the article insults these brave people of faith. It is also an insult to me and my fellow Jews. And it should be felt as an insult to the sensibilities and to the intelligence of Presbyterians and to Christians of all denominations who are attempting, out of their deep faith and sense of humanity, to act for justice.

I have met these Christians. I met them in Fort Worth, Texas, at the General Conference of the United Methodist Church, waging their persistent (and still ongoing) struggle to have the UMC stand behind its ethical investment rules and take initial steps to selectively divest from American companies profiting from the occupation of Palestine. I have met Christians of many denominations in their congregations in Washington, DC, Maryland, Illinois, California, Virginia, Alabama,

---

and Connecticut, sponsoring sales of olive oil and embroidery, inviting Palestinians to speak from their pulpits about their lives and struggles, and, most important, organizing pilgrimages to the Holy Land to witness the occupation and to meet with Israelis and Palestinians who are working across the lines for peace. I myself have been honored to address them from their pulpits, and I have received their gratitude and solidarity in hearing from me, a Jew, about my commitment to justice for all peoples of the land.

When anyone—Jew or Christian—tells you that you must be careful to avoid any appearance of anti-Jewish sentiment when you open up the issue of Israel's actions toward the Palestinians, be wary. It is an easy card to play, and—to shift metaphors—you are being sold a bill of goods. Don't buy it. You know injustice when you see it, and you know that legitimate concern about the human rights abuses of the State of Israel does not add up to being anti-Jewish. Yes, you can find Jews who will exploit Christian guilt over the persecution of the Jews throughout history. These Jews, speaking for major Jewish organizations and lobbying groups, will tell you that they speak for the Jews of America. They don't. They will tell you that the survival of Israel, and indeed of the Jewish people itself, depends on the maintenance of America's unconditional and massive flow of financial and political support for the continuation of Israel's expansionist and colonialist policies. The opposite is true. Israel's policy, remarkably consistent and relentless for the past forty years, to obtain complete political and economic control of all of Palestine, is killing Israel—its young people, its economy, its soul, its very future.

I am deeply concerned about the future of Israel. My roots are there—close to half of my family lives within its borders. I want peace and security for the inhabitants of the land, and I know that this will not be achieved by the dispossession and subjugation of half of its population. Even if, in some way, Israel could achieve a measure of security by some combination of exiling and controlling the Palestinians, this would be unacceptable to me, as it should be for all Jews, and indeed for all people.

You are right to revisit the brave actions you took in your General Assembly four years ago—for going back into the fray, for reengaging the struggle. What the Presbyterian Church began in 2004 and will continue this month is extremely important work. It represents the best hope for peace. I tell you now what you can see with your own eyes: the political process has failed to bring about a just resolution of this conflict, one that will be fair and that will bring peace. As evangelist and political activist Jim Wallis of Sojourners tells us, when politics fail, great social movements emerge to bring about the required social and political change. This must come from the bottom up. Look at the civil rights movement, born in the church. Look at the struggle to end apartheid—again, the churches were critical in mobilizing and organizing popular activism and in providing the leadership to mobilize and focus the grassroots movements necessary to create political and social change. Politicians test the wind and react accordingly, but it is the people who change the wind. This is what your resolutions are about, nothing less. That's how important this is.

Change the wind. Do the right thing. Don't be afraid. When someone—Christian or Jew—tries to stop you by saying that this action partakes of anti-Semitism, or even that it may *look* anti-Semitic, the proper response is to be offended and to correct that person, firmly and respectfully. And to then go on to do the right thing, including educating them. Over and over again: in your churches, at your dinner tables, in your conversations with friends. And in your General Assembly.

In its call for "vigilance," the article raises up the specter of anti-Semitism, based on a false characterization of liberation theology. It then urges us not to "cloud complicated issues" with the "rhetoric of ignorance...or the language of hate." Criticism of Israel is not the language of hate. It is the language of love. Jesus, like the Old Testament prophets who were my inspiration in my formative years, teaches us that the language of love is often not gentle. Speak it with courage.

Mark Braverman
June 4, 2008

I sent this response to my friend, and I believe that it circulated to some extent. But I was not alone in my objections to the piece. It apparently had evoked considerable negative reaction within the ranks of the Presbyterian Church itself. Members objected to some of the theology and claimed that it did not speak for them. Within a short time, the original piece was removed from the web site and replaced by a modified statement². The revised statement removed or softened some of the language about Palestinian Liberation Theology and added language to validate the efforts of the church to seek justice for Palestinians. When the modified article was published on the web site, it drew this response from the heads of three American Jewish denominations in the form of a letter to the Stated Clerk of the General Assembly of the PC(USA):³

Dear Reverend Kirkpatrick—

Candor compels us to respond immediately and clearly to the "expanded" and "revised" publication of "Vigilance against Anti-Jewish Ideas and Bias," and to tell you as plainly as we know how that the new statement marks a new low-point in Presbyterian-Jewish relations.

While we received what now seems to have been a draft of the statement with optimism and appreciation for its clear awareness of the sensitivities in the Jewish community, the revised statement that was just released is deeply troubling theologically, politically, and personally. The revised statement, which is currently prominently displayed on your web site, does more to excuse anti-Semitism and foster anti-Jewish motifs then it does to dispel them. And to speak frankly, the revised statement leaves us with a deep suspicion regarding the motivations behind replacing the initial statement—which the Jewish community warmly welcomed—with a document which you surely knew would cause deep angst. Friends, or even dialogue partners, do not engage in actions that can so easily and plausibly be seen as "bait and switch" tactics.

The initial statement contained many important elements that are now absent, including: an acknowledgement of complicity in existing anti-Jewish attitudes, a deep and thorough analysis of Palestinian liberation theology and the adverse characterization it often projects on the Jewish community, and most importantly a tone that is conciliatory and reflect-

---

2. The modified statement can be found at http://www.presbyweb.com/2008/News/June2008Statement.pdf.

3. Published on the Union for Reform Judaism web site, June 13, 2008.

ing the spirit of true dialogue and respect. Now we have a statement that is completely unbalanced in its appraisal of the Israeli-Palestinian Conflict, which contains veiled threats of "divestment", and which completely undoes much of the positive language and progress that were presented in the initial draft. Indeed, this document reads as a blueprint for how to engage in anti-Israel activity without being accused of anti-Semitism.

On a personal level, we think the most troubling revision to the entire letter is the deletion of one sentence: "We Presbyterians aspire to build positive and respectful relations with our neighbors in the Jewish community, based on an honest exploration of the close ties between our two faith traditions and our shared concerns for peace and justice." While we still deeply hope that this spirit is alive and well in the Presbyterian Church, the elimination of this statement surely gives us pause. If we are to "build positive and respectful relations" we need to do so in an atmosphere of trust and friendship, and in a spirit that truly encapsulates our prophetic duty to work together in honesty and in peace.

Sincerely,

Rabbi Jerome Epstein, Executive Vice President United Synagogue of Conservative Judaism

Dr. Carl Sheingold, Executive Vice President Jewish Reconstructionist Federation

Rabbi Eric Yoffie, President of the Union for Reform Judaism

Several days later, having read both the revised Presbyterian statement and a copy of this letter, I wrote the following:

On the "Expanded" Presbyterian Statement on "Vigilance Against Anti-Jewish Bias in the Pursuit of Israeli-Palestinian Peace"

The revised version of the original document is a significant improvement over the first effort. The author (or authors) of this revised piece have responded to the criticism of the original document and have produced a thoughtful piece that brings the discussion forward much more effectively. Indeed, the document deserves to be renamed from its original title, "Vigilance Against Anti-Jewish Bias," because it corrects the fundamental problem with the previous piece, which was to put concern about anti-Semitism before the actual issue—justice in Israel-Palestine. This shift in focus is reflected in the very opening of the statement, which states, clearly and simply, that Presbyterians "must stand unwaveringly for Justice and Peace."

What is most important about this new statement is that it leads with just that—a principled stand on the injustice being perpetrated against the Palestinian people by the State of Israel. Significantly, it clearly differentiates between criticism of the State of Israel and anti-Jewish feeling or statements. The author stands his ground on the central importance for Presbyterians of opposing any statements or positions that might partake of anti-Jewish feeling, and of the equally central importance of preserving the respectful relationship between Presbyterians and Jews. But he is respectful of this without backing off from a principled stand on the Israel-Palestine situation.

It is a very careful document. That's a good thing, because for Christians this is a complex issue, raising highly conflicting feelings. As such, it requires care. It also requires clarity, and this revised document achieves clarity on several key issues, issues that are often blurred and which create considerable confusion and distress as a result. There are two critical issues that the document covers well, correcting the problems with the first one:

1. It makes a clear distinction between the responsibility of the Israeli government and the Jewish people. Indeed, the Jewish establishment would do well to study this example, as Jewish organizations deliberately confuse Israel and its interests with that of all Jews.
2. Second: the statement presents a much more balanced and considered statement about Palestinian Liberation Theology. Although the author continues to insist that "most Jews" see in Palestinian Liberation Theology an "echo" of the accusation of Christ killing—a statement that I strongly question, and further challenge the author to provide evidence to support this claim—the author has presented a much more sensitive and sympathetic picture of Palestinian

Liberation Theology. This is important because it represents a significant backing off from the specious and destructive argument linking Palestinian Liberation Theology to the ancient charge of deicide.

So this is a great improvement, one that is likely to be more helpful than the original piece for Christians who are confronting the challenge of deciding what kind of action to take on this complex issue. It is also more likely—if not now, then perhaps in the future—to promote positive dialogue with the Jewish community. Jews and Christians alike must grapple with the difficult, painful process of deciding how to confront injustice and evil. They will not get there by focusing on the false issue of anti-Semitism. The issue here is not anti-Jewish feelings, but the injustice being perpetrated by the Jewish state. To make anti-Semitism the issue is to confuse the discourse—it leads nowhere. We must focus not on the sins of the past, but on the crimes of the present.

This statement is not the last word on these issues. What is important here is that in finding a way to grapple with these issues and the conflicting feelings they evoke, Christians do not yield to the temptation to allow the feelings to cancel one another out. This is typically expressed in statements that read something like this: "On the one hand, we abhor the actions of the State of Israel—on the other, we honor the desire of the Jewish people to overcome millennia of oppression." The way the conflict is all too often resolved is to avoid the issue altogether, to dilute the criticism, or as in the case of the original document, to miss the point entirely in eagerness to establish pro-Jewish credentials in the interests of "interfaith" reconciliation. When that is allowed to happen, the Presbyterian commitment to justice is betrayed. So this is a good process. Given the complex feelings raised by the situation in the Holy Land, and the history that it is freighted with, an iterative process is to be expected. It should be honored and allowed to go forward. And it should not be allowed to degrade into shouting.

This is why the response of the heads of the Jewish Reform, Conservative, and Reconstructionist movements is so shocking and disappointing. These Jewish leaders did not like this revised statement, calling it "a new low point in Presbyterian-Jewish relations." No—they preferred the first one, the one that shouted about anti-Semitism, the one that emphasized the need, *above all,* to hold up the mere suggestion of anti-Jewish feeling as a clear and present danger. They preferred the first statement, that promoted the specious argument that support of the struggle for Palestinian dignity and self-determination somehow leads to the charge of Christ-killers. The writers of the letter do not value the difficult and honest struggle of the Presbyterian Church as it grapples with the issue. Rather than participate in the process so painfully entered into by the Presbyterians, they apply litmus tests, take statements out of context, and imperiously demand a kind of rectitude. Rather than honoring the process, and indeed entering into the dialogue so earnestly sought by the Presbyterians, they sit in judgment. With regard to Palestinian Liberation Theology, they preferred the first statement, the one that slandered Sabeel. We prefer the first one, they say, not this second version which attempts to understand the struggle of Palestinian Christians to maintain a nonviolent, dignified stance in relation to their oppression.

But here is the real shocker. As all who have followed the story know, the history of this "dialogue" between the Presbyterian Church and the American Jewish establishment on the question of Israel and Palestine is the story of the enormous pressure exerted on the church not to pursue divestment from companies involved in the illegal occupation of Palestinian lands. In 2004, the church encountered what can only be characterized as a juggernaut of opposition to any notion of divestment. It was to a large extent due to pressure from Jewish organizations that the Presbyterian Church in 2004 removed the word "divestment" from their resolution and replaced it with a notion of "constructive engagement." The revised Presbyterian statement makes reference to this issue by referring to the need to pursue dialogue with these companies—*the word "divestment" is not mentioned*—as one of several actions that should be considered as part of a principled stand against injustice. But the authors of this scolding letter will have nothing to do with nuance or with principles. Ever "vigilant" about the suggestion that a church could take a principled stand through its investments, the letter shamelessly puts words into the mouths of the authors of the church statement, characterizing the statement about "constructive engagement" as "veiled threats of divestment." The authors of this letter want it both ways: they bully the church into removing the word "divestment" from its resolutions and into seeking more conciliatory (and, in the minds of some, less effective) measures, and then accuse the church of making "veiled threats" when it replaces the "hot button" term with an alternative strategy aimed at preserving a positive and respectful relationship with the Jewish community.

In closing, I address these heads of the Jewish denominations directly: As a Jew, I am appalled by your letter. Do you want it both ways? Do you want it all ways? What are you after? Certainly not interfaith dialogue. To your shame, you are keeping alive the despicable notion of Jews as Christ killers, the charge that has caused such suffering for us over the ages, because it serves your purpose now in seeking to intimidate Christians from taking a principled stand against the self-destructive policies of Israel. You want to encourage American Christians to besmirch the noble work of Sabeel, work supported on a wide-ranging basis by Christian leaders here in the U.S. You want to hold progressive Christians hostage to the sins of the past—women and men, laypersons and clergy, who are trying to find a way to move beyond the horrors of church anti-Semitism. You want to drag them back into this archaic theology through degradation and abuse of the Israel-Palestine issue. You don't want dialogue—you want to preach and to intimidate.

I honor the efforts of the people of the Presbyterian Church. They may not have found the answer yet, but they are grappling with the issue. And the issue is injustice. The issue is right and wrong. To them I say: do not allow yourselves to be distracted. Are there anti-Semites in your midst? Perhaps. But surely they are not steering the ship. This is a false issue, a distraction, a bullying tactic. Do not be distracted. Injustice is injustice. Wrong is wrong. Go, as you have, courageously, despite the bloodying you received in 2004, back into the fray. I applaud and support your persistence. I pray that someday the leaders of the American Jewish community will be ready to have the conversation you seek with them. In the meantime, continue to do the right thing: Seek justice; struggle to find the path. The authors of this letter do not speak for me, nor for tens of thousands of Jews who are with you in this journey. God bless you on your way.

Mark Braverman
June 16, 2008

Appendix C

Sermons[1]

A Trustworthy Prophet
Sermon for the Second Sunday after Epiphany

Ravensworth Baptist Church
Annandale, VA
January 18, 2009

Pastor Steve Hyde
Mark Braverman

First Samuel 3:1–20

Mark

As Steve and I sat together earlier this week to talk about this sermon, Steve asked the question, "What's it like to be a prophet?" In thinking about Steve's excellent question, I realized this: It's not about the prophet. It's not about, "Look at me, I am speaking the word of God. I have the truth." No—it is the experience of *speaking the truth* as it becomes inescapably clear to you. It is not a planned or willed act; it is simply something you must do. Three times, as the young Samuel lies in his room in the Temple, God knocks on the door. The fourth time,

---

1. These and other sermons and additional writing by the author can be found at www.markbraverman.org and www.jewishconscience.org.

he gets it. It's God on the other side of the door, hammering on the chambers of his heart. The scripture says, "Samuel lay there till morning. Then he opened the doors of the house of the Lord." [2] Samuel had been living there, in the Temple, since childhood. But only after passing through this dark night of the soul was he able to enter the house of God. And what does that mean, to enter into the House of God? It means to exercise our free will to do what is right. It means to follow the precepts: "Justice, justice, shalt thou pursue,"[3] and "Love thy neighbor as thyself."[4] Then you are in God's house, and the doors open, and they don't stop opening. As for Eli, he was the man in charge of God's house, right? The priest, the rabbi, the pastor, the bishop. And to his credit, he sees what is going on, and says to Samuel, "This is the Lord, let him in! Let it happen!" Eli's blindness is lifted. Eli sees that he is not the boss, or the gatekeeper, or even the intermediary. His job is to help keep the doors open, and to make as little noise as possible so that the Samuels of the world can hear the sounds of their own hearts beating. At that moment, Eli's blindness was lifted. In our scripture for today, God is knocking at the door, saying, "I am going to make the ears of the whole house tingle." Translation: the word literally means ears will ring—you will *hear something*.

And what was he going to do? Well, God was doing what he does— he was calling on a prophet. And what was this all about? The text tells us in the previous chapter that Eli's sons were bad actors: they were eating the fat from the sacrifices rather than just keeping the lean meat for their food. Translation: they were eating up the resources of the people. They were exploiting their power. And when the people protested, these same priests threatened them with violence. In the Temple of that day, force held sway. We will take what we want, and if it is not given, we will take it by force. Sound familiar? It's the same scenario that Jesus confronted when he came to Jerusalem eight centuries later, answering his own prophetic call. Empires, nations, do this, and—sometimes—the religious establishment aids and abets the oppression or just shuts its

---

2. First Samuel 3:18

3. Deuteronomy 16:20

4. Leviticus 19:18

eyes. And then this arrangement is sold to the people as something that is for their own good, that will bring security and prosperity. In the ancient world the sell is that we are keeping God (or the Gods) happy. In the modern world, it is that we are keeping you secure, we are fighting the enemies that threaten our country, our culture, our way of life. Theologian Walter Wink calls it the myth of redemptive violence. This was Eli's blindness. He had shut his eyes to this reality, and what is more important, he had shut his heart. He had let this happen to his people.

And so today we must ask the question: can the blindness be lifted? Can we say, as did Eli to Samuel, "What is it that God has told you? Do not hide it from me!" I received an e-mail the other day from Gila Svirsky, an Israeli activist, one of the early leaders of the movement for justice in Israel and founder of Women in Black—Women in Black, who still get out their signs and protest the occupation of Palestine, every Friday afternoon in Tel Aviv, Haifa, and Jerusalem. Gila writes: "I was listening to the radio interview of two teens from the south of Israel, both of whom had been living under intolerable conditions for several weeks, caught in the crossfire of the adults.

'Oh my family never watches the foreign TV stations,' said one. 'They're not as accurate as the Israeli news.'

'My father forbids it,' said the other. 'It could be demoralizing.'"[5]

Polls show that 80 percent of Israelis support the invasion of Gaza. The Israeli media plays a big role in presenting a heroic, sanitized picture of the war. The media tells a story in which the people of Gaza are not starving families but implacable enemies intent on destroying Israel. But accurate news reporting is not all that is needed to change hearts and minds. Someone has to knock on the door. There need to be prophets. Gila continues:

> Throughout these horrific weeks, the most carefully documented reports inside Israel of what is and what isn't actually happening have been those of the human right organizations. You know there have been serious human rights abuses when eleven organizations come together to do something. B'Tselem even took the unprecedented step of issuing a call for a cease fire. All have done important work in getting the message out to Israelis.

---

5. E-mail from Gila Svirsky, January 16, 2009.

Last but not least, the peace organizations continue raising their brave and lonely voices to the ongoing vilification of patriotic passersby and motorists. Here's what I wrote on my sign yesterday: "We have become our own worst nightmare."

We need prophets. We need them to help us see ourselves. Here is Gideon Levy, the Israeli journalist, writing in *Haaretz* on what he sees when he looks in the mirror:

"There was a massacre of dozens of officers during their graduation ceremony from the police academy? Acceptable. Five little sisters? Allowed. Palestinians are dying in hospitals that lack medical equipment? Peanuts," he wrote. "Our hearts have turned hard and our eyes have become dull. All of Israel has worn military fatigues, uniforms that are opaque and stained with blood and which enable us to carry out any crime." [6]

"We trust violence because we are afraid," writes liberation theologian Walter Wink. "And we will not relinquish our fears until we are able to imagine a better alternative." [7] The God of the Old Testament has a lot to answer for, take it from me. But in the history of his relationship with the people of Israel—in God's own words in Exodus 32 "a stiff-necked people"—we can always rely on God for one thing: his persistence. He will keep knocking on the door. Will we listen? Will we get up and open that door?

Steve

"As Samuel grew up, the LORD was with him and let none of his words fall to the ground. And all Israel from Dan to Beer-sheba knew that Samuel was a trustworthy prophet of the LORD."[8]

Mark, this is the LORD's work, not ours—so I will begin with the hope that none of the words of this text and none of your words will fall to the ground. But I'm going to be a realist for a moment, and acknowledge that some of them already have. We would have to hear what you have just said two or three times before beginning to hear it, and even

---

6. Levy 2009.
7. Wink 1992, 231.
8. First Samuel 3:19

multiple hearings would not guarantee that the truth in what you are saying will not fall to the ground.

So instead of merely hoping, I'm praying that the LORD will do what only the LORD can do…speak to us in these days when "visions are not widespread."

When the Elis of our time—the spiritual elders in synagogues and churches whose job it is to pass on wisdom and hope to the next generation—have grown blind and resistant to new visions and revelation…only the LORD can "lift the blindness" and find a way to reveal truth to us today so that we can both see and hear. The LORD says in I Samuel, and we can pray the LORD is saying today: "See, I am about to do something in Israel that will make both ears of anyone who hears it burn."

What could the LORD do in Israel…in Gaza…in the United States…in the world…that would make our ears ring? What will God who is knocking on our door say to us when we get up from our dozing to open the door and our hearts?

Now I should leave it at that, because I really want to hear your response, Mark.

But I will, of course, say a couple of things first.

Martin Luther King's last Sunday sermon was preached at the National Cathedral, only a few days before he was killed. He called his sermon that day "Sleeping through a revolution," and it's interesting that in our text, both the old man and Samuel—who is just a boy—are trying to sleep. Eli was "lying down in his room," and Samuel was "lying down in the temple of the LORD, where the ark of God was."[9]

But the LORD interrupts their sleep—not once but four times. I doubt very much that Eli slept any more after telling Samuel what he needed to do in order to hear the words from God. He lay awake the rest of the night, I'm guessing, waiting to hear what the LORD had said…knowing, I'm pretty sure, that he was not going to like what he heard.

After hearing the message from the LORD, Samuel "lay there until morning"…until it was time to open the doors of the house of the LORD. According to our text, "Samuel was afraid to tell the vision to Eli."

9. First Samuel 3:3

In his famous speech at New York's Riverside Church on April 4, 1967, in which he spoke about the Vietnam War, Martin Luther King Jr. said that "the calling to speak is often a vocation of agony."[10]

Samuel, lying there until morning with his eyes wide open and his heart pounding, afraid to tell the vision to Eli, is a more true-to-life picture of a prophet than our romantic images of someone with a booming voice eager and unafraid to speak the words of the LORD, when those very words will strain relationships, invite hostility, and create danger. The ones we remember as great prophets would, in the context of their troubled days, have preferred to stay in their cozy beds.

In looking at David Garrow's biography of Martin Luther King Jr.[11], I came across a conversation between King and Howard Baugh. Baugh was a childhood friend of MLK, a Marine veteran and policeman in Atlanta who found King's antiwar statements hard to take. I'm mentioning this instead of King's magnificent oratory because this is an encounter that happened between two old friends, away from the crowds and the cameras. It was a Saturday morning, King was in his study at the church, and his friend showed up at the door.

Howard Baugh tells what happened.[12] King came to the door. Baugh said, "M.L., I'd like to speak to you."

"Yeah, Howard, come on in. You caught me at a good time. Nobody's here but me."

He said, "What's on your mind?"

I said, "You know, last night I listened to your speech, and I think you know how I feel. You know where my sincerity is."

He said, "Listen, if there's anybody I trust, it's you."

"Well, I'm not sure whether I deserve that or not."

He said, "What are you talking about?"

I said, "M.L., I listened to you last night tell this multitude of people that you cannot condone the war in Vietnam, and our people are over there dying."

---

10. King 1990, 231–244

11. Garrow 1987

12. In the following dialogue, Baugh speaks in the first person, and Martin Luther King Jr. is referred to as "he."

He said, "Well, Howard, has that got you to this point?"

I said, "Yes."

He said, "Let me tell you something," and we sat down.

He said, "You've never really given this organization full credit for what it really stands for...It's a *nonviolent* organization, and when I say *nonviolent* I mean *nonviolent* all the way...Never could I advocate nonviolence in this country and not advocate nonviolence for the whole world...That's my philosophy...*I don't believe in the death and killing on any side, no matter who's heading it up—whether it be America or any other country, or whether it be for black folks...Nonviolence is my stand, and I'll die for that stand.*"

Howard Baugh then said to David Garrow, "And at that time I understood for the first time in my life what was meant by nonviolence."[13]

He didn't hear it the first time, or the second and third, maybe not the fourth, but in that moment with Martin Luther King Jr. in the privacy of his study, it got through. The truth knocked on the door; he woke up, opened the door, and let it in.

Mark, I know you don't object to Jesus talk. I can hear Jesus as he stands in that prophetic space that Samuel woke up in...saying to us what are words from the LORD: "You've never really given this synagogue or church full credit for what it stands for...They are meant to be about nonviolence, and when I say nonviolence, I mean nonviolence all the way. I don't believe in the death or killing on any side, no matter who's heading it up—whether it be America or any other country... Nonviolence is my stand, and I'll die for that stand."

I can hear Jesus saying in clear and uncompromising words, like Fr. Elias Chacour: "God does not kill."

So Mark—What could the LORD be saying to us...what could the LORD do in Israel...in Gaza...in the United States...in the world... that would make our ears ring? What are we likely to hear when we get up and open the door?

Mark

You are quite right, Steve, when you say that I don't object to Jesus talk, but I would not put it that way. I would say that I actively embrace

---

13. Garrow 1987, 572–573

Jesus talk. Right here, in this house of God, we are standing in Jesus's synagogue. I was reading a Christian theologian the other day who observed that it is an odd accident of history that the Gospels are not being read every Sabbath in the synagogue. That it is ironic and unfortunate that because Paul ran into trouble with the Jewish establishment of the day, the split occurred between the Jewish establishment of the first century and those Jews who followed Jesus. Because Judaism, at its heart, feels, as did Paul, that the work of faith is to guide us here, *in this world,* to the realization of the as yet unrealized, unforeseen future. And today, of all days, on the birthday of MLK, and as we contemplate in horror yet another example of the murder of innocents, today of all days we need to hear the voice of that visionary Jewish prophet and mystic.

Jesus was a courageous revolutionary, squarely within the prophetic tradition, calling out the abuses and iniquities of Rome and the client rulers of Judea who served her interests—in the words of Isaiah, "grinding the faces of the poor."[14] The Gospels are a blueprint, a manual, for how to repair that world—how to bring about the Kingdom of God, a kingdom, not of another world, but of the world that can be made real here. When Jesus said, "My kingdom is not of this world," he was not saying that he belonged somewhere else, in some heaven or other world. He was saying that the world order that I have come to help create is a world different than the kingdom of Rome. It was the world he describes on the Mount of the Beatitudes. We now know—and MLK understood this and the people working for nonviolence in Palestine and Israel and around the world understand this—that when Jesus said, "turn the other cheek" he didn't mean to stand passively and accept violence and oppression and racism. At the time of Jesus, you asserted your dominance and authority over someone by hitting him with the back of the hand. If the persecuted person, having been thus struck on the right cheek "turned the other cheek," the discipliner was faced with a dilemma. Turning the other cheek means forcing the other person to either strike you full on with their open right hand or fist, which would mean acknowledging equality, or to hold back. Either way, by

---

14. Isaiah 3:15

turning the other cheek, you force the aggressor to recognize his own violence and your humanity.

Nonviolence is not about the presence or absence of physical violence. It is about the nature of the relationship—how the other is perceived—and how one understands oneself. When you turn the other cheek, and open the way for the other to recognize his own violence, you are acknowledging and honoring his humanity. And when you do this—when you make this choice—in a strange, wonderful, and some-times frightening way, you recognize your own violence, your own responsibility for how things turn out. If you fail to do this, if you insist on seeing the problem as always outside of you, then you inevitably, unavoidably, become what you fear.

This is the challenge facing the Jewish people in Israel now. I heard Tzipi Livni on the radio on Friday when she was in Washington. Israel wants peace, she said, it is Hamas that has to be stopped. Israel is on the same side as the U.S.—we want to stop terrorism. She said this at least five times in five minutes. Israel has bought in completely to the myth that violence will end violence. Israel—a country of people still suffer-ing from the effects of one of the most horrible instances of collective violence visited upon one people on another—is still in denial of this: that the lesson of the Holocaust must be that one must never turn into that which has damaged one and which one fears. Here is Sara Roy, a miraculous contemporary American Jewish voice for justice:

> My mother and her sister had just been liberated from concen-tration camp by the Russian army. After having captured all the Nazi officials and guards who ran the camp, the Russian soldiers told the Jewish survivors that they could do whatever they wanted to their German persecutors. Many survivors, themselves emaci-ated and barely alive, immediately fell on the Germans, ravaging them. My mother and my aunt, standing just yards from the ter-rible scene unfolding in front of them, fell into each other's arms weeping. My mother, who was the physically stronger of the two, embraced my aunt, holding her close and my aunt, who had dif-ficulty standing, grabbed my mother as if she would never let go. She said to my mother, "We cannot do this. Our father and mother would say this is wrong. Even now, even after everything

we have endured, we must seek justice, not revenge. There is no other way." My mother, still crying, kissed her sister and the two of them, still one, turned and walked away.[15]

We have to take a look, and we have to hear God knocking on our door. When tens of thousands march in world capitals bearing banners with the Star of David next to a swastika, we need to look. When the comparison is made between Gaza and the Warsaw Ghetto, we have to look.

So, Steve, you ask, what can we do? I believe that the church here in the U.S. has been called. I stand here at Ravensworth and feel, as I have now in perhaps dozens of other churches of many denominations, the hunger for prophecy, for that voice. As we Jews have to acknowledge our complicity in the violence we have brought upon ourselves, so Christians need to allow themselves to walk through the door that stands open in the fight for peace based on justice. Don't be afraid. To be sure, the barriers are there, it's scary to go to Eli and deliver the message from the Lord. But this is happening. This week a Jewish member of the British Parliament, heartsick and outraged at the carnage in Gaza, made one of those knocks on the door. Gerald Kaufman sharply criticized Israel in a House of Commons debate on Gaza, arguing that the Jewish state has exploited the world's guilt for allowing the slaughter of six million Jews during World War II.

Don't be afraid. Speak the word of God, the word you clearly can see and know, acknowledge our humanity and call us to account.

The church is well on its way to healing the Holy Land through nonviolence. When you sell Palestinian olive oil and crafts, when you welcome Daoud Nassar of Tent of Nations, when you travel to Israel and Palestine to meet and support Israelis and Palestinians working for peace and coexistence, when you introduce resolutions to divest your pension funds from companies involved in human rights violations in Palestine—you are opening the doors of the house of the Lord and you are hastening that yet to be realized future.

The challenge is alive today as it was in the time of MLK. In his "Letter from a Birmingham Jail," he wrote, knocking, oh so hard, on the door of the church, the Temple of his day that was so asleep and so blind:

15. Roy 2007

There was a time when the church was very powerful—in the time when the early Christians rejoiced at being deemed worthy to suffer for what they believed. In those days the church was not merely a thermometer that recorded the ideas and principles of popular opinion; it was a thermostat that transformed the mores of society. Whenever the early Christians entered a town, the people in power became disturbed and immediately sought to convict the Christians for being "disturbers of the peace" and "outside agitators." But the Christians pressed on, in the conviction that they were "a colony of heaven," called to obey God rather than man. Small in number, they were big in commitment.

The judgment of God is upon the church as never before. If today's church does not recapture the sacrificial spirit of the early church, it will lose its authenticity, forfeit the loyalty of millions, and be dismissed as an irrelevant social club with no meaning for the twentieth century.[16]

Steve

One of the most influential figures in the civil rights movement was a student, Diane Nash. She was not a publicity-seeker, so her name is not that well known. But to those in the movement, she earned great respect. She is quoted on the cover of today's bulletin: "If people think it was Martin Luther King's movement, then today they are more likely to say, 'Gosh, I wish we had a Martin Luther King here today to lead us'…If people knew how that movement started, then the question they would ask themselves is, 'What can I do?'"[17]

Can you imagine how thrilling it would be for Martin Luther King Jr. to see an African-American sworn in as President of the United States? I have wondered at times if Barack Obama might have been channeling King when he said things like, "We are the change we have been waiting for."[18]

---

16. King 1963
17. Garrow 1987, 625
18. Obama 2008

Could it be that instead of God knocking on the door of a single person, whether a boy like Samuel or a young man like Martin Luther King, God is knocking on our doors, calling all of us to be spectators no longer, making our ears burn with the truth that a long look in the mirror will reveal who it is that God is calling?

How many times must God call us before we wake up, and say, "LORD, speak to us, for we—your people—are listening."

If Martin Luther King were around for the Inauguration on Tuesday, he would say something that would catch us off-guard. If he had a few minutes with the new president in the Oval Office, just the two of them without crowds or cameras, there would be something Barack Obama would see and hear that he had not seen and heard before.

That's what prophets do. They bring the Word of the Lord into our lives, and they speak truth to power. I can imagine Martin Luther King Jr. looking at us today, and saying, "Remember the Beloved Community? Don't lie around half-heartedly waiting for God to call another prophet. Be what you're waiting around for. Be what your world is desperate for—a beloved, prophetic community that hears God knocking, and throws the doors wide open."

Amen.

The Elephant in the Room
Sermon for Second Sunday of Easter
St. John's Episcopal Church of Georgetown
Washington, DC
March 30, 2008

Mark Braverman

Acts 2:14a 22-32
John 20:19-31

We're all familiar with the metaphor of the elephant in the room. A group of people has gathered together—for a meeting, a social gathering, perhaps for worship. An elephant is standing in the middle of the room, and no one mentions it. All agree, without having discussed it openly or at all, not to mention it or even to acknowledge its existence. We have such an elephant in the room with us this morning, as do congregations in tens of thousands of other churches across the world—it is the anti-Jewish words to be found in this morning's lessons from scripture. Pastors and Christian theologians across the religious spectrum continue to face the challenge presented by this aspect of the Christian scriptures. We live in an era of progressive theology, an era in which the church has attempted to reach out to and reconcile with the Jewish people. It is a project that was spurred in no small degree by the almost inexpressible horror of the Christian world at the consequences of anti-Semitism, exposed for all to see at the close of World War II.

Passages such as those we read today, together with other infamous passages which vilify the Jews, have been put to nefarious and tragic use over the millennia. In recent years, these passages have often been sanitized and explained away. For example, in Matthew 27, when the Jews demand that Pilate order Jesus's crucifixion, and in response to his protest answer him by saying, "Let his blood be upon us and upon our children!" Some interpreters claim that "the people" doesn't refer to the Jews but to the Jewish leaders who sought to neutralize Jesus's threat to their power by any means necessary. But a look at the text shows that this is not the case. The writer of this narrative wrote (and meant) *the*

Jews as a group—*all the people* (for you seminarians, *pas ho laos*) put up to it by the priests and the scribes. This counts as anti-Semitism, just as talking about blacks, or Hispanic immigrants, or Muslims as a group counts as the same ugly racist phenomenon. *It's in there.* And I put to you that in these days, especially in these days, we do ourselves a disservice by not grappling directly with the challenge of such passages.

Let's look at these lessons.

> Peter, standing with the eleven, raised his voice and addressed the multitude, "You Israelites, listen to what I have to say: Jesus of Nazareth, a man attested to you by God with deeds of power, wonders, and signs that God did through him among you, as you yourselves know—this man, handed over to you according to the definite plan and foreknowledge of God, you crucified and killed by the hands of those outside the law. But God raised him up, having freed him from death, because it was impossible for him to be held in its power."
> *(Acts 2:14a, 22–32)*

> When it was evening on that day, the first day of the week, and the doors of the house where the disciples had met were locked for fear of the Jews, Jesus came and stood among them and said, "Peace be with you." After he said this, he showed them his hands and his side. Then the disciples rejoiced when they saw the Lord. Jesus said to them again, "Peace be with you. As the Father has sent me, so I send you."
>
> But Thomas (who was called the Twin), one of the twelve, was not with them when Jesus came. So the other disciples told him, "We have seen the Lord." But he said to them, "Unless I see the mark of the nails in his hands, and put my finger in the mark of the nails and my hand in his side, I will not believe."
>
> A week later his disciples were again in the house, and Thomas was with them. Although the doors were shut, Jesus came and stood among them and said, "Peace be with you." Then he said to Thomas, "Put your finger here and see my hands. Reach out your hand and put it in my side. Do not doubt but believe." Thomas answered him, "My Lord and my God!" Jesus said to him, "Have you believed because you have seen me? Blessed are those who have not seen and yet have come to believe."
> *(John 20:19–31)*

There are two elements in these passages that I want to focus on this morning. The first is that the Jews are set up as responsible for the crucifixion of Jesus and, in fact, continue to be a danger to Christians. We'll get back to that. The second has something to do with what it means to see and to witness something that is life-changing. They are about opening eyes, and opening ears. Easter is about experience that transforms—that changes us fundamentally.

One of the most famous encounters with Jesus after the resurrection, of course, was that of Paul. In Luke's account in Acts, what Paul sees is not the image of a man, but a blinding flash of light. Paul himself in his own account in Corinthians reports that Jesus spoke to him, implying more of an actual encounter, but in his letter, in his characteristic style, he sets up a question and then answers it, chastising his questioner for implying that seeing Jesus would be like an ordinary earthly encounter: "the splendor of heavenly bodies is one thing, the splendor of earthly bodies another." *Don't ask me what he looked like*, Paul is saying. *You clearly don't understand what I'm talking about!* Elsewhere, he writes: "God shines a light in our heart so that we can understand the splendor of God."[19]

In other words, true seeing happens within, in response to experience, when we are open to it. It's what Rudolf Otto called "the numinous," and it is outside the realm of the everyday. And it is the heart of the religious experience.

This is what the Bible, in these passages concerned with the immediate aftermath of the crucifixion, is teaching us: what it means to wake up, to be transformed, to be, if you will, resurrected, reborn from a previous level of existence. The purpose of Jesus's crucifixion and resurrection, the Bible is telling us, is to teach us the true nature of seeing so that we may participate in this new life. Interpreters of the Gospel talk about John in particular as saying that the resurrection was not a single event, but a process that continues, for all of us, throughout our lifetimes. This is what it means to have our eyes open, this is what John is telling us in the story of Thomas.

Yes, the book of John sets the Jews up as the killers of Jesus Christ. But it is not murder they are accused of—John makes it clear, as do

---

19. First Corinthians 4:5

the Synoptic Gospels, that it was the Romans who executed Jesus. But, make no mistake, the Jews had a part to play in this story. They *are* implicated in the death of Jesus. But what they are accused of is not his actual execution, but, as John makes so clear here, of *blindness*.

The early followers of Jesus—still identifying as Jews—said to their fellow Jews: *Jesus has shown us something new, something outside of our established tribal, cultic framework. In order to make that entirely clear, that this is new and available to all of humankind, we are going to throw off the dietary laws, and the Sabbath, and, most significantly, circumcision.* And the point was made, and the Jews said, *no.* This is the story that John was telling in his Gospel, and is the basis of his depiction of the Jews of the time: as enemies of what would become the new faith.

Today, we reject the idea of blaming the Jews for the death of Jesus. Theologians are working hard to somehow undo the consequences of Christianity having set itself up as the true faith that superseded Judaism. But we must take heed of the lesson that is taught here, which is the message of Easter.

We all, in one way or another, at one time or another, suffer from Thomas's malady of spiritual obtuseness. And, as John depicts them, we are all at times like the Jews of his day, who did not want to be shaken out of their complacency and their established order, no matter how oppressive and unjust it was. John picks on the Jews—he does!—and there were reasons why he did that, and we can understand this but not justify it, and we know, now that the twentieth century is history, what incalculable damage his depiction of the Jews has caused. The Christians of the first century were not perfect. But what really happened back then in first-century Palestine?

Something of enormous historical significance took place in the earliest days of our Judeo-Christian history. Gary Wills called it a family quarrel,[20] and it set up a rift that had horrible consequences throughout history. The early followers of Jesus split from the Jewish establishment, eventually threw in with Rome, set up the Jews as the politically expendable outcasts, and ultimately rode that wave to dominance. The Jews retreated into their insularity. And so it went—for two millennia, until

---

20. Wills 2006, 127

it reached its unimaginably horrible climax in the twentieth century. Yes, you as Christians feel the pain of that sin, and you strive to take appropriate responsibility for it and take the lessons from it. And I as a Jew today mourn all the suffering and loss and horror that came from that. But I need to know *how* to mourn that Holocaust and, like you, to look critically at the choices my people has made.

And so let us not be afraid of looking squarely at the anti-Judaism in the Gospels, no more than we are afraid of confronting anti-Semitism or any form of racism today. It is wrong. It must be corrected. But to do so we must acknowledge the presence of the elephant, because it opens us to a deeper understanding of the people, their times, and the lessons they have to teach us. To switch metaphors, let us not throw the baby out with the bathwater. Seen in the historical context in which he lived, John was not saying anything that Isaiah, Jeremiah, Amos, and Hosea have not said: trust in God, not in kings or priests, generals or empire builders. Open your eyes. See the light and the revelation before you. The followers of Jesus had seen something that had changed them forever. But, and this is one of the great paradoxes of history, their job, having seen what they had seen, their instructions, from Jesus himself, was to teach people to look, not with their eyes, but with their hearts.

We need this call today, because blindness kills. Open our eyes!

Two years ago, and your fellow congregant John Van Wagoner was there to see it, and it happened to him too, I saw something that changed me forever.

I am a Jewish American. I was born in 1948—a month before the State of Israel. I was taught that a miracle—born of heroism and bravery—had blessed my generation. The State of Israel was not a mere historical event—it was redemption.

I first visited Israel as a boy of seventeen, and I fell in love with the young state. I was proud of the miracle of modern Israel—of what my people had done, creating this vibrant country out of the ashes of Auschwitz. My Israeli family—religious Jews—warmly embraced me. But even as I embraced them in return, I realized that they talked about "the Arabs" in the same way that whites talked about black people in the pre-civil rights Philadelphia of my birth. I knew then that something was fundamentally wrong with the Zionist project. Still, I held to the Jewish narrative: the occupation, although lamentably abusive of human rights, was the price of security. Then I went to the West Bank.

Traveling in Israel and the occupied territories that summer, my defenses against the reality of Israel's crime crumbled. Witnessing the Separation Wall; the checkpoints, the network of restricted roads; the assassinations, midnight raids and collective punishment; the massive, continuing construction of illegal Jewish settlements and towns; and the vicious acts of ideological Jewish settlers, words like apartheid and ethnic cleansing sprang to my mind, unbidden and undeniable. That summer, forty years after my first encounter with the Land, I saw all that, and my relationship to Israel changed forever. My eyes were opened.

I am often characterized—sometimes it's an accusation—of being "Pro-Palestinian." This, of course, is in contrast to being "Pro-Israel." I reject these labels. I reject the category as applied to my beliefs and my experience. What happened to me when I went to Palestine is that I discovered what I had already known, deep in my bones but not yet in my conscious awareness, what I knew to be true—that the Palestinians are every bit as much my brothers and my sisters as my coreligionists in Israel, that the land is theirs every bit as much theirs as it is mine, if we can learn how to deserve it, and that I cannot accept, cannot tolerate, cannot live with, a situation in which my people has dispossessed this other people (any other people) in order to possess the land ourselves. Furthermore, I do not believe that this can work—the attempt to establish a state by and for Jews, with all that this requires—and we are seeing, all too clearly, that this ultimately will spell the destruction of the state itself. The occupation, the attempt to maintain Jewish dominance in a land shared by another people, is unsustainable, wrong, and self-destructive.

Open our eyes!

In a few weeks, we Jews will observe Passover. We will eat unleavened bread and drink wine as Jesus did with his followers on his last night on earth. And we will recite, as we do every year, the story of our going out of Egypt, of our liberation from bondage. And we are taught not to enslave, for we were slaves. We are admonished: deal justly, for you know what it is like to be oppressed.

We Jews are in danger of having forgotten this fundamental tenet of our faith.

It is clear to me, as a Jew, that Israel has lost its way. We must learn to see again, to have our eyes opened. We brought to the world the teaching of a universal God, a God who seizes us by the arm, binds us to his covenant, demands justice—and we are now enacting the creed of a tribal God who commands conquest. We lay claim to our tradition of social justice and the requirement to relieve suffering, but we have left the Palestinians out of it—it is only about *our* suffering. We have unleashed dark forces, exemplified not only by criminal government actions but by the vicious acts of fanatics. Blessedly, there are those among us in Israel and Palestine and here in the U.S.—many—who shine light upon this shadow, this darkness, who are taking on the mantle of prophecy, who are the living stones. They are the living stones. There is Daoud Nassar who visited you here just six months ago at the invitation of Father Albert to share his story, Daoud who—confronted with oppression and guns drawn—turned away from bitterness and violence and worked to create a place of peace and fellowship. There are Rami and Nurit Elhanan who, brokenhearted, reach across the walls of concrete and fear to create a new community of shared grief and hope. There are the Israeli soldiers forced to dehumanize others in their homes, villages, and byways, and Palestinian political prisoners, who shed their army uniforms and emerge from their jail cells to embrace one another and together visit schools to bring a message of nonviolence to the children of both peoples. There are religious leaders here, Christian and Jewish, who, risking the disapproval and nervousness of congregants who want to stay safely courteous, nonpolitical, and not offend anyone, courageously train a strong light on the darkness of injustice and indifference. There are modern-day pilgrims, like your own John Van Wagoner, who visit the Holy Land not to look at the dead stones, the religious sites, but to visit the living stones, those who labor to bring peace, to tear down the walls.

Open our eyes. Take away our fear of seeing with our hearts, even though it destroys our equanimity, upends our lives, makes our families think we've lost our senses. Visit the Holy Land, see the living stones, be changed. And I say this in particular to you seminarians: You are training to be spiritual leaders. It's the most important job in the world today—

go the Holy Land, see the living stones, have your eyes opened.

The Bible is the story of humankind's journey toward a peaceable kingdom built on universal love. Today, here, we continue on this journey. Each of us, if we open our eyes, is Jesus entering the Temple and, in horror, realizing that it has become a den of thieves. It is Jeremiah standing on the Mount of Olives, as Jesus did eight centuries later, weeping for the city, for the destruction he knew it was calling down on itself. It is the person of faith—Christian, Jew, Muslim, Buddhist, Hindu—confronting the question of what to do when confronted with evil in his or her time, confronted with a House of God turned into a machine to dispossess the powerless, rob the poor, despoil nature.

Open our eyes. We have choice. Where are we going? We live in a world which gives us every reason to hunker down in our bubble of prosperity, to say we can do nothing about the juggernaut of globalization that rapaciously exploits 90 percent of the world's population in order to drape the remaining 10 percent in luxury. We live in a world that encourages us to define ourselves according to how different we are from others—from other cultures, other countries, other faiths. We live in a world which prompts us to be full of fear, to hold on, and to close down, rather than to let go and open up. We live in a world that is tottering on the brink, a world very like the world of first-century Palestine into which walked an itinerant Jewish mystic who changed history forever.

Teach us to see. Teach us to understand the lesson of Easter, the lesson brought to the world by one of my own, who said to his own people, the poor, the rich, the farmer, the merchant, the priest, the emperor: Wake up! Open your eyes to the gift of newness that partakes of the divine, that is the gift of the divine.

Walter Wink, writing about this says, "Jesus the man, the sage, the itinerant teacher, the prophet, even the lowly Human Being, while unique and profound, was not able to turn the world upside down. His attempt to do so was a decided failure. Rather, it was his ascension, his metamorphosis into the archetype of humanness that constituted a remaking of the values that had undergirded the domination system for some three thousand years before Jesus. The critique of domination continued to build on the Exodus and the prophets of Israel, to be sure. But Jesus' ascension to the right hand of the Power of God was a supernova in the archetypal sky. As the image of the truly Human One, Jesus became an exemplar of the utmost possibilities for living. The religious task for us today is not to cling to dogma but to seek a personal experience of the living God in whatever mode is meaningful."[21]

Teach us to see. Teach us all—Christians, Jews, Muslims, people of all faiths—to see and to follow that light. To know that we face the choice, to see or not to see, every day, to know that resurrection is happening every day.

Amen.

---

21. Wink 2008

Reference List

Abrams, Jeremiah, and Connie Zweig. 1990. *Meeting the shadow: The hidden power of the dark side of human nature.* New York: Archer Penguin.

Agha, Hussein and Robert Malley. 2001. Camp David: The tragedy of errors. *New York Review of Books,* 48 (13), http://www.nybooks.com/articles/14380.

Amichai, Yehuda. 1995. *A life of poetry, 1948–1994.* Trans. Benjamin and Barbara Harshav. New York: Harper Perennial.

Arendt, Hannah. 2007. The Jewish state: Fifty years later, where have Herzl's politics led? In *The Jewish writings,* ed. Jerome Kohn and Ron H. Feldman, 375–387. New York: Schocken.

Ateek, Naim S. 1989. *Justice only justice: A Palestinian theology of liberation.* Maryknoll, NY: Orbis Books.

———. 2008. *A Palestinian Christian cry for reconciliation.* Maryknoll, NY: Orbis Books.

Avishai, Bernard. 2002. *The tragedy of Zionism: How its revolutionary past haunts Israeli democracy.* New York: Helios Press.

Back, Rachel Tzvia. 2007. *On ruins & return: Poems, 1999–2005.* Exeter, UK: Shearsman Books.

Bechler, Rosemary. 2005. Nation as trauma, Zionism as question: Jacqueline Rose interviewed. *Open Democracy,* August 18.

Ben-Gurion, David. 1950. The forefathers of the Jewish nation. TS, Jerusalem, 1. Quoted in Rose 2005, 46.

———. 1972. *Israel: A personal history.* London: New English Library. Quoted in Rose 2005, 25–26.

Beit-Hallahmi, Benjamin. 1993. *Original sins.* New York: Olive Branch Press.

Borg, Marcus J. 2006. *Jesus: Uncovering the life, teachings, and relevance of a religious revolutionary.* San Francisco: HarperOne.

Borg, Marcus J. and N. T. Wright. 1999. *The meaning of Jesus: Two visions.* New York: HarperCollins.

Brown, Stephen. 2008. Theologians warn on "biblical metaphors" in Middle East conflict. *ENI Bulletin* September 24.

Brueggemann, Walter. 2001. *The prophetic imagination.* Minneapolis: Augsberg Fortress.

———. 2002. *The land.* 2nd ed. Minneapolis: Augsberg Fortress.

———. 2008. Prophetic ministry in the national security state. *Theology Today* 64 (October): 285–311.

Burg, Avraham. 2008. *The Holocaust is over and we must rise from its ashes.* New York: Palgrave MacMillan.

———. 2008. *Zionism, Israel and human rights.* Presentation at the Second North American Conference on Human Rights sponsored by Rabbis for Human Rights North America, December 7.

Carroll, James. 2001. *Constantine's sword: The Church and the Jews.* Boston: Houghton Mifflin.

Carter, Jimmy. 2006. *Palestine: Peace not apartheid.* New York: Simon and Schuster.

Chacour, Elias and David Hazard. 2003. *Blood brothers.* Grand Rapids, MI: Chosen Books.

Dunn, James D.G. 1990. *Jesus, Paul, and the law.* Louisville: Westminster John Knox Press.

————, ed. 2003. *The Cambridge companion to St Paul.* Cambridge: Cambridge University Press.

Ellis, Marc. 2001. On the Jewish civil war and the new prophetic. *Tikkun Magazine.*

———— . 2004. *Toward a Jewish theology of liberation: The challenge of the 21st century.* Waco: Baylor University Press.

Epstein, Jerome, Carl Sheingold, and Eric Yoffie. 2008. American Synagogue Leaders Decry Presbyterian Church's "Revised" Statement on "Vigilance against Anti-Jewish Ideas and Bias." Union for Reform Judaism, June 13, http://new.urj.net/about/union/pr/2008/presbyterian_jewish_relations/index.cfm?

Epstein, Yitzchak. 1905. The Hidden Question. Quoted in Halper 2008, 268–69.

Evron, Boaz. 1981. The Holocaust: Learning the wrong lessons. *Journal of Palestine Studies* 10 (3): 16–26. Quoted in Ellis 2004, 54.

Falk, Richard. June 29, 2007. Slouching toward a Palestinian Holocaust. The Transnational Foundation for Peace and Future Research. http://www.transnational.org/Area_MiddleEast/2007/Falk_PalestineGenocide.html.

Forster, Arnold and Benjamin R. Epstein. 1974. *The new anti-Semitism.* New York: McGraw-Hill.

Gaillardetz, Richard R. 2008. *Ecclesiology for a global Church: A people called and sent.* Maryknoll, NY: Orbis Books.

Gager, John G. 1983. *The origins of anti-Semitism.* New York: Oxford University Press.

Goren, Arthur A., ed. 1982. *Dissenter in Zion: From the writings of Judah L. Magnes.* Cambridge: Harvard University Press.

Garrow, David. 1987. *Bearing the cross: Martin Luther King, Jr., and the Southern Christian Leadership Conference.* New York: Vintage Books.

Goren, Arthur A. 1982, *Dissenter in Zion: From the writings of Judah L. Magnes.* Cambridge: Harvard University Press.

Gorenberg, Gershom. 2007. *The accidental empire: Israel and the birth of the settlements, 1967–1977.* New York: Times Books/Henry Holt.

Green, Arthur. December 2008. We are all Israel: Thoughts of a religious Jew and a secular Zionist. Lecture given at the second North American Conference on Judaism and Human Rights, Washington, D.C. http://www.rhr-na.org/resource/ we-are-all-israel-thoughts-of-religious-jew-and-secular-.

Greenberg, Irving. 1977. Cloud of smoke, pillar of fire: Judaism, Christianity, and modernity after the Holocaust. In *Auschwitz: Beginning of a new era? Reflections on the Holocaust,* ed. Eva Fleischner, 7–55. New York: Ktav.

———. 1981. The third great cycle in Jewish history. *Perspectives,* September.

Hagee, John. March 11, 2007. AIPAC Policy Conference 2007. http://www.aipac.org/Publications/SpeechesByPolicymakers/Hagee-PC-2007.pdf.

Halper, Jeff. 2008. *An Israeli in Palestine: Resisting dispossession, redeeming Israel.* London: Pluto Press.

Harris, David. 2008. A Jewish political platform. In the Trenches: The Jerusalem Post Blogs, October 9, http://cgis.jpost.com/Blogs/harris/entry/a_jewish_political_platform_posted.

———. 2009. Shame! In the Trenches: The Jerusalem Post Blogs, January 11, http://cgis.jpost.com/Blogs/harris/entry/shame_posted_by_david_harris.

Hertzberg, Arthur. 2003. *The fate of Zionism.* San Francisco: Harper-Collins.

Heschel, Abraham Joshua. 1962. *The prophets.* Philadelphia: The Jewish Publication Society of America.

Hijab, Nadia. 2009. Olmert's nightmare. *Counterpunch,* April 8, http://www.counterpunch.org/hijab04082009.html.

Horsley, Richard A. 2003. *Jesus and empire: The Kingdom of God and the New World disorder.* Minneapolis: Fortress Press.

———, ed. 2008. *In the shadow of empire.* Louisville: Westminster John Knox Press.

Khoury, Elias. 2007. *Gate of the sun.* Trans. Humphrey Davies. New York: Picador, 348–349.

King, Martin Luther, Jr. 1963. Letter from Birmingham Jail. *The Christian Century,* June 12.

————. 1990. Sermon: A time to break silence. In *A testament of hope: The essential writings and speeches of Martin Luther King, Jr.* ed. James M. Washington, 231–244. New York: HarperCollins.

Kook, Abraham Isaac. 1963. Eretz Yisrael. In *Orot Hakadesh*, 9. Jerusalem: Mosad Harav Kook. Quoted in Rose 2005, 23.

Kovel, Joel. 2007. *Overcoming Zionism: Creating a single democratic state in Israel/Palestine.* London: Pluto Press.

Levy, Gideon. 2009. And there lie the bodies. *Haaretz*, January 26, http://www.haaretz.com/hasen/spages/1052348.html.

Magnes, Judah. 1929. Letter to Chaim Weizmann. Quoted in Goren 1982, 62.

Mearsheimer, John J. and Stephen M. Walt. 2006. The Israel lobby. *London Review of Books* 28 (6), http://www.lrb.co.uk/v28/n06/mear01_.html.

————. 2007. *The Israel lobby and U.S. foreign policy.* New York: Farrar, Straus, and Giroux.

Obama, Barak. February 8, 2008. Presidential campaign speech. Seattle, WA.

Osborn, Robert T. 1990. The Christian blasphemy: A non-Jewish Jesus. In *Jews and Christians: Exploring the past, present, and future*, ed. James H. Charlesworth, 214. New York: Crossroad.

Pappe, Ilan. 2006. *The ethnic cleansing of Palestine.* Oxford: One World.

Peled-Elhanan, Nurit. June 8, 2001. A speech to Women in Black. Tel Aviv, http://www.nimn.org/Perspectives/international/000132.php?section=.

Pettit, Peter A. 2008. Pain and God are on sides in Middle East. *Allentown Morning Call*, February 11.

Remnick, David. 2007. The apostate: A Zionist politician loses faith in the future. *The New Yorker*, July 30, http://www.newyorker.com/reporting/2007/07/30/070730fa_fact_remnick.

Rabbis for Human Rights. http://rhr.israel.net/rabbis-for-human-rights.

Rosen, David. June 2006. "The Churches and the Battle Against Anti-Semitism." Address, http://rabbidavidrosen.net/Articles/Christian-Jewish%20Relations/The%20Churches%20and%20the%20battle%20against%20antisemitism%20June%202004.pdf.

Rosenfeld, Alvin H. 2006. Progressive Jewish thought and the new anti-Semitism. *American Jewish Committee*.

Rose, Jacqueline. 2005. *The question of Zion*. Princeton: Princeton University Press.

Roy, Sara. 2007. *Failing peace: Gaza and the Palestinian-Israeli conflict*. London: Pluto Press.

———. 2007. How can children of the Holocaust do such things? *Counterpunch*, April 7/8, http://www.counterpunch.org/roy04072007.html.

———. 2009. Israel's "victories" in Gaza come at a steep price. *Christian Science Monitor*, January 2, http://www.csmonitor.com/2009/0102/p09s01-coop.html.

Ruether, Rosemary R. 1997. *Faith and fratricide: The theological roots of anti-Semitism*. Eugene, OR: Wipf and Stock.

———. 2008. The why's of Holocaust denial. *National Catholic Reporter*, April 4, http://ncronline.org/node/591.

Ruether, Rosemary R. and Marc H. Ellis, eds. 1990. *Beyond occupation: American, Jewish, Christian and Palestinian voices for peace.* Boston: Beacon Press.

Ruether, Rosemary R. and Herman J. Ruether. 2002. *The wrath of Jonah: The crisis of religious nationalism in the Israeli-Palestine conflict.* 2nd ed. Minneapolis: Augsberg Fortress.

Said, Edward W. 2005. *From Oslo to Iraq and the road map: Essays.* New York: Vintage.

Schwartz, Regina M. 1997. *The curse of Cain: The violent legacy of monotheism.* Chicago: University of Chicago Press.

Shlaim, Avi. 2009. How Israel brought Gaza to the brink of humanitarian catastrophe. *The Guardian,* January 7, http://www.guardian.co.uk/world/2009/jan/07/gaza-israel-palestine.

Soulen, R. Kendall. 1996. *The God of Israel and Christian Theology.* Minneapolis: Augsberg Fortress.

———. 2004. Michael Wyschogrod and God's first love. *The Christian Century,* July 27, 22–27.

———. 2008. Review of *According to the scriptures: The origins of the Gospel and of the church's Old Testament,* by Paul M. van Buren. *Theology Today,* April, http://findarticles.com/p/articles/mi_qa3664/is_200004/ai_n8887732/?tag=content;col1.

Spong, John Shelby. 1999. *Why Christianity must change or die: A bishop speaks to believers in exile.* San Francisco: HarperCollins.

———. 2005. *The sins of Scripture: Exposing the Bible's texts of hate to reveal the God of love.* San Francisco: HarperOne.

Stainer, Michael Bungay. 2008. *Find your great work.* Toronto: Box of Crayons Press.

Van Buren, Paul M. 1984. The Jewish people in Christian theology: Present and future. In *The Jewish people in Christian preaching*, ed. Darrell J. Fasching, 19–33. Lewiston, New York: Edwin Mellon Press.

Volf, Miroslav. 2006. *The end of memory: Remembering rightly in a violent world.* Grand Rapids, MI: Eerdmans.

Wagner, Donald E. 1995. *Anxious for Armageddon.* Scottsdale: Herald Press.

Wallis, James H. 1997. *Post-Holocaust Christianity: Paul van Buren's theology of the Jewish-Christian reality.* Lanham, MD: University Press of America.

Wallis, Jim. 2005. *God's politics: Why the right gets it wrong and the left doesn't get it.* San Francisco: HarperCollins.

Walt, Stephen M. 2009. Treason of the hawks. Foreign Policy, April 28, http://walt.foreignpolicy.com/posts/2009/04/28/the_treason_of_the_hawks.

Washington, James M. 1990. *A testament of hope: The essential writings and speeches of Martin Luther King, Jr.* New York: Harper Collins.

Wills, Gary. 2006. *What Paul meant.* New York: Penguin.

Wink, Walter. 1992. *Engaging the powers.* Minneapolis: Fortress Press.

———. 2003. *Jesus and nonviolence: A third way.* Minneapolis: Fortress Press.

———. 2008. Easter: What happened to Jesus? *Tikkun Magazine,* March.

Williamson, Clark M. 1993. *A guest in the House of Israel: Post-Holocaust Church theology.* Louisville: Westminster John Knox Press.

Wyschogrod, Michael. 1986. Christology: The immovable object. *Religion and intellectual life* 3. Quoted in Soulen 1996, 79.

———. 1989. *Body of faith: God and the people Israel.* San Francisco: Harper and Row.

About the Author

Mark Braverman's roots are in the Holy Land—his grandfather, a fifth-generation Palestinian Jew, was born in Jerusalem and emigrated to the U.S. as a young man. Growing up in the United States, Braverman was reared in the Jewish tradition, studying the Bible, Hebrew literature, and Jewish history. Trained as a clinical and community psychologist, he consulted to federal agencies, private companies, and international humanitarian assistance nonprofits on crisis management policy, staff mental health and wellness, and disaster recovery. He has authored two books and over thirty articles and book chapters on psychological trauma, crisis management, and organizational health. Visiting the Holy Land in 2006, Braverman was transformed by witnessing the occupation of Palestine and by encounters with peace activists and civil society leaders from the Muslim, Christian, and Jewish communities. Since then, he has devoted himself full-time to the Israel-Palestine conflict. He has spoken about Israel/Palestine before diverse groups, focusing on his journey as a Jewish American committed to peace and dignity for all peoples of the land, the role of religious belief in the current discourse in the United States, and the impact of the conflict on both Israelis and Palestinians. Braverman is the executive director of the Holy Land Peace Project, an interfaith and ecumenical organization that promotes education about and action for Middle East peace in the U.S. faith communities. Braverman is a co-founder of Friends of Tent of Nations North America, a nonprofit dedicated to supporting Palestinian land rights and peaceful coexistence in historic Palestine. He serves on the Board of Directors of the Israeli Committee Against House Demolitions-USA, the steering committee of Friends of Sabeel North America, and the advisory council of the Washington Interfaith Alliance for Middle East Peace. Braverman lives in Bethesda, Maryland, with his wife, Susan.

For information on appearances and other writing by Braverman, and more on *Fatal Embrace*, visit www.MarkBraverman.org.

Index

244, 282, 293, 303, 306, 315, 335, 338, 341-342, 348, 366
transition from tribal to universal, 98, 115, 118, 144, 172-173, 181, 204, 221, 223, 227, 234, 238, 256, 268, 335, 367
Jonah, Book of, 138, 172-175, 184, 227-229, 254
Judaism
and exceptionalism, xiii-xiv, 116, 306
as a universalistic religion, 6, 12, 93, 98, 115-116, 120, 139, 144, 146, 172-173, 180, 204, 206, 211, 213, 215, 222-223, 226-227, 234, 238-239, 256, 335, 367
differences from Christianity, 116, 130, 132, 180, 305
need for reform, x, 44, 64, 112, 119, 123, 126, 131-132, 138-139, 143, 145, 147, 164, 187, 197, 229, 246, 256, 262, 344, 346
tribal elements of, 97-98, 114-116, 118, 124, 180-181, 221-223, 227, 268
Judt, Tony, 72

K

Khoury, Elias, 309-310, 375, 387
King, Jr., Martin Luther, 78, 138, 154-155, 207, 252, 268, 278, 294-295, 338, 353-355, 359-360
Kook, Abraham Isaac, 88, 185

Kovel, Joel, 97-98, 180, 238, 317

L

Law of Return, 198-199
Lerner, Michael, 68, 296
Leviticus, Book of, 251, 274
Levy, Daniel, 65, 283
Levy, Gideon, 18, 235, 242, 352

M

Magnes, Judah, 64, 97, 99, 189, 268, 280
Mark, Gospel Of, 237
Malley, Robert, 19, 371
Meir, Golda, 31, 81, 94
Messianism, 58, 67, 82-84, 88-89, 91-92, 177, 179, 182, 185

N

Nakba, 41, 61, 67, 74, 85n, 96n, 198, 286, 309-310
Nassar, Daoud, 3-4, 75-76, 78, 80, 85, 315, 317, 327, 358, 367
Netanyahu, Benjamin, 271-272, 280, 283-284, 305
Neumann, Michael, 218-219, 244
Nonviolence, 12, 16, 41-43, 47, 81, 174, 234, 238-239, 246, 264, 267-268, 274-275, 294, 296, 340, 347, 355-358, 367

O

One-state solution, xviii, 184, 279, 285
Osborne, Robert T., 125
Oslo Accords, 11n, 78, 95, 183, 273